The Picador Book of Contemporary
NEW ZEALAND FICTION

Fergus Barrowman was born in 1961 in Wellington, where he lives with his wife and son. He has been Editor of Victoria University Press, a leading publisher of New Zealand fiction, since 1985, and founded the biannual literary magazine *Sport* in 1988.

Edited by
FERGUS BARROWMAN

The Picador Book of
Contemporary NEW
ZEALAND
FICTION

PICADOR

FOR ELIZABETH

This book has benefited from assistance and advice from many people. I would particularly like to thank Bill Manhire, Damien Wilkins, Iain Sharp, Lawrence Jones, Mark Williams, Nigel Cox and Rachel Lawson.

First published 1996 by Picador

an imprint of Macmillan General Books
25 Eccleston Place London SW1W 9NF
and Basingstoke

Associated companies throughout the world

ISBN 0 330 33996 6

Introduction and this selection copyright © Fergus Barrowman 1996

The right of Fergus Barrowman to be identified as the
editor of this work has been asserted by him in accordance
with the Copyright, Designs and Patents Act 1988.

9 8 7 6 5 4 3 2 1

A CIP catalogue record for this book is available from
the British Library

Typeset by CentraCet Limited, Cambridge
Printed and bound in Great Britain by
Cox & Wyman Ltd, Reading, Berkshire

Contents

Introduction

THIS ANTHOLOGY REPRESENTS New Zealand fiction
published from 1979 to the end of 1994 – a time of extraordinary
richness. In 1979 eight New Zealand novels and three collections
of stories were published. These numbers were not unusual; the
figures for 1978 and 1980 are almost the same. In February 1995,
as I tried to persuade my selection to lie down and be still,
Wellington's *Evening Post*, in a preview of publishers' lists for the
year, said that 'about two dozen' novels would appear. The tone is
business-as-usual, and the estimate low anyway – a little phone-
research established that the final total would be forty.

The boom was in large part ignited by Keri Hulme's novel
The Bone People. First published in 1984 by a feminist collective, it
quickly achieved levels of sales previously recorded only by the
autobiographies of Sir Edmund Hillary and All Black Colin Meads,
never by serious local fiction. When this home success was
validated by the award of the 1985 Booker Prize and spectacular
international sales – New Zealanders are always readier to trust
overseas experts than their own elbows – publishers were suddenly
hungry for new New Zealand fiction. At the same time, the supply
of this fiction was guaranteed by huge increases in the sums of

public money available for subsidies to writers and publishers through the Arts Council of New Zealand. And the two main book awards, the Montana (previously the Wattie) Book of the Year and the state-sponsored NZ Book Awards, began to receive levels of media attention that would have seemed unimaginable a few years before.

If it is difficult in this account to avoid slipping into the tone of a state literature body functionary, or a books programme presenter, or the editor of an anthology for export, it is also worth recalling a paradox noted by the American critic Allen Tate, 'that not even literary nationalism could abort a genuine national literature when it is ready to appear.'

I began with the conventional construction 'were published', but that is unhelpfully passive and anonymous. Of those eleven 1979 volumes, six were published by large overseas firms: four in the UK and one each in Australia and the US. Of the five published locally, two were from mainstream firms whose central interests were definitely not literary, and three from tiny firms owned by enthusiasts.

This had been the pattern since fiction began to be written in New Zealand shortly after European settlement early in the nineteenth century. Local publishing was sporadic and uncertain, so that a writer who wanted to build a career had to find a publisher in London or New York. Many writers have commented on the drawbacks of this situation. While there were opportunities for periodical publication in New Zealand and Australia by which a writer could get a career going, the step to book publication in London proved too great for many to make in one stride, and few found that local publication provided sufficient income or encouragement. But a distinction between writers who struggled on at home and the lucky few who achieved Home publication is too simple. The latter might come under pressure to remove 'local' elements to suit the work for a British audience. They might find that the publisher lacked the local knowledge to market the book properly in New Zealand, so failing to exploit the major potential sale. If a book did sell in New Zealand, the writer would then receive a reduced 'export' royalty. A drawback for *readers* was the difficulty of obtaining New Zealand books. For years the majority of Janet Frame's books existed only in US editions which were almost impossible to get in New Zealand. For New Zealand fiction to flourish, the first requirement was a local publishing industry.

All of the New Zealand fiction published in 1995 was published in New Zealand – although some was also published overseas simultaneously or subsequently. The publishers were the local branches of four multinationals, Penguin, Random House, Hodder Moa Beckett and Reed International; Victoria and Otago University Presses; and an array of independents including Tandem, Godwit, Hazard, Daphne Brasell, David Ling and Longacre. Every year since *The Bone People* yields a list of similar size and range, though the names change often. While on the one hand it has been a period of great volatility in New Zealand publishing, with mergers, takeovers, failures and new enterprises occurring at a rate to match London or New York, on the other hand it has been one of remarkable stability in terms of the gross publishing resources available to serious fiction. The stories of these firms and their personnel since 1979 would be a fascinating essay in itself, and would tell us more, perhaps, about New Zealand fiction than a traditional critical history treating the texts as if migrating directly and mysteriously from writers' imaginations to their places in Literature.

This volume is arranged by the date of the first book publication by the thirty-one writers it contains. They can be divided into rough generational groups – generations based on entry into literature rather than entry into the world – which establish a rough literary history. At the same time, reading through it in that order will highlight the unhelpfulness of any contestatory model of literary history, of new generations sweeping out old, of avant gardes and old lags. No distinctions can be made between the older and younger writers here in terms of subject matter or stylistic innovation; and it is significant that while half the writers have emerged during the period the anthology covers, all are still active at its end.

Janet Frame's 'Insulation' stands at the head of the book. She is such a powerful and unusual figure that she is often treated as *sui generis*, a little outside the central history of New Zealand literature, rather in the way her publishing history kept her for so long outside New Zealand bookshops.

Frame is followed by Maurice Shadbolt, Maurice Gee, C.K. Stead and Vincent O'Sullivan, four writers whose literary careers began in the late 1950s or early 1960s. The Provincial Period, as it has been dubbed, is discussed fully by Lawrence Jones in his chapter on the novel in *The Oxford History of New Zealand Literature in English* (1991). In this version of the development model often applied to the histories of Commonwealth or other 'new' literatures, the Provincial Period represents a third phase of confident belonging in a place, which follows a first phase of armchair travel literature bringing exotic places to a Home audience, and a second phase of anxious assertions of belonging in the new place.

The characteristics of Provincial Period fiction are its oppositional stance towards society, which is defined as both puritan and materialistic, and the prevalence of critical realism, the literary form which most readily conveys this message. The structural weakness of Provincial Period fiction, its paradox really, is the mutual dependency of confidence in the nation and the oppositional stance to society. The critical stance is inseparable from the effort to bring the place and people into imaginative being, to define them in a pattern of essences and exclusions. Such unstable insularity implies a fourth phase, when the security of boundaries is lost and confidence in a nation is followed by a more fluid sense of *region*.

Provincial Period fiction had an unfortunate tendency to narrow down to a model that was Pakeha, male and realist. The inevitable reactions became visible from the late 1960s, in particular with the emergence of significant numbers of women writers, and Maori writers, and in a general exploration of a greater range of formal possibilities. Patrick Evans, in *The Penguin History of New Zealand Literature* (1990), characterizes this as the 'end of a literary monoculture and the beginnings of a time of abundance and multiplicity'.

The first post-Provincial Period is represented here by a group of twelve writers – four Maori writers: Witi Ihimaera, Patricia Grace, Keri Hulme and Apirana Taylor; the Samoan New Zealander Albert Wendt; five women: Margaret Mahy, Fiona Kidman and Sue McCauley as well as Grace and Hulme; and four Pakeha males: Bill Manhire, Ian Wedde, Russell Haley and Owen Marshall.

An essay which fell into the trap of treating these as exclusive categories might begin with the metafictional techniques of the Pakeha men; go on to how loudly different women writers beat the feminist drum; and end with the educative, didactic and fabular modes of contemporary Maori fiction. But the boundaries are unsustainable. For instance, many of the features derived by Maori writers from traditional oral forms – use of oratory and myth, the presence of the dead, collective narrative voices – are very similar to innovations credited to post-modernism or magic realism.

I take the first post-Provincial Period as ending in 1984 with the publication of *The Bone People*, its signature book. Fourteen of the writers in this book – almost half – have published their first books in the decade since. Their work doesn't show any radical break with the preceding period, and it would be wrong to impose any category other than the liberating pluralism of forms and styles. Indeed, the insouciant lightness of much recent fiction is in contrast with the aggressive tone of the period's literary debates, and the level of change and conflict within society.

The New Zealand of the Provincial Period was complacent and self-satisfied. We had the third highest standard of living in the world. We had the best race relations in the world. We were a classless society. These 'facts' were told us repeatedly by our politicians and newspapers. By the late 1970s, as the economy faltered and the gap between rich and poor widened, the steady divergence of the real life of the country from this pretty picture was impossible to ignore. It had become plain too that the poor were disproportionately Maori, and the campaign by Maori for redress of past wrongs and a greater share in society's power structures, which had continued unbroken since the signing of the Treaty of Waitangi in 1840, had become so urgent none could pretend to ignore it.

But the 1970s in New Zealand turned out to be a long decade – a conservative National government under Sir Robert Muldoon kept the lid on until 1984.

The six years of the fourth Labour government were a time of astonishing change, the effects of which have been deeply contradictory and difficult to assimilate. New Zealand's economy went from being one of the most regulated outside the communist world (as regulated, it was said, as many within the communist world) to one of the least regulated. The level of real poverty and hardship increased at the same time as signs of material luxury proliferated – changes to import controls saw a much wider range of goods in the shops, and relaxation of licensing laws brought café life to New Zealand.

At the same time as rushing into the modern world, New Zealand was preparing to celebrate its history – 1990 would mark the 150th anniversary of the birth of the nation with the signing of the Treaty of Waitangi. But this was at a time when the viability of the notion of 'New Zealand' itself, let alone celebrating it, given the history of injustice Maori were forcing into public awareness, was in question. In the end, while many useful things were achieved under the cloak of the sesquicentenary that might otherwise have been shelved for lack of funds or public commitment, there was a half-hearted, disconnected air about it all. And 'sesqui' ended up equated with 'disastrous incompetence' in a 1994 dictionary of New Zealand English.

The National government that was returned in 1990 brought no change of direction – all New Zealand's National governments have been caretaker governments, their agendas set for them by the Labour governments to whom they leave significant change. But there seems to be some possibility of significant change with the introduction of a proportional representation electoral system in 1996.

Janet Frame's 'Insulation' captures the decline of New Zealand in the late 1970s: 'The country is not as rich as it used to be.' But more than this, it captures the inauthenticity introduced into the lives of those who have been used to a pragmatic culture of hard work and material rewards:

> We both knew we were playing a game, he trying to sell what he didn't possess, and I imagining I could ever install it, to deaden the world.

The tone of Janet Frame's work changed about the time 'Insulation' was published. The dominant note of her prodigious output from *Owls Do Cry* (1957) to *Daughter Buffalo* (1972) was of unbearable pain, the source of which was both without – she was once described as 'having one skin too few' – and within – the critic Mac Jackson has her 'caging her inner life in words in order to avoid being devoured by it'. In the sequence of work that began in 1978 with *Living in the Maniototo* is a new note of irony, coming perhaps from an acknowledgement of the 'insulation' afforded her by her art – but this is not so much a compromise of Frame's sense of reality as a different modulation of it.

'Insulation' sets a tone that one hears often in New Zealand fiction of the next few years:

> I find it hard to go on. Not because of terror, I can face that. Because of shifts, because of dizziness. Nothing will be still. Poverty and abundance transmute. And this is that and that is this. And *it* was so, but yet not *so*. What other option but silence do I have? Imperfections strike at me like hail. And there, you see, this double focus, which is a kind of seeing round corners, a view through mirrors cunningly placed, when all I want is to look *straight* at the *single* thing. Obliquity makes me dizzy, multiplicity smothers me. Yet I'll go on. I think that if I'm silent I'll soon die.

This could be read as a statement of a writer's existential dilemma, a version of Beckett's 'I can't go on. I'll go on.' Yet put it back in its context – Maurice Gee's *Prowlers*, in which a New Zealander in his eighties in the changing New Zealand of the 1980s, looks back on his life – and it looks extraordinarily specific. The New Zealand novelists formed in the Provincial Period who have remained powerful through the 1980s and 1990s are those who have always been writing to some extent against the assumptions of that period and have been alert to changing imperatives. They have responded to the culture's obsession with history. And they have all, in different ways, enlarged the model of critical realism by acknowledging a crisis of narrative authority.

With the passing of the certainties of the Provincial Period the question for New Zealand writers had become, as Ian Wedde puts it, 'Where is here?'

*

'New Zealand,' one lucid voice said. 'Who sodding needs it now?' Maurice Shadbolt does not identify the owner of the lucid voice on board a ship approaching the Bay of Islands, just after the signing of the Treaty of Waitangi. It could belong to a British army officer returning to duty, or perhaps the Yankee bosun who says that New Zealand has been 'buggered' by the British flag. It could speak too for many in the 1980s and 1990s: those, not only Maori, who would adopt the name Aotearoa to signal the start of a truly post-colonial era; or those amongst southern Maori who would assert closer ties with Sydney than with Auckland; or those, not only Pakeha, who want to assume a cosmopolitan identity free of the anxieties of nationalism, to live easily in the world without leaving home. The New Zealand so arduously brought into focus by the Provincial writers threatens to come apart into fragments, or lose itself in something larger.

Maurice Shadbolt signalled his large Provincial ambitions by titling his first collection of stories *The New Zealanders*. Later, he described his longest novel, *Strangers and Journeys*, as an epic designed 'to illuminate the textures of New Zealand life as it has been lived in the last sixty years'. The trilogy of historical blockbusters which began in 1986 with *Season of the Jew* surprised some, but it is in fact completely consistent with those earlier ambitions. Shadbolt has said that he was in part trying to fill a gap in the canon – the rip-roaring frontier yarns he was unable to read in his teens because they did not exist – and into this mould he poured the revisionist history of the 1980s, the most prominent examples of which are books by James Belich, Claudia Orange and Anne Salmond. Old narratives featured the inevitable military defeat of the Maori by the British Empire, the new narrative military statement or partial Maori victory, followed by gradual domination by weight of Pakeha numbers.

The tone changes through Shadbolt's three novels. The most straightforward is *Season of the Jew*, which has a cliffhanger at the end of each short chapter and is populated with bumbling

Imperialists, anxious colonists and potent Maori. In *Monday's Warriors* the comic note prevails, but by *The House of Strife* Shadbolt's scepticism about all human pretension leads him to depict Maori as the Europeans' equals in avarice and pride as well as proneness to pratfalls (while still far superior in strategy it must be said), and the comedy and adventure are decidedly squalid. The visitor and potential colonist Ferdinand Wildblood, who is also Henry Youngman, author of *Monarch of Maoriland* and other blood-soaked romances, is led to the realization that any involvement in the conflict – whether Ferdinand's well-meant meddling or Henry's bestselling books – implicates him dangerously. Ferdinand/Henry could be speaking for the author when he says that his 'interest in colonial warfare appeared to be on the wane'.

The New Zealand Wars of the mid-nineteenth century were a major factor, along with the booming settler economy and birth rate, in the formation of a national Pakeha identity separate from that of the mother country. However, this mood gave way, for various reasons including the depression of the 1890s, to what Belich has called a period of recolonization, a move to reassert New Zealand's filial relationship with England, which reached its zenith in the jingoism of the First World War.

The octogenarian looking back in Maurice Gee's *Prowlers* is Sir Noel Papps, a distinguished scientist. Too much lingering on personal history comes hard to him, seems immoral almost, but once the image of a piano exploding into flames sets him off his past unfolds. *Prowlers* is constructed out of a pattern of oppositions like that between personal and 'real' history. In this primal scene – which recalls the real history in which the bells of Christchurch Cathedral were melted down on account of their German manu-facture – it is first of all between the rabid yet shallow intolerance of most of the community for the German piano teacher, and the greater compassion of a few. Others spiral out from it, such as that between Noel Papps and his friend and nemesis Phil Dockery, between the embryonic men of science and business. But nothing is as simple as it first seems; Papps repeatedly celebrates his scientific achievements in terms of the apples he has caused to grow in barren lands – in overtly materialistic terms, that is – and as he follows the stories of his past he becomes increasingly aware not only of the limitations of his scientific rationalism, but also of impulses behind it which are scarcely any more rational or scientific than the crowd's intolerant passion.

Maurice Gee first used the narrative structure of *Prowlers* in his 1978 novel *Plumb*, which won a clutch of awards (the James Tait Black Prize for the best novel published in Britain in 1978 as well as the two major New Zealand awards) and was a local bestseller. The Plumb family saga was continued in two sequels; the trilogy is a rich social and cultural history of twentieth-century New Zealand. *Plumb* is a key book both in its author's development and publishing history, as it marks the beginning of the wave which crested with *The Bone People*.

C.K. Stead's *All Visitors Ashore* is set in 1951, a year known for a major industrial dispute on the waterfront – most often referred to as a strike but in reality a lockout – which paralysed the economy, polarized the community and was the occasion for extraordinary legislative infringements of civil rights. This public affairs backgound is vital but muted; more immediate is the literary background suggested by the book's dedication: 'To whom it may concern'. New Zealand readers were quick to translate: Curl Skidmore into the young Karl Stead; Melior Farbro into Frank Sargeson, New Zealand's most celebrated and influential short-story writer after Mansfield, whose short stories of the 1930s and 1940s laid the foundation for Provincial Period fiction; Cecelia Skyways into Janet Frame – the story of Frame's residence in Sargeson's shed is told in both their autobiographies.

New Zealand's most successful stage work is Bruce Mason's solo piece *The End of the Golden Weather*, in which the idyllic world of childhood is shattered by the social pressures caused by Depression and war; the pattern is similar to *Prowlers* and many other New Zealand works. Stead has likened *All Visitors Ashore* to the Haydn symphony in which the players one by one leave the stage. For many artistic Pakeha and European immigrants, it seems it is still impossible to sustain a cultured life in New Zealand, and the loss of Curl's summer idyll will not be caused by acute pressures of history, but by a gradual loss of energy in the form of the nation's best and brightest. The strains of the will-to-definition are absent from the erotic, elegiac mood of Stead's novel.

In Vincent O'Sullivan's 'The Last of Freddie' we find ourselves in the present, and the only context is personal; history has fallen away unobserved. The past of private life is never more present than at a funeral. Freddie's three lovers share the telling of this story, his story – and there is no real distinction between their voices, nothing to help you remember whether it was Lydia or June or Maddy who had the critical thought: 'There was something wrong with everyone, if only you knew about it.' The point of course is that knowing is unimportant. When culture is so thin that it comes down to personal life, then yes, of course every life is unique, but also scarcely distinguishable from another. It is only the passing place names which tell us this story is set in New Zealand – this cultured, artistic middle class is responding to history by not thinking about it.

The absence of any mention in 'The Last of Freddie' of Maori is true to the life of the society depicted. I have mentioned before New Zealand's pride in excellent race relations. But this has been based on the liberal virtue of colour-blindness; polite society making a virtue of non-discrimination, in the sense of not drawing attention to the Maoriness of an individual when met in the role, say, of lawyer or teacher. The corollary of this, that it requires Maori to pass as white, has become untenable with escalating social and historical pressures. Maori have demanded recognition of their special status as tangata whenua, people of the land; of the need to acknowledge cultural difference in all areas of life; and of their social disadvantage, of the fact that while it *is* possible to encounter a Maori teacher or lawyer, their numbers compared with the Maori proportion of the population (13 per cent and rising) are far too low.

The public policy that reflects this pressure has been labelled 'biculturalism'. An engine of necessary and positive change, when captured by the natural tendency of policy-makers to try to freeze change:

> biculturalism . . . usually comes down to the requirement that Maori assert a generalized identity (and be encouraged to do so); and that they be encouraged, and even obliged, to assert a cumulative economics. To speak with one voice, and to invest. Unity, and resource management.

For biculturalism to remain dynamic, Ian Wedde continues, it has to 'keep a certain kind of problem alive'. From this perspective, much of the fiction about Maori and Pakeha seems, as Vincent O'Sullivan puts it, 'simplistic and gauche' at best. Maori have usually existed in Pakeha fiction as colourful Other. A summary list of roles would include noble savage, Aryan Maori, dying chief, ornament of New Zealand, loafer, fine footballer and soldier, good bloke who only drinks beer, oppressed victim of the West . . .

This is the dilemma for the contemporary Pakeha writer: how to avoid appropriation of Maori material for decorative or moral effect while still representing the full New Zealand reality. One response has been not to depict Maori at all; one of the notable features of Pakeha fiction of the last fifteen years has been the low incidence of Maori characters and issues. This is what we see in 'The Last of Freddie', the exact representation of Pakeha society with Maori as a felt absence. Where Maori *are* present in recent Pakeha fiction, representation has been scrupulous and exact.

In a telling instance in *Prowlers*, Noel Papps's views on the despoliation of New Zealand by corrupt materialism lead him naturally to acknowledge Maori land grievances:

> We have gangsters, and Wall Street men, smart-money men, and footpads, hunting packs, and there are fights in the streets, with real knives. And the original owners are acting up. They want back what was theirs and I don't blame them.

Towards the end of the novel occurs one of the few bits of Maori lore known to most New Zealanders: 'A fantail in the house foretells a death (Maori belief?) but I put no credence on that sort of thing.' What is especially interesting is not so much that the image should arise, as that despite the man of science's dismissal it arises at a point in the novel where it does act as a portent of death, predicting also perhaps the coming end of automatic Pakeha scorn for Maori superstition.

In *All Visitors Ashore*, C.K. Stead uses Curl Skidmore's lover's part-Maori ancestry to make subtle jokes on the parts Maoriness has played in some Pakeha fantasies: the dusky maiden sexual fantasy; the fantasy of aristocratic lineage – she is Tuhoe; and the fantasy that access to Maori creative forces will provide the unique element in New Zealand artistic creation. These fantasies are given a much fuller workout in Stead's later novel *The Singing Whakapapa*.

But the big story is the emergence in the 1970s of Maori voices into New Zealand fiction written in English. Various suggestions have been made as to why it was so delayed; they all come down to variations on the incompatibility between the forms of oral narrative and written literature, and the silencing effects of passing as white.

The question of whether Maori *should* write in English and in European literary forms has been as hotly debated in New Zealand as it has in other colonial societies where the future of an indigenous language has been threatened by the dominance of English. The case against was made clearly in a review of the fourth volume of Witi Ihimaera's anthology *Te Ao Marama*, which was devoted to recent writing, most in English, by Maori for children:

> If writers claim to be Maori story writers and poets then compositions should be written in the Maori language. Themes (contemporary or traditional) should be displayed by traditional imagery.

The challenge in this statement has been taken up, with much of the drive coming from Maori language education initiatives, kohanga reo (kindergartens, literally 'language nests') and kura kaupapa (schools). The period since the emergence of Ihimaera and Grace has seen a great deal of new writing in Maori, in traditional, contemporary and hybrid forms, which goes unrecorded by this anthology. And C.K. Stead's 1985 prediction, 'If any modern literary writing has been done in the Maori language, next to none has been published, and that is likely to continue to be the case,' has proved wrong — new firms devoted to Maori language publishing are doing excellent business and established firms have begun Maori language lists.

Witi Ihimaera was the first Maori writer to publish a book of fiction in English, with *Pounamu, Pounamu* in 1972. Its simple stories of country childhood fitted neatly into the pastoral tradition, and enlarged it with their exact depiction of Maori society, and transcription of Maori English. Ihimaera's later work has shown a greater stylistic range than perhaps any other New Zealand writer. He has broadened his social range into more urban and modern settings; and gone back into colonial history; he has made use of Maori myth, both in classical and contemporary settings; and political polemic. The book which made the biggest impact was

The Matriarch, an historical epic published in the same year as *Season of the Jew*, telling the same story from the Maori perspective and showing how it lives on in modern Maori political and spiritual life.

Bulibasha, King of the Gypsies illustrates Ihimaera's strengths very effectively. In the extract here, the narrator's childhood experiences travelling with the family shearing gang are all the pastoral should be; but at the same time, the historical and political iniquities of the New Zealand heartland of the 1950s provide a firm backdrop, never forgotten however wild the comedy or moving the family drama becomes. Ihimaera also contrasts 'the master's study filled with leather-bound books' (an environment which in New Zealand has produced no Patrick White) with the energy of an oral tradition taking and remaking whatever it finds to its taste: traditional ghost stories, family legends, movie melodrama ... The vitality of the resulting fiction bears out Allen Tate's dictum, 'the arts everywhere spring from a mysterious union of indigenous materials and foreign influences'.

Patricia Grace emerged at the same time as Ihimaera, and has published four collections of stories and three novels. Her range of strengths is harder to represent in a single piece than Ihimaera's. Her stories are exact in their record of lives and voices, but they do not proclaim as loudly the historical and political dimensions with which they are pregnant. There is a line of New Zealand criticism which finds them lacking in 'life's larger conflict and tragedy' – this not hearing what is not said is typical Pakeha obtuseness.

Grace's novel *Potiki* is based firmly in pastoral life; but rather than the past, it is the back-to-the-land movement which has arisen in the present partly in reaction to economic pressures. The threat to this recreated life comes once again in the form of Pakeha incursion – Dollarman, would-be developer of a new marina, who when legal avenues are exhausted, and cash offers declined, resorts to sabotage and subterfuge. This is an allegory of the Treaty of

Waitangi and subsequent New Zealand history as well as a true story of today.

Potiki is shaped by the myth of Maui. All New Zealanders are familiar from their schooldays with the exploits of Maui, the youngest child adopted from the sea: how he fished up the North Island of New Zealand (the South Island is the canoe and Stewart Island the anchor); how he slowed down the sun so that the people could work the land; how he stole fire so that the people could be warm and cook; and how he died while attempting to defeat death − Hine-nui-te-po, the great woman of the night − by crawling into her vagina and back out of her mouth. She was awakened at the critical moment by a fantail's laughter and Maui was crushed to death.

Fiction by Maori writers poses formal challenges to critical orthodoxies to match the moral and economic challenges of Maori politics. One is the straightforwardly polemical nature of much Maori writing; the messages of the fiction match those of political figures with a closeness seldom found in the Western tradition. Another is the insistence that readers take the supernatural element as *literally* true − not as a literary device in the way that a writer like Angela Carter makes use of European fairytales. The opening paragraph of Apirana Taylor's 'Te Tohunga Makutu' makes clear what the Pakeha reader must suspend to join the audience addressed:

> This is no fairy-tale, I tell you. Let us remember the ancestors of we Maori were a warrior race who feared nothing but witchcraft. This tale is true. Passed on to me by word of mouth. Perhaps it happened not long ago. To this day, give or take a few years, we Maori have known Christianity for barely a hundred and fifty years.

There is no other clue given in this pitiless, cruel tale as to how its apparent message of the powerlessness of human agency and the inevitability of all things passing might reflect on New Zealand's present and future.

The school version of the Maui legend fudged the last detail – the first time it was published for a mass Pakeha readership, in 1971 in the part-encyclopedia *New Zealand's Heritage*, there was a public outcry – and indeed is a crude simplification of a vast body of often conflicting oral lore. 'It all depends / on what story / you hear' as Keri Hulme puts it in 'Headnote to a Maui Tale', the Afterword to the collection named after that Maui tale, 'Te Kaihau / The Windeater'.

The Bone People, also a Maui tale, is the culminating work of the first post-Provincial Period, icon of biculturalism. But I have chosen to represent Hulme here not by an extract from that work – there is none which successfully suggests its range and power – but by a story which followed it a few years after like a whisky chaser. 'Te Kaihau/The Windeater' displays the riches of *The Bone People* in small compass. Hulme concludes her foreword to the collection: 'You'd be a brave human who would say where all the influences come from . . .' There is an element of autobiography – she has elsewhere confirmed details such as the short-sightedness (but you'd be a brave human to speculate much further) – refracted into a variety of fables. The language shows a wide range of influences, from Tennyson to New Zealand vernacular to science fiction; with a few words you'll struggle to find anywhere else.

Maui appears in his role as trickster and shape-changer, a mischievous demi-god, and his doings can be read as a metaphor for the influence of Maori ancestry on the narrator's life. She has grown up passing for white; it is only at thirteen that she asks her father about her Maoriness and is given the sentence 'Ko Pakate-whainau te iwi, no Wheatewhakaawi' ('I am of the tribe Buggered-if-I-know, from Where-the-fuck-are-we' – there is a joking reference here to the generations of Maori children who were punished for speaking Maori at school, in a misguided attempt at integration). Yet Maui has acted on her early life like magic in her blood, and keeps intervening to turn her to her Maori side, in deeds that borrow as much from science fiction and tales of the Celtic twilight as they do from classical Maori tradition. The Maori cultural renaissance of the 1980s is sometimes criticized for radical inauthenticity, that it is in fact the sentimental, pretentious borrowing of Maori garb by people almost entirely Pakeha by early upbringing and schooling, as well as by blood. 'Te Kaihau / The Windeater' is one of many works disproving such a crude conclusion, works in which the complex relations between tradition and modern conditions are explored.

'Te Kaihau / The Windeater' unfolds into one of the most effective recent images of the instability of 'New Zealand':

> And just before the fish shatters into an archipelago, the incandescent cloud will roar helterskelter over Auckland and boil all the northern sea to a frenzy. And all along, the line, the volcanoes will gout and the wild tsunamis rear up and speed in huge glassy walls over every innocent island there is. And the canoe will rock and most of it slide under the waves.

The innocent islands in the northern sea are both the mythical ancestral homeland of Hawaiki from which the Maori came, and the islands of the South Pacific with which New Zealand has close and complicated relations. A number of small nations have been New Zealand's or Britain's colonial dependencies until recently, and some still are. They are still economically tied, dependent both on New Zealand aid and remittances from their citizens living in New Zealand – often in numbers approaching or even greater than those remaining at home. There are thus a number of sizeable communities – principally Tongan, Samoan, Niuean and Cook Island Maori – which are part of New Zealand's social fabric.

Albert Wendt was the first writer from one of the small Pacific nations to appear, with the novel *Sons for the Return Home* in 1973. An openly autobiographical account of Samoan childhood and New Zealand education, and the resulting dual identity and divided appetites and obligations – the Samoan extended family and the self-creating artist – it established the themes Wendt has continued to probe in a dizzying mix of formal modes. Wendt is a difficult writer to see clearly. Towards the world of Samoan village life his individualist message seems almost revolutionary; to 1990s New Zealand he speaks of Polynesian collectivity. 'The Balloonfish and the Armadillo' sets these themes of divided ancestry and unstable identity in a drama of memory and inheritance.

Grace and Hulme are also part of the emergence in the 1970s of a significant body of writing by women. Women have always been prominent in New Zealand fiction of course – the status of Katherine Mansfield and Janet Frame has always been recognized – but the combination of the social temperature of the 1950s and the agenda of the Provincial Period obscured other women writers, such as Robin Hyde, most of whose remarkable novels of the 1930s only came back into print in the 1980s.

Sue McCauley's *Other Halves* (1982) was the first novel published by the local branch of a multinational to build on the market opened up by *Plumb*; and its success was crucial in establishing the conditions for *The Bone People*'s two years later. An autobiographically-based story of a love affair between a middle-class Pakeha woman in early middle age and a Maori streetkid, *Other Halves* has the virtues of the style of fiction sometimes known derogatorily as journalistic. Its record of the texture of society in the early 1970s is exact, and it confronts an area of public anxiety head on, and explores it in the terms in which the public knows it. In this it recalls a quality in William Faulkner's fiction praised by the black American writer Ralph

Ellison: a willingness 'to start with the stereotype, accept it as true, and then seek out the human truth which it hides'. Fiction criticizing Pakeha racism and complacency about race relations has often been 'simplistic and gauche' in its clumsy reversal of old clichés of lazy Maori and virtuous Pakeha into new clichés of cheerfully amoral Maori and anxious, repressed Pakeha, or of impoverished Maori and their Pakeha oppressors. *Other Halves* offers no easy resolution to the tensions in Tug and Liz's relationship, which touches on all of these roles before ending on a convincing note of tentative but uncomplacent optimism.

Another writer to bring a feminist consciousness to the established mode of critical realism is Fiona Kidman. The society recorded in 'Hats' is a little further down the ladder of social class than that of 'The Last of Freddie' – the consolations of art are not so apparent – but very similar in the way that its history is present not as something grasped and understood but in rituals that exert quite ridiculous emotional pressure. This is the society, familiar from earlier fiction, committed to getting things done. The narrator keeps thinking 'No time to go on reflecting . . .' but the gaps between how she feels and how she knows she is supposed to feel have widened to the point that realization must dawn. Indeed the conclusion suggests that it has dawned – 'Hatted and hatless, that's us, blesséd are the meek, it's all the same now' – but the narrative voice, true to itself, passes briskly on without drawing attention. Kiwi understatement has its virtues, in fiction as in life.

Critical realism remains at the heart of fiction of the first post-Provincial Period, but the narrow model has been replaced by a broader and more various range of possibilities. Maori fiction has included myth and non-naturalistic events within the realm of the real as experienced by Maori. Questions of apprehension and narration – epistemology and metafiction – can also be seen as part of realism, how we receive and order the world. There is a continuum from 'Hats' to the farthest shores of post-modernism.

Owen Marshall's first collection, *Supper Waltz Wilson*, might have looked very conservative in 1979, an offering from a disciple of Sargeson, with none of the fireworks of the avant-garde. Yet in a glowing review, Sargeson himself drew attention to Marshall's 'creating a verbal density which according to all the rules could well play havoc with any clear narrative line'. And in his subsequent work – he is more prolific by far than any other short-story writer of the period – Marshall has continued to draw out the formal implications of this linguistic density as well as the possibilities of realism. 'A Day With Yesterman' stands at the conventional end of Marshall's spectrum. It is essentially a finely-nuanced character study shaped by a happy coincidence of events and people on a trip from Christchurch to Dunedin and back – this is a road story to read alongside others in this volume. Marshall is always concerned to draw out a story's moral. Chatterton is reconciled to the imminence of death when 'the knowledge that relationships had no necessary continuation ceased to disconcert him', a concern with continuity and community sounded often in contemporary New Zealand fiction.

Russell Haley's first collection, *The Sauna Bath Mysteries*, appeared only a year before Marshall's. Patrick Evans notes the paradox that while Haley has been regarded as one of New Zealand's most experimental writers, he sounds like a conventional realist. 'Fog' exemplifies this. His formal concerns – seen here particularly in his nervous corrections and hesitations, his patient tracing of the accidental resemblance or pun as well as the obviously meaningful – are simply what you have to do to have a hope of getting vital matters like ancestry and geography right. In these obsessions Haley resembles not only other recent migrants from the northern hemisphere, but many whose New Zealand lineage goes back several generations who still find it of vital importance to specify their Orkney or Scandinavian roots.

Ian Wedde's *Symmes Hole* is a book obsessed with history to the point of paranoia – although it appeared in 1986, its stylistic affinities are with the American 'literature of exhaustion' of the previous decade. In the extract here Wedde's researcher, exhausted in part by his inability to conclude his great work, and in part by the bad food and cheap wine of a State arts bash, finds himself at once extricating himself from a difficult situation involving police and drug-smuggling Russian seamen and battling ghosts – including, along with Katherine Mansfield and a crowd of nine-teenth-century politicians, the novel's two biggest ghosts, Herman Melville and Worser Heberley. Melville haunts Wedde's book as the first great Pacific fictioneer, a writer who didn't try to squeeze the broad new reality in front of him into pre-existing forms, but allowed it to lead him into new forms that would necessarily prove failures; and of course an American, and therefore outside the British literary heritage. The business of Wedde's great book is imagining a different New Zealand history from the one that beached us at the 1990s celebrations. To the official New Zealand Company settlement organized by the Wakefields, Wedde opposes Worser Heberley as an example of those maverick Europeans who established themselves during the time of the great whale fisheries and early missions, when survival was dependent on living with the Maori on fluid terms.

Bill Manhire is located in this anthology by his emergence as a poet at the beginning of the first post-Provincial Period, but he didn't begin publishing fiction until the late 1980s; his is the name critics reach for first when referring to post-modern tendencies in recent fiction. 'Ponies' is set at the end of the magical year 1984, although the reference which makes that clear is not to any of the notable local events but to the assassination of Indira Gandhi. The story presents itself in the guise of critical realism. The narrator, Kevin, is in the line of young people beginning to make their way in a world they can't quite make sense of. Kevin is aware of this in a desultory way:

Well, there we were. As they say. I am inventing the words, for I have no clear memory of what they actually were. But I am doing my best to reconstruct the *tone* that I recall.

This tone recalls Janet Frame's 'Insulation', which had its characters in a charade of commerce in a collapsing economy. By 1984 the economy had got much worse, but the Labour government's reforms created a large number of entrepreneurs out of thin air (Prime Minister of the time David Lange called them reef fish), of whom Jason Michael Stretch is the archetype. His name, given in full like a newspaper report of court proceedings, indicates he might be one of the less fortunate or adept of the highflyers, one of those who ended up in jail after the bubble burst.

But there is more to the story than deconstruction of the complacent voice of critical realism and illustration of the paper-thinness of the economic revolution. New Zealand's proximity to the Antarctic and its role in one of the century's great heroic tales, Scott and Oates, is connected with the scientific theory of nuclear winter. This points to the other thing for which the Lange government is famous, its anti-nuclear policy, and to the tradition of post-apocalypse fiction in which New Zealand's isolation makes it humanity's last refuge – Government policy and public imagination coinciding in an image of New Zealand as the future of the world.

Margaret Mahy is a very difficult writer to fit into a sober history of New Zealand fiction. Just as well she writes for children, so no one needs to. 'The Bridge-Builder' was published in *The Door in the Air*, a collection of stories which, shorn of the 'for young teenagers' tag on the jacket and the misty illustrations, would fit neatly into the tradition of modern fabulists like Calvino. 'The Bridge-Builder' is firmly grounded (like all good bridges) in autobiographical fact: Mahy's father was a bridge-builder. Knowing this helps us to see how her fable parallels the fable often told of New Zealand literature, and other 'new' literatures, which goes something like this. The harsh circumstances of early settler New Zealand produced a harshly pragmatic society. This both delayed the emergence of a literature, and gave it a utilitarian character when it did emerge. It was only with a kind of maturity that forms of delight were able to flourish, to the consternation of the culture which is nonetheless rescued by them.

Australia has always held a problematic place in the New Zealand imagination. New Zealand was once one of a group of more-or-less equal Antipodean colonies, but Australian federation reduced it to the role of minor relation. Around the turn of the century there was a brief possibility of New Zealand joining Australia, but that passed and through the century the two nations have turned away from each other like two siblings just a little too far apart to play together naturally. New Zealand has defined itself as more British, less vulgar, kinder than Australia; while envying Australia's size and economic potential. At times of economic strain in New Zealand, Australia looms larger – politically, with New Zealand promotion of Closer Economic Relations, and for individuals in search of jobs (some demographers in fact treat Australia and New Zealand as a single labour market). Criminals too have traditionally been attracted by the promise of anonymity in the larger population. But Australia has been a paralysing dream – Oz, and the place just over the ditch.

The 1980s was a time of migration to Australia – particularly, for the struggling classes of workers and small business-people represented by the family in Lloyd Jones's 'Swimming to Australia', to the frontierland of Queensland, with its property and tourist developments. For many the reality has been a disappointment, like one of those cautionary tales where running away to the circus turns out to mean cleaning up after the animals. Such intertwining of the fabular and the journalistically descriptive to the point that they are scarcely distinguishable has been a feature of Jones's work, notably with *Biografi, An Albanian Quest*. As a technique, it perhaps has its local roots in the bush yarn – of which Australia has all the best examples although it is a New Zealand tradition too.

Mrs Pratt's flight from New Zealand in Shonagh Koea's story is motivated not by material longing continuous with the main-stream culture, but by fundamental rejection of it. However, that culture is so gross – Arnold's family so consummately selfish and insensitive with a jealously-guarded tribal history that has frozen into ritual, sentiment and greed – that the sensitive soul hasn't had the opportunity to develop her own imaginative purchase on her world and its history. Therefore, her longings turn to 'somewhere that reminds me of nothing'. All of Koea's fiction has been about widowhood, both as a literal state and as a metaphor for alienation. 'Mrs Pratt Goes to China', one of her earliest stories, provides the pattern for subsequent work, at least up to the novel *Sing to Me, Dreamer*. But flight of course is not always literal; it can be into the world of the imagination, or the solitude of a house or garden, or ritual, or connoisseurship. Koea's is an extreme version, to the point of parody, of one of the key narratives of critical realism, in which the appallingness of the society and the infantilism of the sensitive soul society imprisons seem so complete as to preclude hope of change. Yet her sympathies are wider than her stark oppositions suggest. The builder with his coin collection stands for other pillars of materialism – tradesmen, policemen, sportsmen – with their shy, saving flaws.

The example of Katherine Mansfield has led to an especially strong tradition of fiction centring on the lives of children. Elizabeth Knox has published two short novels in this line, *Pomare*, which sees the Wellington suburb of Pomare through the eyes of seven-year-old Lex and her family and friends – Knox uses a Mansfieldian floating narrator – and *Paremata*, in which Lex is ten. The books are packed with period detail, but the effect is not nostalgia. Knox has said that 'the fictional world must be a dense enough medium to float all odd or heavy vessels', and that fiction 'should imitate the fullness of the world; like a hunter lying in a swamp imitating duckcalls, the writer must make the right noises to attract some blood and heat down into the work'. *Pomare* and *Paremata* use their recreation of a child's world to float big matters, respectively death and faith. But these themes are not pressingly on the surface. In *Pomare* the death does not occur in the narrative; its effect is conveyed by a gradual withdrawal of the point-of-view from the sufferer, as if through a series of valves.

Knox has alternated these short books with very different longer novels. She is one of a number of New Zealand writers – Fiona Farrell and Albert Wendt are others – to use formal devices such as multiple storylines, non-naturalistic events and genre styles, which are often seen as characteristic of the leading writers of post-colonial literatures – Marquez, Rushdie and Carey, to take three. But there are domestic models for these too. Janet Frame is the most obvious, but in 'A Story About Skinny Louie', amongst a flurry of delightfully gratuitous half-allusions (a farmer called Warren Baty is another) is mention of a character called Ethne Moran. This recalls the opening sentence of the great example of New Zealand Gothic, Ronald Hugh Morrieson's *The Scarecrow*: 'The same week our fowls were stolen, Daphne Moran had her throat cut.' Morrieson died of alcohol in 1972 and two of his four books were published posthumously – he had expressed the hope that he wouldn't be 'one of those poor buggers who's discovered after he's dead'. Though he didn't make it to the time when he would have been celebrated, his distinctive voice can be heard coming through writers as diverse as Lloyd Jones, Shonagh Koea and Fiona Farrell.

'A Story About Skinny Louie' was published first as a story, as it appears here. Later it became the first chapter of a novel in which Louie doesn't appear again, and in which plot, character and imagery spin out from the birth scene and on into the future without any promise of closure or recursion. If critical realist narratives tend to snap shut like locks, *The Skinny Louie Book* doesn't impose a contrived order on randomness: 'And won't we scatter.' Amidst the fictional fireworks, *The Skinny Louie Book* crams as great a density of social history as *Pomare*. Of particular interest is the role of the Queen. The extract from *Prowlers* demonstrated the anxious need of a society insecure in its identity to find it in the Crown. New Zealand has always made a big deal of royal visits. As international travel has become easier and these visits have become more frequent the pitch of excitement might have abated slightly, but they are still the occasion for acts of urgent definition – seen just a few years ago when a Maori activist threw a T-shirt at the Queen; both the act and the absurdly punitive response of the State were good theatre. In fiction, too, being taken to see the Queen is always the occasion for an unwanted revelation – in Peter Wells's short film 'Little Queen' homosexuality, in Damien Wilkins's story 'Out in the Field' general human mendacity. In 'Skinny Louie' it is the anxiety and dividedness of the apparently united and tranquil Pakeha society; and it is from this point at the beginning of the novel that New Zealand starts to disintegrate into a whirl of fetishized tokens of nostalgia. (It is interesting that the book has been welcomed more for its warm surfaces than for the disquieting insight behind them.)

The opening of 'Skinny Louie' catalogues some of the ways New Zealand is unstable physically as well as socially. Three young islands created by the friction of tectonic plates, New Zealand is a land of earthquakes, volcanoes and erosion. A couple of years ago the top fell off the highest mountain, Mt Cook. Human settlement was relatively recent – archaeological and DNA research indicate about 1000 years ago, from Asia via a chain of Pacific islands. The people who would become Maori brought new food plants and animals, including a species of rat, and wiped out a number of species of bird; but it was after European settlement began that change accelerated. A traveller now, such as the protagonist of Gregory O'Brien's road novel *Diesel Mystic*, sees the changes everywhere. In fact they are so thoroughgoing that he or she might fail to see them. Botanists claim that the native flora of New Zealand has been more thoroughly obliterated than anywhere else in the world – except of course for pockets, isolated from larger ecosystems and thus no longer part of natural process, which are now tenuously conserved. The traveller will see plenty of erosion, evidence of over-farming; and, if sharp-eyed, signs pointing to landfills, of which there are said to be as many, leaking poisons, as in the USA. The people who live in this landscape put its instability out of mind; the New Zealand imagination tends to leap straight from home to mountaintop or beach. But 'The verge of losing somebody' is an example of the humanly-altered land as a perfect objective correlative for a life lived in it.

New Zealand is proud of having been the first nation to give women the vote, in 1893, and uses it as a sign of social progress. But things are never quite as they seem. Campaigning by women preceded the granting of the vote; but when it came it was as a desperate attempt by an unsympathetic government to retain power. And if women's opportunities improved in the 1890s and after, they narrowed significantly around the 1950s, and it wasn't until the mid-70s that voices of change were heard clearly again.

Anne Kennedy's story 'The Road to Damascus' is a story of the 1890s, that time of the greatgrandmothers, written in the 1980s, a time of similar possibilities. Greatgrandmother 'had been laundering and starching and airing and laying out all the while'. The Steinian list continues. But she 'wasn't quite as hopeless as she had once been'. The ironies of the result of her action of self-interest are intriguing. By showing the extent to which women have internalized and come to value themselves by their subservient role they indicate the thinness of any promise of merely legislative or occupational change. After all, Greatgrandmother's efforts have only been in the service of a model of self-adornment derived from that position. The story, like a catechism, concludes with a moral: 'Greatgrandmother got it all wrong. It's the men who buy the fur coats.' Either this is profoundly pessimistic or it's a parody-moral; the ironic message is that fur coats, or anything they stand for, are not the prize.

Another story in which a dutiful daughter steps out is 'Miss Hobbs thinks about the peonies at the Kamikaze Pilots' Memorial at Etajima'. Like 'The Road to Damascus', it illustrates some of the real ethnic diversity which underlies the apparent Pakeha monolith. Barbara Anderson has dealt with a wide range of women's experience, especially in her fiction: notably women at work, in the class- and staff-rooms of *Girls High*, as well as science labs, motels and farms. She has also dealt with the home lives of the armed forces in *All the Nice Girls*, and Hawke's Bay farming families – New Zealand's rural 'upper classes' – in *Portrait of the Artist's Wife*. Usually in New Zealand fiction, ethnic or class differences within Pakeha society have only been noticed when most colourful – the Irish Catholic strain has produced and attracted many writers, for instance – as if the genteel, educated English haven't lived real enough lives.

The 1980s and 1990s in New Zealand have seen politicians make statements about New Zealand being part of Asia, which have hardly been reflected in the nation's cultural consciousness. Perhaps it is because Australia is so much closer to Asia geographically, or has allowed more immigration from Asian countries, that that country has seen higher levels of public anxiety and more open discussion. A problem for older generations of New Zealanders has been that any thoughts of New Zealand's future lying with Asia are overcast by memories of the fear of invasion by Japan during the Second World War. Anderson's story deals with the shadow of this difficult history with great subtlety.

Asia has also featured often in the local line in fiction set in the near future. This tradition has a long pedigree, with two notable books being one-time New Zealand premier Sir Julius Vogel's *Anno Domini 2000*, published during the last fin-de-siècle, and Aldous Huxley's *Ape and Essence*. Recent examples are remarkably unanimous about what the near future will be like –

Huxley's post-nuclear apocalypse descent into bestiality rather than Vogel's feminist utopia. One feature they share – even the few published since 1990 are remarkably pre-fall-of-the-Berlin-Wall in tone – is a narrative of recolonization, either from without by a larger power or from within by an elite.

John Cranna's fictions in this mode have always avoided naming this place – the label 'New Zealand' will no longer apply of course – but it remains recognizable in geographical and social detail. In his novel *Arena*, Cranna made the new colonizers explicitly Asian; but the earlier story 'Visitors' is more powerful for leaving this question open: whether the Pale Suits represent US or Japanese colonial government, or trans-national business interests, or local bureaucracy, is quite irrelevant to the manner of their relations with the local population. And it follows from this openness that what is shown in 'Visitors' could as easily be a personal tragedy as a political situation. A grandfather is dying, slowly and by fragmentation, leaving the scarcely-comprehending child to take up 'the intolerable burden of memories' – an updating of the post-colonial coming-of-age story into a world where 'New Zealand' no longer signifies strongly, and there is no certainty of any future.

By contrast, Ngahuia Te Awekotuku, looking back to the 1950s in 'The Basketball Girls', is as concrete and particular as she can be. This story is an act of memory, an act of love. In this, and in the society it depicts, it strongly recalls both *Bulibasha* and *Pomare*; and like them, it sounds a complicated note which is both loss and discovery. Tahuri's discovery that Ahi is Cindy, that Tihi's boyfriend is really her old girlfriend, reveals to Tahuri her own secret. But her immediate impulse – 'I was dying to run away and tell someone' – is checked. Her new knowledge of herself removes her from full spontaneous participation in her immediate community.

In the midst of the confused national celebrations of 1990, Alan Duff burst on the literary scene with *Once Were Warriors*, the only recent novel to rival *The Bone People* in public impact. *Once Were Warriors* is an unlikely mix for such a hit. On the one hand it is a stark portrait of a family living on the scrap heap – an absolute point, in a way, of what one critic has dubbed 'inexorable realism'. On the other hand, it is written in an astonishing, self-created style, comprised of spicy local idiom, American tough-guy lingo and Modernist interior monologue (actually bought as an off-the-shelf mix from Hubert Selby Jr), and a taste for Gerard Manley Hopkins. Yet this style seems at home here – the inside of Jake Heke's mind is rather like Joe's in *The Bone People*, when the latter is at his most self-accusatory.

The general accuracy of the novel's portrait of the community has not been disputed (though the artistic wisdom of piling it on so thickly has). Witi Ihimaera in an interview has said that the families of Duff's Pine Block – based on Rotorua, the setting of 'The Basketball Girls' – are only one generation removed from the family he portrays in *Bulibasha*. But that generation covers an urban migration (in 1951, 18 per cent of Maori lived in cities; in 1981, 79 per cent) and an economic boom and bust cycle.

Once Were Warriors comes with contradictory messages. It shows the economic injustices which have put many Maori in this abject condition; and says it is their fault for not rising to the challenge. Hope of social recovery through return to traditional ways is illustrated in some characters and events; while traditional ways are explicitly scorned. The novel's rhetoric constantly stresses individual freedom and responsibility, and the members of the Heke family – even Jake and Nig – are often suggested to be of more sensitive fibre than the mass of their neighbours; but the narrative voice, like that of 'The Last of Freddie', tends always towards a collective point of view, and the suggestion that individuals are less special than they'd like to think. Ultimately, much of the novel's power comes from these unresolvable conflicts. The rollercoaster experience it gives a reader is scarcely suggested by the cartoon versions of its 'message' which have circulated in the media.

It is striking that the special tragedy of the Maori, which is depicted so unsparingly in *Once Were Warriors*, is at the same time very similar to the tragedies of millions of people in societies across the world; and that the language the novel finds for this New Zealand reality clearly displays its foreign influences. This condition of being simultaneously in New Zealand and everywhere, or nowhere, might be called post-colonial or post-modern. It can be seen in recent New Zealand versions of several contemporary modes: coming-of-age story; gay fiction; road story; romance.

Patrick Evans has said Damien Wilkins in his first novel, *The Miserables*, 'writes as if no one has written a novel before and his is the only way to do it'. Yet at the same time Wilkins's prose displays clear affinities with writers like Thomas Bernhard and Gerald Murnane. *The Miserables* is straightforwardly a writer's coming-of-age story, a *Bildungsroman*. It is as if Wilkins has chosen to meet head on the challenges of the obvious themes: the novel's gaze opens out from the central character's self-absorption to include family and friends and ultimately the nation – near its end is a recollection of an attempt to explain New Zealand to a group of fellow international students at a US university. The present action takes place on the deck of the ferry which joins New Zealand's two main islands; the real substance is an intricate pattern of flashbacks which take the form of ascents or descents – in 'Cable' of the Wellington cable car, the city's tourism signature, and a mountain. The action of cutting a cross-section is framed within one of joining. *The Miserables* ends with the word 'tenderness', signifying the central character's acceptance of his and others' shared humanity – a state achieved not by action, or a handyman's fix, but by seeing the present self fully imbued with the past.

Coming-of-age narratives have also been common in gay fiction. This genre was slow to develop in New Zealand – perhaps because of the society's smallness and intolerance of difference (sodomy was only decriminalized in 1985) – but a number of writers have emerged recently, of whom Peter Wells is most prominent. 'Outing', even in its punning title, gathers some of the key themes: the need to be visibly gay, and the inner wrenching this causes after years of learning otherwise; the importance of family, and of reimagining/inventing family where families have failed; the presence of death in life. None of these is unique to gay writing of course, but they are brought into special focus by the AIDS epidemic.

Less prominent in 'Outing' is the overt eroticism that is such a feature of Wells's writing; but it is latent in the strongly sensual apprehension of the world of flowers, furniture and people, and perhaps in the rather exaggerated delight in language, the desire to conjugate 'fucking' and 'inscrutable', to use 'queried' instead of 'asked'. This raises interesting questions of authenticity, or of what it means to evoke authenticity as a measure. It marks perhaps an attempt to create voice or identity where there is little live tradition to build on – planting in thin soil and overfertilizing – and parallels the situation not only of the arty middle-class of 'The Last of Freddie' but also the narrator of 'Te Kaihau'.

'from Motel View' is the title of a stand-alone story by Forbes Williams, which also opens his collection, Motel View. 'from Motel View' is a fragment of a journey, and is one of several road stories in this anthology representing a common New Zealand trope. For instance, the film that kick-started the New Zealand film industry in the way that The Bone People did publishing was Goodbye Pork Pie, in which a disintegrating Mini is driven the length of the country in a race with police. Williams elsewhere in his collection comments on this tendency to ritual: 'All long thin countries have these end-to-end quests.' Motel View is a place totally packaged for tourists who are not wanted, a place almost devoid of people but with no vacancies, a place you know only from the road but which proves full of menace if you ever get stuck there. This is a dark, sardonic view of New Zealand, in which the paranoia foregrounded in the 1970s in the work of Ian Wedde and others has become normalized, muted perhaps, but omnipresent – in much the way that Thomas Pynchon seems to lie somewhere behind Raymond Carver.

Emily Perkins, the youngest writer in this book, articulates as clearly as Williams the paradox of place. 'Not Her Real Name' is notable for its exact observation of young urban life in 1990s New Zealand, yet at the same time we feel we could be anywhere Doc Martens are worn. The story of Francis and Cody is a romance. The plot's improbabilities – happy coincidences and out-of-character acts – proceed in the dogged naturalistic steps the genre demands. Yet it is a post-modern romance: the characters are at once worldly and innocent. And the close – a happy ending for today, no comment on tomorrow – is anything but naive, as Perkins displaces the anxiety of ending on to a deft narrative trick: a shift into second-person point-of-view which casts the reader as Francis, just as the reader began the romance as Cody: a perfect mixed note of tentative optimism and formal poise.

Two images have occurred to me as I have read for this anthology: a stop-action film of a blooming flower, and on darker days a slow-motion film of an explosion. I have tried to picture a literature in a time of great energy and rapid change – to freeze it at its point of maximum expansion and offer a promise of its final shape.

Fergus Barrowman

Janet Frame

INSULATION

IN THE SUMMER DAYS when the lizards come out and the old ewes, a rare generation, a gift of the sun, gloat at us from the television screen, and the country, skull in hand, recites To kill or not to kill, and tomatoes and grapes ripen in places unused to such lingering light and warmth, then the people of Stratford, unlike the 'too happy happy tree' of the poem, do remember the 'drearnighted' winter. They order coal and firewood, they mend leaks in the spouting and roof, they plant winter savoys, swedes, a last row of parsnips.

The country is not as rich as it used to be. The furniture in the furniture store spills out on the footpath and stays unsold. The seven varieties of curtain rail with their seven matching fittings stay on display, useless extras in the new education of discernment and necessity. The dazzling bathroom ware, the chrome and fur and imitation marble are no longer coveted and bought. For some, though, the time is not just a denial of gluttony, of the filling of that worthy space in the heart and the imagination with assorted satisfied cravings. Some have lost their jobs, their life-work, a process described by one factory-manager as 'shedding'.

'Yes, we have been shedding some of our workers.'

'Too happy happy tree'?

The leaves fall as if from other places, only they fall here. They are brittle in the sun. Shedding, severing, pruning. God's country, the garden of Eden and the conscientious gardeners.

Some find work again. Some who have never had work advertise in the local newspaper. There was that advertisement which appeared every day for two weeks, full of the hope of youth, sweet and sad with unreal assumptions about the world.

'Sixteen year old girl with one thousand hours training at hairdressing College seeks work.' The *one thousand hours* was in big dark print. It made the reader gasp as if with a sudden visitation of years so numerous they could scarcely be imagined, as if the young girl had undergone, like an operation, a temporal insertion which made her in some way older and more experienced than anyone else. And there was the air of pride with which she flaunted her thousand hours. She was pleading, using her richness of time as her bargain. In another age she might have recorded such time in her Book of Hours.

And then there was the boy, just left school. 'Boy, sixteen, would like to join pop group as vocalist fulltime' – the guileless advertisement of a dream. Did anyone answer either advertisement? Sometimes I imagine they did (I too have unreal assumptions about the world), that the young girl has found a place in the local Salon Paris, next to the Manhattan Takeaway, where she is looked at with admiration and awe (one thousand hours!) and I think that somewhere, maybe, say, in Hamilton (which is to other cities what round numbers are to numbers burdened by decimal points), there's a pop group with a new young vocalist full-time, appearing, perhaps, on *Opportunity Knocks*, the group playing their instruments, the young man running up and down the stairs, being sexy with his microphone and singing in the agony style.

★

But my real story is just an incident, a passing glance at insulation and one of those who were pruned, shed, severed, and in the curious mixture of political metaphor, irrationally rationalized, with a sinking lid fitted over his sinking heart. I don't know his name. I only know he lost his job and he couldn't get other work and he was a man used to working with never a thought of finding himself jobless. Like the others he had ambled among the seven varieties of curtain rail and matching fittings, and the fancy suites with showwood arms and turned legs, and the second circular saw. He was into wrought iron, too, and there was a wishing well in his garden and his wife had leaflets about a swimming-pool. And somewhere, at the back of his mind, he had an internal stairway to the basement rumpus. Then one day, suddenly, although there had been rumours, he was pruned from the dollar-flowering tree.

He tried to get other work but there was nothing. Then he thought of spending his remaining money on a franchise to sell insulation. It was a promising district with the winters wet and cold and frosty. The price of electricity had gone up, the government was giving interest-free loans – why, everyone would be insulating. At first, having had a number of leaflets printed, he was content to distribute them in letter boxes, his two school-age children helping. His friends were sympathetic and optimistic. They too said, Everyone will be wanting insulation. And after this drought you can bet on a cold winter. Another thing, there was snow on Egmont at Christmas, and that's a sign.

He sat at home waiting for the orders to come in. None came. He tried random telephoning, still with no success. Finally, he decided to sell from door to door.

'I'm going from door to door,' he told his wife.

She was young and able. She had lost her job in the local clothing factory, and was thinking of buying a knitting-machine and taking orders. On TV when they demonstrated knitting-machines the knitter (it was always a she, with the he demonstrating) simply moved her hands to and fro as if casting a magic spell and the machine did the rest. To and fro, to and fro, a fair-isle sweater knitted in five hours, and fair-isle was coming back, people said. Many of her friends had knitting-machines, in the front room, near the window, to catch the light, where, in her mother's day, the piano always stood, and when she walked by her friends' houses she could see them sitting in the light moving their hands magically to and fro, making fair-isle and bulky knit, intently reading the pattern.

'Yes, door to door.'

The words horrified her. Not in her family, surely! Not door to door. Her father, a builder, had once said that if a man had to go door to door to advertise his work there was something wrong with it.

'If you're reputable,' he said, 'you don't advertise. People just come to you through word of mouth, through your own work standing up to the test.' Well, it wasn't like that now, she knew. Even Smart and Rogers had a full-page advertisement in the latest edition of the local paper. All the same, door to door!

'Oh no,' she said plaintively.

'It can't be helped. I have to look for custom.'

He put on his work clothes, a red checkered shirt, jeans, and he carried a bundle of leaflets, and even before he had finished both sides of one street he was tired and he had begun to look worried and shabby.

This is how I perceived him when he came to my door. I saw a man in his thirties wearing a work-used shirt and jeans yet himself looking the picture of disuse, that is, severed, shed, rationalized, with a great lid sinking over his life, putting out the flame.

'I thought you might like to insulate your house,' he said, thrusting a leaflet into my hand.

I was angry. Interrupted in my work, brought to the door for nothing! Why, the electrician had said my house was well insulated with its double ceilings. Besides, I'd had experience of that stuff they blow into the ceiling and every time there's a wind it all comes out making snowfall in the garden, drifting over to the neighbours too.

'No, I'm not interested,' I said. 'I tried that loose-fill stuff once and it snowed everywhere, every time the wind blew.'

'There's a government loan, you know.'

'I'm really not interested,' I said.

'But it's new. New. Improved.'

'Can't afford it, anyway.'

'Read about it, then, and let me know.'

'Sorry,' I said.

My voice was brisk and dismissing. He looked as if he were about to plead with me, then he changed his mind. He pointed to the red print stamped on the leaflet. There was pride in his pointing, like that of the girl with the thousand hours.

'That's my name and phone number, if you change your mind.'

'Thank you, but I don't think I will.'

He walked away and I shut the door quickly. Insulation, I said to myself with no special meaning or tone. How lovely the summer is, how cosy this house is. The people here before me had carpets that will last for ever, the ceiling is double, there are no cracks in the corners, that is, unless the place decides to shift again on its shaky foundations. How well insulated I am! How solid the resistance of this house against the searching penetrating winds of Stratford. The hunted safe from the hunter, the fleeing from the pursuer, the harmed from the harmer.

'How well insulated I am!'

★

That night I had a curious ridiculous dream. I dreamed of a land like a vast forest 'in green felicity' where the leaves had started to fall, not by nature, for the forest was evergreen, but under the influence of a season that came to the land from within it and had scarcely been recognized, and certainly not ruled against. Now how could that have been? At first I thought I was trapped in a legend of far away and long ago, for the characters of long ago were there. I could see a beggar walking among the fallen leaves. He was the beggar of other times and other countries, and yet he was not, he was new, and he was ashamed. I saw a cottage in the forest and a young woman at the window combing her hair and – a young man with a – lute? No, a guitar – surely that was the prince? – and with the guitar plugged in to nowhere he began to play and sing and as he sang he sparkled – why, it was Doug Dazzle – and he was singing,

> One thousand hours of cut and set
> my showwood arms will hold you yet
> baby baby insulate,
> apprentice and certificate,
> God of nations at thy feet
> in our bonus bonds we meet
> lest we forget lest we forget
> one thousand hours of cut and set. . . .

The girl at the window listened and smiled and then she turned to the knitting-machine by the window and began to play it as if from a 90 per cent worsted, 10 per cent acrylic score. I could see the light falling on her hands as they moved to and fro, to and fro in a leisurely saraband of fair-isle. Then the beggar appeared. He was carrying a sack that had torn and was leaking insulation, faster and faster, until it became a blizzard, vermiculite falling like snow, endlessly, burying everything, the trees and their shed leaves, the cottage, the beggar, the prince, and the princess of the thousand hours.

The next morning I found the leaflet and telephoned the number on it.

'I'd like to be insulated,' I said.

The man was clearly delighted.

'I'll come at once and measure.'

We both knew we were playing a game, he trying to sell what he didn't possess, and I imagining I could ever install it, to deaden the world. All the same, he measured the house and he put in the loose-fill insulation, and following the Stratford custom, although it was summer, I ordered my firewood against that other 'drear-nighted' winter.

Maurice Shadbolt

from THE HOUSE OF STRIFE

MUSTER OF MEN for the storming parties began at two. The Duke's pinpricks were having the desired outcome. The British lion, with ruffled mane, was about to lumber into his field of fire. Silence grew in the fortress, taunts and challenges fading away. One might surmise that firearms were being cleaned and shot tallied. Behind British lines men had been fed with such edibles as harassed cooks could summon; Despard was insistent that storming parties served their monarch best with full bellies.

Timothy Walker Nene, after fretting through the morning, made a last appeal to Despard. He requested an interpreter so that Despard should not mistake his meaning. That meant me. The assault was insane, Nene said; the mere thought of it left him sick at heart. Better that Despard personally shot his own soldiers one by one, he argued, than that he push brave young men into an abyss. I ensured that this plea lost nothing in translation.

'What is he saying?' Despard demanded. 'That he wishes no part of this?'

'Nor his Maori,' I explained.

'I knew all along natives were not to be trusted,' Despard said. 'Bloody cowards one and all.'

I endeavoured to express this more charitably. It proved impossible to launder it.

'Tell the colonel that he is a very stupid man,' Nene said.

I found that no feat; I even coloured it a little.

'Tell the savage to march his men off,' Despard roared. 'I regret that it is not in my power to have him arrested and flogged.'

I conveyed such of this as suited the occasion. Nene withdrew a few yards to confer with lieutenants. Then he planted himself before the colonel again.

'What does he want now?' Despard asked. 'Hasn't he heard me?'

'Indeed he has, sir,' I said. 'He offers you a favour.'

'Favour?'

'Of bold nature, if I am not mistaken.'

'Continue,' Despard ordered.

'He says that if madness must be, he will do his best to see that disaster is kept within bounds. In brief, sir, he offers to lead his Maori in a feint to the rear of the fortress. That may not only distract the Duke; it might also lessen the damage his muskets can do from the front.'

'What do you hear in that, Wildblood?'

'A philanthropic proposition,' I risked saying.

'I hear the bleat of a spineless barbarian who wishes to keep a finger in the British pie. I am no fool. I suspect his hope is to wrest land from the rebels from behind British guns.'

'Is that your reply, sir?'

'Indeed,' Despard said.

I did not interpret. Mayhem, at this point, would serve no purpose. 'The colonel,' I advised Nene, 'does not request your services.'

'Then may he request God's,' Nene said.

He marched his Maori to the rear. With him went the last prospect of an unpretentious bloodletting.

*

The remaining hour was the longest in the lives of most present; for the imaginative it also looked to be the last. I climbed to the least imperilled location in the vicinity. It afforded me a view of preliminaries. The silence was ventilated by shots from the rejuvenated 32-pounder. In the end it proved no better than its leaner cousins in demolishing the palisades. At five minutes to three, when the last round fell, the Duke's defences were as forbidding as before. Then the Duke made himself heard. He was steeling his men for the fray. 'Stand firm,' he called. 'Let the red tribe march into our ovens.'

He may have been expressing himself figuratively; but who was I to say? I did not offer to interpret. The men of the forlorn hope, the martial euphemism for those foremost in a storming party, had enough to contemplate. Most of the volunteers for that fateful role were men of Cyprian's beloved 58th. He managed to watch them without wincing as they filed into place. So that honours might be divided, however, the front ranks were interspersed with ageing workhorses of Despard's 99th. Despard gave command of the first storming party to a sufficiently obsequious major of his own regiment. Cyprian, to his chagrin, had to make do with the second. Last to make a showing was a mixed contingent of sailors and militia equipped with axes, hatchets, grappling hooks, ropes and ladders, implements to ensure that the palisades presented no further obstacle. This nondescript group was in the command of George Philpotts; Despard mistakenly imagined him out of harm's way among military merchandise.

All in all, Despard's army could not have presented a worrying sight to the Duke's warriors. Men were ragged and filthy, their uniforms soiled and faces drawn; many were barefoot, or had their crumbling boots tied together with strips of flax. Their trousers were tattered and patched; their red jackets were dulled to the colour of brick. Their bayonets alone suggested them serious.

Men finally assembled in dead ground, in a broad gully a hundred paces short of the fortress. Judging a short pause adequate,

Despard instructed his bugler to sound advance. The problem was that he had neglected to notify most of those in his command of his intentions; even lieutenants had been overlooked. Sergeants, corporals and rankers were meant to be clairvoyant. For the first five minutes, as a result, the bugler's sound produced an unhappy *mêlée*. Officers tended to move off in one direction, their men elsewhere, until recalled and persuaded to find each other. Fortunately most of this confusion was out of view of those entrenched in the fortress; otherwise the Duke's marksmen might have had an even more noteworthy day.

The bugler sounded advance again. This time the result was less mixed. 'Prepare to charge,' officers commanded. Then 'Charge'. Men of the forlorn hope moved off at a trot, rank after rank, in close order. Their elbows were touching; there were no more than the regulation twenty-three inches between ranks. Despard was not going to countenance unsightly procedure in this battle: there were no untidy probes, messy feints, or ambling skirmishers. There was merely infantry in tight formation, muskets loaded and bayonets bristling, about to war as well as they knew.

In the hollow a second storming party formed as the first lifted away. The pioneer and naval party was preparing too. Among tradesmen George Philpotts was as conspicuous as ever. His attire for the day included not only a forage cap but also army issue black trousers with a red stripe, and a blue sailor's tunic; a sword swung from his waist. On first sight of proceedings ahead he had second thoughts about his garb. 'Damn me if I'm going to die a soldier,' he decided. With that he tossed away the cap, divested himself of the trousers, freed his sword, and hurried forward to give fight in flannel drawers, his monocle still marvellously in place.

Meanwhile the first party was closing steadily with the fortress. Fifty paces out, men heaved into a run with a hearty British hurrah. It was a signal to death to begin reaping. The citadel of vengeance came to life, with fire flashing along its front face. Then bastions right and left flared too. Finally there was a boom loud enough to speed the devil back to Bible class. As smoke cleared, it became apparent that the fortress was defended by more than muskets. Hidden in a flanking angle until that moment was a veteran 9-pounder purloined from a passing whaler. Liberally stuffed with old chains in lieu of conventional shot, it trimmed away most of the men of the first storming party; the second had to pick a path through bodies sundered and sometimes headless. Then they began toppling too. Not a man of them saw a Maori face. Rank after rank cheered themselves on; rank after rank reeled off into eternity or, if they were luckier, lifelong infirmity. Their uniforms smoked as shot burned into them again and again at short range. The few men who reached the fortress wall began slashing at ties ineffectually with bayonets, or tearing at timber with bare hands.

Militia and sailors were ordered forward to force an entrance. Most of the militia, on meeting a tide of metal, went judiciously to earth. George led a small group of sailors on with a lone scaling ladder. Miraculously ducking shot, they managed to prop it against the fortress wall. George then dismissed the party and urged them to do something happier with their lives. With a last salute to things of this world, George mounted the ladder and flourished his sword. Even in his long flannels, even as he filled with the lead of a Maori fusillade, he managed to cut a monumental figure; he seemed to float above the palisades before winging into the fortress. His fear of dying the undistinguished death of a ranker was baseless. The stain of Blackguard Beach was forgiven and forgotten. To this day, as I understand it, the Maori of northern New Zealand recount the tale of George Philpotts's demise with awe; he was the only Briton that day to view the interior of the Duke's fortress, albeit in his last moment. Passing travellers even place flowers on his grave, under a tall English oak. They believe it brings luck. There are too few heroes in this world, they say, for such as he to be unremembered. Amen.

★

By then in de facto command of the assault – with Despard's favoured officers immobile or breathing their last – Cyprian was making equally stylish efforts to win fame and a funeral. With a few men of muscle he even hauled away some of the fortress's lighter fencing only to find two fences more. Despard himself, jigging from one foot to the other, appeared to be petitioning heaven as he watched much of his army mince itself on Maori architecture. In an absent-minded fit of diligence, he suggested to his bugler that retirement might be sounded. As the notes fluttered above the battle, he turned to the bugler in poor temper.

'Who ordered that?' he demanded.

'Why, you did yourself, sir,' the baffled bugler pointed out.

'Did I indeed?'

'I fear so, sir.'

'That is damned curious. Tell me, young fellow, do you observe the fortress taken?'

'Not at this juncture, sir,' the bugler confessed.

Despard mused while more men died. 'So why should I have done that, pray?'

In fear of court martial, the bugler replied, 'I cannot imagine, sir.'

'Very well. Call the buggers back if you must.'

So much for generalship. The ensuing retreat was no more masterful. Britons had forgotten how to depart a battlefield in disciplined fashion. Soldiers bolting from blazing loopholes found their weapons an impediment and discarded them as they ran. This did not necessarily save them. Feuding over proprietorship of loopholes, Maori marksmen placed shot among a forest of fleeing legs. A few brave Britons staggered home with wounded and dying on their shoulders. The Duke's men crept from the palisades and among Britons abandoned. Their swinging tomahawks won an impressive silence.

★

The attack lasted no longer than five minutes. At its end there were forty Britons lifeless on the field and others slowly expiring. More than a hundred were mangled in ways large and small. Not a rebel could be heard suffering.

Quiet grew. Both sides seemed dumbfounded.

I found Cyprian resting such of his regiment as he managed to retrieve from the inferno. The seriously damaged were being borne off to surgeons in stretchers and makeshift litters. Short-range shooting meant minor wounds were few. Cyprian himself was intact, though this was not apparent. His uniform was bloody and blackened, his voice a bleak whisper.

'George too?' he asked.

'George too,' I confirmed.

'Is this war?' He was still breathing hard.

'Our wishes sometimes confound us,' I suggested.

'Tell me it is not true,' he pleaded.

At his most venturesome Henry Youngman would have found that difficult. The best that could be expected from Ferdinand Wildblood was a civilized elegy for the fallen. The fact is that the day was as desperate as any in the history of British arms.

Nor was it finished. The Duke's recipe for humble pie required him to assemble his men where they were most visible to the red tribe and there lead them in an athletic war dance. The picturesque character of this performance – the stamping feet and flashing tongues, the pitiless chanting and wild leaps with weapons high – eluded me as dead cooled by the dozen under the winter sun. I knew what it meant at last. There was nothing in the least quaint in this pagan polka. It spoke defiance, exultation, triumph, and above all contempt of death; it spoke of men mastering the world and the worst it could do. Need I say that my soul shrivelled? My genitals likewise? Consider it said.

Cyprian, reluctant to leave the field, shepherded the last of his casualties to safety. His eyes were still stunned.

'Come,' I said, and offered my shoulder.

'I am not a victim,' he protested.

'I am the best judge of that,' I argued.

He leaned on me after all as we limped after his men. Engrossed in finding a path unmenaced by shot, I failed to note another impediment. Freed from Despard's quarantine by the sound of strife, the Reverend Williams had arrived to do his duty by Christendom's dead. His face said he was still struggling to comprehend the magnitude of his task. He acknowledged my presence only so far as I formed part of a charmless spectacle.

'I cannot believe it, Wildblood,' he confided.

'Your difficulty is shared,' I told him.

'Meanwhile we have a familiar mission.'

'We, sir?'

'You and I,' he agreed.

'If you mean recovering the dead, sir, you would be well advised to let battlefield fever pass.'

'Never,' he said. 'Strike while the iron is hot. The Duke may be a pagan, but many in his entourage are more enlightened. Should we approach the fortress they may hear our plea charitably.'

'If John Heke were among them, perhaps.'

'Confound the fellow,' Williams said. 'I am beginning to miss him.'

Later that afternoon we approached the fortress in full view of the Duke's marksmen. A shot discharged in the air stopped us short of our goal.

'Say your business,' an authoritative voice shouted.

'I come for Christian heroes of all colours,' Williams replied.

There was a lengthy silence. A conference was evidently in progress. Meanwhile we were marooned in a sea of human fragments. Soldiers and sailors were strewn among streamers of viscera and a slime of drying blood. Shock lingered on the few faces intact, resignation on others. And that is not to tally the least agreeable sight of all. George Philpotts's monocle dangled poign-antly from the point of a palisade. The rest of him was missing.

The same voice said, 'Come for the dead when your Colonel withdraws his army and promises peace for a month.'

'You ask him to confess defeat.'

'He cannot boast victory.'

'In that respect he may amaze you,' Williams promised.

'Then peace for a week,' the rebel bargained generously. 'Return with the colonel's answer tomorrow.'

Midwinter dusk was falling as we made our way back to the camp. 'Thank you, Wildblood,' Williams said. 'I daresay you have been expecting harsh words from me.'

'Such words should not have surprised me, sir.'

'You will not hear them today,' Williams explained. 'Mortality on such a scale encourages a different perspective.'

'Indeed, sir.'

'Angela is well?'

'Safe in Heke's camp.'

'You would do well to think of her soul,' he suggested. 'And for that matter of yours.'

'I shall give it thought,' I promised.

'The communion rail is ready for you. Similarly the altar. Not to put too fine a point on it, God is.'

'That is a tall order, sir.'

'May you soon hear it,' Williams said.

'What is it now?' Despard asked.

Relieved of his boots, if not of command misery, he sat in his tent. An attentive manservant filled his glass to brimming, plainly not for the first time.

'It is in respect of the dead, sir,' Williams said.

'Been counting them, have you?'

'My brief is to ensure Christian burial.'

'Shall I tell you what I think?' Despard downed his grog and indicated his need for more.

'By all means,' Williams said.

'There is more to this than meets the eye.'

'God's intentions are seldom apparent,' Williams agreed.

'I talk of perfidy,' Despard explained.

'Perfidy, sir?'

'Rank treachery. Whoever heard of natives who refused to back away from Britain's bayonets? Whoever heard of a heathen fortress halting us? I smell renegades at work.'

Williams was as nonplussed as I.

'Renegades?' he asked quietly.

'White men,' Despard disclosed. 'Mercenaries. Traffickers with the enemy. Perhaps treason-loving Yankees.'

'This far,' Williams observed gently, 'such renegades have failed to make themselves apparent.'

'That is their cunning,' Despard explained. 'Would you expect such fiends to show their faces? The proof of their existence is before us.'

'Proof, sir?'

'On the battlefield. The good men fallen there cry betrayal by their own kind. This has not been the work of untutored savages.'

'Who knows?' Williams asked, as piously as he could.

'I know,' said Despard, beginning to quiver.

'And you will confide as much in your report?' Williams said.

'You understand me,' Despard said. 'To argue otherwise would be disloyal to our dead.'

'Speaking of the dead,' Williams said, 'I bear a rebel proposition.'

'It is not my intention to offer mercy,' Despard announced.

Wherever he was campaigning, it was still elsewhere.

★

The day had been bitter; night was no improvement. The busiest location in the British camp was the surgeon's tent. Bullets were extracted, bones set, and limbs amputated. The surgeons slaved in a soup of mud and blood. Elsewhere, in tent after silent tent, men lay felled by rheumatism, cramp and shock. Many a young lieutenant lost interest in his vocation that day; many a captain began contemplating the sale of his commission.

As if there were not enough to unnerve them, there was war dance after war dance performed in the fortress; there were no uplifting hymns of the kind John Heke favoured. There was also, from time to time, satanic shrieking, which may or may not have been pagan priests possessed by spirits. At all events it was preferable to think so. Terrified men on piquet duty deserted their posts and had to be persuaded back again by officers still capable of pointing a pistol.

Despard's lamp burned till late. For his superiors he dictated the following to a tactfully silent subaltern: 'It would be difficult to give an impression of the enthusiasm with which troops advanced to the attack. The struggle was who would be foremost. My troops returned to camp undaunted in mind and spirit, wishing only that another opportunity of attack might be offered them.'

You think that dispatch this chronicler's invention? Not a syllable is mine.

The Duke had composed a more reliable report for tribesmen far and near. It was short of flourishes and succinct in character: 'One wing of Britain is broken and hangs dangling on the ground. Who will help break the other?'

Cyprian, after touring tents and consoling his wounded, finally made his appearance in the accommodation we shared with George Philpotts; the silence there was crushing. He sat for a time with head in hands.

'If it is any comfort,' I finally informed him, 'you were not beaten by mere savages.'

'No?'

'Your commander attributes today's disaster to renegades.'

Cyprian remained silent for a time.

'That means he may have to find one,' he pointed out.

'Like whom?' I asked.

'Like you,' he warned.

My interest in colonial warfare appeared to be on the wane.

Maurice Gee

from **PROWLERS**

I

I DO NOT LIKE HER. She's beautiful without any contrivance
and I don't trust nature to that degree. Nasty things lie under
surfaces. That's the sum of my wisdom learned through lenses –
my lifetime of squinting through bits of glass. Tup said magnifi-
cation banished fear. So it seemed to me for many years. Now I
know it shows empty places, endless recession, and how can we
hope to travel there? We're trapped at the intersection of two
planes (is and ought, there's two good names), we're buried at
a crossroads with the stake of our limitations through our heart.
An evolutionary dead-end, my opinion. Said as much to that girl,
but she was kind, gave me a verbal pat and a smile like a sticky
sweet. She's blue of eye, a Lotte Ogier eye, and pink of cheek,
and honey-tongued, and oh so patient with this smelly dod-
derer, myself; but whispers, 'Shit!' under her breath when her tape
plays up.

I don't like that. Don't like her. I wish she'd leave me alone
and stop this infernal scrape scrape with her questions. It gets her
nowhere with me that she's grand-daughter of my sister Kitty, and
this job, all she can get with her fine degree! keeps her from
drawing unemployment benefit. I don't care if she starves. I don't

care if she goes on the streets. That won't bother a girl so free with faecal expletives.

Calm down. Read your pulse. Is it still there? Do I still have a pint or two of blood? See the yellow dent the biro leaves in the ball of my thumb. It's beyond my resources now to plump that bit of flesh out.

Beauty lies under surfaces. There's a contradiction. So soon? It does not matter. Contradictions are beautiful. Tensions are beautiful. And beauty is inadmissible! So, all my life, to the very end, I kick the feet from under myself, and pick myself up. What fun it is knocking these bits of skin off. The blood flows, see?

Start again. I do not like her; like you not, Kate Adams, your plumped-out lip and bright kind eye and snake-hissed lavatory word. The skin peeling on your arms – don't you know the dangers? Your moving breasts. That's too much cheek. Put on a brassière, you slut, before you come questing here again.

Questing is a good word. It's inadmissible. Confusion is a good word. Extraordinary to be confused after a life so full of magnifications and clarity. And mysteries penetrated. And governing principles understood. Kitty used to infuriate me by saying of Lotte Ogier, piano teacher – a Meissen shepherdess, pink, befrilled, a weeping German monster, greedy, cruel – that her eyes were so blue and clean she must take them out at night and wash them in a basin of cold water. Bile rose in my throat to hear her say it, a bitter taste came on my tongue, and pulses made a flutter in my temples. I cried, 'You can't take out eyes, you're being mad,' and I got my new anatomy chart and showed Kitty the human eye in horizontal section, a structure I had *understood*, and made my property, and showed her how it was continuous, from sclerotic and cornea and crystalline lens to the optic nerve which carried the impressions to the brain, and it was mad, *mad*, to talk of washing it in basins of water. The thing would be dead then, you could never put it back. Kitty defended herself. She had not been talking of optic nerves but Lotte Ogier, a different matter. You couldn't cut her down the middle and make a chart of her ('Oh yes you can' – and I flipped pages), and eyes, after all, were things you looked at, not just with, and they could have meanings of all sorts. And she quoted some line about 'speaking eyes', which made me screech, 'Eyes can't speak'; and then we grinned, for we had moved into self-caricature, a saving place; and Kitty looked at my chart then, for she had wide interests, and understood the eye in a trice, though she let me explain, and marvelled at the good sense of it all. That pleased me immensely, for it was my good sense. Yet Lotte Ogier's clean blue eyes always made me tremble after that.

Kate Adams has that eye. Washed and bright. She's a thing of lovely surfaces. How complete the young are, you never think of bits when faced with them. Organs, blood, bowel – that Burma road – murky secretions by the kidney-bowl; none of that. They seem all joints and surfaces and their parts are teeth and hair, no parts at all, but continuous. Yet this one peels. Is she starting to come apart, as I come apart? The last thing I want is to pity her. Admiration, dislike, interest, lust, fear, as I watch from my multiple eyes. Pity with all this? I'm glad she's gone, reduced to neuronic shifts in my brain.

I take my handkerchief (it crackles like paper, and how that made her twist her nose) and wipe the sore grooves that run from my clown's mouth down to my jawbone – which I consider now turning into the jawbone of an ass and hacking at friends and enemies with. She did not kiss me there but on the forehead. My mother used to kiss me on the lips, full on the lips, and Kitty too, and even Dad. We were a kissing family and must have put armies of germs about. But Kate has taken my germs, no doubt at all, from the chair she sat in, from my fingers' touch, and touch of my mind. Minds, the boy Noel screeches, cannot touch, but I tell him to shut his gob, he's had his say. Kate stowed her tape-recorder in her ethnic bag – embroidered sugar-sack it looked to me – pecked me at the hairline, ran prophylactic finger on her mouth, and off she swayed. She'll edit this weekend and bring her transcript round to me next week. It's all lies. I gave her a batch of sterile slides, but touched her with my mind, its many parts, and will see if we can get a culture there.

I've flown apart. There are bits of me floating off as I spin and spin. Can I persuade them back by being still?

Here they come, the asteroids, the basalt moons.

2

I don't want them. Start again. The girl upset me. I'm not like this, not a mad old man. I'm Noel Papps. I'm dux of Jessop College. I'm Pettigrew Scholar. Here I come, I'm Dr Papps, I'm head of Soil Science. I, alone, discover what is wrong with the Plowden Hills, why they won't grow, and I, Noel Papps, repair that error (Whose? I ask the bishop). I put in what they haven't got; and look at me now, I'm Director of the Lomax Institute, I'm Sir Noel.

Have I reached the end? Is that all? One paragraph and a joke? My God, is this my entry? Where are the days? They were brimful. They burst like crates of apples. They ran off down the lawn like apples spilled, I have not the hands to grab them all. Where are they gone, lying in the long grass, lying in the hydrangeas. Slaters crawl in brown caves pecked by birds. I crush cider-flesh with my feet, walking by.

Piffle! Rot! I'm not Kitty. This is her stuff. Get yourself out of my head now, Kit. Go on. Minds can't touch. I know my days, they're marked on calendars, eighty years. Not one is lost, not one lasts a moment longer than I allow it to. I'm in control and all those forces outside law – fear, grief, desire, comedy, ambition, hatred, love – are cellular in me and know their place and wait until I stain them to their lawful show; and that's no boast. Amazement and clear sight go hand in hand.

So what shall I choose, where am I now? Shall I be with Tup Ogier in the playground, leading him to where a praying mantis eats a fly? It's a blue one, iridescent, oil-sheeny, and its buzz half-hearted and its legs giving life away as hooked arms hold it dinner-wise and jaws chomp its head. 'A beauty,' Tup breathes. 'God-horse in some places, Papps. Lovely creature, eh?' The mantis eats the fly's head like an apple, stopping only to munch a leg like a celery stick. 'See how its jaws work. Mandibles. They're lateral, not horizontal like ours.' He has his little glass out from its hinged leather case and lets me look. I see yellow jaws that work unhurriedly in time with the crunch of fly tissue. 'The strength there, Papps. If he was as big as us he could chew iron bars.' 'She,' I say, looking at her abdomen; and he pats me and says, 'Good boy. Look, here's pudding.' The mantis eats unborn maggots from the fly's abdomen. They wriggle, tiny grubs, but there's nowhere to go. Untimely ripped, my father would say; born into the monster's iron jaws.

If mantises could burp this mantis would. Her lovely arms wipe her lovely mouth. There's not a fly-scrap left, and she's cross-eyed, she's blotto, and will fall off her twig if she doesn't watch out.

'A bird should come along and eat her now.'

'Ha! Good boy.'

That was the first lens I looked through, Tup Ogier's magnifying glass, which he called 'my truth-teller'. 'No more superstition, Papps, when you look through this.' 'No, sir,' I said, not understanding. Years later, he gave the glass to me, and I joked, 'She tells the truth but she can't prophesy.' He stroked her with the ball of his thumb. 'She does enough. The end of fear, Noel. Look after her.' I took her — let's say *it* — home and dropped it in a drawer; and it lies there now, with a litter of specimens I'll never classify — marble from the valleys and granite from the hills I play the game of name and number with; or would if I had the interest; and gold, a tiny nugget, and a splinter of black basalt speckled with olivine.

Tup's glass and all her kind tell me nothing now.

3

When he gave you his attention you couldn't tell which eye it was that saw. Which eye must you fix yours on, like a man? One was always out of line and though it wasn't that you chose it always came to fix on you and make you blink, and the other was the one over your shoulder. Tup, the least shifty of men, shifted them. Yet I believe that's impossible. Impossible, too, that it was the outward sign of an inner flaw, his maculation, for moral health made a running fire on his skin. He wore a ragged ear, but that was no flaw, that was a prop – mauled by a wildcat in Peru, bitten by a Burmese pirate in the China Seas. His teeth were under pressure from each other, they jutted or lay back like head-stones in an old cemetery. With all this, an energetic springing of coarse hair, pads of it on cheeks and wrists and fingerbacks; horse-lips, ape-man jaw, yeti-feet; and you had a man of ugliness so majestic that children new at his school had been known to hide their faces at the sight of him. 'Imagine having to kiss him,' little Irene Lomax breathed. Tup was a walking contradiction, and a lesson for me in deeps and surfaces.

He took the four of us – a Blyton four, said clever Kate, not an hour ago, and was miffed at having to explain – into the little lab he'd made in a storeroom at school and gave us a lesson in blowpipe analysis. The occasion comes spinning back to my centre. Beauties of shape and significance make me a little breathless as I set it down to study it; and speculations threaten me about chance and fate. None of that. I will not fall down that hole.

We were Kitty and Noel Papps, Irene Lomax, Phil Dockery, and Phil and I had helped capture Edgar Le Grice, the Jessop fire-raiser. Our story appeared in the *Daily Times* alongside news of the landings in the Dardanelles. I'd better get us down in our right balance. Algebraic symbols would help, Kitty as x, Phil as y, and so on, and then I could compare and bind together, and display us in our proper magnitudes; and Tup and Le Grice could come in; others too, Lotte Ogier (a subtraction from Lotte Reinbold), and the Gasman, Les Dockery, a negative number, and a dozen others, and I might end up with an axiom. Instead I have these powers that won't obey, and a sense that individual being rests on lawlessness. So I'll enter the maze without that help, and the only cotton thread I'll hold is me.

Noel Papps was a boy just turned thirteen. An ugly fellow – like this sick baboon, old Sir Noel. He gave an impression of sootiness, sooty eyebrows, sooty hair, and dark blood in his cheeks; and a rubber face, lips you could stretch and let fly back, an ill-formed nose, a squashed potato, and eyes very dark, smart-alec eyes that signalled the boy's anxieties too well. He asked himself how he would get on, having, so to speak, no exterior. He declared what was inside without moderation, desperately. He was clever. Like fat boys he must be a character, and he was part way to it when things happened in Jessop that made him something else.

That's Noel Papps, a bit of him. Or is it marks on paper? One begins with an axiom, one doesn't end. Begins with a truth self-evident. Say *Noel Papps* and leave it there. What's the place of all this attribution? Sooty. Ill-formed. That stands already, doesn't it, in *Papps*? Smart alec though. That is better. That somehow changes the rules. It prods the thing into a jerky step. We advance some way into the dark with that. I could have some interest in this game. There's a buzzing in my ears. I could become a devotee. There are things I'll never see again, not now; shadowy forms I'll never reach. But *smart alec* – yes. And *desperation*. Progress like that makes one ambitious.

Let's get on.

★

If I hadn't been a scientist I would have been an actor. I made up my mind that's what I'd be. I practised stretching my face, I practised snarling. I laughed, heh! heh! heh! and I did murders. Sometimes at the bathroom mirror I'd try Robin Hood, but I was a clever boy, as I've said, and I wasted only a moment before inflating into Friar Tuck. I was very good as the Sheriff of Nottingham too. My eyebrows came down to hide my eyes and my teeth grew points. When I played the Kaiser in our school's patriotic pageant I had a face all ready to use.

Kitty was Britannia. She sat on a throne and held a trident, just like the lady on the penny. Irene was Gallant Little Belgium. 'Britannia, Britannia, oh pity our distress . . .' And Phil Dockery, the Port Rat, barefoot boy, flea-bag Phil in his ragged pants, was New Zealand. That came about from my cleverness. I was chosen for New Zealand, and being hero tempted me, and the rifle and uniform, but not as much as the spiked Hun helmet and the moustache. 'I tear this poppy Belgium from her stem!' I knew my part. There was something else though, and sometimes it increases me and sometimes diminishes. Although it's a fact I can't focus on it, which is upsetting. I'll put down this: I was sorry for Phil. We were not friends, but Mrs Beattie had marked him down as Hun, and I saw what he would lose. So I pointed out how tall he was. She stood us back to back and even without shoes he had an inch on me.

'New Zealand should be tallest, Mrs Beattie. I can do the Hun. You watch.' I stretched my rubber face and lunged so fierce at Irene that she screeched, and I made as if to twist her head from her neck. Mrs Beattie, fat and silly – silly in behaviour, fat in her mind, but clever in a number of pin-pricking ways – recognized me; saw the centre of strength that would hold up the shaky structure she assembled, and was left with Phil Dockery as New Zealand. Turning this grubby Port Rat into our soldier boy brought her cruelty out. She tweaked his ear and tugged his greasy hair, and wiped his germs from her fingertips with a folded handkerchief. 'Whait cliffs, Dockery, whait, not whoit. You sound like a navvy from Liverpool.' How all the goody-good girls, in their pinafores and pink ears, laughed. Irene laughed, though she would have to stand by him and have his arm around her in the end. The bolder girls pretended they had seen fleas jumping over.

I fought with Phil Dockery in a corner of the school grounds. Crazy with insult, he tried to twist my head from my shoulders. But I was rubber, I changed shape, he could not hold me. I stayed alive until Tup Ogier came and broke us in half as though breaking an apple, and marched us by our necks off to his room to tan our hides. But there he only let his strap roll out like an ant-eater's tongue and rolled it up again and put it away and spread a chart of the human brain on his table and showed us where the evil passions lived. He told us the brain was a flower, see how it opened like a rose — the cerebellum — but down here in the stem a worm was eating, here in the medulla oblongata, the reptile brain. That's where Phil and I had been, splashing with the crocodiles in the swamp. I thought that was unfair. Phil had been trying to kill me but I had only been trying to stay alive. I didn't protest though, because the chart had taken my breath away and I had no time for unimportant things. Tup strikes again. Every time he aimed at me he scored a bull's-eye.

'Sir,' I said, 'sir' — and I could smell a strong sweet scent — it penetrated me. Life was a series of shocks and recognitions. I had perhaps a dozen steps to make, and this was one; and when Tup rolled the chart up and sent me away, keeping Phil back to swab iodine on his knee, where my loose toe-cap had razored him, I felt as if I had been given a taste of some new food and its flavour lingered in my mouth and penetrated my cerebellum. In lunch-hours I sneaked inside and opened Tup's drawer and studied the chart; played games with it, sailed down this river and that, explored the hemispheres like continents and found scaly birds and man-eating fish; but came always back to names and outlines, for the real adventure started there – in control. That was the thing I smelled like a rose.

And I sneaked up to the belfry and spent my time with Miss Montez, stroking her, poking my fingers in her apertures. She had lovely fingers, she had lovely toes, and a pelvis like a gravy-boat. Beautiful joints – Tup rubbed them with mutton fat – and a curve in thigh and forearm no woman with flesh on her has ever equalled, not for me. The measured knitting on her skull could not have been done better with a machine. Her eyeholes had a symmetry and balance that made me want to weigh and measure them. She was yellow. Tup told me later she was probably a man.

Phil and I carried her down for a lesson. She was wired to a wooden frame and Tup moved her arms and legs with a set of levers at the back. 'Children, say hello to Miss Montez. She's my good friend of many years. I met her first on a river steamer in Brazil. A Portuguese lady, a soprano at the Manaos opera. She threw herself into the river for hopeless love of an Italian tenor—', and so on, aimed at the girls. The piranhas ate her – 'look, you can see the marks of their teeth on her bones' – and the tenor sang an aria that made everyone cry. Then Tup bought her from the captain for seven shillings.

'That's all lies, sir,' Kitty said.

'When we don't know the facts we're entitled to invent,' Tup replied.

There were facts enough for me, her bones were facts. He raised her arms like mantis arms – but likenesses were nothing beside names. Tup told me them: occipital and parietal, clavicle and scapula, humerus, ulna, femur, fibula, and lovely toes and fingers, phalanges. Mouthing these, I possessed Miss Montez. I entered a world shining with order, bright with controls, where two follows one and three follows two. To know the name of things is my desire; our only proper knowing is through names. Circles are completed in the noun, margins and boundaries are clear, and we are free from vagueness, free from fear, with every object known from every other. The name, the name, is the single proper epithet.

And having said that, what about the verb? Isn't breaking down and building up the thing that chemistry is all about? For I'm a chemist. Nouns create a landscape without movement or sound. Nothing happens. Verbs bring activity and change. Yes, I agree with that argument. But I see predication as closer naming. Noun and verb unite in my craft or science.

I say this as though it remains true all my life. It started long ago when I was young, uncertain of what was real and what was not, afraid, and glimpsing powers (seeming to glimpse) – ready for religion, that is. The answer did not come from there, and never can for me, not now, even though the answer that I found doesn't hold. The name's a lovely shell, lovely container, but outside and in, chaos, harmony, unknowable. I remember now, better than occipital, parietal, the hollows in her skull, the aching void.

I go on too long about Miss Montez. Miss Montez was not my bride, the oxidizing flame was my true bride. Let me come to her by even steps. And in all these words find one big name? I don't hope for it. Nor is my question theological. Anything considered, but no theology, never that. By big name I simply mean my life. I'll be selective – direct, evasive – and perhaps come close to it, a shadow shape. I'll go along by predication. That's the method. But acting shall be my vehicle. I've placed that talent second long enough.

How I shall howl! How I shall laugh!

4

But I shall also say things quietly and try to put them in their proper place. Howls and laughs will be imperatives, chronology will be my discipline. So – the patriotic pageant, that comes next.

I can say my speeches to this day: 'No scrap of paper binds me. Might is right. The weak I feed into my iron jaws. What care

I for truth and peace and justice? I tear this poppy Belgium from her stem. I trample her red petals in the mud—'

Mrs Beattie wrote it with the vicar of St Bede's. The Kaiser had the best lines. Kitty, on her throne, might cry, 'Fight we must and fight we will. Who will follow? Speak!' and Egypt, India, Canada step forward – 'I', 'And I' – and poor Phil, rifle shouldered, at attention, 'Mother of Empire, furthest are we from Home of all your sons, far far we lie from those dear *whait* cliffs—' but that was all just wind and I had words. My moustache went crooked and I tore it off and held it like a blade in my hand, killing laughter. And in the end, though I squatted shrinking at Kitty's feet, though she held me snarling till I died, with her trident digging in my back, while everyone sang 'Land of Hope and Glory' and the hall joined in, I knew there had been one peak in the night and I, Noel Papps, had stood on it alone.

Before we could take our bows, Jacklin, our MP, came bounding on stage. 'Friends, people of Jessop, children of Jessop school . . .' He was a doggy fellow, oh how he wanted to be patted, to be loved. And how ready he was to snarl and bite and prove this way his devotion and worth. He pumped with his little fat arms. We smelled him – tobacco and ripe meat – and heard, the nearest, Phil and I, a bubbling in his guts, and heard him fart, poot, poot, poot, three little woofs. 'What a glorious night! And what a lesson we've learned! Out of the mouths of babes, eh? True patriotic feeling.'

Tup Ogier, in the front row, shook his head. He'd had words with Mrs Beattie about the jingoistic huff and puff in her pageant. Lomax, the mayor, who had filled Jacklin with the food that caused his borborygmus, began to pull his lower lip. And perhaps Jacklin had not meant to speak real words but lost his judgement. Real words came out in the end. 'Which of us wouldn't like to shoot a Hun right now? A Hun or Turk? For Empire. For Mother England. Remember those lads in Gisborne, how they wrecked that German pork butcher's shop? He'll never show his face again.

And that one in Wellington, with the name no civilized person can pronounce. Von this! Von that! We'll show 'em, eh? We'll show 'em, with these young soldier lads and lasses at our backs. Von, two, three, out!'

When the laughter had died down he put his hands on his knees, he almost squatted, and leaned his face into the audience. 'What a pity it is we haven't got any pork butchers in our town.'

A man at the back said in a loud voice, 'We've got that piano teacher down the road.' It was Edgar Le Grice.

Now there's a name. I feel when I've put it down I've said enough. Jacklin I need a lot of words for and at the end he's barely there. Edgar Le Grice though – that's enough. He comes spinning back like a moon. And he's black. He's red and black. And he has fire in his head. You see it burning there behind his eyes. He's on his feet below neat-lettered Sunday School texts and the paragraphs make his head start out of a page. A hulking fellow, silent. I've seen him once before, squatting beside his hydraulic ram and watching over his shoulder as Tup marches us up the river bank for swimming in Bucks Hole. We're on his property but have right-of-way and Tup keeps us strictly to the path. The thump-thump of the ram is the beat of Le Grice's rage. He never moves, he's like stone there.

Now here he is, with 'love' and 'Lamb of God' about his head, but different words coming from his mouth. 'Why should she grow fat here when we've got soldiers dying over there?'

Others took it up, young fellows mostly. Cries, thick and brutal, filled the air.

Lomax mounted halfway up the steps. 'Now, wait a minute, boys, wait a minute.' He tried to say we didn't want any trouble in Jessop, not tonight; but Le Grice said, 'Shut up, Lomax. Your daughter goes there for piano lessons.'

'Not any more,' Lomax cried.

Le Grice took no more notice; ignored Jacklin too, flapping on the stage. He said in his passionless way, while rage leaked from his eyes, 'We're not having her, so follow me,' and I seemed to hear again the ram's thick beating.

Although I did not know it, my father had gone, which was brave of him. With a name like ours it would have been more sensible to go home quietly and lock the door. But he ran down the road with Tup Ogier and found Frau Reinbold at her piano. He threw his coat on her and took her along the alley by the park and hid her in the bakehouse, with Kitty and Irene to look after her.

Tup faced Le Grice's mob from the middle of Frau Reinbold's garden path. Phil and I arrived in time to hear the end of his speech and had not heard his voice so lost before. He was a man of too many words. On the other side of the white picket fence was Edgar Le Grice.

'She's your fancy lady, teacher, so shut up.' He kicked the toy gate and sent it spinning off its hinges. They knocked Tup Ogier down and ran over him. Sunday-suited for our pageant, black and dense, they wedged through the door, one stopping to wrench Frau Reinbold's plate from the wall and spin it like a discus into the street.

We helped Tup Ogier up. His tattered ear was bleeding. I felt the bottom fall out of one of my certainties. We sat him on the garden seat and he panted, 'Stay away, boys, they've gone mad.' My father came back. 'It's all right, Tom. She's in the bakehouse. She's all right.' A smashing of glass came from the house. The noise seemed to fracture my teeth, I felt them throbbing. Tup tried to stand up but my father held him. 'They'll tear you to bits. Get the police, boys.'

'Mr Lomax went for them.'

The French doors bulged and burst. Le Grice appeared, with curtains draping his torso. He tore them in handfuls from their rings and balled them and flung them into the garden, where they opened out and floated like scarves and settled on the round-headed shrubs. He leaned back inside and gave a heave and seemed to lift the Bechstein over the step. Men with white mad faces came beetling round its sides. They beat it across the flower beds, kicked it like a donkey and tipped it three feet into the sunken garden. One jumped on it and struck it with an axe. The letters of the name sprang out and looped to my feet. (And my father lifted the spiked Prussian helmet from my head and put it down behind a daphne bush.)

The axe made kindling of the ebony wood. The keys came out and made a waterfall. Wires sighed, and hammers did a caterpillar walk. Edgar Le Grice had gone back into the house. Now he appeared in the doorway, with a bottle held stiff-armed above his head, and throat lined up as though he meant to swig. He jumped on the piano, shouldered the axeman away, stood wide-legged in the broken keys. Liquid spun like glycerine and fractured into glass at his feet. He held the bottle until it was empty, then flung it back-handed at the house, where it burst on the wall and rained his mob with splinters. Le Grice had sucked motion, speech, intention, even fear, from us all. We were like the sleepers in the castle and could not move as he passed among us, but could see. The rattle of his matches brought us awake.

'No!' shouted Tup Ogier.

'Ha!' cried the mob – a breath in time with the fire's explosion. Le Grice seemed lifted by it and thrown back. He landed on his feet on the garden wall, and stood wide-legged, lit-up, facets of him flashing red and yellow. I think of him now as pleochromatic, but that's a defence, that's a retreat, it leaves out black. And as the piano crackles and the flames turn crystalline, it's black I see: Le Grice spinning at me, basalt moon.

5

'A tragic family,' Tup Ogier said; and that was with their story only half told. Everybody knew it but my mother told it best, especially stirring pots at the stove or beating dough on the kitchen table, when her busy-ness became a kind of counterpoint to the story. The Le Grices had been lazy and proud, treating their farm out there in the river bend as a country estate, and he, Edgar's father, not doing a hand's turn but strolling with a walking stick – called it his ash-plant – and pointing out this and that wanted doing. He owned property in town and ran for mayor but failed because he was too snooty to ask for people's votes. He thought the highest place should be his by right.

Mrs Le Grice, the old lady? Well, my mother said, fixing us, then slapping dough, she wasn't always old, remember that. A beautiful woman, in her day – if you go for the sort without any flesh on their bones. And of course she could spend as much as she liked on clothes. A fashion-plate, and very social too. They had garden parties there, and English lords and ladies to stay. But all that changed, my mother said; and could not be satisfied, for it came about from the death of a child. Lucy was her name, Lucy Le Grice. To hear my mother tell it, she was a kind of fairy or woodsprite, flitting about the farm, among the lords and ladies, picking flowers. She drowned when she was nine, in a river pool, called Girlies Hole later, where classes from our school had swimming lessons. Her brother, Edgar, was meant to be watching her, but he had gone off fishing with his mates. They found her in the deep part, down past the rapids, floating under the water like a fish, with her eyes wide open.

'Oh, the poor thing,' Kitty said, her own eyes brimming.

'I've seen her photograph. It's all over the house,' Irene Lomax said.

My mother gave her a puzzled look. She disapproved of Irene, that confidence and knowingness, yet was pleased Kitty should have the mayor's daughter as a friend. A part of her story, too, was robbed from her – that no one ever saw Mrs Le Grice after Lucy drowned. I waited to see if she would work it in. Cecil Le Grice, she went on, became a shadow. He wasted away and died from grief. As thin as a matchstick, she said, and his skull nearly breaking through his skin. And, she said doggedly, not looking at Irene, no one saw Mrs Le Grice after Lucy drowned, not close up. They saw her on the porch sometimes, but she went inside if people called. She wore sandshoes and a garden party hat. The tennis court grew weeds and the fences rusted. All the workmen left and Edgar Le Grice tried to run the farm. Gorse came down the hills. He grew into a hulking silent fellow.

And at forty-five (it's not my mother now) he started burning buildings round the town. He burned a grocer shop and a quarry shed and the band rotunda in the park and Dargie's Livery Stables. He tried to burn Lomax's seed and grain warehouse, but Phil and I stopped him. It happened on the night after the pageant. The day too had its terrible event.

I find it hard to go on. Not because of terror, I can face that. Because of shifts, because of dizziness. Nothing will be still. Poverty and abundance transmute. And this is that and that is this. And *it* was so, but yet not *so*. What other option but silence do I have? Imperfections strike at me like hail. And there, you see, this double focus, which is a kind of seeing round corners, a view through mirrors cunningly placed, when all I want is to look *straight* at the *single* thing. Obliquity makes me dizzy, multiplicity smothers me. Yet I'll go on. I think that if I'm silent I'll soon die.

Frau Reinbold then. She sat at our breakfast table, and, 'Oh, you are spoiling me,' and, 'I shall grow fat,' she cried as my mother ladled porridge into her plate. Plump and pink and sugar-spun Frau Reinbold, with eyes so sparkling blue they looked as if she took them out at night etc. etc. 'Outside it was Walpurgisnacht. But Kitty and Irene – two angels.'

'She was more like a devil with that fork,' I said.

'Ha!' The Frau seized her spoon and poked my ribs. My mother frowned.

'If you've finished, Noel, go and get ready for school.'

I was reluctant. I'd worked out what a fancy lady was and I

was a little drunk with Frau Reinbold. My father came in and said Tup Ogier was in the sitting room and wanted to talk to her. 'Ah, dear Thomas,' she cried, dabbing her lips with a hanky and tweaking her cheeks to colour them up, though already they were as pink as cherry icing. Dad showed her out, winking at Mum; and according to Kitty, who peeped through the door, Tup Ogier held Frau Reinbold in his arm – like this, she demonstrated – and wiped tears from her cheeks with his own hanky. Mum looked into the hall then and made a charge at Kitty with the flyswat, so she saw no more. But, 'Fancy having to kiss him,' Irene Lomax breathed.

We sat in our desks with fingers folded and looked at Tup with interest and respect. His ragged ear was yellow with iodine. Ladypowder smudged his black waistcoat. 'Tup tup, tup tup,' he sang as he moved about.

'Sir,' Phil said, 'my father reckons Mr Le Grice must be the fire-raiser.'

'Well, Dockery,' Tup replied, 'we mustn't start rumours. We must leave the fire-raiser to the police.'

'Sir,' Kitty said, 'those bumps you told us about, on people's heads—'

'Phrenology,' I said.

'It's not a science remember, it's like astrology, a pseudo-science.'

'Yes, sir. Would a fire-raiser have a special bump?'

'If we believed in it, Kitty, he certainly would. Just here, above the ear. Destructiveness. Quite close to music, strangely enough. I wonder what harmonies he hears.'

'Sir, can we see Miss Montez?'

'Ah no, not today. Arithmetic.'

'Do Germans have a special bump?' I asked, meaning fancy ladies.

'No, Papps, certainly not.'

'Germans have got square heads,' said a boy called Ray Stack. (Hay stack.)

'Who told you that?' Tup said.

'My father. He says it's square with a hole where the brains should be.'

'Ha, ha,' we laughed uneasily.

Tup breathed through his nose. 'Arithmetic.'

'Was Frau Reinbold's piano worth a lot of money?' I asked. I could not stop rubbing myself against her.

'Enough. Enough. Books out.'

'It was a Bechstein,' Irene said. Her own Bechstein was sold and replaced with a Broadwood. And her music teacher was Mrs Wilson now. Irene had been Frau Reinbold's Wunderkind. 'Bechsteins are the best in the world.'

'They can't be if they're German,' Ray Stack said.

'Sir,' Phil said, 'what about the war? Are the Turks still floating mines down the Bosporus?'

Tup Ogier held his finger up. 'Another word and out comes Dr Brown. Arithmetic.'

In the afternoon we went swimming in the river. Mrs Beattie led the way and Tup came in the rear, watching to see no boys sneaked into the tomato gardens. The girls turned down the path to Girlies Hole and we crossed a wooden one-way bridge – for English lords' and ladies' carriages – and went up the river bank to Bucks Hole. Over the paddocks the Le Grice house sat brown-sided, rusty-roofed, with yellow gorse behind it on the hills. The rocking-chair on the veranda was the one Mrs Le Grice was sitting in when they carried Lucy home. She rose and put her hands on her throat and squeezed a peacock scream out of herself. (That's my embellishment. I've no idea if it's true, but now it's down I'll leave it, for it seems to include judgement as well as decoration – though why should I judge?)

Mrs Le Grice, Irene Lomax said, never cut her nails. They

curled over her fingertips and clicked like knitting needles when she touched anything. Her hair came down to her knees and sometimes she plaited it and used it like a club to hit her son. I don't need to say that's a lie. Irene must have enjoyed herself telling Kitty. It's true her mother took her there several times and made her play the piano for the old lady. And it's likely the music room was full of photographs of Lucy Le Grice, and five-finger exercises were on the piano still, and the piano had dead notes and played like a wire mattress (she was oddly mature in some of her language, Irene), and dust rained from the curtains if you tried to pull them back, and came from the sofa in little puffs when the old lady patted it for Irene to sit down. Irene claimed Mrs Le Grice mistook her for Lucy, and that's likely too. 'You must practise harder, Lucy,' she said, which made Irene cross, for her mistakes were the piano's fault.

We watched the house and kept to the path and passed the hydraulic ram going thump thump thump. At Bucks Hole Tup took the temperature of the water while we stripped on the shingle fan. 'Sixty-eight, nice and warm,' he called. Chicken-scrawny, most of us, white-bummed, with patterns printed by singlets on our backs. But one or two, like Phil, were already men, and stood hands on hips, showing it. A bit of a midget there, I ran for the water, with hand neatly cupped. Later on none of us cared, the water shrank us all to tiddler size.

Tup took Phil and me and several others along the bank to the deep part of the pool and tested us for our diving certificates. He flipped a tobacco tin, hammered flat, into the water. It fluttered like a leaf going down and vanished in the translucent green; and in I went, second, after Phil, and the bottom of the pool was magnified as though I looked at it through Tup's glass. I went along the gravel like a crab, with puffs of sand springing from my hands. The element enclosing me was death. Meniscus silvery, it bulged and bent. No guarantee of my world still in place. It might have been snuffed out while I was gone. Other things, not people, waited there. I had the tin, and kicked, clawed up fast; and broke into my natural element, and must have looked, with open, haunted eyes and hollow cheeks, like some traveller from the underworld. That, anyway, is my fancy, for I'm not looking straight ahead.

Tup reached for the tin, but never took it. Two girls came running on the path.They stopped at the shingle fan and stood side on, not to see us naked boys, and cried their messsage at the trees: 'Sir, come quick. Mrs Le Grice has fallen in the pool.'

The scramble for clothes then! Tup, with a shout, had gone. 'Get dressed, all of you. Meet me on the bridge.' We ran along the path but did not stop. The bridge drummed under our happy feet. We ran through the head-high scrub to Girlies Hole. Tup had Mrs Le Grice lying face down on the grass and was giving her artificial respiration. Water trickled from her mouth and liquid flecked with blood from her English nose. A tiny wax white ear bloomed on her head. Her false teeth lay on the stones as though she had coughed them out.

'Is she still alive, sir?'

'I'm not sure. I told you boys to wait on the bridge.'

Kitty was kneeling by Mrs Le Grice's head. She had patted the old lady's hair into a bun and placed it on the base of her neck. Now she tried to squash a balloon of air caught in her dress but it moved somewhere else. So she took the old lady's sandshoes off and tipped the water out.

Tup stopped his counting. 'Get an ambulance, some of you boys.'

'I sent for one,' Mrs Beattie said.

'Well, Dockery and Papps, you'd better go up to the house and fetch Le Grice.'

We went up the path and over the bridge and ran side by side along the road to the gate. A drive curved to the house, a perfect arc, with dust as white as flour in the wheel-ruts. We passed a square of blackberry enclosed in rusty wire, where bits of a tennis net were wrapped about a post. Ripe berries hung in clusters over the walls of a fallen pavilion. The rocking-chair was on the house veranda. It was woven seagrass, ravelled like knitting. A doorway opened into a hall where glass tear-drops gleamed on a chandelier. We climbed up and knocked on the jamb.

'Maybe he's not home.'

'What's that noise?'

We jumped from the veranda and walked round the house to the back yard. Edgar Le Grice was sharpening a sickle. He held the blade two-handed, working a treadle with his foot, and sparks streamed from the wheel and ran up his arms. White sparks, black-haired arms. Red tartan shirt. Belt of heavy leather, buckled with brass, and a spike like a dog's tooth through the hole. His belly and chest were barrel-hard.

We moved to let him see us. The wheel stopped. He set the sickle down by his feet. We heard him breathing through his nose.

'Your mother fell in Girlies Hole, Mr Le Grice.'

'Mr Ogier's doing first aid.'

Le Grice took a step, somehow drunken. He was stunned by the arrival of a moment – but I'm guessing. I must say what he did, which was to run. We followed him like dogs at heel, and he ran with a long limping stride, his feet beating dust from the ground, past the house and tennis court, along the road. We saw an ambulance beyond the bridge, with its doors wide open, and children standing in a group, and Mrs Beattie pushing them away. Ambulance men brought Mrs Le Grice from the path, lying on a stretcher.

Le Grice shouted, 'Ma!'

They slid her in the way my father slid trays into the oven, and waited at the doors as he galloped up. 'Ma!' He went up clumsily and banged his head, but did not notice. I could not see Mrs Le Grice but saw his hands reach out and hold her face.

Tup Ogier came up the path. He held the old lady's teeth, and offered them. I had been refined and drawn by a kind of osmosis into Edgar Le Grice's grief. I was outraged, and drew myself away from Tup. One of the ambulance men hooked the teeth on his finger and dropped them in his pocket. They closed the doors and drove away.

'Will she die, sir?' Kitty asked.

'I don't know. She's very ill. But you did very well. You were very brave. Irene too.'

'Everyone into lines now,' Mrs Beattie said.

'Oh, I think they can make their own way back.'

We went in a cluster round Kitty and Irene. They had pulled Mrs Le Grice from the pool.

'She just walked into the rapids,' Kitty said.

'She thought I was Lucy. She called out,' Irene said.

The old lady tumbled through the chute and floated into Girlies Hole. She kept raising her head, and giving little bleats like a lamb. Then her face stayed under water. The girls swam up and tried to turn her on her back but a bubble like a pudding in her dress got in the way. So they floated her along, trying to hold her head on one side. Kitty nearly drowned, she said, when the old lady's hair wrapped round her throat.

Mrs Beattie tucked up her dress and waded in – 'up to her bloomers,' Melva Dyer said – and helped pull Mrs Le Grice to the bank.

'She sicked up.'

'She had dribbles coming out her nose.'

So the others. Irene and Kitty, knowing their value, kept out of it. If I understand the word right, they'd had a Blyton time.

Phil's and mine came in the night. Chronology holds, images fatten up. Here we are, standing on a street corner under a gaslamp, eating pies. We've come from helping in the bakehouse, where Dad has made Phil soap his arms up to the shoulder, and put him in an apron and tucked his forelock under a cap, then washed his own hands a second time; and Phil has been neat and small in the presence of food and has worked with his arms at his sides, minimized, not to put the mysteries in danger. Wolfing his pie, he becomes himself, and grabs and gulps the crust I offer him. (He brings no lunch to school but scrounges sandwiches from other boys.) 'Your old man makes good pies,' I hear him say. I'm sickened by his open-mouthed chewing, the glue of mince and pastry on his tongue. I don't really want him as a friend, but the intimacy of our fight won't go away.

Wind rumbles in the swollen night. Palms clash their branches in the park and the lamp at the entrance lights up the polished wood of a children's slide. Beyond the river the dome on Settlers Hill gleams like a head. Tup Ogier is working there tonight, but clouds swelling up from the east will cover Mars and spoil his view.

'Old Tup gave me a look through the telescope. We looked at the moon.'

'When?'

'Monday night. We saw the craters. We looked at Mars too. Tup reckons there's no real canals.'

Jealousy and rage make me dizzy. Tup is mine. I'm betrayed. Phil is stink-bag Dockery from the Port, with horse shit on his ankles and snot wiped on his arm. I put my hand on the lamp-post to keep from falling, but the sky dislocates and turns on its side. There's an external agent in this: the breaking of glass. I reach out now and tap my tumbler with the paper-knife. A sound, clear as bells; but it's no good. I want that sharp fracture, icy silence, and I'd like to throw the tumbler at the fire grate.

Phil says, 'Glass!'

'In Lomax's.'

We're threaded on the sound and can't get off. 'Come on,' he says.

We run down an alley between brick walls. A pile of dirt lies half in the light, with shapeless footprints climbing into the dark. Phil puts his foot in one but I don't dare. 'He's a giant.' He climbs to the top and puts his head over the wall. 'Long way down.'

'It might have been a cat.' I remember the cat, a ginger Tom with yellow eyes and a torn ear. He's my invention. He burns like a flame, which Phil snuffs out.

'With feet that big? Hey, a broken window.'

I climb the pile of dirt and look at it. A black hole, a nostril, shows in the pane. 'Get your cissy shoes off,' Phil says. I sit on the dirt and take them off and stuff my socks inside.

Phil straddles the wall and lets himself over. He drops and his feet slap on paving stones. 'Come on, Papps.'

I howl silently, dropping down. It's come into my head I'm on my way to being killed. We cross the cobbles, slinky as cats, and rub along the warehouse wall. Phil puts his head through the broken pane and I squint along the side of his cheek. Blades are poised to slice our throats. Our arteries are delicate and bare.

The warehouse is a brick shed half as long as a football field, with skylights in the roof, from which starlight and gaslight diffuse through the room. Huge bins, head-high, stand along one wall and sacks of grain are stacked along the other, plump as loaves. At the far end is a loft where empty sacks are stored. No light penetrates, but we see a movement there, and hear the tinny boom of an empty can. We hiss with fear. I see Phil's tongue come out and wet his lips.

Edgar Le Grice strikes a match. His red balaclava blooms like a rose. He pulls a piece of rag from his pocket and sets it alight and his hand is on fire; but he doesn't feel, he looks as if he means to eat the flame. Then he leans down and touches sacks and they spring alive, he's printed on the ground of his fire. His red round head and black coat make him bird, and down he jumps, or flies, with coat-wings spread and one hand flaming, and lands on sacks by the ladder's foot. He touches bags of seed and makes them flower. Flame runs along and he lopes with it, keeping pace and yodelling delight. He looms at us in the window. He has no ambulatory motion I can see, and I screech and jump away. Glass has sliced my fingers (not the only time in my life looking through windows makes me bleed), but I don't feel. I run and Phil runs with me, along the cobbles to the double gates, where we can climb.

A door opens in a larger door. Le Grice comes into the bay where drays load up. The burning rag is gone from his hand. He jumps from the lip into our path and sends Phil tumbling with a whack of his arm. I scream like a swamp hen as he faces me. I don't know whether he's going to wrap me round or break me in pieces. There's a tearing noise and a stink and my pants fill up.

Le Grice looms over me. I puzzle him; and perhaps he knows what I've done and sees a child and is sorry for me. Just for a moment our eyes meet. A grunt comes from his throat; a twisting – is that grinning? – on his mouth. He puts out his arm and moves me aside. Then he's running, and back from his detour into normality, for he looks over his shoulder at Lomax's and raises his arm and yells at the flames. He jumps and catches the top of the wall and hauls himself up. Phil, limping past me as I squat, grabs his leg, but Le Grice scrapes his fingers off with his other boot, and straddles the wall, and looks a last time at the fire gargling in the warehouse. He jumps down and smacks away up the street.

'Come on,' Phil yells, but I crouch holding my belly and my rubber face signals agony. He climbs the gates and runs to give the alarm.

What do I do? That warm filthy weight is in my pants, and stink about me; and horror in my brain. I musn't be found. I see a hose looped over a tap and I run bandy-legged and stick the nozzle in my pants and turn it on full-blast and hose the shit out, front and back. The force of the water nearly tears my penis off – but I'm clean, I'm clean, and nobody knows. I know, of course.

Men arrive. By that time I'm at the door in the big door, holding my arm against the blast and hosing water on the nearest sacks.

Tons of grain and seed are lost, but the firemen save the

building. Phil and I are heroes. We tell them who it was and police drive out to the farm and arrest Le Grice.

I'm full of self-importance. But also I have secrets on my mind.

You see, Kate Adams, why I dislike your language?

C. K. Stead

THE DREAMTIME
from ALL VISITORS ASHORE

LET'S BEGIN with the tea towel – it's hanging over a string and damp so the string curves downward under the sink bench and Melior Farbro, the old master, who is not so old, a little over fifty like the century itself and in good shape despite his limp and his endless complaints about corns, piles, tinea, peptic ulcers, migraine, bends down to dry his fingers on its brown checks. He has been making a salad and now he limps with it to the counter that separates his kitchen from his studio and puts it down in front of Curl Skidmore who is thirty years younger and hungry and likes salad and fresh fruit but doesn't think of them as food. Farbro squeezes a lemon over the salad and tosses it so oil and lemon mix through and Skidmore is watching Farbro's fingers which are long and broaden at the nails, spatulate, while all the time Farbro is talking and the sun is shining in and shining down on the garden beds out there where the lettuce and tomatoes and green peppers that are in the salad grew alongside the lettuces tomatoes and green peppers that are still growing. The sun is shining on red peppers drying on the peeling window sills and on sunflower heads bristling with black seeds you pluck out and chew for the oil and what it does for your corns, piles, tinea, peptic ulcers, migraine while Farbro is putting out cold smoked fish with the salad and telling

Skidmore there's nothing a young man needs a woman for, nothing his pals can't provide and make it better, let's not go into details, and Skidmore is regretting that it's brown bread, healthy and rough and good for the bowels but with salad and fish he would have liked unhealthy white floury light warm doughy bread fresh from the bakery on the corner you can smell even down at the beach when the wind blows the right way on a yeasty night and he has her against the retaining wall her skirt in his teeth to keep it from falling down over the business and her bush in his palm. Nothing, Farbro is saying, not noticing that the young Skidmore who has gone back a moment to the beach and the night and the easing of thighs this way and that against the slope of the retaining wall is shifting from buttock to buttock on the stool on the studio side of the counter and hand in pocket is making an adjustment. Farbro has put a plate in front of him, is putting cold potato salad beside green salad and he's saying he has some cold sausage — salami — if the fish isn't enough and then he's back to the subject of what boys can do for one another, thinking of himself as a young man and of little Kenny, tough little bugger, knowing everything right from the start and taking it all in his stride without ever a qualm or a tremor or a worry, and is that maybe what's holding up this lanky Skidmore whose hands move so daintily over his food (but nothing dainty about the quantities he's putting away) and he's saying yes, some salami would be nice. In Farbro's day it was 'the fear of God' they used to say they would 'put into you' to keep (he used to think) the pleasures of the prick out. So slicing the salami with little yelps of pain pretending it's a piece of himself he reaches over to push the pieces on to the plate of young Skidmore who is losing his sense of that yeasty beach scene and is now looking up and around. He takes in again the easel and the work bench and drawing board, the stretched canvases and sketches and watercolours, the pinned-over walls and the long shelf of art books and folios of prints, and the long strips of heavy paper, on which Farbro says his new work will be done, hanging over the arms of the canvas chair. Through the door and another door both open Skidmore catches sight of the green over-arched enclosure of the back garden filled with bird-sound and the faint clatter of the typewriter of Cecelia Skyways unseen in the garden hut writing her *Memoirs of a Railway Siding*. And Farbro taking a moment to look at this young visitor while the visitor is looking around him is thinking This lad has an eerie charm and he talks well and probably has talent but there are so many with talent and what becomes of them?

And now the tea towel with the brown checks is again heavy on the string, the string curving further towards the floor, the dishes washed and dried and put away, and Melior Farbro is seated in the canvas chair having thrown the long strips of heavy paper like a suit of clothes on a hanger across his day bed and moved the easel into a corner and guided Curl Skidmore to a comfortable chair. He has rolled himself a cigarette and passed the makings to Curl who is expertly following suit, keeping the paper moving at the tips of his ginger fingers, pinching the strands from either end after the last deft roll-and-lick-and-roll. The light passes from one to the other and there is the silence of the satisfied in-breath while they hold it there, letting the smoke hang a while in the lungs, pleasantly agitating, and with no sense in either of vast dark consequences to come, this being 1951 and it being the mark of manhood and the seal of friendship to exchange the poison weed and set it smoking down there inside you. Cecelia Skyways' railway words clattering on a distant surge of her typewriter flow a moment into the silence of the indrawn breath conjuring sidings, steam and the clank of joining wagons, and then Skidmore and Farbro breathe out and the pallid smoke, deprived of its best tars, flows forward in two greeting dissolving streams. Farbro is looking at the back of his hand held up against the light from the windows, turning his spatulate fingers this way and that, and already Curl knows from this sign that the old man is considering.

'You have intelligence,' Farbro says, 'and a good appetite, so there's nothing you can't do if you go about it in the right way.' There is a heavy stress on that phrase the right way and Curl Skidmore knows, half-knows, has picked up but won't let himself quite recognize it, won't do more than glance at it obliquely, that the right way for the old master doesn't mean Patagonia (he thinks of her as Pat) against the sea wall on a yeasty night. It might include a bit of that but only and always recognizing that cruising the loos and the docks for gentlemen partners is living dangerously but not half so dangerously as cruising where Farbro guesses Curl may be situated now on the borders of the vast bog of domesticity, the average, the norm, mothers and fathers and kiddies and debts, no canvas or heavy paper or (as it would be in Skidmore's case) galley proofs draped over the camp bed, no clatter of the railway siding words of Cecelia Skyways flying up among the passion fruit and pawpaws, no art, because there is no art of the average, no art of the mean, of the mean in heart (Farbro is in full flow) and there is besides (he avers) the fact that all art is androgynous and you have the hands, my boy, you have the hands. Curl's eye is fixed on a cobweb in a cobwebby corner but he has shot down his flying hands, brought them home to base where they lie awkwardly on his lap playing dead with a bad grace. It is with a desperate honesty, feeling he's climbing a high stone wall, heaving himself over it, that he brings out the fact (his eye still on that broken web stirring in a breeze from the open windows) that he has a girl, that she has moved in with him in his glassed-in verandah down on the beach, that her name is Patagonia (he calls her Pat), that she would like to meet Farbro because she is a painter, a student of art.

Silence, while the old man considers the back of his hand, his spatulate fingers turned this way and that, and then a formal invitation like a card on a tray. Next time Curl comes he must bring her.

★

Curl Skidmore walks dejected at the water's edge, barefoot on the wet sand that the small waves slide over. He doesn't know why he is dejected. It is summer, the sun is shining, the Gulf is blue and calm, there is a sense of space, the sea spreading away to and around the islands of the Gulf and one big ship going out past Rangitoto through the immense wide gateway to the world. He walks, hands behind his back, his stomach comfortably full of Farbro's lunch, his head comfortably light with Farbro's wine, the sun feeling its way through his shirt to his shoulders, the sliding water cooling his feet with a hissing sound over the coarse-grained yellow-orange sand, full of some vague yearning that might be for anything – God, Fame, Nirvana, Great Love, Extinction – and only (Skidmore thinks in the wisdom of his twenty-one years) a fool would tell you that one of these words with a capital letter fitted the feeling better than another, or that it ought to be just one of them, but the world is full of fools and nothing is more entrapping, more enticing, than a word with a capital letter and there is a triple-fool in Skidmore (he knows this too) who can dispense with God and Nirvana but would like Fame, Great Love and Extinction all together and in equal measure. The beach is deserted, the mothers are shopping the fathers are at work the children haven't been let out of school and there is only Skidmore and a capering dot that grows as the distance between them diminishes and becomes a dog, a brown-black dog, a bedraggled mongrel spaniel which chases sticks for Skidmore out into the calm water and returns, shaking itself on the sand, and grips the stick more tightly and growls and twists when Skidmore tries to take it and in a moment releases it and as it flies from his hand turning and seeming to float against the blue sky before falling to the gently rising water, runs yapping and bounding and swimming to retrieve it. So it is out of a flurry of sand and dog and stick and water that Curl looks up to see a couple walking hand in hand at the water's edge and as they near him and hesitate and turn away and turn back he registers that it is Felice, the wife of Nathan

Stockman the violinist, and that the little hand of Felice (who is a soprano) is resting in the large red hand of their cook. Not that they have a cook as people have cooks in novels or in history or in England, but the beautiful house of Nathan and Felice Stockman designed by Nathan's architect brother among the pohutukawa trees and looking over rock and water at the end of the beach has been turned into a restaurant where, it is advertised, you can eat and look out to sea and listen to 'Nathan and his Gipsy Violin'; and since every restaurant of quality needs not so much a cook as a chef it is in fact (correcting the fact) in the hand of their chef that the tiny hand of a potential Mimi called Felice is at present unfrozen and indeed entirely unthawed. And Skidmore thinks it's odd they should turn away like that and he feels (wrestling with one end of the stick while the spaniel whose name is Rosh growls and hangs on grimly to the other) something like disappointment thinking of Felice's high pure notes floating out through the branches of the moon-filled pohutukawas and of Felice's big swelling soprano bosom and of her white neck and her round red mouth moulding the notes. Not that he thinks of her very precisely (throwing the stick so it turns end over end against the sky while the spaniel skitters to the water) because she is at least twenty-five and perhaps more and there is something (he suspects so) motherly about the way she pats his shoulder and his bottom and pinches his cheek when they meet. They are walking away now, she and the cook, no longer hand in hand. Perhaps he's her brother, Curl thinks, making a dash at the spaniel as it comes out of the sea.

Melior Farbro rests on his hoe between the bean rows his mind running between the skinny Skidmore who ate so much and talked more and the memory of Kenny as a young man eating very little and talking less but always observing – the two of them so different Farbro wonders why they should go together in his mind. He twists the hoe so the brown volcanic soil that would blow away in summer dust if it were not enriched with compost parts and crumbles around the bean stalks and begins yet again to compose a letter to Kenny he won't write warning him that the Government means business this time, he's sure of it, and that Kenny should stay out of it, not take part in executive decisions because the police will be looking for anyone well up in the union they can bring any sort of charge against and that if Kenny goes cruising just once while the heat is on . . .

But of course he won't write it because Kenny would think it was the old jealousy rising again trying to keep him off the streets, trying to make him all Farbro's own – and would that, Farbro asks himself, be entirely untrue? Leaning on his hoe again he listens to the bird notes which he can't identify but which have the feel of the warmth of the day about them, and then he notices that there is no sound from the hut, Cecelia has finished her stint for the day, her typewriter is silent. And as he looks towards the hut the door opens and a Botticelli face enhaloed by ginger-gold curls through which the sunlight for a moment astonishingly strikes looks out, sees itself looked at from the bean rows and with a gasping-in of breath withdraws again. Silence but for the bird calls until slowly the door moves, inches open again and slowly the bright head puts itself forth and a voice as sweet and clear and remote from this world as the heavenly head it issues from says, 'It's you Melior' (Who else? he thinks, smiling however), adding that she thinks she will make a cup of tea and would he like one? He nods, yes he would like one, and she gathers herself at the still only half-open doorway and then in a flash she is down the two steps into open ground that might be raked with machine-gun fire and crisscrossed with mine-fields, across it and up the three steps into Farbro's house, banging the door behind her.

At the concrete steps that lead up to the white gate Curl Skidmore stops, his feet sinking in the dry sand, and throws the stick. The brown-black spaniel who is called Rosh bounds a few yards and stops. Skidmore is darting up the steps. Rosh follows but the gate snaps shut. Skidmore looks over it and down into brown doggy eyes. The docked tail moves faintly from left to right, enquiring. Skidmore says No, trying to sound as if he means it, and the ears go down and the tail stops moving. No animal, Skidmore thinks, has a right to look so human and so entirely deserving. As he goes along the side of the glassed-in verandah he admires the look of the island matting he has nailed over the weatherboards inside, and Pat's painting of them, him and her, cubed into the angles of the sea wall but unmistakably and sexually spliced together, which hangs over the matting. She is not in the verandah room nor in the little kitchen which is also the verandah, partitioned. She is in the bedroom which opens off the kitchen and which is just big enough to hold the double bed she is lying on and the wardrobe with the mirror on its door and the chest of drawers with the mirror above it. And because the mirrors are exactly propped and angled and because she is lying in exactly that place on the bed and because she hasn't jumped up to greet him and thrown her arms around his neck or punched him on the arm or kneed him in the balls he knows she has been waiting for him to come home and that she is wanting to play the Game. Her eyes you would say were shut but he knows they are slits and from that angle she can see her mirror, the one on the wardrobe door propped open to suit her, and that when he is in position he will be able to see his mirror, the one over the chest of drawers. So he plays his part now, tiptoeing into the room and finding her asleep, someone he has never seen before whose name (for all he knows) might be Patagonia or Aorewa or de Thierry or Bennett and whose wavy black hair is spread over the white pillow and whose ancestry might be Maori or French or (as it is in fact if the fact were only known to this unknown intruder skirting the bed's edge loosening his belt) something of both. He checks the window and seeing no one in the dazzling white yard with the cabbage tree at its centre he draws the blind leaving the sash window up. Then slowly quietly he returns to the girl on the bed who shows no sign of knowing he's there. Her skirt is over her knees and he lifts it a little and a little more revealing a smooth olive thigh and a little more revealing more of the firm curving smooth olive thigh and a little further revealing thin pants through which the dark bush darkly looks, and below which the thin pale transparent cloth is wrinkled and absorbed into the bulges and folds and declivities of a vulvar landscape – a sight so palpable even without touch he at once removes his trousers and underpants to make room for the occurrence that troubled him last at Melior Farbro's board . . .

So that's how it was you remember Aorewa, and as I look up from my leather-topped desk to the stuccoed wall and the clerestory light that was done in imitation of Nathan's house along the beach I can see two of Farbro's cartoon series (two of the best of those that survived) and beyond them on the wood-panelled wall that runs off at right-angles there's my early de Thierry, derivative but full of promise the experts say, and it was called the Game, you pretended to be asleep and I pretended to be a stranger and I removed my clothes and your clothes and you watched in your mirror and I in mine (as the hymn used to say). It was your favourite wasn't it, Patagonia? Why the silence? Are you refusing to answer?

Since this is going on inside your head Curlyboy, it's up to you whether I answer or not.

Curlyboy. I'd forgotten you called me that. And Earlybird. They were both in that letter . . . But we'll come to that. Yes, I require an answer.

I don't remember.

You don't remember the Game?

No.

The mirrors?

Vaguely.

We had a mirror each. It was the slowness that counted. Inching in you called it.

Eighthofaninching . . .

So you remember. It took a long time – the longer the better. And it took control. (Both senses!) Just one entry.

No I don't want to hear about it. I don't remember . . .

You do, Aorewa.

It – I mean the Game – it was what Cecelia Skyways would have called a Zen exercise . . .

The disastrous Dawn!

You could feel it approaching in me and I could feel it in you – the climax – from a long way off. We were so perfectly attuned . . .

'It is tone that makes music.'

The school motto! You remember that too.

May I go now?

Not yet. I want you with me.

Impossible.

I mean back in 1951.

Any particular location?

Still Takapuna but up the ridge again, right through Hurstmere Road shopping centre and Halls Corner and away along the . . . And off to the . . . And around the . . .

You mean back to Farbro's studio.

Yes. Hold tight . . .

Kenny, old boy (Farbro writes in his clear black script) I was thinking of you just now hoeing the beans and it must be time I dropped you a note. I was pleased to see you got elected to the union executive but I wish it wasn't that union or not that union at this time because Sid Holland means business, I can feel he's going to crack down, knowing that's what the public wants, and

some of you boys will be in the firing line. What is it has gone
wrong with the place, already I'm looking back on the Slump as
the good times and I don't think it's just me who feels that is it?
Of course they were good times for you and me and I still
remember our gardening jobs in Remuera and even the days when
we didn't manage to get a bob together for one square meal
between us seem good when you look back on them. You know
I'd like to see you and have a good talk and if there's trouble of
any sort and you feel for any reason you want to lie low there's
always a bed for you here. Not in the hut but I'm always
comfortable on the day bed in the studio and the bedroom's all
yours. Not the hut because I've got a sort of lodger – it's hard to
explain about her (yes, old boy, it's a she – I wish I thought I'd
made you jealous for a moment there but I know it's no such luck
for me). She's a little tyke girl, a real sweetheart who spent as far
as I can get it out of her nearly six years training to be a nun and
then decided she couldn't stick it or wanted to do something
different. Anyway she ran off to her aunt's place which is quite
near mine and the aunt introduced me because Cecelia (that's the
ex-nun) wants to be a writer and the aunt knows me – she's a very
enlightened lady who buys my pictures sometimes and we chat at
the greengrocer's – and knows I have literary friends like Rex. It's
hard to get the whole story because the girl is so shy, frightened
too (I don't know how she got up steam to make a break for it)
but anyway there she is, I offered her the hut and she accepted and
now she's writing a book in there. Her hair has grown out since
she got out of the nunnery (or whatever it was) and it's bright
ginger-gold just like a bush all around her head. You'd like the
look of her, she'd make you think of some of those lads who used
to be your favourites and used to make me so jealous. I had a
skinny youth here today (another would-be writer – the world's
full of them) and he reminded me quite a lot of you although I
don't need to add he didn't have anything like your special charm.
Well, old pal, I'd better get on with it (my little ex-nun has just

brought me a cuppa) so I'll be seeing you but remember what I said about Sid and be careful now you're on the executive – they'll be hot on your tail if they can, this Government, so don't go taking any of your old risks. Look after yourself, Kenny, because you know I don't get any less silly as I get older (fifty-one this year, same as the century – as always!) and that means your old friend still loves you, boy.

The white concrete yard was no longer dazzling, the sun sloping beyond the ridge had gone off all but the topmost points of the cabbage tree, the spaniel had gone from the gate, the gulls were silent, and across the yard in their little whitewashed two-roomed flat Jim and June could be seen packing. Curl Skidmore, half sitting and half lying sprawled across the table at the end of the glassed-in verandah looked alternately across the yard to watch Jim and June through their uncurtained windows bouncing on the lids of over-stuffed suitcases and tea-chests, and out to sea where a cargo ship was sailing down the Gulf along the shoreline of Rangitoto that was catching full-face the light of the declining sun. Out there across that spacious surface of the Gulf was the gateway to the world towards which the ship was sailing and in a day or so another would sail and in it would be Jim and June. Curl had never wanted to join the godwits but now at the thought of Jim who was going to learn bullfighting in Spain and of June who was going with him and of them both drinking from wine skins and listening to castanets and flamenco singing and eating spiced food and walking under the hot sun in crowds where nobody spoke a word you could understand, Curl felt stirrings of unrest. Around the side of the house he could hear in the stillness between the hesitant breaking of small waves the dragging left foot of Mrs Battle who owned the house and let the glassed-in verandah and the little two-roomed flat across the yard and now her best-foot-forward-left-foot-drag step was joined by her throttled and yet somehow projected articulation of his name: 'Gurr-l' (step, drag) 'Gurr-l' (step, drag) as she rounded the corner into the darkening yard that still pulsed its stored sun-heat upward into the purpling velvet sky. 'Gurr-l' (step, drag) — her eternal dressing-gown dragging at mottled ankles and pom-pommed feet. Jim and June have stopped bouncing and are poised unsteady one on a tea-chest the other on a trunk, both on the edge of hysteria. Patagonia is craning forward at the sink bench to look down on the thinning grey hair, but holding back so as not to be seen. 'Gurr-l' (step, drag) — and by now Skidmore is moving to the door, dragging not one of his feet like Mrs Battle but both. In the darkening yard she gives him a lemon from her tree and an egg from her son's fowl house ('For your breakfast,' she says, keeping up her pretence that he lives alone and that the sounds which come through the wall from his bedroom to hers are some kind of athletics) and they talk about the weather ('*phew!*') and that dog loose on the beach ('I'll call the Council if he gets in here') and the new restaurant along the beach ('They say it's run by a gipsy') and has he heard the news because for sure Mr Holland's not going to let the harbour fill up with cargo while those lazy good-for-nothing communists spend all day fishing off the wharves. And while she runs on about the Watersiders and what Sid Holland is going to do to them Curl Skidmore, his eye on the deepening velvet of the heavens above the cabbage tree, discovers a hole in his right trouser pocket and inserting two fingers, then two fingers and a thumb, widens it, and with further finger-work subtle and unseen by the impassioned Mrs Battle, draws his cock from his underpants out and up until it is sitting in his pocket . . .

She has run her course now and is step-dragging back around the corner of the house and Curl goes to the open door of the little flat and tells June to get down off the tea-chest and come and discover what he's got in his pocket.

*

'Sentimental prick,' says Melior Farbro, reading over his letter to little Kenny. But he seals it up and addresses it care of Mrs Hinchinghorn.

Jim and June had stopped packing to watch the white ship going out past Rangitoto. At first the sun was on it and it shone brilliantly but then the shadow that was racing across the Gulf intercepted it and began to edge up the narrowing slope of Rangitoto towards the crater. In two days' time they would be sailing down that same stretch of water looking out to see if they could pick out Takapuna beach and Mrs Battle's house and the whitewashed outhouses around the courtyard – their flat facing Curl and Pat's verandah, the seaward side enclosed by the outhouse containing the bathroom and laundry shared by the four of them, and the little square completed by the steep slope behind the house. Would they be able to pick out the white gate at the top of the steps up from the beach, and the tamarisks blowing along the fence-line? Jim took out a packet of Capstan, lit two and handed one to June. She was sitting on the lid that was supposed to close over one of their tea-chests but despite her weight springing woollen things bulged out all around. He drew on his cigarette watching the shadow climb the even slope of Rangitoto as the sun went down somewhere behind the ridge at their back, thinking of the last time he'd left New Zealand, sixteen years old and freshly kicked out of school with just his fare and five pounds in his pocket from his father and the idea that there was adventure to be had or money to be made in Australia on the cattle stations shooting kangaroos and snakes and riding under the gum trees. One suitcase had been enough, more than enough, it had rattled. Now there had to be blankets and sheets and pots and pans and cutlery because June said you couldn't be sure what a furnished flat would mean in Spain and if they decided to live a while in London first they would need all the blankets they had to keep warm. Also warm clothes and clothes for dressing up on the ship and you had to work out what went into the Hold and what went into the Baggage Room marked 'Wanted on Voyage' and what went into your cabin . . .

Curl had come out into the yard, he was talking to Mrs Battle. The ship had gone, the last of the light was on the summit of Rangitoto, June was laughing listening to Mrs Battle and watching Curl shifting from one foot to the other staring up into the cabbage tree and fiddling in his pocket. Mrs Battle was talking about the strike threat down on the wharves and Jim wondered whether it would happen and if it did when and would it be within the next few days and if it was would passenger liners be affected or only cargo ships. The wharfies had been offered an extra fourpence ha'penny an hour that would bring them up to about nine pounds a week without overtime but they wanted something nearer to ten and that seemed fair enough but more than the wharfies wanted ten pounds a week Jim wanted to get out of New Zealand. He had been reading Hemingway and as much as he'd ever yearned for Australia and the Outback and dingoes and wallabies and kookaburras and the big stations and opal mines and Death in the desert Jim yearned now for the heavy breath of the wounded bull and the graze of its horn making a last lunge along his tight-trousered matador's thigh and he up on his toes making a clean job of it with a single thrust of his sword up and over the horns and deadly into the heart. Did matadors travel with women who crammed blankets and pots and pans into tea-chests and then sat on them to nail down the lid? One suitcase and five pounds in the pocket seemed a more likely start. But Jim and June were married, she had worn a white dress, he had worn a dark suit, and for two years they had both worked as clerks living on her wage and saving his and now they had their tickets, they were packing and in two days' time they would be sailing out there, north towards the equator.

Mrs Battle was dragging her way back towards the corner of the house and now Curl was at their door leaning in and telling

June to come over and see what he had in his pocket. She jumped down and went to the door where he was standing side-on holding his pocket open and she pushed her hand into it and drew away with a squeal. Curl said there was something almost as good in the other pocket and he pulled out two pound notes. That was for tonight, he said. He'd booked a table for the four of them at Nathan Stockman's restaurant, it would be a flash farewell, it would be the last supper.

Blessed Virgin (wrote Cecelia Skyways) it will interest you to know we are having a Language Release here in Takapuna this summer or you might call it just a plague of the verbal squitters. Even my friend Melior says he's finding it hard to resist the impulse to put words into his paintings, and of course I am hard at my Railway Siding memoirs every morning. And today Melior had a visit from a young writer called Skidmore who (Melior tells me) says he has two complete novels in his head. I looked at him through a gap in the curtains as he was leaving and I thought it was a nice head and that there might have been another novel or two tucked away inside his trousers as well. (I'm glad you enjoy a joke. I've always thought a woman in your position who lacked a sense of humour would be sunk.) It's getting dark and I'm writing by the light of a kerosene lantern because there's no electricity in this hut and I'm glad of that because the last place I was in my head was so electrified my hair still stands out all around it, a kind of halo that makes me feel akin to you, B.V., whenever I see your picture. I haven't told Melior about the electrification of my head, people take fright so easily, I've told him I was in a convent which is near enough to the same thing. You know as well as I do this is a man's world and a woman has to tell some little lies and some bloody whoppers to get by. But Melior is kind to me, he's a sort of woman-man anyway, and right now he's cooking over there, I can smell it wafting across among the pawpaws and tree tomatoes and lemons and pears and grapefruit. And while he cooks he has the radio on and there's something that might be Bach or Telemann something baroque or rococo with a flute and a violin and one of those twangling instruments that Caliban heard (I'm a lady Caliban, my isle is full of noises) and that music fills the shadows between the trees that usually fill me with fear. But I am attending to my Zen Master who inhabits a web just over the door and he instructs me not to draw back from my fears but to go forward into them, to become my fear because it's the division in me between self and self that is the cause. Last night I lay in bed with my door ajar and out there lay the shadows and I looked at the shadows and the shadows looked at me and neither of us moved and when I thought I was going to die because my breath had stopped Melior's door opened and shot a long shaft straight into the shadows killing a couple of the worst of them dead and then out came Melior with a torch and he worked his way here and there pointing the ray this way and that shooting holes in shadows to left and right only stopping now and then to pick a snail or a slug off the leaves of his vegetables. It's a strange life people lead in the suburbs, B.V., and I enjoy watching them come and go at exactly the same time, they look so full of purpose. I've got quite out of the way during my years indoors of seeing how they live inside their lives like sausages inside a skin. Melior's section is enclosed by trees and overgrown hedges, just perfect for someone like myself who is full of fear but needs to look out, and my Zen Master in the web tells me to observe is good, to interpret bad, so I become (like Christopher Isherwood) a camera pointing out at the suburb from Melior's trees. But there's a lady across the road who has a camera, a real one, and another lady on this side of the road who has a dog, a spaniel I think, called Rosh, and the camera lady says it's the dog lady's dog who is fouling her front lawn while the dog lady denies it. So the camera lady plants herself last week in her garden shed with the door ajar and when the dog lady's dog comes to deposit his business on her grass she snaps him once, twice and then a third time in full crouch and with the offending matter in emerging stages and now she says (they argue outside Melior's hedge) she has sent copies to the Council and she wants the dog destroyed. Destroyed! Doesn't that word send shivers into you, Blessed Virgin, it's what they did to your Son and I think the camera lady would welcome it if dogs could be crucified but as it is she'll settle for the gas chamber. Melior is calling me to dinner and he has opened the door so there's a straight yellow path through the shadows and I shall fear no evil but as I write that my Zen Master from the web says Go forward Cecelia Skyways, look for no protection but become your fear.

Where are you now, Nathan Stockman, somewhere 'over there' leading an orchestra, occasional soloist and with your own quartet noted for its recordings of Beethoven and Bartok, how would you like them to know (or do you tell them and laugh?) about your restaurant and the advertisement for 'Nathan and his Gipsy Violin'? How you winced when you thought of your friends who said you ought to be in Wellington leading the National Orchestra and imagined them reading the sign and the advertisements! But Felice was firm, she wasn't going to Wellington. Who could sing (she wanted to know) in a town where the wind blew as long and hard as it does in Wellington? It was too depressing. So there you were putting all your Jewish melancholy (that was how you described it) into your playing of a Bach sonata and there hadn't been much all that evening of the jolly gipsy in your playing. The light was dim in the restaurant so you could see out to the Japanese lanterns among the pohutukawas and catch a glimpse of the long curve of the beach with light from the houses shining down on to the sand and now and then the lights of a ship going along the line of Rangitoto towards or away from the harbour entrance. There were only two couples at a table by the window, the other five who made up the total for the night had gone, but it wasn't the small number of customers that made you melancholy and it wasn't even the thought that you should be down there in Wellington at the National Orchestra's number one desk, it was something else that was very near to you but just outside your range of vision, a sinking you might have felt if, as hereditary receptacle of that Jewish melancholy, you had been somewhere in Europe ten years earlier and someone had inadvertently knocked a little louder than necessary on your door in the night. It was a certainty that the bottom was going to drop out of everything, the trap was about to be sprung, the noose was in place, the gas canisters were ready, the wagons were rolling (Hitler made the cattle trains run on time!) and it – the big threat – it wasn't in Wellington or across the harbour among the silent stalks of the wharf cranes pointing up at the night sky or even out there in the suburban street, it was right here in the room with you. You felt sick with it, sick with the fear and worst of all with not knowing what it was and as you felt it it went through your fingers to the strings and the bow and you registered that the young writer, Scamper, or Skinflint, from along the beach had detached himself from the three he was with, he was leaning back in his chair taking in your music, and for a moment seeing what you heard heard also by the young Skillsaw from along the beach you soared into an ecstasy that didn't leave the melancholy behind but took it with you into the upper reaches of the empyrean. And that, my God, you deplored it, it was absurd, your own veering intensities, and as a protest against them and to deflate yourself and young Skidmore too who was looking so dewy-eyed in his appreciation of what your fingers were doing you bounced almost without a break into the 'Flight of the Bumble Bee'.

Full of wine now and wavering together and apart and two steps forward and one step back as they make a steady nearly no-progress along the sand from the restaurant these four are Curl and Pat and Jim and June and to keep not entirely out of sight but at a comfortable distance all thought of departures bullfights goats guitars Curl is reciting and running together aloud and along the beach the endless long runnable lines that are stored in his head (together with two unwritten novels) offering up to the heavens and into the wind *It was my thirtieth year to heaven woke to my hearing from harbour and neighbour wood and the mussel-pooled and the heron-priested shore the morning beckon with call of seagull and rook and the knock of sailing boats on the net-webbed wall* – and as that runs its course turning as quickly and unhesitatingly as Nathan Stockman turned from the Bach to the Bumble Bee replacing soon-to-be double-dead Dylan with the unmanned Manley Hopkins of *this morning's minion kingdom of daylight's dauphin dapple dawn-drawn falcon in his riding of the rolling-level-underneath-him-steady air.*

A breeze is coming across the Gulf making the warm night strangely chill as they pause at the gate under the blowing feathery tamarisks to say goodnight and to go to their separate flats that face one another across the moon-white courtyard with the spiky cabbage tree at its centre. And it is Pat now (Patagonia de Thierry Aorewa Bennett, as she sometimes says to the night, telling the moon her name) who thinks He is so remarkable with his head full of poems that unfold like scrolls and with two whole novels just waiting to be unwound and with that brilliant sensitive ferret face. He is her mystery-man and her brilliant-future-man and her lover-man and her child-man with a little of the husband too for formal occasions and even sometimes something like a father – one kind of father – for doing arithmetic and warding off ghosts. But tonight she wants to take with her into the big double bed the best of all Curl Skidmores which is not the real one but her idea of him, that golden boy of whom the horny intractable reality is only a drunken gabby and imperfect shadow. So Curl pawing at her in the dark, feeling for buttons and loops and openings, finds himself in his wine-haze pushed down on the divan under the verandah room's matting while the elusive Aorewa de Thierry, artist of the future with the Tuhoe-Parisian past, not for the first time but no less obscure to him in her motivationsretires alone and smiling to their bedroom and locks the door.

Nathan Stockman lies very still looking through the clerestory glass angled under the roof to the upper branches of the pohutukawas stirring slightly against the starlit sky. He's tired but he can't sleep and he doesn't know whether Felice who lies beside him is asleep or only pretending to be. Lying there it has come to him, he knows, feels sure he knows, what has caused it — that nameless fear. It's that Felice is having an affair with that young Skidmore the writer from along the beach. Nathan wants to wake her now, if she's asleep, to challenge her, tell her he knows. But at the same time that he's certain, and feeling sick with the certainty, he knows he hasn't anything like proof, she will deny it, he might believe her denial and he doesn't want to believe it, because although the pain of knowing is so bad it's not as bad as the pain of not-knowing . . .

It seems to Nathan that he is wide awake, he won't sleep, must lie there unrelaxed all night torturing himself with his new knowledge and for a long time he does lie staring up through the arms of the pohutukawas into the infinite and uncomforting spaces between the stars. But at last Felice who has been lying waiting, staring into those same empty spaces, hears unmistakably the change in his breathing, the steady regular faint whistle of his breath that signifies he is asleep.

Melior Farbro turning his book face down on the table beside his bed reaches over to switch off the light. The two black cats at his feet, Agatha and Christie, stir and settle. He has listened out as the last bus from the last ferry has gone by, waiting as he does most nights for the footsteps of little Kenny that used to come from it and one of these days, when Kenny has had enough of freedom, Melior thinks might come again. Looking out into the back garden he sees Cecelia's lantern in the hut turned down and then extinguished. And in her hut with the door again bravely ajar Cecelia says — tries to say aloud so the shadows will hear but her voice shakes down to a whisper — goodnight to the Zen Master, and goodnight to the Blessed Virgin.

Unable to sleep under the blanket on the divan below Patagonia's cubist painting of lovers against a sea wall Curl Skidmore lies listening to the sound of the sea which has changed with the wind from a steady breaking of small waves interspersed with a rustling of shells to what is now a general unpatterned uninsistent agitation as of the chattering of a crowd in the dark. He tries to centre his mind on that sound, on its rises and falls, so sleep will come to him but it's no use. He wants Pat but he doesn't dare break in on the dream in which she's locked with her ideal unreal perfect and eternal Curl Skidmore to whom he, the real thing, the dinkum oil, Urlich Amrose Skidmore, known to his family and friends as Early (though he's usually late) and more recently as Curl (though his hair is as wave-less as a dam in summer) bears some but insufficient resemblance.

He gets up from the divan and goes out into the yard where the long points of the cabbage tree clatter quietly against one another in the breeze. No sound from Jim and June. They are sleep-ing, dreaming Andalusian or Catalan dreams. He walks down to the beach breathing the beautiful fresh shellfish-and-seaweed smell that blows from the reef. Out there is the sprawling dark dreaming shape of Rangitoto, a beacon flashing from its western extremity. Under the pohutukawas around Nathan Stockman's restaurant he stops. Two figures have come out into the darkness, one small and fluffy, the other heavily built, and of course he remembers now as he watches them through the trees, sees them pushing two suitcases behind the bucket seats of the open MG and driving away without lights — the sight of them on the beach that afternoon. It is Felice and the chef and they appear to be running away.

Vincent O'Sullivan

THE LAST OF FREDDIE

WHEN HE WENT at sixty-four his friends could hardly believe it. Indestructible old Freddie! They all knew his paintings had not been up to so much these last few years, but as for dying – if Freddie came to that, then who couldn't? Although that was said discreetly. Critics liked to say – now he wasn't there – what a gap he was going to leave. On *Kaleidoscope* Bonnard would be mentioned as his master and a constant influence, as a quick comparison of selected canvases confirmed. Bonnard of course through the eyes of the Moderns. But that same preference for intimate domestic scenes, the shortened perspectives, the delicate sense of colour. If the phrases came rather too easily, as Maddy suspected they did, this was not the time to point it out. Oh yes, she thought – he painted, he screwed around, he drank himself to death. Caesar's neat little triplet hardly matched that as an epitaph. But it was a limb lopped off, wasn't it, hearing his death announced that morning over the nine o'clock news? She had poured herself a stiffish drink and switched the radio off. And she thought at once, oh won't they be swarming now, the academic maggots. Not even waiting until the meat had time to go off.

When June phoned her a little after ten she said that to her friend, although she knew June's son was at work on a *catalogue raisonné*. A few weeks before she had said, 'You can't *raisonné* before someone's dead, for God's sake.' She had been amused. But now she was angry, and a little drunk. She thought of Freddie wearing a green paper hat and not a stitch else as he lumbered down on her after a party at the old place in Kelburn. Angus already was out to it in the lounge, a gold cardboard crown slipped over his forehead as he lay squashed into the piled cushions of the sofa. It was after Freddie's finest show. They wore silly hats because it was Angus's birthday as well. Earlier in the night they had blown whistles that unfurled long paper tongues. They had danced to a Glenn Miller record and Maddy livened up her husband's drink with something somebody had brought in a black stone bottle. All it did was tumble him like a tree trunk. Then the artist had raised his long pale arm and groped for the glass-bead cord, like a row of raindrops, beneath the yellow shade. 'Painting be stuffed,' he told her. He said it vehemently. Then he had collapsed on the bed beside her.

'So you've heard?' June asked her.

'I heard it on the news.'

'When you think how well he was looking.' Then after the slightest pause, 'Had you seen him lately?'

'Not for a while,' Maddy told her. (*Madeleine*, Freddie used to enunciate back in those days. Why the hell can't people call you that, why that ridiculous abbreviation?)

'Last time he was that frisky. You'd have thought any of us might have gone before he did.' June reminded her how Freddie of course visited every second Friday. Surely she couldn't have forgotten that? 'We always had such *rapport*.'

Maddy could see her friend, red-eyed and big-busted, sucking at grief like a child at an orange. She thought, you ridiculous old cow, Freddie was into anything. But she said the required things until June had to tell her, 'I can't talk about it now. Not this close. I'll have to go.'

'Take three or four Disprin.'

'As if that'll help.'

'They worked when John went missing, didn't they?' Maddy thought, I'm a bitch saying that, aren't I? June had told her time and again how she hadn't shed a tear when the police came to her after the accident. It had taken weeks before it sank in. She had taken all those Disprin and simply gone to sleep. But this morning she had drawn the curtains and cried until she knew her face would be puffed for days.

'You never know how death will strike you,' Maddy said. After they had talked, she sat by the window that looked out across the valley to the irregular line of hills, her comforting glass beside her. She stroked at the glossy cover of a book she had for review, as though it were a cat. Each of them had forgotten to say so on the phone, but the women took it for granted Lydia would drive down for the funeral. How could she not? The three of them together again, to put their man away.

They met in the porch of the crematorium chapel. A northerly blasted along the valley and across the gravestones, driving people into the porch. 'How he'd love those hills,' June was saying. She nodded to the darkened slopes, the cloud shredding along their tops. 'If he could see them he might,' Maddy said. Why, she thought, do people have to talk such damned rubbish? Then at the same instant she and June called out, 'Lydia!' There was a brief trio of embracing among the mourners.

'We'll talk afterwards,' Maddy said. 'We're late as it is.' She took the smaller woman's arm and directed her to where they should sit. June walked on her other side. 'Oh,' she was saying, even as they stepped into the pew. 'Our meeting up like this!' Lydia smiled without looking at either of them. Then they sat, two tallish women with a shorter between them, listening to what was being said about Freddie, who lay on a slightly raised platform, a few inches of stained pine coffin showing beneath the flag that draped him. Maddy thought of him lying in bed, watching her dress with his feet extended outside the bedclothes. Once her clothes were back on he would say, 'A gin'd go quite nicely for afters. Know where everything is?' She heard the minister talk of his war service and his art. Then more importantly in the eyes of God, his generosity, his lack of malice. 'Balls,' she thought. In over thirty years, how often had she heard him say a good word about a painter younger than himself? Although he could be very open-minded with the dead. 'Weekes was brilliant,' he used to say. 'He was so very close to being good.'

Lydia heard June sobbing beside her into a handkerchief tugged from the top of her frock. It was one of the handkerchiefs Freddie had made in that period when he used to say, in his best proletarian voice, 'What are us buggers painting pictures for anyway? Why don't we make things people *use*?' This had meant at different times curtain fabrics, wooden toys, neck-pendants with local polished stone. And that spate of handkerchiefs – coarse linen made by a friend in Levin, then treated by Freddie with his own vegetable dyes. Lydia wished for a moment that she had brought hers, a sombre green that Freddie insisted was as natural a dye as it was possible to get. No one could mistake them for anyone else's work. Their size, their big hems that the artist himself had stitched on an old Singer treadle machine. Then she saw a woman at the end of the row in front of them – a woman in a fur coat and with heart trouble it must be, the way she panted, breathing through her mouth. Or asthma. She was dabbing at her throat with the same kind of coloured square, only dun brown. Freddie had given Lydia a tablecloth he must have dyed at the same time. It had been on the table the last time he visited her. He had taken it between his fingers and said it wasn't lasting so badly, the colour had kept quite nicely too. Must be twenty years, he said, since he made those things. Nineteen, she remembered. The year she went to Sydney.

'Get on with it,' she heard Maddy say beside her. Lydia felt confined between her friends. She looked straight ahead, at the pillar of sun that fell from the windows high in the wall. It picked out the line of powder on the sweating woman's throat, and made the ears of the man next to her quite transparent. The tiny veins and splotches seemed unpleasantly naked. What was that story about June and Freddie on the riverbank or something? A light shone on them by surprise? She had an image of their white limbs, of June's rotundities and Freddie's lankiness, caught in the flicker of a policeman's torch. The torchlight falling then and the sunlight now. June's wedding ring blinked where she crushed her handkerchief in her lap. Then Lydia noticed too that Maddy's fingers drummed on her crossed knees, a sign of irritation.

After the prayers and the eulogy a curtain was drawn across so theatrically that a bow would not have been out of the question. Then there was a hymn chosen by Freddie's wife. Everyone sang the words from a printed sheet, and the chapel swelled.

> There is a blessed home beyond this land of woe
> Where trials never come, nor tears of sorrow flow.
> Where faith is lost in sight, and patient hope is crowned,
> And everlasting light its glory throws around.

'He'd be bored shitless!' Maddy said at the end of the verse. June looked over sharply, her eyes interestingly pink, as Freddie might have thought, against the dark linen held at her cheek. Lydia continued to gaze ahead, at the stirring in the front pews as the family prepared to leave. That odd little smile of hers, June thought. I wonder if she quite knows what is going on? God knows none of them were any younger. It was senility with some, that was simply the way things were, just as it might be a weight problem unfortunately with others. Though the last time Freddie grabbed at her he had said for the umpteenth time, 'Can't stand these bloody women with no upholstery to them.' He had nuzzled into her as eagerly as at the University Extension weekend all those years ago. It had been a life-study class. Rather a pert little woman sat partly draped on a desk in front of them, her breasts as small and sharp as the last inch or two of ice-cream cones. That was exactly what she had thought of then, and it came back to her now. It was so silly, June smiled. And the way life goes on, she thought. She watched Freddie's wife walk down the aisle, her arm linked with her son's. What a gift, a wife as innocent as that had been! You'd have thought, though, wouldn't you, that a relative or someone would have told her the little cap thing she'd been wearing for years wasn't quite the thing for a funeral? It made her look like a jockey. And years ago when her own husband took her to the races, June had noticed the little men used to carry their saddles in the birdcage rather as Jos now carried that big old leather handbag across her arm. She wished she had thought of that while Freddie was still alive. He had liked her flair for putting things.

'Outski,' Maddy broke in on her. She jerked her head in that rather masculine way of hers, as though it was simply the movies they were leaving, or the end of a concert. Then for the first time since coming into the chapel together, Lydia looked from one friend to the other. She smiled shyly at both of them. She was thinking how they had all lain and sighed with and been loved by Freddie, hadn't they? There were times when June at least had become unfriendly about it, having to share him around like that. Although Maddy always laughed when they met and his name came up. 'He's fun the old wretch, isn't he? If you want more than that of course you go to someone else.'

They moved slowly from the chapel, the man with the thin pale ears shuffling in front of them. Perhaps a stroke, each of them supposed. There was something wrong with everyone, if only you knew about it. In a few moments they would be in the porch, then out again into the pelt of the northerly, the dappled scudding of the afternoon. There would be a quick embrace with Jos and others in Freddie's family, and words with people Lydia had not seen for so long perhaps she would have forgotten their names, and she would feel awkward because of it. Then the laughter that always began soon after a funeral. She and Maddy and June would separate, come back together, observe at more leisure the encroaching signs of age that marked them. And a man in a vaguely imagined room at the back of the crematorium would turn a jet – she supposed it was something like that – and flames would leap up, a bright engulfing calyx with Freddie at their centre. While they were talking, glancing out of windows. It struck her as very strange.

Lydia was a widow as her friends were, but the widow to nothing spectacular. June's husband had quite a name as a surgeon, then drowned a few years ago when he fell from a yacht off Banks Peninsula. Maddy's became a big wheel in theatre design. He had dramatically up and disappeared because of some homosexual flurry just after the War, and died before he was fifty. In other company Lydia perhaps would mention Cliff's Cambridge degree and the edition he had been working on for years when he died. Compared with the others, she supposed, Cliff didn't cut much ice. He now seemed so far away in any case.

'All of us widows!' June said rather gaily, just as Lydia was thinking that.

Young Richard came up to them and said, 'I'm glad you could make it. It's nice so many of his friends could be here.'

'As if we wouldn't have!' Maddy said. As if we'd miss out on seeing how the others were taking it.

Richard was the only son. He was tall like his father, with the same hank of hair falling across his brow. It had always made the self-portraits look lop-sided, that sheet of thick ochre slapped across the thinnish face. The young man smiled at the three elderly women, saying enough for each of them to think yes, what a charming boy he was. They could quite see Freddie coming through in him.

'That same profile,' June said. 'Can't both of you just see it?'

'At the same age!' Lydia said. She had been the first to know his father. 'You'd swear you were twins.'

'You knew him that long ago?'

'When we were students, would you believe that?' There was a vivid memory of swinging along with a group of friends, their arms about each other's waists, across a Gothic quadrangle forty years before. It was late in the evening, after a party. Between the cloisters and the ginkgo tree in the middle of the quad, Freddie had put his hand under her skirt.

'You saw him recently, did you?' Richard's question was to all of them. 'Saw Freddie?' June hesitated then said, 'Oh, not so long ago.'

'I hadn't seen him to talk to for a year or so,' Lydia had to admit. Then she asked herself aloud, 'Would it have been that long?' Richard had taken their wine glasses to refill, holding them between the fingers of one hand like a clump of transparent tulips. Maddy said, 'After our last *contretemps* it was probably better for everyone if we kept our distance. After that portrait.'

A couple of years ago Freddie had exhibited a nude, the female figure ageing but attractive in a butch, chunky way. And anyone with half an eye could recognize Maddy. The figure was sitting cross-legged on a chair, in a splash of greenish light, starkers except for a pair of long suede boots. Silly old bugger, she had said when she saw it. He hasn't seen me like that for ten years! It still made her hot to think about it.

'Well, as if you didn't have reason to,' June said. She was thinking thank God the one he did of me was *The Pink Hat*, the one the National Gallery had snapped up. It was impossible to guess who that one was. The tilted plane of the hat was all that interested Freddie that day. He had come in the morning, painted, had lunch, painted, then even after John came in he turned down a gin to get it through in 'one bash', those were his very words for it. Until, 'That'll do,' he said. Then he sat down in front of the telly and went to sleep. It was romantic though, June considered. It was how artists should work. She could have paraded about that day in boots and suspenders and it wouldn't have mattered twopence to him. She had reminded him of it only a year or so ago. They were sitting in the garden, it was in the early weeks of spring. They had been there for an hour and he had not even suggested that they go inside. 'Fancy a bit of the old one two?' was what he usually said. It always amused him that June would have liked him to put it more delicately. 'Christ,' he used to shout at her sometimes. 'Your whole life's like those bloody pink doo-dah things you've got over the spare dunny roll in the jakes. All frills and puff and cover-up.' But this day he simply sat in the white cane chair under the lime tree and tapped first the sharpened end of a pencil on the table, then the flat end, over and over until June had said, 'I was just working it out, Freddie. It's exactly fifteen years since you did that picture of me in the hat. That was October too. There's that same light falling across you now.' Freddie had looked at her, surprised. 'You've got a good eye,' he complimented her. Then he told her something else. 'Fifteen bloody years since I've done a decent picture in that case.' But as though saying that was a door he had partly opened and at once regretted, slamming it before June had time to enter, he leaned forward and pressed the swell of her thigh beneath her new wrap-round skirt. 'Still there, is it?' he asked her. He threw his head back and bellowed when she slapped at his hand and looked across, quickly, to where a neighbour's window might have given someone a view of her entertaining.

With the same slight smile she had kept throughout the service, Lydia said now, 'I don't know how I'd feel if it was me. I mean a picture like that, Maddy.' Then she added, 'I suppose as long as people are only thinking of it as art.'

Maddy looked at her friend, at the neatly parted grey hair and the grey suit and the benign fey expression like an ageing doll's. What the hell Freddie ever saw in *that* one. But here came Richard with their glasses again, there was no need to answer her.

'You *are* a darling,' June told him.

'There we are, ladies,' Richard said. Carefully he handed each of them a brimming glass. 'I know they're not supposed to be that full. But it cuts down on travel.' There was such a press of people around them that Lydia wondered how he had carried the glasses so well.

'You'll be all right?' he asked them.

'We won't go dry,' Maddy promised. She gave him one of her broad rare smiles, showing the perfect teeth that had made his father sometimes call her the Piranha. June watched her friend and the young man who now laughed with her about something that was lost in the hubbub of the wake. No wonder Freddie had that nickname for her. Here she was devouring Richard, drawing him off so that she and Lydia were simply left standing there. That'll make her day, June thought. Although not quite a victory like the old days, not like that writer's funeral in Auckland when a much younger Maddy had waltzed off with the dead man's brother on to the side of One Tree Hill. She had come back inside without even brushing the twigs or whatever from the back of her dress.

'Oops!' Lydia broke in on them. Someone had jolted against her arm, so that half her wine leaped from its glass. Richard was with her at once, mopping at her skirt, telling her he didn't think it would stain, in fact he was quite sure it wouldn't. Red might but not white. Then the man from behind the bar was there as well, handing her a dampened cloth. June raised her eyebrows as she caught Maddy's glance. But Lydia was turning from one friend to the other, asking 'Why me?', her face crinkled comically, her little-girl voice that hadn't done so badly for her over the years either, Maddy thought.

*

They had not met so often over these last five or six years, but Freddie always used to tell her, 'By God you're the one who matters, Lydia.'

'Oh yes,' she would smile.

'You are,' he insisted to her.

'And the others?'

'The others?' He would raise his arm from where it lay above the bedclothes and snap his fingers. He always did that about 'the others'. It made her think of a bank teller, contemptuous of the notes he was counting out.

'You believe me?'

'Yes and no,' she used to say. She said it about liking pictures or people that they knew or in this case what she meant to Freddie. And he so easily became angry when she answered him like that. 'There's not a mind inside there,' he would tell her, pointing at her head. 'There's a bloody see-saw.' He told her she was like the whore he had heard about during the War, who had 'Mild' tattooed on one breast and 'Bitter' on the other. 'You try to please everybody, that's your trouble.' He was so jealous. Then she would put on a face like the one when the wine spilled and Richard sweetly made such a thing about attending to her. 'I please you, don't I?' she used to ask. She would draw herself across him and Freddie always spread his hand across the back of her neck, gripping her as one might hold down the head of a kitten so it couldn't move. 'I love that,' she would tell him.

June broke in on her with the coffee she placed on the table next to her.

'I was just admiring this,' Lydia said. She tapped the marble table beneath her cup.

'Florence,' June said. 'John should have been an auctioneer, the stuff he picked up.'

Maddy took her coffee and said, 'I hope this isn't the strongest drink you're giving us, June?'

'Scotch then? Glenfiddich?'

'That'd do nicely,' Lydia said. Then they sat without switching on the lights, the three women facing the broad window that commanded half the harbour.

'Even on a dull day like this,' June told them, 'it's worth watching.' The northerly still pushed the clouds in ragged packs along the hills behind Eastbourne. The harbour itself might have been made of pewter.

'It depresses me,' Maddy said.

'What does?' June asked. She was kneeling at the gas heater, adjusting the bright whispering flues.

'This view. This weather.'

'Freddie used to say that if we could remember things exactly, things like colour tones and the movement of shadows and the rest of it, there wouldn't be more than half-a-dozen days in a life-time probably that were exactly the same.'

So the talk came back to the man who had died. They spoke of him warmly, without envy of each other, as the evening darkened outside. Maddy at least was thinking, he is never going to exist so fully as this again. Next time we meet we may talk of him, but not with this ease, this intensity. Our talking is letting him go slowly, slowly. The last time a man is spoken of is when he finally dies. Then she clucked her tongue sharply. It annoyed her that the vague pool of dimming silver in the mirror behind June's head, and that luminous lift that comes to the harbour when the sky itself is all but completely dark, were making her sentimental. How much she disliked June's own love for 'atmosphere' she thought. Her friend's finicky arrangement of camellias and looped Italian candlesticks and such. Those frothy blouses and pastel shades that June wore because they were the 'kindest' to her years. The moment you give way to sentiment, Maddy had always instructed herself, you blur the present as much as the past. You lose the lot. For a moment she held the hot swill of malt in her mouth. Then she asked, 'Can't we have the light on?'

'Is this making you jumpy?' June said. She liked the way the panel in the gas heater glowed there in the darkened room, while outside the night came down. 'There we are,' she said. She had touched a switch beside her. Two carefully angled lights were thrown across the paintings on the large expanse of wall. Only one of them was Freddie's, a gutsy still life of simple brilliant forms. What treasure that is, Maddy thought, after sitting in the gloom. Coming back from Hades. She thought of those favourite lines of hers, the great hero unrecognized in the swirl of fog, the twittering voices as remote as birds.

'The way he gets that orange,' Lydia said. 'Doesn't he?'

'The whole thing's *alive*. That's what matters about it.'

'Drinks again all round?' June offered them. She went to the kitchen for ice. Lydia knew she should refuse if she was sensible. She looked up at the painting and saw the fruit was already slipping when she tried to focus. The orange kept losing its roundness, smearing towards the bottom of the frame. She took a handful of nuts from the dish Maddy held towards her.

Lydia thought what a pity the light went on when it did. She had liked the sense that they were suspended somehow, as though in a transparent bell with the outside world pressing against its curves, a place where their voices came to each other clearly yet mysteriously, where surfaces ran with shadows and the last silvery core of light. There was no way she was able to put it, really. And she had almost made the mistake of confiding in them. It was good that hadn't happened. To have almost said, 'When I woke on Friday morning before it was light I knew he was there with me.' *Who?* she could hear them say. Who are you talking about, Lydia? *Freddie*, she would have had to say. They would not say much back, how could they? 'I opened my eyes, I often wake just before light, but the moment I woke I felt his weight.' Because it couldn't be anyone else. And they might ask her then, 'You'd already heard he was dead?' And she would answer them, 'How could I have heard? He wasn't even dead then. He was dying.'

'You're a quiet lot in here,' June said. She carried through a tray with sandwiches as well as the bowl of ice with claw-shaped tongs lying across it. She placed the tray on a table at the end of the room. Then before she attended to their glasses or handed each a plate, she briskly drew the curtains. She snapped on other lights, the room lifted into a glare of colour, of vases, bookshelves, more pictures on other walls, a brilliant clump of proteas.

'My God!' Maddy said, when she saw the flowers. She stretched out her hand to touch the stiff waxy blooms. With the press of dark leaves that backed them, they made her think of a burst of skyrockets, frozen and held against the night.

'They are lovely aren't they?' June said.

Yes, Lydia was thinking, what a lucky stroke that she hadn't tried to tell them that.

Then June went on, 'He never painted flowers. That's odd, isn't it?'

'It's because he couldn't draw them,' Maddy said.

'Couldn't draw them?' June looked down at her friend. 'But he drew beautifully.'

'He said he couldn't ever do flowers the way he wanted to. They don't have dimension the way fruit does.'

They certainly wouldn't have believed her. June would have become puzzled and flustered, her hand running along the chain of her gold Victorian locket. *There was this weight, how could she explain that?* And Maddy might have said, but isn't it only a coincidence anyway? That she had this feeling and thought of Freddie which was natural enough for *her*, she had hardly played the field? Then later that morning she had heard. It was curious, but not so much more than that.

June was adjusting the wall-lamp, directing it more clearly across the painting of the fruit. 'Haven't I seen that jug?' Maddy asked. 'I'm sure I remember it.'

'That one?' June looked more closely at the canvas, at the few brush strokes that gave the shape of the jug, a dab of whitish-blue along its rim that made you think all the light in the picture was gathered just there.

'It's the one he kept his brushes in,' Lydia said. 'Isn't that the one?'

'As if it matters now.' Maddy spoke quietly, her impatience tailed off. But Lydia was looking at her own hands, thinking again that it was not a thing to tell to others. How her bedroom had been completely dark when she had closed her eyes. Then after — how long, five minutes, ten? — the weight was withdrawn and when she looked again the morning already had come with that feeling of such stillness, and yet such energy too. The furniture and the mirror and her clothes across the chairback near the window, the frames on the photographs even and that oddly sad painting he had done when they spent an entire week in Akaroa, her red dog in grass as stiff as spears — how they had all been steeped in life, immersed in it. Full of that exuberance she had lain there and thought of him. *Dear Freddie.*

'Come on!' June was ordering her. Her friend stood in front of her, holding the fresh glass and with her other hand offering a plate of sandwiches. Maddy was standing too, one knee supported on the arm of a leather chair. She rooted about in her handbag, saying she was after a photograph she had brought to show them, the three of them in summer clothes outside the Takahe, three young women Christ knows how long ago.

'Dreaming, eh?' June had always teased her about that. Lydia smiled up, the 'drifting' smile as Freddie used to tell her, that bloody batty look as he had joked about it to Maddy and to June, there was a screw loose somewhere, there had to be.

She took the glass and an anchovy sandwich. 'Yes and no,' she said.

Margaret Mahy

THE BRIDGE–BUILDER

MY FATHER was a bridge-builder. That was his business — crossing chasms, joining one side of the river with the other.

When I was small, bridges brought us bread and books, Christmas crackers and coloured pencils — one-span bridges over creeks, two-span bridges over streams, three-span bridges over wide rivers. Bridges sprang from my father's dreams threading roads together — girder bridges, arched bridges, suspension bridges, bridges of wood, bridges of iron or concrete. Like a sort of hero, my father would drive piles and piers through sand and mud to the rocky bones of the world. His bridges became visible parts of the world's hidden skeleton. When we went out on picnics it was along roads held together by my father's works. As we crossed rivers and ravines we heard each bridge singing in its own private language. We could hear the melody, but my father was the only one who understood the words.

There were three of us when I was small: Philippa, the oldest, Simon in the middle, and me, Merlin, the youngest, the one with the magician's name. We played where bridges were being born, running around piles of sand and shingle, bags of cement and bars of reinforced steel. Concrete mixers would turn, winches would wind, piles would be driven and decking cast. Slowly, as we watched and played, a bridge would appear and people could cross over.

For years my father built bridges where people said they wanted them, while his children stretched up and out in three different directions. Philippa became a doctor and Simon an electrical engineer, but I became a traveller, following the roads of the world and crossing the world's bridges as I came to them.

My father, however, remained a bridge-builder. When my mother died and we children were grown up and gone, and there was no more need for balloons and books or Christmas crackers and coloured pencils, his stored powers were set free and he began to build the bridges he saw in his dreams.

The first of his new bridges had remarkable handrails of black iron lace. But this was not enough for my father. He collected a hundred orb-web spiders and set them loose in the crevices and curlicues of the iron. Within the lace of the bridge, these spiders spun their own lace, and after a night of rain or dew the whole bridge glittered black and silver, spirals within spirals, an intricate piece of jewellery arching over a wide, stony stream.

People were enchanted with the unexpectedness of it. Now, as they crossed over, they became part of a work of art. But the same people certainly thought my father strange when he built another bridge of horsehair and vines so that rabbits, and even mice, could cross the river with dry feet and tails. He's gone all funny, they said, turning their mouths down. However, my father had only just begun. He made two bridges with gardens built into them which soon became so overgrown with roses, wisteria, bougainvillea and other beautiful climbing plants that they looked as if they had been made entirely of flowers.

Over a river that wound through a grove of silver birch trees he wove a bridge of golden wires, a great cage filled with brilliant, singing birds; and in a dull, tired town he made an aquarium bridge whose glass balustrades and parapets were streaked scarlet and gold by the fish that darted inside them. People began to go out of their way to cross my father's bridges.

Building surprising bridges was one thing, but soon my father took it into his head to build bridges in unexpected places. He gave up building them where people were known to be going and built them where people might happen to find themselves. Somewhere, far from any road, sliding through brush and ferns to reach a remote stretch of river, you might find one of my father's bridges: perhaps a strong one built to last a thousand years, perhaps a frail one made of bamboo canes, peacock feathers and violin strings. A bridge like this would soon fall to pieces sending its peacock feathers down the river like messages, sounding a single twangling note among the listening hills. Mystery became a part of crossing over by my father's bridges.

In some ways it seemed as if his ideas about what a bridge should be were changing. His next bridge, made of silver thread and mother of pearl, was only to be crossed at midnight on a moonlight night. So, crossing over changed, too. Those who crossed over from one bank to another on this bridge, crossed also from one day to another, crossing time as well as the spaces under the piers. It was his first time-bridge, but later there was to be another, a bridge set with clocks chiming perpetually the hours and half hours in other parts of the world. And in all the world this was the only bridge that needed to be wound up with a master key every eight days.

Wherever my father saw a promising space he thought of ways in which it could be crossed, and yet for all that he loved spaces. In the city he climbed like a spider, stringing blue suspension bridges between skyscrapers and tower blocks – air bridges, he called them. Looking up at them from the street they became invisible. When crossing over on them, you felt you were suspended in nothing, or were maybe set in crystal, a true inhabitant of the sky. Lying down, looking through the blue web that held you, you could see the world turning below. But if you chose to lie on your back and look up as far as you could look and then a bit farther still, on and on, higher and higher, your eyes would travel through the troposphere and the tropopause, the stratosphere and the stratopause, the mesophere and the mesopause, the Heaviside layer, the ionosphere and the Appleton layer, not to mention the Van Allen belts. From my father's blue suspension bridges all the architecture of the air would open up to you.

However, not many people bothered to stare upwards like that. Only the true travellers were fascinated to realize that the space they carelessly passed through was not empty, but crowded with its own invisible constructions.

'Who wants a bridge like that, anyway?' some people asked sourly.

'Anyone. Someone!' my father answered. 'There are no rules for crossing over.'

But a lot of people disagreed with this idea of my father's. Such people thought bridges were designed specially for cars, mere pieces of road stuck up on legs of iron or concrete, whereas my father thought bridges were the connections that would hold everything together. Bridges gone, perhaps the whole world would fall apart, like a quartered orange. The journey on the left bank of the river (according to my father) was quite different from the journey on the right. The man on the right bank of the ravine – was he truly the same man when he crossed on to the left? My father thought he might not be, and his bridges seemed like the steps of a dance which would enable the man with a bit of left-hand spin on him to spin in the opposite direction. This world (my father thought) was playing a great game called 'Change', and his part in the game was called 'crossing over'.

It was upsetting for those people who wanted to stick to the road to know that some people used my father's hidden bridges. They wanted everyone to cross by exactly the same bridges that *they* used, and they hated the thought that, somewhere over the river they were crossing, there might be another strange and lovely bridge they were unaware of.

However, no one could cross all my father's bridges. No one can cross over in every way. Some people became angry when they realized this and, because they could not cross over on every bridge there was, they started insisting that there should be no more bridge-building. Some of these people were very powerful – so powerful, indeed, that they passed laws forbidding my father to build any bridge unless ordered to do so by a government or by some county council. They might as well have passed a law saying that the tide was only allowed to come in and out by government decree, because by now my father's bridge-building had become a force beyond the rule of law. He built another bridge, a secret one, which was not discovered until he had finished it, this time over a volcano. Its abutments were carved out of old lava and, along its side, great harps, instead of handrails, cast strange, striped shadows on the decking. Men, women and children who crossed over could look down into the glowing heart of the volcano, could watch it simmer and seethe and smoulder. And when the winds blew, or when the great fumes of hot air billowed up like dragon's breath, the harps played fiery music with no regard to harmony. This bridge gave the volcano a voice. It spoke an incandescent language, making the night echo with inexplicable songs and poetry.

'The bridge will melt when the volcano erupts,' people said to each other, alarmed and fascinated by these anthems of fire.

'But none of my bridges are intended to last for ever,' my father muttered to himself, loading his derrick and winch on to the back of his truck and driving off in another direction. It was just as well he kept on the move. Powerful enemies pursued him.

'Bridges are merely bits of the road with special problems,' they told one another, and sent soldiers out to trap my father, to arrest him, to put an end to his bridge-building. Of course, they couldn't catch him. They would think they had him cornered and, behold, he would build a bridge and escape − a bridge that collapsed behind him as if it had been made of playing cards, or a bridge that unexpectedly turned into a boat, carrying his astonished pursuers away down some swift river.

Just about then, as it happened, my travelling took me on my first circle around the world, and I wound up back where I had started from. My brother, the electrical engineer, and my sister, the doctor, came to see me camping under a bridge that my father had built when I was only three years old.

'Perhaps you can do something about him,' Philippa cried. 'He won't listen to us.'

'Don't you care?' asked Simon. 'It's a real embarrassment. It's time he was stopped before he brings terrible trouble upon himself.'

They looked at me − shaggy and silent, with almost nothing to say to them − in amazement. I gave them the only answer I could.

'What is there for a bridge-builder to build, if he isn't allowed to build bridges?' I asked them. Dust from the world's roads made my voice husky, even in my own ears.

'He can be a retired bridge-builder,' Simon replied. 'But I can see that you're going to waste time asking riddles. You don't care that your old father is involved in illegal bridge-building.' And he went away. He had forgotten the weekend picnics in the sunshine, and the derrick, high as a ladder, leading to the stars.

'And what have you become, Merlin?' Philippa asked me. 'What are you now, after all your journeys?'

'I'm a traveller as I always have been,' I replied.

'You are a vagabond,' she answered scornfully. 'A vagabond with a magician's name, but no magic!'

Then she went away, too, in her expensive car. I did not tell her, but I did have a little bit of magic − a single magical word, half-learned, half-invented. I could see that my father might need help, even a vagabond's help, even the help of a single magic word. I set off to find him.

It was easy for me, a seasoned traveller, to fall in with my father. I just walked along, until I came to a river that sang his name, and then I followed that river up over slippery stones and waterfalls, through bright green tangles of cress and monkey musk. Sure enough, there was my father building a bridge by bending two tall trees over the water and plaiting the branches into steps. This bridge would, in time, grow leafy handrails filled with birds' nests, a crossing place for deer and possums.

'Hello!' said my father. 'Hello, Merlin. I've just boiled the billy. Care for a cup of tea?'

'Love one!' I said. 'There's nothing quite like a cup of billy-tea.' So we sat down in a patch of sunlight and drank our tea.

'They're catching up with me, you know,' my father said sadly. 'There are police and soldiers looking all the time. Helicopters, too! I can go on escaping, of course, but I'm not sure if I can be bothered. I'm getting pretty bored with it all. Besides,' he went on, lowering his voice as if the green shadows might overhear him, 'I'm not sure that building bridges is enough any longer. I feel I must become more involved, to cross over myself in some way. But how does a bridge-builder learn to cross over when he's on both sides of the river to begin with?'

'I might be able to help,' I said.

My father looked up from under the brim of his working hat. He was a weatherbeaten man, fingernails cracked by many years of bridge-building. Sitting there, a cup of billy-tea between his hands, he looked like a tree, he looked like a rock. There was no moss on him, but he looked mossy for all that. He was as lined and wrinkled as if a map of all his journeys, backwards and forwards, were inscribed on his face, with crosses for all the bridges he had built.

'I'm not sure you can,' he answered. 'I must be *more* of a bridge-builder not *less* of one, if you understand me.'

'Choosy, aren't you?' I said, smiling, and he smiled back.

'I suppose you think you know what I'd like most,' he went on.

'I think I do!' I replied. 'I've crossed a lot of bridges myself one way and another, because I'm a travelling man, and I've learned a lot on the banks of many rivers.'

'And you've a magical name,' my father reminded me eagerly. 'I said, when you were born, this one is going to be the magician of the family!'

'I'm not a magician,' I replied, 'but there *is* one word I know . . . a word of release and remaking. It allows things to become their true selves.' My father was silent for a moment, nodding slowly, eyes gleaming under wrinkled lids.

'Don't you think things are really what they seem to be?' he asked me.

'I think people are all, more or less, creatures of two sides with a chasm in between, so to speak. My magic word merely closes the chasm.'

'A big job for one word,' said my father.

'Well, it's a very good word,' I said. I didn't tell him I had invented half of it myself. 'It's a sort of bridge,' I told him.

All the time we talked, we had felt the movement of men, not very close, not very far, as the forest carried news of my father's pursuers. Now we heard a sudden sharp cry – and another – and another. Men shouted in desperate voices.

'It's the soldiers,' my father said, leaping to his feet. 'They've been hunting me all day, though the forest is on my side and hides me away. But something's happened. We'd better go and check what's going on. I don't want them to come to harm because of me and my bridge-building habits.'

We scrambled upstream until the river suddenly started to run more swiftly, narrow and deep. The opposite bank rose up sharply, red with crumbling, rotten rock, green with mosses and pockets of fern. My father struggled to keep up with me. He was old, and besides, he was a bridge-builder, not a traveller. Closing my eyes for a moment against the distractions around me, I brought the magic word out of my mind and on to the tip of my tongue – and then I left it unspoken.

The soldiers were on the opposite bank. They had tried to climb down the cliff on rotten rock but it had broken away at their very toes and there they were, marooned on a crumbling ledge – three of them – weighted down with guns, ammunition belts and other military paraphernalia. Two of the soldiers were very young, and all three of them were afraid, faces pale, reflecting the green leaves greenly.

Below them the rocks rose out of the water. Just at this point the river became a dragon's mouth, full of black teeth, hissing and roaring, sending up a faint smoke of silver spray.

It was obvious that the soldiers needed a bridge.

My father stared at them, and they stared at him like men confounded. But he was a bridge-builder before he was anybody's friend or enemy, before he was anybody's father.

'That word?' he asked me. 'You have it there?'

I nodded. I dared not speak, or the word would be said too soon.

'When I step into the water, say it then, Merlin!'

I waited and my father smiled at me, shy and proud and mischievous all at once. He looked up once at the sky, pale blue and far, and then he stepped, one foot on land, one in the water, towards the opposite bank. I spoke the word.

My father changed before my eyes. He became a bridge as he had known he would. As for the word – it whispered over the restless surface of the river and rang lightly on the red, rotten rock. But my father had taken its magic out of it. No one else was altered.

The curious thing was that my father, who had made so many strange and beautiful bridges, was a very ordinary-looking bridge himself – a single-span bridge built of stone over an arch of stone, springing upwards at an odd angle, vanishing into the cliff at the very feet of the terrified soldiers. He looked as if he had always been there, as if he would be there for ever, silver moss on his handrails, on his abutments, even on his deck. Certainly he was the quietest bridge I had ever crossed as I went over to help the soldiers down. There was no way forward through the cliff. Still, perhaps the job of some rare bridges is to cross over only briefly and then bring us back to the place we started from.

We came back together, the three soldiers and I, and I'm sure we were all different men on the right bank from the men we had been on the left.

Our feet made no sound on the silver moss.

'They can say what they like about that old man,' cried the older soldier all of a sudden, 'but I was never so pleased to see a bridge in all my life. It just shows there are good reasons for having bridges in unexpected places.'

Together we scrambled downstream, and at last, back on to the road.

'But who's going to build the bridges now, then?' asked one of the young soldiers. 'Look! You were with him. Are you a bridge-builder, too?'

They knew now. They knew that unexpected bridges would be needed.

But someone else will have to build them. I am not a bridge-builder. I am a traveller. I set out travelling, after that, crossing, one by one, all the bridges my father had built . . . the picnic-bridges of childhood, the wooden ones, the steel ones, the stone and the concrete. I crossed the blue bridges of the air and those that seemed to be woven of vines and flowers. I crossed the silver-thread and mother-of-pearl bridge one moonlit midnight. I looked down into the melting heart of the world and saw my reflection in a bubble of fire while the harps sang and sighed and snarled around me with the very voice of the volcano.

Some day someone, perhaps my own child, may say that word

of mine back to me – that word I said to my father – but I won't turn into a bridge. I shall become a journey winding over hills, across cities, along seashores and through shrouded forests, crossing my father's bridges and the bridges of other men, as well as all the infinitely divided roads and splintered pathways that lie between them.

Bill Manhire

PONIES

IT WAS JUST after the assassination of Indira Gandhi that I came into the employ of Jason Michael Stretch. Wellington is a city of hidden steps and narrow passages, dark tributary corridors which are rapidly being translated, courtesy of the new earthquake codings, into glittering malls and arcades, whole worlds of space-age glass and silver. Inside these places, on their several levels, there is a curious calm, which is now beginning to extend out on to the footpaths. No one points excitedly; people drift along, pale, ice-cold, gazing into windows in a way which is almost tranquil, or ride escalators which take them up and down but not quite anywhere. A few years ago – as, say, a first-year student – I think I might well have scorned these aimless citizens, or felt sorry for them: a bit superior, anyway. Now they strike me as somehow beyond distress or temptation or anyone's genuine concern – as if they are busy at something which the city itself expects of them, and which they do rather well merely by moving from one place to the next.

A few people behave as if they know their way around. They lack the general air of glazed serenity. They don't quite merge into the crowd. They move marginally faster, like swimmers going downstream, outpacing the current; then they duck clear and vanish into a doorway or make a sudden dash across the road into the downtown traffic. For a few weeks I was running so many errands for Jason Stretch that I began to fancy that I myself must have looked like this. A man who stood out a little from the crowd. A *busy* fellow, someone with intentions and a destination.

Pepperell and Stretch was in Upper Cuba Street — down an alleyway, up a flight of steps, several turns along a corridor. The footpath in that part of Cuba Street has a richness which not only assaults your nostrils, it manages to hit you right at the back of the throat — as if having soaked up a full variety of human juices over the years it is eager to give something back. (You will see that in my weaker moments I would like to be a writer, not a part-time student of anthropology who has got himself lost somewhere between courses.) But maybe it is only because of the Chinese restaurant on the corner that someone with a spraycan has written Pong Alley just next to Drop the Big One — two messages which I had the opportunity to contemplate several times a day as I went by lugging a bag filled with items for the mail or yellow leaflets for one of Jason's suburban letterbox runs.

There wasn't a Pepperell, not in the office. One of my jobs, though, was to take the Number 1 bus out to Island Bay once a week and remove from the letterbox of a house in Evans Street the about-to-be-current issue of *Pepperell's Investment Weekly*, a stockmarket tip sheet, all immaculately typed and centred on a sheet of white A4 paper. Then the thing would be to take this back to town, over to Easiprint in Taranaki Street, and get fifty-seven copies run off ('Pepperell and Stretch's charge account thanks'); and that same day if there was time, or the next morning if there wasn't, I'd trundle back out to Evans Street, ring the doorbell, go and stare at the island for half an hour — and back again to find each of the fifty-seven sheets signed, 'All the best! Bob Pepperell', in a ragged blue ballpoint.

Mrs Watson said that the woman before her had told her that

Jason had acquired *Pepperell's Investment Weekly* when he took over
the firm, and that he had actually been a subscriber himself when
he was still in Balclutha. Mrs Watson typed subscriber addresses
on envelopes for me to slide the individually signed sheets into.
She did one or two other jobs of the same sort; otherwise she
typed student theses, paying Jason Stretch a 20 per cent commission
fee. She said this figure was 'very fair'. Jason looked after the
horoscopes himself.

'A terrible business, this shooting in India,' said Jason Stretch.
'Two of Mrs Gandhi's bodyguards shot her seven times as she was
walking from her home to an interview with the British actor
Peter Ustinov. One of the assassins had been one of Mrs Gandhi's
bodyguards for eight years. The entire security unit of Mrs
Gandhi's residence has been taken off duty and is undergoing
intensive questioning. Unquote.'

He put down the *Dominion* and reached across the desk. I
reached out my hand, since this was what he seemed to be
expecting, and he took it. He shook it. (Was the grasp firm or
limp?) 'Executed in cold blood by her own employees,' he said.
'These all have to be read for clipping and filing.' He gestured
towards a pile of newspapers. 'Still, I doubt if you'll have time for
that sort of thing. I very much hope you won't. Well, there we
are. Nine o'clock tomorrow, then. Let's see how things go,
Kevin.'

Well, there we were. As they say. I am inventing the words,
for I have no clear memory of what they actually were. But I am
doing my best to reconstruct the *tone* that I recall. Jason Stretch's
communications to his employees (me and Mrs Watson) tended to
jump about a lot but were somehow without energy or final form.

I had been expecting some sort of interview but apparently
the job was mine. 'Editorial and administrative responsibilities,'
the ticket at the job agency had said: 'Applicants must be steady

and reliable but should also be comfortable with innovative thinking.' Apart from rotten pay, this added up to the expeditions out to Island Bay; a lot of time spent sitting in an old armchair next to Mrs Watson's desk and doodling on a clipboard; and looking after the post – which meant at least one cable-car ride a day up to the Kelburn Post Office to clear the private box which Pepperell and Stretch kept there.

Then there were the leaflet runs in the afternoons. 'But nothing too arduous,' said Jason Stretch. 'The experience of walking the footpaths is going to stand you in good stead I'm sure, but there's no point in wearing yourself out.'

Here he comes, the suburban packhorse . . .

Some afternoons I took a sheet advertising *Pepperell's Weekly*, and sometimes I had one headed 'Astral Readings!', which started off with a whole lot of stuff about the Future and ended with an invitation to write in confidence at once, giving your date of birth.

'Send no money now but be sure to include a stamped addressed envelope for immediate return of your free Astral Interpretation. Confidentiality guaranteed. Jason M. Stretch.'

The 'Jason M. Stretch' bit was a genuine signature. Each leaflet was individually signed. Jason spent a couple of hours every morning writing his name at the foot of his promotional leaflets. Perhaps it made him feel he existed more securely, perhaps the personal touch was company policy. Perhaps it came down to the same thing.

An odd thing: I must have glimpsed Jason's signature any number of times in an afternoon, but unless I was actually looking directly at it I could never summon up an image of it. Was it large or small? Neat? Listless? A jovial flourish? What colour ink?

Come to that, as I trailed around suburban Wellington, pushing Astral Readings into the letterboxes of Kilbirnie or Thorndon or Hataitai, I couldn't quite summon up Jason himself,

I couldn't get him plainly in the forefront of my mind. He was in his late thirties, I'm pretty sure, certainly a good deal older than me. His hair was shortish, fairish . . . but was he balding or just closely cropped? Did he wear glasses all the time, or only for reading? Now I find myself wondering if he wore glasses at all.

All I can call into being is the outline of a body and a head above a desk. There is no colour which I associate with the eyes of Jason Stretch, or with his complexion; not even with his clothing. He barely has being, for all the hundreds of times he wrote his name.

He ought to have seemed to me then – and no doubt ought to seem to me now – grotesque, colourfully Dickensian; but he is ordinary and indeterminate and unemphatic, like a dark brown desk viewed against a light brown wall, like the office furniture he sat at.

So there we were, and the truly grotesque discovery was learning that Jason's occasional references to the value of walking had a point. During January and February, he thought, I might like to lead small walking tours around Wellington. All the major cities had them, he said. There were more people than you might imagine – tourists, visitors from out of town – who *liked* to move around a city more or less at ground level, maintaining a leisurely, unhurried pace, yet all the while being kept amused and informed by knowledgeable and entertaining guides.

Jason already had two tours mapped out ($15.00 a head) and some provisional copy for the brochures. 'Historic Thorndon: a leisurely ramble through pioneer Wellington – home of prime ministers, birthplace of Katherine Mansfield.' 'Harbour City: come with us on a stroll around Wellington's busy waterfront; see views of the harbour that even Wellingtonians don't see; visit the historic Maritime Museum.'

'We'll improve the descriptive stuff; it needs to sound about two hours' worth, wouldn't you say? How's "Secret Wellington" coming along, Kevin?' 'Secret Wellington' was a walk which Jason felt we needed to have up our sleeve in case Wellington's weather made 'Historic Thorndon' and 'Harbour City' doubtful prospects. An indoor, under-cover route which stuck to Lambton Quay, Willis Street and Manners Street (for example) would be just the thing.

'Keep it in mind as you go about the city, Kevin. All the little nooks and crannies. A few historic sites. Some of the new malls and plazas. What about the new BNZ underground place? There might be something there. Check it out when you go for the post.'

So there we were, me and my prospects, sitting on the cable-car in mid-November, worrying about January and how I could possibly handle the problem of knowing enough to be able to say anything at all to tourists and out-of-towners. And what if I bumped into someone I *knew* on one of these outings? I whimpered inwardly.

'You can always take them on the cable-car,' a small inner voice whispered to me; and suddenly I knew what it meant to be able to say that your whole being glowed with pleasure. I turned over one of the airmail letters which came addressed to Jason Stretch from Pundit Tabore, 'India's Most Famous Astrologer', of Upper Forjett Street, Bombay, India. I beamed at it in all its beauty. The flimsy brown envelope blazed out with coloured stamps. There was a woman doing gymnastic movements against a sky-blue background; against a red background a powerfully muscled man lifted weights. Five linked rings: the Olympics! But the odd thing about Pundit Tabore's letters (and here it was again) was that the stamps were always on the wrong side of the envelope. I mean, on one side of the envelope the man grunted and strained and the woman was graceful, while on the other was Jason M. Stretch's name and Wellington address.

'They always seem to get through, though,' said Mrs Watson. She was taking a break between chapters of a Communication Studies thesis. 'It must be their way of doing it. I'd love to know what that Indian's telling him.'

'Do you think he believes in it?' I said.

'Well,' said Mrs Watson, 'there must be about a dozen inquiries each week, and three or four of them end up sending the $75.00 for the full reading. I suppose they must learn something to their advantage. You need the place of birth for that, though, and the time of day as near as you can get it.'

Next morning I mentioned the cable-car to Jason.

'Well, Kevin,' he said, 'let's hang fire on that one just for a little while, shall we?'

He seemed tired, but very excited.

'You know,' he said, 'an old bloke in the Catlins once told me that if you're a real bushman and it's about to rain, then you can hear the drops hitting the leaves at least a couple of minutes before the rain itself starts coming down. Even before it starts spitting, that is. Well,' he said, his voice pleased and lowered and confidential, 'I like to think I can hear people who are about to spend their money in just the same way. You can quote me on that when I'm famous.'

Of course, I am inventing the detail of Jason Stretch's words again, but not, you may be sure, out of nothing. Jason needed words like these as background and preamble to his main point, which was that he had seen on television the night before a panel discussion about nuclear winters. He had seen a way of making money.

'Horrifying. Makes you think. But it's a chance at last to

combine real service to society with our own information skills. And it means real research work for you, Kevin. You'll have to move quickly, though.'

There must have been a look of reluctance on my face.

'I grew up in Balclutha,' he said, 'but here I am' – as if this would solve whatever it was that was making me so diffident.

He was jumping up and down like the man who invented hokey-pokey ice cream.

I sat in the Wellington Public Library, researching survival techniques in sub-zero temperatures. I read about the Antarctic. Mrs Watson's uncle had watched the *Terra Nova* sail from Lyttelton in 1910.

'He said it was the next best thing to Noah's Ark. I never was much interested in the dogs really, it's the ponies I feel sorry for.'

'Ponies?' I said.

NUCLEAR WINTER
War between the superpowers grows more and more likely every day!

It is well known that in the event of a nuclear exchange human life will become extinct in many areas of the planet.

Are you aware that things may be nearly as bad outside the immediate blast areas? Do you know that even a small nuclear war in the Northern Hemisphere may spell disaster in the South?

Smoke from fires burning in hundreds of cities will spread rapidly into the troposphere and stratosphere, severely limiting the amount of heat reaching the earth's surface from the sun.

A thick sooty pall. Darkness at noon. Temperatures will plummet. Imagine the cold and ice of an Antarctic winter. Many plant and animal species will be threatened with extinction.

Many communities in the Northern Hemisphere will perish from the extreme cold.

In the Southern Hemisphere some of us may survive. Within three days, scientists have forecast, concentrated jet streamers of smoke and pollutants will have poured into the atmosphere above Australia and New Zealand. Those sufficiently prepared to cope with the sudden fall in temperature may win through, but many will not – the problem is beyond the limited resources of Civil Defence. The only answer is individual initiative and forward planning.

Write at once for your 'Nuclear Winter Kit'. It contains information essential to your personal survival. Make sure you will be ready to meet all eventualities. You owe it to yourself. You owe it to your children. Send $29.95 (cheque or postal order) to 'Nuclear Winter Foundation', Box 831-240, Wellington 5. We will send your 'Nuclear Winter Kit' by return post.

There were nineteen Manchurian ponies on board the *Terra Nova*, taken to Antarctica to haul sledges. They were crammed aboard the tiny ship. 'One takes a look through the hole in the bulkhead,' wrote Scott, 'and sees a row of heads with sad, patient eyes come swinging up together from the starboard side, whilst those on the port swing back; then up come the port heads, whilst the starboard recede.' The ponies' boxes were two or three feet deep in manure when the *Terra Nova* came in sight of Antarctica.

The ponies were Manchurian, white or (a few of them) dappled grey. They cost £5 each. Captain Oates, famous for other things, was hired to look after the ponies. There are photographs taken by Ponting of the ponies aboard ship and on the ice. They are so white, the ponies, that they must often have been hard to see against the landscape they had been taken to.

There is a photograph of Oates standing on the upper deck of the *Terra Nova* with four of the ponies. Man and animals are all perfectly still, posed for the image. Among the shore photographs there is one of a pony called Chinaman with his leader, Wright. Wright faces the camera while Chinaman is in profile. There is a photograph of Oates standing with Snippets. There is Cherry-Garrard with his pony, Michael, of whom he said, 'Life was a constant source of wonder to him.' Michael is rolling on his back in the snow. Cherry-Garrard holds him on a long rein.

The ponies are greyish-white against the massive surround of ice and sky. They have coal-black eyes. The men are darker. The ponies seem to be moth-eaten; but maybe this is an effect of Ponting's photographs, or of the very rough photocopies which I made of them.

'A bit of fine tuning, but it's mostly there,' said Jason. 'We won't worry about any suburban deliveries with this one. People will be flocking into town for Christmas shopping over the next few weeks. We'll distribute directly, pass the stuff out in central Wellington.'

(Bowers records somewhere that old pony droppings, distorted by a trick of the Antarctic light, could look like a herd of cattle on the horizon.)

Oates was the man who looked after the horses. He was a taciturn man, known as the Soldier, who wrote letters to his mother. He gave two lectures on the management of horses to the men wintering over in Antarctica, ending each with a joke or anecdote. On the journey to the glacier he wrote: 'Scott realizes now what awful cripples our ponies are, and carries a face like a tired sea boot in consequence.'

Of the original nineteen horses, only ten were alive when Scott and his party set out on their journey to the Pole. Some had died on board the *Terra Nova* on its journey to Antarctica. Some had died on overland training trips. Others fell from ice floes into the ocean.

Only ten survived the winter and all of these were to be shot when the sledge parties reached the Beardsmore glacier; subsequently the men would haul their own sledges. The ponies were old, at the end of their working life; they had been bought cheap by a man who knew nothing about horses. 'Poor ancient little beggar,' Bowers wrote of Chinaman. 'He ought to be a pensioner instead of finishing his days on a job of this sort.'

On 24 November 1911, Jehu was shot. His body was cut up and given to the dogs.

On 28 November, Chinaman was shot. Oates remarks, 'He was a game little devil, and must have been a goodish kind of pony fifteen years ago.'

Scott and his men were now having pony meat in their hoosh. They found it much improved.

On 1 December it was the turn of Christopher, a pony who had been 'nothing but trouble', requiring four men to hold him down whenever his harness was to be placed upon him. 'He was the only pony who did not die instantaneously,' wrote Cherry-Garrard. 'Perhaps Oates was not so calm as usual, for Chris was his own horse though such a brute. Just as Oates fired he moved, and charged into the camp with a bullet in his head. He was caught with difficulty, nearly giving Keohane a bad bite, led back and finished.'

Oates now took over the leading of Scott's pony, Snippets. Scott roved about on skis, photographing the ponies as he went.

The next pony shot was Victor. Bowers wrote: 'Good old Victor! He has always had a biscuit out of my ration, and he ate his last before the bullet sent him to his rest.'

On 4 December Michael was dispatched.

A disastrous blizzard raged for several days. On 9 December the party reached the glacier. It had been a fourteen-hour march. One member of the party later recalled the condition of the ponies, 'Their flanks heaving, their black eyes dull, shrivelled, and wasted. The poor beasts stood,' he wrote, 'with their legs stuck out in strange attitudes, mere wrecks of the beautiful little animals that we took away from New Zealand.'

The last five ponies were shot on 9 December.

When Scott and his party were dispatching the remaining ponies, more than a month of overland sledge-hauling lay ahead of them. Amundsen would reach the Pole in a matter of days. It was Oates's work with the ponies which so impressed Scott that he asked him to join the smaller team which now made the ill-fated final 'dash'.

Rajiv Gandhi stood by his mother's flaming funeral pyre, surrounded by the dignitaries of the world.

As the flames spread, India's new Prime Minister stood with his hands clasped in prayer, receiving the condolences of official mourners. Behind barriers, tens of thousands of people also mourned the death of the woman they knew as Mother India.

Nearly an hour after setting the pyre ablaze, Rajiv was still on the surrounding platform waiting according to Hindu custom for the body's head to explode.

Mourners touched their foreheads to the platform.

'Tomorrow,' said Jason Stretch, 'I think we'd better make a start on distributing these, Kevin.'

There were half a dozen big cartons of leaflets.

'I very much hope we'll need to run off a few more than this before we're finished. I think the thing will be to stick around the new shopping plazas. And we'll need to begin finalizing copy for the Kit itself. How's it coming along?'

I said that I'd picked up quite a lot of material on some of the Antarctic expeditions.

'Right. And it might be worth checking with Civil Defence. They may have a few words of advice. Or tramping clubs and things like that. There must be plenty of stuff available. But see if you can get rid of a box of these first.'

I stood with my armful of leaflets outside the new AA building in Lambton Quay for forty-seven minutes before it came to me that I was never going to work up the courage to stick Nuclear Winter sheets under the noses of passing Christmas shoppers. At the same time I realized that it wasn't that I particularly disapproved of what Jason Stretch was up to. I probably did, but the real truth was that I felt silly – or was scared I would look silly. Each moment that went by, I felt a little more potentially ludicrous. From time to time someone would look at me curiously. I tried to look as though I was waiting for somebody. Help! I tried to stand there as though I wasn't there.

I wrote out my resignation on the back of a Nuclear Winter sheet and posted it to Jason's box number. 'All the best to Bob Pepperell,' I added. I dumped the pile of leaflets at the end of an empty counter in the Chews Lane post office. I don't know why I should have forgotten the ponies. You grow up knowing all that stuff about Scott and Captain Oates. Oates was in charge of the ponies. That's why he was there in the first place. They called him the Soldier. I am just going outside and I may be some time.

The ponies' names were James Pigg, Bones, Michael, Snatcher, Jehu, Chinaman, Christopher, Victor, Snippets and Nobby. After I had written Jason Stretch's name and address on the envelope, I stuck the stamp on the opposite side.

I actually saw Jason about half an hour after I'd posted the

letter. He was on an escalator at the new BNZ Centre. I half tried
to catch his eye, but he looked straight through me – not because
he was choosing to ignore me but because he wasn't quite looking
at anything. I can't remember now, just a few weeks later, whether
he was rising up out of the earth or descending into it.

Ian Wedde

from SYMMES HOLE

HE'D HAVE TO WATCH how he told this story. Somehow it wasn't just an . . . *incident*. That man in the overcoat had run as though he'd had no real target — 'As though I wasn't really there?'

> ''Cos, you've, got
> Per-sonality
> > > disorders . . .'

. . . performing an elaborate dance-step along Oriental Parade — lifting one foot over the other, arms raised above his head in a Spanish, make that Mexican, Me*h*ican, manner . . .

Shaking imaginary maracas he tried it again, arse and chin tucked in, flashing wetback teeth at the veering car lights . . .

'You see *that* . . .?'

'Some young pisshead . . . dope fiend . . . dole bludger . . . sex pervert . . . subsers', subversive . . .' — how did they know he wasn't a, Courtenay Place bus-shelter sherry boob-head? . . . executive for the Challenge Finance Corporation? . . . McDonald's Fast Foods franchisee?

. . . nah, got that one sorted out. How could they possibly not recognize, ta-dah! – Herman Melville!

Take a bow.

. . . in one or another of the handsome portraits of him by Asa W. Twitchell in the Berkshire Athenaeum, Pittsfield, Massachussetts, U.S.A. . . . thick dark hair with a virile wave above the left temple, broad high brow, wide straight dark eyebrows, dense dark beard (one version has him with no moustache: bottom lip prominent, a thumb-sucker), big straight bony nose, wide pale 'Gansevoort' cheekbones . . . brawny shoulders in good dark cloth, necktie of some extravagance, well-laundered collar . . . and dark eyes looking away at . . . or, when you measured their focus, looking *through* you, at something behind . . .

And what's this, 'personality disorder'? Why not 'higher consciousness'?

> Monk: What happens when the leaves are falling, and
>   the trees are bare?
> Unmon: The golden wind, revealed!

He again spotted the light of some small craft out in the roadstead. It had moved oddly closer . . . the light flickered unsteadily, why? . . . more like a torch signal than . . . and what would it be doing in the hour before midnight, on a course for the art-deco band rotunda in Oriental Bay?

Customs and excise man (now) Herman Melville turned from the consideration of minutiae around himself – half-focused gazing at bits of wood and stone, small bituminous coils of lapdog shit on the parade, the miscellaneous refuse of affluent boredom: half-cigars, discarded newspapers . . . a bright yellow scarf . . . a mislaid kahawhai spinner – hang on. He picked up the spinner and put it in his pocket then went back for the scarf – it had a delicate aroma, was it coconut soap?

And his dreamy attentiveness to what was true and insignificant vanished − behind the veil of vision he was again with Marquesan Fayaway in the secret valley of Typee ... the water of the swimming hole shook from her oiled skin ... dark haloes around her nipples roughened into goosebumps at the cool ... his own body, with its inheritance of Gansevoort paleness, seemed translucent beside hers, even the heavily freckled sailor's arm he threw around her waist. Where her small teeth nipped his shoulder the indentations filled with red colour, while the marks his left upon her neck showed purple, purple also the trail between her breasts, and the half-moon bite with one upper canine missing, upon her smooth belly ...

− Uh, cann', *cannibalism*? And they always said sailors was too salt from eating junk horse. But as his teeth nipped into the fragrant meat of her body, the soft flesh inside her thigh, his erection sprang into weightlessness at the temptation to feast upon the dark plethoric juice of her sweet ... to feel his teeth meet through her protein. Why not − the thought blazed up in him as he went for her gravy − why not *devour each other simultaneously*?

'Have a piece of arse.'

'Swap you for ...', wait on, *arse*? Now if it was veal you'd say, was it *chump*? ... for pork, *leg short-end*? ... for lamb, *leg loin-end*? ... for mutton, *saddle*? ... for beef, *rump, aitch-bone*, or *buttock*?

His loud laughter bounced back at him from the buildings across the parade. 'Have a piece of chuh, a piece of, ha-have a piece of chu–*chump* ...!' − screaming weakly because ...

And the aproned man on the other side of the road, popping a milk-crate out in front of the Pâté Shop Restaurant, sidled inside to his telephone in a hurry.

'I want to report ...', my God just look at him, back against that Norfolk pine, seems to be ... howling? And before that, kind of dancing, talking out loud, then looked as though he was going to ... 'Expose himself? No he didn't *actually* but ... All right all right ... Yes, probably drunk or ... Acting *very* qu',' read that again, 'very *strange*, wild . . . Now? He's just leaning against a . . .', God! *Biting* himself in the, seems to be trying to turn himself around and bite himself in the . . . Un*bal*anced, yes . . . I'd say that. Definitely unbalanced . . . Against property? No, not actually *violent*, but . . . I mean, if he crossed the road I'd . . . You bet your sweet, you bet I'm going to stay here! . . . Your regular patrol? But don't you think this is a little more, unusual? . . . than your *normal*? . . . All right, tha' . . . thank you ossif', officer. Thank you very much!' Flouncing down the phone, he checked back at the weirdo across the parade.

Out there with his back against the strange antediluvian skin of the great conifer he was screaming weakly, he was only just still laughing because beneath his teeth it was as though, Herman? . . . Herman's mouth and face encountered a non-Marquesan angularity, depleted sparser squiff of hair, hips with rims like bone china, a parched odour of civilization and impatience . . . lightness of hollow ornithoid bones . . . bunt of loins against him without languor or luxury . . . shroud-white belly . . . gaunt ribs and white, white breasts with little puckered colourless nipples . . . delicate clavicles . . . one long neck-tendon standing out with the head turned sideways . . . ironic angry passion of the wasted profile . . . damp, dark fringe of hair . . . charnel breath . . .

'Kathleen . . .?'

'*Herman*, well . . . well, well . . .', arid methedrine glare in those dark eyes, fingers that couldn't keep still anywhere on him. 'Remember, I am a very *modern* woman . . .', her laughter speeding up until it threw out grief like a heavy distillation, the little weightless trembling body hanging upon him.

'What do you mean, you're a very . . .?' – the pressure of those arms around his neck as light as silk. . . shrinking, fading . . . 'What do you mean, a very *modern* . . .?' And he took off the perfumed scarf he'd hung around his neck and held it against his cheek. 'Kathleen . . .?'

The lights out on the water had moved closer. From the pâté

shop across the road came the sound of Donizetti turned up loud, *Lucia di Lammermoor*? He thought he recognized it . . . Beverley Sills? There was almost no traffic on Oriental Bay, the parade. He inhaled the sweetish coconut aroma of the scarf. Fear not nausea moved him to a bench by the sea-wall. He could see that light flashing out there, hear the faint sound of oars. The Marquesan Fayaway fantasy was okay, but this other . . .

It was a feeling like dread that made him shove the scarf against his mouth . . . 'In love?', his voice muffled by the coconut-scented silk, 'With, Kath' . . .? *Kathleen*?' He couldn't struggle through to a sense of what it meant. She was . . . where would he find her? She was dead.

He could now make out a rowboat about fifty yards offshore. And no torchlight. Nothing fitted.

He went back over it: the space closest to him was . . . confused. Back from it the street lights along the parade stepped away from him around the curve of Oriental Bay. The boat with lights. Herman Melville the customs clerk squinting at it with a dark suspicious melancholy official eye (could it be a boat-load of significance upon the deep?) from a portrait by Asa W. Twitchell. A burst of gaiety, sound of Latino, salsa or something? Then it was another boat, a 'little steamer all hung with bright beads', sound of the moaning buoy on Barrett's. *That* he'd . . . imagined. Unreal charnel breath as he passed the Freyberg Pool, the modern reek of chlorine. Rattle of halyards at the marina. Against his back a bulwark from which he faced the dark street in which nothing moved any more. Then he saw the overcoat flapping across the road on that weird diagonal . . . as though running between invisible sheets of glass. FINE said the ticker below the clock. The pulp of *National Business Review* skidded out beneath his heel. Through the dark of Parliament grounds he hurried. Why should he have felt so furtive? The word eavesdrop was a pivot around which he spun, flap of nausea and claustrophobia in the revolving doors, back to the babble of the . . . He saw poets, he saw novelists, he saw critics and academics, he saw 'arts administrators', he saw cigarette ash and a trampled crust of canapé on the carpet, he saw a purple suit and a green scarf, well-polished lenses flashed at him . . . turning from the reflection of his own self-satisfied haggard face he went back to it . . . He couldn't see her anywhere. He couldn't *find* her. She'd gone.

'Kathleen . . .'

Regnava net silenzio / alta la notte e bruna . . . burst of coloratura marksmanship as the door of the little pâté restaurant opened. Oh my *God*, he tutted, untying his apron – there he still was . . . 'The deep dark night reigned in silence', indeed! – I should be so lucky! And what would the cops do with him if they got their hands on him? . . . sitting over there, seemed to have a, something yellow? . . . had it pressed against his face. Maybe I better . . . He snibbed the door, was about to walk over when a Holden Commodore pulled to the kerb.

Little squeal of rubber – what? . . . turning his face from the scarf he looked back across the road, his vision was still hunting for Kathleen in the reception crowd . . . when he saw the large funereal saloon car his heart gave a heavy thump . . .

And over there, 'Whaddaya lookin' at ya fairy?' from the kerbside window.

'Nothing, I . . .', butting the restaurant door open with his backside, retreating to Act One Scene Two of *Lucia di Lammermoor* – flag it *all* away tonight . . .!

'Who's the weirdo on the bench over there . . . 's right where I wanna park!'

'How the fuck should I know, relax willya Harry, wanna toke on . . .?'

'Fuckin' idiot!' knocking the giant squiff from the other's hand. 'They'll be here any minute, an' that fucker's . . .', opening the driver's door. 'Hey, shit, where'd the weirdo *go*?'

'Carpet's on fire, man,' the other bent double with his head under the glove-box groping for the joint where smoke arose from the dark maroon pile carpet. 'See what you . . . ow, Jesus!' crack of his head against the console as the driver hauls him upright . . . 'Harry!'

'Shut the fuck up, you . . .!'

'. . . you cunt, you can't . . .!'

'*Shut up*!' slamming him against the door.

The car was rocking as they shoved at each other. From within the pâté shop the aproned man watched it all . . . the Commodore was leaking smoke. And, and our fair friend across the way, he'd . . . hey, he'd gone? The stereo was fixed to repeat on Scene Two of the first act, and now Lucia was seeing the ghost all over again, in the night '*alta . . . et bruna*' . . . as the door burst open on the passenger side and the man spilled out dragging a floor rug with him . . . a billow of smoke blew away up the parade . . . the other hood was coughing out the driver's window. – This was better than . . .

Below the promenade on the pebbly beach he looked up with sudden dread as the splash of water signalled the approach of the rowboat – sudden whine in his bowels had sent him scuttling to the dark on the beach beneath the parade wall . . . kicked his pants off, scraped a wee hole, just in time – a loose turd followed a hock-lubricated detonation of painful gas. Must've been the, those – fighting a little nausea at the thought of the pastry cases with the fishy fillings . . . Plus too much of that God-awful cheap hock they . . . and now he was going to get caught with his . . . maybe the boat wasn't coming round this . . .? But then he saw the rowboat nose around the side of the art-deco band rotunda.

'Where's Harry, he was supposed to . . .?' – stage whispers.

'Don't worry he's cool just get up on the . . . nobody can see you from the road . . . *fuck what's that*?' as the squad car squeaked to a halt, slam of two doors, alert burst of coloratura soprano, light flooding suddenly through the pâté shop window – and the man poised with the smoking rug raised ready to beat on the pavement, looking at the diamond-patterned headband on the cap coming over at him fast.

'Fuckin' hell Harry it's the cops!' The passenger door slammed shut of its own accord as the Commodore peeled away from the kerb with a scream of tyres leaving ten-yard burn marks on the asphalt and a little pall of acrid rubber smoke.

On the beach: 'What, Jesus, listen . . .!'

'Don't move, give us the . . .!'

Above: 'He was over here, only *seconds* ago, this other lot . . .', bright ever-so-helpful voice crossing the road from the pâté shop.

'. . . give us that, give us the shit, *Christ* . . .!' – the rowboat rocking as he lobbed a parcel carefully back into the shallows by the base of the rotunda.

'I haven't done nothing . . .!' whining. 'Cigarette caught fire in the . . .'

'Okay then why'd your mate take off in such a hurry?'

'I dunno, he . . .'

'. . . youngish blond chap, he was acting very . . .'

'So you've told us *Mary*, now why don't you just pipe down for . . .'

'*Wait*, what's this *Mar*', now look . . .'

'Listen turdburg I've got my hands full, now shut up and get out of the . . .'

'What the fuck are we gonna tell them . . . we were *fishing*?' – the whisperers trying to fend off the base of the rotunda.

'What with, your shoe? Listen, jus' say . . .'

'What was that?' from the parade, as the boat bottomed. 'Sounded like . . .'

'Go for it Galky, cops've . . .' The Commodore fireman let out a yell before the second policeman shoved him against the bonnet of the squad car. The other's flashlight probed accurately down. The rowboat was drifting beam-on to the waves as one man grabbed for a floating oar. His head came up full into the shaft of light – heavy slightly Asiatic face, smile like a hastily opened sardine tin, some gold in it.

'Come in there you in the boat.'

'Oh hello officer, we were just . . .'

'Fishing? Come and meet your friend here, he was putting out a fire.'

'. . . *nel silenzio / alta la notte e bruna* . . .', and then the reprise cut off as the pâté shop door slammed.

'Talk to the fag later. Get the fireman in the car – he's coming voluntarily for a wee chat, aren't you pal? Now you lot . . .', striding down to the beach, flashlight trained away from the shadows under the wall. 'Come on in here sailor boy, your pal too, pull that boat up – *Christ*, what's . . .?', as his regulation shoe skidded off the fresh turd in its little hole.

And it wasn't Herman Melville who now watched the officer hop on one foot to the rocks and scrape shit off his shoe. Back in the deep shadows he crouched. He'd tried at first to get his feet into the legs of his trousers. But now he hunkered motionless as the crowd around him grew – arriving by sea and by land, musical accompaniment by Beverley Sills and, the Vienna Volksoper maybe?

. . . it wasn't Herman Melville excise man who watched the packet sink back there against the rotunda foundations . . . nor was it any longer Herman who saw the slightly Asiatic eyes of the man called, was it Galky? . . . Galkin? *What?* . . . saw the flat eyes look through the darkness and *see* him at the same moment as the name *Gálkin* clanged into place in his cowering head – But, *that's the name of the doctor on the sloop Vostók which came to Queen Charlotte Sound with the Bellingshausen-Lazarev Antarctic Expedition in 1820, he's a, a dead Russian?*

'The Russian' looked straight at him and saw a cowering man with no pants on . . . by the rocks the cop with his back turned was cursing as he scraped smelly crap off his shoe. No expression moved the large flat features of 'Gálkin'.

The Russian placed two fingers against his temple, one saurian eye winked shut as he pulled the trigger: as in, '*Got it?*'. . . and a very minimal flash of gold in his mouth. Then he turned away from the cowering man and stepping efficiently around the squashed turd walked briskly to the steps as the cop's flashlight swung back.

The beam missed the lair by inches – Hey, thanks Gal' . . . And then the gratitude at not having his cover blown away into the lit thoroughfares of disgrace – Promising Young Writer Caught With Pants Down? Scribe in Scatological Scandal? Poet's Public Poop Puts Paid To Prospects? Dung Disgrace Dogs Doodler? – the gratitude which had been the first emotion to register in his poor . . . his scared mind flooded next with icy anticipation of the bullet The Russian's short hairy fingers had smilingly pointed into it. 'He knows that I . . .', I'm the *only one* who knows?

– I blow whistle on odd comrade with no pants, next thing cops get packet because *he* tells them . . . I don't, no one's the wiser . . . only *he* has to understand: leave that in its one or two *sazhen* of water or else hole in bottom of your body won't be only one giving you trouble . . . as it stands you can up pull your pants and count yourself lucky, Tovarich.

On the parade they'd run out of interesting conversation. The squad car squealed through a television drama U-turn and left in a downtown direction. He watched its red tail lights proceed around the curve of the bay. There were no voices left up there, not that he could hear. Donizetti had shut down also: 'the Ravenswood Ghost' had thrown her phantom switch.

He waited for a tell-tale cough, anything. There was only the splash of little waves. How far would waves move that, the . . .? And the tide when it went out . . .?

He pulled on his pants . . . little grit in the grundies, and his shaking fingers had trouble with the zipper. It was then that he thought, *They might want to kill me anyway*! And then certainty, stamped out the message: A Russian from the 'Homage-to-James-

Cook' Bellingshausen-Lazarev Antarctic Expedition of 1819–1821 is going to kill me?

There was a test: the packet. Only way to find out if you're dead, is to find out if it was worth anybody's while to kill you. And now's . . . because later . . .

Funny how it goes, he was thinking – don't get it turns into get it . . . alive turns into dead. The water was nearly up to his waist. Reaching down into the cold sea, his whole front submerged. He felt around the sea-bed among the complicated striae of long-gone mussels, some mud, litter of shells and pebbles over the rocks.

But the water was at least freshening him, and when he felt the packet under his fingers he even let out a little whoop . . . clutching it to his chest he wallowed ashore. The packet was well sealed. He shoved it into a pocket of his coat, encountering a reservoir of sea-water. His clothes hung around his quaking limbs. He could feel The Russian's golden dumdum shattering in slow motion into the cusps of his skull . . .

And this bent figure ran flicking sprays of water across the parade into the up-hill dark by Hay Street. Seawater left a trail clearly visible by street-light. From the silence and shadow he presently peeked out at the promenade . . . saw this trail zagging over the street and ending where his clothes now drained downhill across the pavement. – Christ, why not, why not just, stand in the middle of the road, offer your profile to the muzzle of the smile, the gold fang that will be driven like a little ice-pick into your . . . And then he got the smell too – looking down again at where the trail pointed to his feet he saw the vestigial smear of his own dung-spoor . . . image of Dobermann Pinschers burning pad-smoke as they brake to halts: '. . . quarry *wants* us to find him?'

. . . sneaky-pete back across the road. – Escape by sea! . . . that, or a nude dash up Grass Street in the dark through the trees up the zig-zag, jus' me an' a packet of, frozen guh-guh-guh, frozen trevalli bait – lower jaw wagging as the cold began to rattle his teeth. – And, and ju-just imagine – pushing the boat down to the receding tide-line – just imagine meeting one of those, one of those literary pa-pa-pachyderms up there somewhere en route from a post-Bee-hee-hee-hive party or something . . . and there you go, shrivelled cock wiggling in moonlight, skinny shanks reaching for mossy steps, whoops! . . . right at their feet. 'Hey look, it's that young . . .' And the packet's burst, there you lie stretched out all cold and white and blue, in a scatter of, frozen trevalli . . .?

In his pocket the 'frozen trevalli bait' bulged, his left elbow prodded it as he rowed competently from the beach muttering 'In-out' under his breath. – Little row by, *moonlight?*

. . . the harbour was bathed in the glare of the late-risen moon . . . the near-full orb wobbled above Point Jerningham . . . on three sides of him the lights of the parade and of the quays glittered: stalls, dress-circle, gallery. And there's your entertainment: marine clown, little man in a boat churning moontrail toward the darker reaches of the roadstead, dead on for the glass mountain – there he goes! . . . only moving, clattering, splashing thing on the entire harbour surface, like a solitary Back-swimmer *Anisops assimilis* water-bug, actually *Anisops wakefieldi!* – with a whole shoal of starving trout just under the meniscus . . .

But the tide was running full out and as he settled to his stroke and began to feel warmer he found himself making good progress. The boat was a kitset double-kelson dory . . . the low surface chop smacked against its pram bows. He was skirting the end of Oriental Parade, coming up on Point Jerningham about a hundred yards offshore. A thin vapour arose from his clothes. – Got a boat, got away, got about half a kilo of . . . got a, got a contract out on me . . .

. . . 'Two-three, in-out.' *Calm* thoughts. – The thing about the sea was, it was a-historical. He was now pulling steadily up to the broad reach where Evans Bay opened to the south and west. He'd passed the Point Jerningham, *click*: Edward Jerningham Wakefield, nephew of the colonel, same lad that set fire to a whole mountainside of virgin forest in the Pelorus Sound winter of 1839

because he wanted to see what a *really* big blaze looked like . . .
Queen's Scout material that young man, and Uncle had him
collecting signatures for land-deals too . . . wrote a book *Adventure
in New Zealand* . . . ripping yarns . . . *fade out* – passed the Point
Jerningham Light 'on the starboard beam' . . . the lights of the city
well astern as he leaned into his stroke.

There was the Beehive . . . tower of Williams' Deathtrap on
Plimmer Steps . . . Bob Jones Building leaning its sleek cheek in
. . . intricate sprawl of the container mega-hive . . .

. . . back in the other direction, up Evans Bay, he saw the
Mount Crawford Prison floodlights low along the top of the
Airforce Defence Base at Shelly Bay – from his room he could
hear the sound of gunfire from the practice range . . . helicopters
would rise into the air from the lz at the base, and batter the calm
atmosphere above the prison, or, tilting forward, would traverse
the bay where in summer he often lay back against the gunwale of
an old dinghy.

And from out here it looked as though the dark were a fabric
with rents through which shone disordered illumination from a
power source which had barely changed in a million years – the
present a sombre, viscid magma pierced by spears of light and heat,
imperceptibly flickering in the winds of entropy . . . and he was
now drifting before it, alone 'upon the surface of the deep'! A
euphoric feeling swept over him, out there in the great roadstead.
For a moment he thought, I'm exposure-happy. But then he
shipped the oars and drifted, feeling safe. – Because time was,
differential? . . . it was a differential calculation that would plot the
movement of this tide on which you drifted? . . . the true study of
time was, hydrographic?

– And vengeance? . . . revenge? Its consequence was going to
happen through time, but it was still going to start hitting you
*some*where: choose the locale, the time doesn't matter.

Funny: he still didn't feel scared. He hunkered below the
gunwale.

Now he could see down the main seaward arm of the harbour past the scatter of late lights at Fort Ballance, *click*: Ballance Ministry – the one with R. J. Seddon and J. Carroll, *and* W. P. Reeves . . . and J. McKenzie the landgrabber . . . he ticked them off, themes that faded in and out – late lights at Fort Ballance, stepping-out of street-lights around the bays: Scorching Bay, Worser Bay named for 'Worser' Heberley when he became pilot there, before great-grandfather Heinrich Augustus – how did it go? . . . 'Ai! Tangata whata haere mai mou te kai!' and 'tangata whata' turned through whaler-Maori into 'Worser', Worser Heberley, Couldn't-be-any-Worser Heberley . . .

Nowhere to go on land or sea without gilling yourself in the cross-hatch of stories. Who could think of apologizing for walking over the graves of, Hannibal's mahouts at Trasimene? . . . but your uncles that fell into the Italian furrows, yes the Maori Battalion Loves that were dropped in World War Two, sure. Only a handspan back to Jackie Love or Haki Rau as they called him, Queen Charlotte Sound 1830s and '40s, Taranaki before then . . . and spoor back from then still fresh too, right back through Pacific history into its classical distances, ages back from where your little tributary trickles into the stream . . .

He was drifting out into the roadstead channel as the tide ebbed from Evans Bay. Down beyond Worser Bay and the remaining houselights at Seatoun was Barrett's Reef named for Dicky Barrett . . . ocean horizon opening out past Pencarrow and Baring Head into the eastern limit of Cook Strait and the Southern Pacific. In the great silver-lit expanse of harbour, the south-east ocean horizon seemed to have sucked all the darkness out with the ebb tide . . . gathered it under the pale rim of the sky – few stars in that part of the heavens . . . comforting cluster of Pleiades in the north-east . . . but south-east a great dark vacuum into which he felt he was about to be voided. – And Great-Grandfather Heinrich Augustus . . . a pilot also on the same run, bringing in shiprig when he refused to work steam . . . all so close . . .

He'd begun to shake again. He knew he'd have to pull back to Evans Bay against tide *and* the wind . . . if he could get up to Evans Bay again he'd at least have the wind behind him. He looked down-harbour at the dark ocean horizon. The harbour was plenty wide enough for one *Anisops wakefieldi* idiot in a pram dinghy. He began to haul back across the flow. Sighting off a light by Fort Ballance he could see that his progress was minimal. The main channel chop fouled his stroke . . . he felt water in his shoes. Shipping the oars he crouched to feel around for a bailer. There wasn't one. He began to scoop water out with his cupped hands . . . he could see the light he'd sighted off slipping by.

– And you from seafaring stock, mooning your way out into the mid-channel on a cold night with wet clothes . . . man, they wouldn't even find you, you'd be gone 'without trace', the black-backs would peck out your eyes at first light, barracouta the rest, and if the sealice left your skin the way they leave rags of fishskin on set-line hooks, then the gurnard and the little spotties would soon suck it up out of the bottom silt.

His scoops flew out over the lee side . . . then he pulled off his shoes and used one, his back to the freshening breeze. All at once the surface of the water darkened . . . the breeze had blown clouds across the moon . . . he felt the dark and cold close around him. He imagined a wave slapping into his mouth as he struggled to get a breath past the acrid blockade whose curfew now came into effect – hearing an unfamiliar throbbing that seemed to come up at him from the dark water . . . from the air all around . . . and a grinding . . . 'all hung with . . .'

The squidder had its Christmas-tree bunting of work-lights glaring along its length. From the in-board p.a. came the aggressive nasal sound of Korean. The rusty flank reared above the little dinghy, bilge-water jetted sluggishly from a pipe near the foul waterline . . . throb of half-throttle marine diesels. The oxide-streaked squidder shuddered past with a metallic internal clanging as though some great bearing were being ground and beaten

shapeless . . . its bow-wash lifted the dinghy where he clung yelling
into the racket of the engines . . . sea bucketed over his legs . . .
reek of, *kimchi*? – and fuel oil . . . hissing wake of bubbles . . . a
light that briefly struck him, meaningless squawk of amplified
language . . .

And then the searchlight cut off leaving him staring dazzled
into utter darkness. Finally he could see the ship receding – its
dingy stem was blocking the view down to the ocean horizon. His
teeth were chattering as he bailed with the shoe. Then he began
to row. With the last scoop he'd also flung the shoe wildly
overboard. – Don't stop, '*Don't* stop!' gibbering as he pushed the
ridiculous oars through the rowlocks and bent his back into the
stroke, turning the dinghy beam-on to the chop and churning
straight for shore near the point below the Mount Crawford prison
farm and the Massey, *click*: forget it . . . Massey monument . . .

Good of the chaplain to enter Lone Bay, how? . . . oh yeah . . .
yeah, it was, wait on . . . *And down on his marrowbones here and pray*
. . . forgotten it, wait on . . .

Fathoms down, fathoms down, how I'll dream fast asleep.
I feel it stealing now. Sentry, are you there?
Just ease these darbies at the wrist,
And roll me over fair!
I am sleepy, and the oozy weeds about me twist.

'. . . *and the oozy weeds about me twist*!' he said with desperado relish
. . . the worn out A-crystal scouring like rust along the cold
reticulation of his blood. Real lost soul out there for a minute,
shipmate. What a long, long way it had been. So he began to sing.

I am a young virgin just come on board
And I have as envious a maidenhead
As ever a young man took in his hand
Besides I have forty pounds in land

. . . bedrock fo'c's'le dreams . . .

> The first was a merchant that came in
> He told what a traveller he had been
> He boasted how he could handle his pen
> He said he could write the best of all men

. . . taking two oar-strokes to the line, leaning forward into the caesura, dragging black water aft on the first and third feet of the lumpy unmusical strophes . . .

> The *next* was a doctor, *that* came in
> He *said* what a traveller, *he* had been
> He *said* he'd a lance, that would *open* a vein
> With *pleasure* with ease, with*out* any pain

> The *next* was a poth'cary, with his *pastle* and pills
> He *said* he could cure me, of *all* my ills
> *Then* he took out, his *glister* pipe
> And I *gave* the rogue, a *mighty* wipe

. . . remembering the time he'd worked at Kinleith, bush-gangs jammed into the little cabins at Hillcrest Camp, hundred and fifty men watching TV commercials, you could hear the groans of rage and hopeless longing − and a pretty woman with a sly twitch to her shoulder had turned her back on the men in the TV room, opened the door of the refrigerator, and crouched to demonstrate the superior capacity of the shelves . . . a whole world the fo'c's'le could only sing about.

> The *next* was a sailor, a *sailor* bold
> With *all* his pockets, *lined* with gold
> He *waited* not, but *ended* the dispute
> Sir *here* is my heart, and maiden*head* to boot

. . . like, *settle it*.

Because really, all you heard in lines like that was a groan of deprivation – under the Jack-Tar confidence was the grief of exclusion from the world 'most people' thought fit to take for granted.

Which was why so many seamen-whalers had beached themselves with such sturdy commitment to Maori wives, to their numerous children, to the violent affairs of the tribes, the hapu? Like Worser Heberley had done? . . . because, in Te Awaiti you could be respected for your deeds. Whereas in the world of bourgeois educated vandals like Jerningham Wakefield, you were part of an Adventure . . . whacko, ripping! . . . at best exploitable . . . at worst, scum.

Russell Haley

SIMON FESK'S MOTHER had a sense of humour. There was no denying that. She was seventy-five years old and still wrote to him when she believed the occasion significant. These times were not always personal though they often were. Once she wrote to him on Armistice Day: 'Imagine all the silent people,' she said. Another time he received a telegram on *her* birthday which simply read: 'But for me.'

Today was his birthday. He thought of it as halfway to ninety. His mother, though, felt differently. The home-made card stood on the side-table.

That is less than an exact description. The card could not stand by itself. It was not made from paper stiff enough to support an upright position. It leaned idly against a milk bottle, insolently concave – a spiv of cards with its trilby hat tipped over its eyes working out a paper deal. The breeze set it flapping around the rented room.

Nor was the table an ideal surface. He had bought the thing, knocked-down in both senses, at an auction in Karangahape Road. The legs were shaped like the side frames of a lyre and they slotted into grooves on the underside of the top. A smaller shelf fitted near the feet and prevented the legs from spraying or collapsing inwards. The surface of the top was carved with jungle blossoms of an unknown species and of such high peaks and low troughs that even the milk bottle was unstable.

Fesk bought it because he liked the colour – dark honey. He also needed a table. Simon had a streak of practicality.

Such was the form of the card. Its contents were no less pliable.

'Think only of the future,' his mother wrote. 'You have your whole young life ahead of you.' The card was quarto size, folded once across the centre. These words were written in pencil on the front. His mother's hand was still firm. Inside, however, were two printed charts.

A physical impatience welled inside Fesk. He was sitting in his old brown uncut moquette armchair. The chair was also from an auction. It rattled and chimed mysteriously whenever it was moved. No doubt it contained treasures of small change, lost pens, shopping lists. Fesk did not feel this impatience in his head. It stemmed from his legs. He raised his feet in turn from the carpet as though he were walking in a crouch and then he squeezed his thigh muscles. He wore Donegal tweed trousers. Fesk bought them in a Mission shop.

They were not charts. Inside the card were two tables. If he had been in a better mood he might have laughed. A thin card containing two printed tables slumped on his decisively carved table.

He did smile. His eyes lit up. Simon forgot his legs. His impatience ceased to exist. Like the tree in the forest which falls unseen and unheard. So large in this country that you could make a whole house from one of them. But people would have to come in and out of doors and switch on radios.

Table One described the various classes of fog signals in use on the 1st of January, 1910, in certain countries. Fesk's own adopted country was not mentioned. As far as fog was concerned this country might not have existed in 1910. Hundreds of years of Polynesian voyaging had been made in the clear sunlight of the Pacific. New Zealand was not tabulated. Fog was infrequent in Auckland though it existed in thermal areas. Perhaps too in the Marlborough Sounds. Fesk's meteorology was sketchy. So too his geography. He sailed here on a ship which took many weeks to arrive. Since then he had not moved. His memories of Suez and Aden were dim and blurred. He could not remember whether he saw the Bitter Lakes first or the Red Sea. There was an image of the heat-hazed coastline of North Africa.

But in this table England, Scotland, Ireland, France, the United States, and British North America were fully examined in terms of fog and signals: sirens, diaphones, horns, trumpets, whistles, explosive devices, guns, bells, gongs and submarine bells.

To lie there underwater and listen to bells – undersea Sunday – aqua-Christmas!

1910 must have been a festive year if foggy. His mother would have been six years old. He thought of her as a small girl called Lydia clutching a penny. Her maiden name was Martello. But she was born in Ravensthorpe far away from these detailed sea signals. Almost as far away from the sea as you could get in England. Unlike here where he could look out to the island and the Gulf if he opened his curtains.

But the local blanket mill did fire a cannon at ten o'clock every evening fog or no fog. It was called the ten o'clock gun. You could set your watch or close a pub by it. And hooters signalled lunch.

Perhaps she married his father because of the gun – future nostalgia. He was a sailor – shipped out of Hull for Rotterdam and Antwerp. Maybe this card came from his prodigious papers. With senility he had lost the ability to control them. Instead, he grew massive sunflowers in the narrow garden of the new bungalow.

Last Christmas his mother sent him a clipping from the local newspaper. His father, lined beyond comprehension, pouring the dregs of his tea on the earth at the foot of the sunflowers. She wrote a different message then: 'Keep us always in mind.'

Fesk kept them in his head. Where else? They were his prototypes for the future. Though he would have no children to send clippings and obscurities.

His birthday came in cold weather in this country. If he'd remained in Ravensthorpe it would occur in summer. Impossible to blow out the breath like this and make a small cloud of mist. Bigger there then at eleven and a half, winter, a plume from your lips. Adding minutely to the fog-blanket which obscured the poplars on the boundary of the football field. Thicker and closer than that suggested. Run three paces and lose yourself. Or your friends. Screaming in wet wool.

'Nobody can get me!' Lighting a tab with his last match. Woodbine smoke and breath pouring from both nostrils. Perfect freedom.

His cat jumped up on the arm of his chair. It ripped at the upholstery and then forced its head against his hand. There were beads of moisture on its whiskers. Titus turned his head as though it were articulated on a ball-joint. The underside of his chin was white. Ten. Close to senility.

'Grow flowers,' Fesk said. He prodded the cat and it jumped to the floor. Titus landed awkwardly.

Halfway to ninety. Two-thirds of the way to nothing. The last fog. Lying there in your cold sheets with the room dissolving.

There was an unclear patch already. In the top corner of the living-room where last winter's rain soaked through obscuring the pattern of the wallpaper. It looked like a small cloud.

Miniature gun, diaphone, or bell? Some tiny warning signal: bang – hraarnm – ting!

But perfect freedom. The field like iron. They did that game with breathing. Deep. Deep – sucking in the fog. Then hold it with Wally squeezing his chest. Fooo! Falling forwards on hands and knees with the world crashing. Rehearsals.

It was bigger, that blurred patch. A slide of mucus in his eye. It moved when his gaze altered.

Fesk got up and bathed his eyes in warm water at the sink. He put the kettle on for tea and then went to the table to re-read the card.

According to Sir Boverton Redwood (1904), duplex burners which give a flame of 28 candle-power have an average oil consumption of 50 grains per candle per hour.

Grains of oil! Solidified fog. You could reverse anything with words. His mother implanting him in the past. The cat sailing up from the floor, its startled look turning to placidity. The head turning. The white chin. Striations in the moquette fading.

Steam issued from the spout of the kettle. Simon knew less about physics than the little he retained of geography. But he remembered that certain bits of the water were agitated and changed their form. Slow them down and they turn to ice. Tea does not taste the same at the top of Mount Everest. Water boils quicker and colder. So the tea fails to mash, to draw.

He drank his cup in his chair. A knowing smile passed over his face.

She was a cunning old bugger. Fog itself was the warning. Not the signals. She was telling him about change, mutability: fog was the future. Everything gone out of shape. A low ceiling.

He had once caught a bus in thick fog. So dense that the conductor walked ahead, showing the driver the way. And the passengers trudged behind. Walking to keep warm and following the bus so that they did not lose their way. He'd paid full fare. Sixpence to walk!

Whatever light Sir Boverton tried to cast we were walking into darkness. Follow the bus.

It was late now but Simon did not turn on his light. A cruise ship hooted three times as it left the harbour. He had seen flying fish, an albatross, dolphins. The stern and a white trail blazed across the sea. You have been there. You leave your own wake.

After he left home he moved to London. In those days fog was green and frequent. He lived in Archway. Could walk to Hampstead Heath. The fogs drove him wild with desire. He was young. The possibility was held out of meeting a fellow-soul in the fog. Lighted windows took on a special diffuse quality. You could draw close. Who curtained against that blanket?

The city changed shape and decayed under that floor of fog. Lagan to be retrieved in discrete fragments of treasure. A girl dressed in mist — her hair like dark water.

Meetings were an astonishment — looming, distorted, and immediate. And people talked excitedly, their breath catching.

'Are you there? Are you there?'

'Where am I?'

'Haa! I thought I was nearly home.'

'I've passed that corner three times.'

And were there really smudge-pots burning in the roads? One could walk naked and undetected.

There were more deaths. The old and frail gave up when their boundaries dissolved. They simply merged with whatever was to come. Their bits vibrating in the different mode. Passing out into something else. Steam or ice.

The young survived. They kept their shape because their memories were sharper. Matter is solidified memory of form. In fog a key which had been too long a key could slip its form and run as a bright trickle of amnesia down the thigh. So the old flew out from there. Officials called it pneumonia or influenza.

Fesk knew now that he loved it, fog, as some men love danger. He should not have washed his eyes although the room was comfortingly dark now. It was a poor simulation but it would have to serve. He should be colder than he was, his skin transparent to the air.

Simon removed everything he had on and sat in his armchair, nude.

Rather than take those sounds as warnings, one could orchestrate them into a hymn in praise of fog:

> Boom crack wheep bong ding blah hooo
> dong fooo crash ting boom wheee!

Repeat and vary. A fifty-grain candle burning as an offering.

Finally Simon knew what he was celebrating. He would leave this meridian of sun where fog, at the very best, came three times a year. He would seek out some industrial valley in a northern clime where factory chimneys poured out their libations to invisibility. Perhaps Ravensthorpe if it had not been ruined by the Clean Air Act.

Certainly not that bright little suburb on the outskirts of York where sunflowers grew in profusion. It would have to be a mucky place where dark bricks absorbed acid from the air. Where the skin was an osmotic device and not a dry barrier tanned and leathered by the sun.

She had made him homesick after all these years.

He would find desire again. One evening. Some dark girl in a mackintosh. Walking huddled streets glazed with rain, inundated with mist.

Fesk sang, the old song, before he retired:

> Oh I am a bachelor and I live all alone
> And I work at the weaver's trade
> And the only only thing I ever did wrong
> Was to woo a fair young maid
> I wooed her in the winter time
> And in the summer too
> And the only only thing I ever did wrong
> Was to save her from the foggy foggy dew.

He straightened the card against the milk bottle. It bent again. A meniscus of hope.

Before Simon went to bed he emptied the tea-pot outside the back door. He flung the soggy leaves against the agapanthus growing there.

Somewhere or other his father smiled a blank bright unimpassioned smile. His mother prepared a congratulatory sheet.

Fog descended immediately on all points.

Witi Ihimaera

from **BULIBASHA,
KING OF THE GYPSIES**

IN THOSE DAYS THE whole of Poverty Bay, the East Coast
and Hawke's Bay was covered by a grid of roads which wound
further and further from the main towns of Gisborne, Opotiki,
Whakatane, Napier and Hastings along the coast or up the steep
valleys into the interior. On the way were small Pakeha-run
settlements similar to Patutahi. They marked the beginning of
Pakeha history when a whaler or English trader settled there and
began the process of bringing civilization to the natives. Later,
after the land wars and two world wars, the towns became the
focus of more settlers when parcels of land around them were
granted to rehabilitate soldiers who had fought for King and
Country; war memorials of a soldier bending over his rifle sprouted
in every town. The settlements had names like Tolaga Bay,
Tokomaru Bay, Tikitiki, Te Karaka, Mahia or Nuhaka and they
comprised a hotel, petrol station, general store, small community
hall where a dance or film was shown at weekends, church and
graveyard, rural school and stockyards – and their roads were tar-
sealed te rori Pakeha. Further out, and you were in dust country.
There the settlements were villages like Waituhi, Waihirere,

Mangatu and Anaura Bay – brightly coloured houses around a drab meeting house, with not a Pakeha in sight.

Right at the back of beyond, along the even dustier roads which zigged up the valleys and zagged down over culverts, through cattle stops, across fords, through gates that you opened and closed on your way in and out, around hairpin bends and over rickety one-way swing bridges, at the very top of the valleys, were the big sheep and cattle stations. Regardless of their isolation, the big stations and their ability to produce meat and wool for export were the edifices upon which the entire economy of Poverty Bay, the East Coast and Hawke's Bay depended. Without them, and the constant stream of cattle and sheep trucks which brought their stock and produce down the valleys, there would have been no need for the settlements, freezing works, ports, towns and industries which had grown up to support them.

The big stations knew their importance. They were capped by huge two-storeyed houses with names like Windsor, The Willows, Fairleigh or Tara. Some had been constructed of stone shipped from England, France or Italy. They were characterized by wide entrance halls, their floors shining with paving stones that had been hauled in by bullock teams. They had imposing staircases and hallways panelled with English oak. The furniture, four-poster beds, linen and sculptures were all English and had been collected during regular visits by steamship to the Home Country. The master's study was filled with leatherbound books; there was always a deer's head over the fireplace. Gravelled driveways led up to the big houses. Rose trellises and arbours of English daisies bordered the driveway. In the middle, a clipped green lawn. The glass in the windows was handmade and shaped like diamonds. From the windows you could see the big red-roofed shearing shed, cattle yards and sheep yards.

To ensure an appropriate distance between station owner and station worker, the quarters for the foreman, musterers, cattlemen, shepherds and their families and all those who were on regular pay were on the *far* side of the shearing shed. Furthest away were the whares – crude, rough-timbered bunkhouses and kitchen-dining room – for the itinerant workers, the scrubcutters, fencers and, of course, the shearing gangs. They had no ovens, no running water and no electric lights.

My sisters and I loved the shearing season. To this day I don't know why. Why, for instance, would anyone love all those dusty three- or four-hour journeys to the sheds? Usually we had to travel in convoy to ensure support for one of the other cars just in case it broke down, its radiator boiled over, tyres were punctured, batteries ran flat or an axle snapped under the weight of our accumulated baggage. One year Uncle Hone's old car gave up the ghost entirely. Dad hitched a tow line which broke as we were going up a steep gradient and Uncle Hone's car careened back in a wild ride down to the bottom of the hill. It had no brakes. In the second attempt to get the car up the gradient, Dad lashed a spare tyre to the front bumper and our car *pushed* Uncle Hone's car to the top of the hill. Uncle was supposed to wait for us at the top so we could get in front of him and prevent a dangerous no-brakes descent. Uncle must have forgotten, because no sooner had he reached the top than down the other side he went.

I can still remember that car as it rocketed out of control down to the bottom of the gradient. How Uncle managed to hold the road was a mystery – we agreed later that it must have been because the weight of all the people inside kept the car from flipping on the corners. On our own way down we had to stop every five minutes to pick up pots and pans, bedding, boxes of food and tin plates that had come loose on that pell-mell descent. What else could we do except dissolve into gales of laughter when we reached the bottom ourselves?

Then there were the fords, where one car would get stuck in the middle of the river. My aunts would yell out, 'I could do with a swim!' Out they'd get, their muscled arms heaving away until the car was free. My Aunt Sephora discovered that she had natural flotation when she slipped and went arse over kite down a waterfall and along the deep river.

'Help!' she cried. She couldn't swim. She bobbed along, kept afloat by her natural buoyancy, her red dress inflated by trapped air like a balloon.

After that, my uncles used to sing in jest, 'When the red red robin goes bob bob bobbin along—'

More dangerous were the swing bridges when some of the boards gave way and the car's wheels went through. We'd all get out, carefully unload the car to make it lighter, lift the car up from the holes in the bridge and load up again once the car had reached the other side.

Finally there were roads that had been washed out or blocked by slips or peppered with mud-filled potholes. Some places had no roads at all. When such hazards or challenges presented themselves, Uncle Hone would say, 'She's right. Let's have smoko.' Uncle Hone was the boss of Mahana Four. After smoko, while we kids were skinny dipping in the river, he would korero the problem with the adults and, by the time we got back, something had been worked out. Off we would go, backtracking or sidetracking or driving down to the river bed and motoring along it until we could get back onto the road.

We drove, pushed, pulled and sometimes carried our cars piece by piece to get to the sheds.

'It was easier when we had packhorses,' Grandfather Tamihana said.

My mother never liked travelling at night. We had a four-hour drive ahead to the Williamson station and 'Amberleigh' at the back of Tolaga Bay.

'As long as we get there by midnight,' she said.

Like many Maori, Mum believed that kehua – ghosts – were abroad at night; humans were therefore taking their lives into their hands when they traversed the kehua's domain. She was calm enough for the first part of our journey across the red suspension bridge and through Gisborne, but when we left Wainui Beach she started to get nervous. The darkness fell very quickly and the only lights were those from farms floating away like ships on a dark sea. Even the moonlight on the road was intermittent. Dark clouds boiled up from the south. To cap it off, it began to rain.

'E koe,' Mum said, nodding her head. 'I knew this would happen.'

The rain didn't last long – luckily, as we didn't have a tarpaulin for the hens on top of the car – but then there was a *bang* and Pani's car skidded to a halt. A burst back tyre.

'E koe,' Mum said again. All her fears were being confirmed. 'The kehuas want us to go outside so they can jump from the scrub and eat us.'

Dad scoffed at her. He positioned our car close behind Pani's and, in the light of the headlights, they jacked the car and began changing the tyre. No sooner had the engine stopped than we heard the noises of the bush, *alive* with bird calls, wild pigs rooting in the scrub, the sounds of the hunter and the hunted.

I got out to help. Glory wanted to come with me, but, 'You stay in the car,' Mum said to her. 'You're just the right size to be taken by a flying kehua to its nest of hungry chicks.'

We arrived at Tolaga Bay at around eleven that night. Half an hour out of Tolaga, just as Pani's car got to the top of a precipitous road, its radiator boiled over.

'E koe,' our mother said between compressed lips. 'We're never going to get to Amberleigh by midnight.'

That meant that we would all be eaten up by kehua. Ah well, nothing else to do except have our last feed on this earth. So out came the food basket, and we ate and drank as if it was the final supper – Maori bread buttered with margarine and golden syrup, washed down with raspberry cordial.

Out of the darkness, Aunt Ruth began to tell a story about

the family. There were always stories during the shearing; they leavened our work with fun, excitement and a sense of history. The stories recounted the life of the family, our travails and triumphs, defeats and victories. But this was a story I had not heard before, telling the reason why the Mahana and Poata families were always fighting. It had nothing to do with religion at all.

Grandmother Ramona was sixteen and Grandfather was nineteen when they met, just before the Great War, in 1914.

'Your grandfather tried to enlist,' Aunt Ruth said. I already knew this; Grandfather carried a grudge against the army when he was refused. 'It wasn't his fault. His parents wouldn't have let him go anyway. Why should they let him go to fight a white man's war? We'd only just finished one *against* him!'

Grandfather was visiting Grandmother's village. They took one look at each other, and it was love at first sight.

'They were struck by the lightning rod of God,' Aunt Ruth said. 'If that lightning strikes, you're the dead duck.' Poor Aunt Ruth – the Lord hadn't pronged her and Uncle Albie with his divine sign, that's for sure. 'The trouble was, Mother Ramona was already engaged to be married to a soldier who had just joined the Pioneer Battalion in the First World War.'

You guessed it: Rupeni Poata.

'It was all jacked up between Mother Ramona's family and Rupeni's family,' Aunt Ruth said, 'but Mum never loved Rupeni. However, her people told her, "Poor Rupeni, he could get killed and have no children", or "This is a great sacrifice Rupeni is doing, so can't you make his last days in our village happy?" Despite her love for our father, she agreed to marry Rupeni. Of course Dad was heartbroken. He tried to dissuade her. She said it was too late. She had to honour her family's wishes and marry Rupeni. Our mother was supposed to be the innocent sacrifice to Rupeni's lustful desires.'

'What's lustful desires?' Glory asked.

'Ask your brother,' Aunt Ruth answered, casting me a murderous glance. Why me?

'The day of the wedding came,' Aunt Ruth continued. 'Our father rode his white horse over to Mum's village to ask her once more not to go through with the wedding. He arrived just as she was setting off to the church. She was wearing a beautiful long wedding dress, the one she has to this day locked in her memory chest. She was on the verandah with her father and family. Her father was outraged to see our father and got his old rifle. He didn't want any young buck from another village, especially Waituhi, to soil his goods. But our mother restrained him from shooting our father—'

I've mentioned before the two photographs of Grandmother Ramona and Grandfather when they were young. Although badly hand-tinted (Grandfather had been given green eyes and curly brown hair) the coloration cannot disguise my grandmother's innocent beauty or my grandfather's handsome pride. As Aunt Ruth was talking I imagined a scene straight out of a silent movie.

RAMONA IS ON THE VERANDAH OF AN OLD HOUSE. HER PARAMOUR, TAMIHANA, STANDS IN THE STIRRUPS OF HIS WHITE HORSE AND, TEARS STREAMING FROM HIS GREEN EYES, CUPS HER CHIN IN HIS HANDS AND KISSES HER.

TAMIHANA E Ramona, kaua koe e haere ki to marena.
(Subtitles: Ramona, I beg of you, do not do this.)
RAMONA Aue, e Bulibasha, tenei taku whakamutunga.
(Subtitles: Alas, my love, this is my destiny.)
TAMIHANA Engari, kahore koe e aroha ana ki a ia.
(Subtitles: But you do not love him.)
RAMONA Ae engari, ko hoatu te honore ki toku papa.

(Subtitles: That is true, but I do this for the honour of my father and because it is his wish. And Rupeni has only a week before he must journey to the war.)

TAMIHANA (CLOSE UP, IN DESPERATION) Ka pehea atu ki au?

(Subtitles: What about me?)

RAMONA (WITH PROUD RESOLUTION) Ahakoa taku aroha ki a koe, ake, ake, kaore he aroha mo maua. Haere atu.

(Subtitles: Although I will love you for ever and for all eternity our love can never be. Go.)

TAMIHANA (WITH AN AGONIZING CRY) Ramon-aaaaaa—

(Subtitles: Ramon-aaaaaa—)

'Your grandmother and grandfather had one last sweet kiss,' Aunt Ruth said. Hupe was dribbling from her nose — she was such a romantic. 'Then your grandmother pulled the veil over her face. She was never more lovely. "Although another man may own my body," Ramona said to our father, "you will always possess my heart." A single tear trickled like a falling star down her left cheek.'

Meanwhile, Rupeni had arrived at the church. He was an ugly, squat young man with a big bulbous nose, huge fleshy lips and legs so short he looked like he was walking on his knees. He was at least three inches shorter than Grandmother. Whoever heard of a hero who was shorter than the heroine?

'Did you know there was a song named after your grandmother?' Aunt Ruth asked. 'Well, a small trio outside the church — a violinist, pianist and bass player — started to play that song:

"Ramona, I hear the mission bells above, Ramona—"

'The guests were mainly Rupeni's family and all those he had managed to fool. Huh! He was as heroic as my bum! Everybody knows he didn't lob that grenade at the Turks, it was somebody else. Just as he was going through the door with his groomsmen he heard the karanga. He turned and saw his bride coming—'

This is what Rupeni saw. An old kuia, one of the guests,

stepped forward and began to call, 'Haere mai ki te wahine na, haere mai, haere mai, haere mai.' Her voice was high-pitched, formal. Far in the distance, along the road which ran through the maize fields, the bridal party was coming. Ramona was escorted by her weeping mother, father, sisters, brothers and relatives. She was in the middle, her face veiled. A beautiful feather cloak was over her shoulders and white wedding dress.

From that distant bridal party came the reply, 'Karanga mai, karanga mai, karanga mai.' The reply was pitched even higher, and throbbed with emotion. Everybody knew that Grandmother was making a sacrifice. Rupeni was oblivious to all except his own lust and passion.

Ramona walked with her head held high; the rest of the bridal party were watching the road so they could avoid the horse shit and potholes. Ramona was silent, unlike her sisters who were yelling out to the mangy old dogs that dashed out to snap at them. Her pride had made her inviolate to such barking creatures. She was otherworldly, seeming to float above everything crass and mundane.

Rupeni heard the voice of the priest beside him. 'You should come inside now and wait for your bride at the altar.'

Rupeni shook his head. He was entranced by Ramona's beauty and sadness. He waited. Finally she was there. He looked upward into her eyes. The boldness of her stare made him look away.

By this time, Ramona was having a change of heart.

I watched Aunt Ruth's lips. I felt like switching her voice off, as if it was a radio, and mouthing along with her lips.

Rupeni heard Ramona say, 'Mother take the cloak from my shoulders. It is a royal cloak and should not be sullied by such an event as this.'

Rupeni laughed. His lips curled into a sneer. He saw Ramona's tears of anger.

'Although you weep for another man,' Rupeni said, 'you will

always be mine. I own you as surely as I do my horse, my cattle, my sheep, my farm.'

Defiant, Ramona answered, 'I marry you only to give you the comfort of my body for a week before you leave for Europe. Yes, I might have a child by you and, if so, I will love that child. I do this for my family and yours. You could have spoken against the arrangement. Instead you take advantage of me because I am the most beautiful girl you have ever seen and a virgin. You are a rogue, a cur and a bounder, sir, and I hate you. Will you not let me go?'

'Never, *never*,' Rupeni hissed. 'I will take you to my bed and make you mine.'

'So be it,' Ramona said, 'but never assume my throes will be passion. I spit on your bed and I spit on you. Though you may take my body repeatedly in the night, my innermost soul and my heart will never be yours. Never, never, never, *never*.'

'The preacher coughed for attention,' Aunt Ruth said. 'He began to beckon everyone inside the church.'

That is when it happened.

A thrumming of hooves came echoing along the road between the fields of maize. A handsome young lover was seen, spurred on by passion for his woman.

'It was our father,' Aunt Ruth continued, eyes afire. 'The thought of losing our mother was too much to bear. Impetuous, he rode his white horse right to the church steps—'

The tinted oval photograph comes to life again.

'Ramona-aaaa—'

Ramona gives a cry. She sees the sunlight flashing in Tamihana's curly brown hair and the desperation in his sparkling green eyes. She turns to her father.

'Forgive me, e pa—'

Tamihana is galloping in slow motion, scattering the crowd, his horse's hooves scything the air like silver swords.

Rupeni's groomsmen try to stop Tamihana. They grab at the reins of his white horse. He eludes them and in a trice is reaching for Ramona. Only Rupeni is between him and his prize.

A gasp comes from the crowd. Rupeni has a knife and he slashes at Grandfather's face. Blood beads Tamihana's left cheek, spilling dark red rubies on Grandmother's white dress.

'Oh my love—' Ramona cries.

Laughing like Douglas Fairbanks in a swashbuckling movie, Grandfather leans down, knocks Rupeni to the ground with one heroic blow, scoops Grandmother up into his arms and turns his white horse away.

Glory clasped her hands with delight at Aunt Ruth's story. As for me, was I surprised? Was I what!

'True love gave your grandparents the wings of eagles,' Aunt Ruth said to Glory. 'They rode and rode—'

'Into the sunset,' I murmured.

'And Rupeni couldn't find them,' my aunt continued, trying to poke me with her foot. 'He left for Europe and by the time he returned from the war your grandparents were already married and raising the family in Waituhi.' She paused. 'And of course,' she added hastily, 'they lived happily ever after.'

Aunt Ruth's voice drifted into the darkness. The radiator of Pani's car popped and hissed as it cooled.

An hour later we were able to pour some water into it and get on our way again. It was getting on for half-past twelve. Then, *crack*. Pani's second headlamp went out.

'E koe,' we said before our mother could open her mouth.

'Aue,' she agonized, 'Kei te haramai a Dracula ki konei!' Dracula will get us now for sure. She had been to see Bela Lugosi in *Dracula* a month before. Dracula was even worse than kehua because he sucked your neck.

We stopped again. Dad went over to talk to Pani.

'We should shoot your car,' Dad said, 'and put it out of its misery. Never mind. You follow us. And look—' He pointed to the moon, rising full across the sky, lending silver light to the road ahead. 'Who needs lights when we have the moon to show us the way?'

My mother wasn't so sure. A full moon meant that Dracula would find us easy.

By that time our mother's anxiety was affecting us as well. We kept on saying, 'Hurry up, Dad, make the car go faster.' Dracula was already following us. He was coming over the hills. His mouth was opened and his fangs were starting to grow and—

Saved! Ahead was the sign for the Williamson station and, beyond, the track leading along the side of the hill past the two-storeyed house where the boss lived, to the shearing shed and shearers' quarters beyond. But what was that? Luminous green eyes staring at us from out of the darkness! Vampires! We screamed.

Only sheep. Phew.

A lamp was shining in one of the quarters.

'Is that you, Joshua?' Uncle Hone called.

'Ae,' Dad said.

'Good,' Uncle Hone continued. 'Early start tomorrow. You and your family are in with Sam Whatu's family. Pani, you're in bunking with the single men. Sephora, you and Esther are in with Auntie Molly. Ruth? Albie's over in the quarters next door. He's been waiting eagerly for you all night.'

'I'll bet,' Aunt Ruth said.

By torchlight and moonlight we unpacked the two cars – the bedding first, so that my aunts and Mum could make up the beds for us; then our belongings, stores and provisions for the kitchen, twenty-five yards away next to a small stream. Finally, Dad and Pani took out the handpieces, blades and assorted equipment they would need for tomorrow's shearing. I could hear them talking as they worked; Pani sounded unusually anxious. Apparently Mahana One, on their way to Horsfield station, had come across Poata Three.

'Are you sure?' Dad asked.

'That's what Maaka told Hone,' Pani said.

'Could he have made a mistake?'

'No. They came around a bend in the road and, hello, there were the Poatas as plain as day. They looked like they'd just come from the Horsfields. Anyway no sooner had they seen Mahana One than they scooted off in the other direction.'

'They're way out of their territory,' Dad said.

'Ae,' Pani nodded.

'Has Dad been told?'

'Aua,' Pani shrugged. 'That's up to Matiu.'

Dad paused. 'Something must be going on. I don't like the sound of it.' He was pensive. The moonlight glinted on his blades.

'Come to bed,' Mum called, interrupting him.

We had arrived.

Albert Wendt

THE BALLOONFISH AND THE
ARMADILLO

A LONE CICADA in the garden in front of your house is
sucking at the night's succulent thickness; its rhythmic trilling picks
at the silence, like the beating of your heart, while you sit at your
desk in your study, a magazine open on your table, you pay it no
attention, your skin covered with a cool film of sweat. The air is
ponderous with humidity; every time you place your arms on your
desk, your sweat stains it. All the bookshelves that wall your study
are inhabited by books. Neat. Tidy. Expensive. Immaculate proof
of your learning and success. Into this womb you retreat almost
every night now.

Your wife is asleep in your bedroom at the other end of the
house. For a moment you picture her, sheet drawn up to her neck,
arms crossed over her ribs, her pale face shining like marble in the
light of her bedside lamp, eyes shut, her breathing hardly audible.
You've been married for thirty-five years and, always, she has slept
in that position. Some nights, while watching her, you think she is
dead or dying (or more frightening, lying on a sacrificial altar
inviting the priest's stone knife). You've dared not tell her this.
Recently, at a particularly boring cocktail party, you told everyone
that she was still 'the passion of your life'. When you returned

home she chastised you: 'You shouldn't get so drunk!' You refused to tell her that you hadn't touched a drop all night.

You break from your thoughts when you hear a mouse scratching at the ceiling directly above you. A quick, urgent scratching. Must get some rat poison.

It is after midnight. In the air, wafting in slowly from the veranda, you detect the odour of the dark green moss that lives on the barks of the immense monkey-pod trees outside. A rich, medicinal scent that you enjoy. The mouse scratches again. You glance up, expecting to see tiny claws piercing the ceiling.

Yesterday was your sixty-first birthday. For ten years you have refused your wife's offer of birthday parties. Waste of money, you keep telling her. But you don't begrudge her the money spent on her grand birthday celebrations: orgies of food and drink and meaningless conversation and gossip, good for business, though.

You imagine the night is an enormous whale curled protectively around your house up on these slopes, a kindly, benevolent softness into which you can sink, be embraced by. Your son John, who everyone fears as the relentlessly honest and righteous Attorney General, and Nora, his humourless New Zealand wife, whose charity extends to running the newly formed Society for the Intellectually Handicapped, and their two teenage sons, thoroughly spoilt demanders of everything and who respect nothing, came for your birthday dinner last night. You've never been able to think of Nora as your daughter-in-law, and her sons as your grandchildren. To keep them at a distance you give them anything they want. Your wife knows the way you feel about them; you never provide her with the opportunity to discuss it though. Whenever they visit, the conversation, the warmth and rapport is always with your son only. Nora and her sons keep trying to break into the sacred circle but you always ease them out of it politely, firmly.

Your T-shirt, now drenched with sweat, sticks to your body; it feels like a slippery second skin. You get up, peel it off, drop it into the wastepaper basket, walk over to the open windows and, hands on your hips, you let the faint breeze caress your skin with its cool fingers. Soon the acrid smell of your own body invades your nostrils. You suck it in deeply and hold it down. One ... two ... three – you count to fifteen and then ease the air out of your lungs. Your own smell reminds you suddenly of a woman's sap during sexual intercourse. You don't expect a pleasurable reaction from your flesh, and you don't get it. You fondle yourself slowly, deliberately tempting the once almost uncontrollable passions of your flesh. No reaction. It is good, you tell yourself. You live beyond physical desire now. Free of it.

At the edge of the light cast from the windows of your study, the night walks. You think of it as your son, in flowing silk-black robes, pacing the shadow of the Judge's bench, defiantly stalking the guilty, the sinners, the innocent ...

Last Monday night while I was in my study my recurring migraine grew to inhabit, almost to bursting, the whole of my head, and, as usual, I tried to ignore the intense pain.

I have always pictured my migraine as a fully inflated balloon-fish with its spikes extended like threatening spears, bulbous eyes staring unblinkingly at me, its small round mouth opening and shutting in time to its breathing, suspended in the still sun-clear waters of a tropical reef. Why I came to associate this creature with my migraine, I'll never be able to fathom. I can remember though that my migraine first roared out of the depths of my brain the night I watched, with a mixture of horror and fascination, my son being born in Auckland Hospital where my wife, who doesn't trust the local hospital, had insisted on going. All babies, so the stereotype goes, are expected to scream as they are slapped for the first time by the hostile cold of our atmosphere. John's reaction, however, was an unforgiving, contemptuous silence, and, in his eyes, I caught an accusation. He seemed an utterly self-contained being from another planet. Perhaps the round accusing silence of the balloonfish reflected John's birth silence. But even suffering the first full impact of my migraine, my eyes brimmed with tears of joy: the love I felt then for my son was greater than I had experienced for anyone and anything else before. I would tell no one, not even my wife, of how I had felt then, nursing my treasure secretly, afraid that if I revealed it to anyone it would diminish in value.

That night while I foraged in my desk drawers for the flask of brandy to drug my migraine, I rediscovered the folder of papers which my father had left me almost twelve years before when he had died of a stroke, and which I had avoided looking at.

My father, who was nearly ninety when he died, was a self-made man (so he was described in business circles). His parents were humble villagers, so, after pastor's school, at the age of fourteen, he was apprenticed to a German carpenter, and, with his very meagre wage, he supported his parents and six brothers and sisters. He discovered early that to succeed in business in Apia he would have to learn German and English and accounting. He proceeded to master these at night by teaching himself and, during the day, by practising on his employer and any other person who was fluent in English or German. In 1914, he put his knowledge into effective use when the Germans were expelled from Samoa by the English-speaking New Zealanders, and he took over the German carpenter's modest construction business. Throughout his life he was admired, even by his business rivals, for his impeccable English, business acumen, and his inspired sermons as a lay preacher in the English-speaking Protestant Church where he met and married my mother, against her parents' wishes.

Proud of his 'self-creation and self-education', his own description, he refused to throw away anything, especially the literature, which he collected or generated. His spaciously gloomy bedroom came to be stacked on one side, from floor to ceiling, with his treasure of boxes, cartons and crates containing all the books, magazines, papers and the other odds and ends of his education. It was as if he needed all this to prove to himself that he was an educated man. We were forbidden to touch any of it. I was tempted to but after Max, my oldest brother, suffered a severe beating for doing so, I dared not. Often, as a boy, I imagined the stack growing larger and larger, bursting out of the bedroom and filling all the other rooms, then the whole house, even the toilet, and eventually, with a loud thunder-like cracking, the house bursting apart and my father's treasure set out to smothering our country.

My father's hoard remained intact in his cavern-like bedroom right throughout his two marriages, his rise to being described in the papers as a 'prominent businessman', until the week after his funeral when my son and I went to examine it. (He had bequeathed it to me in his will. I was the only surviving son from his first marriage but he had five children by his second wife. I was puzzled, therefore, about his reason for leaving it to me, saying, in his will, that I deserved it.)

At that time my son, John, was a strapping nineteen-year-old who had just returned for the holidays, having graduated from high school (my old school in Auckland) and who was now getting ready to return to start law school in New Zealand.

My stepmother and her family were conveniently absent from the house which is situated on the banks of a stream of brackish water, known in the neighbourhood as the Vaipe, behind the Apia Police Station. It is a two-storeyed wooden building with rows of louvre windows, dark blue and green outside walls and a bright red roof. As tidy and neat as my father had always been. I was reluctant to visit it, fearing my father's hoard and the childhood memories that would entangle me once I was there. Yet I also wanted, with an insatiable curiosity, to explore the mystery that my father had assumed in my life, after he had divorced my mother when I was twelve years old. In the entrails of that treasure, I hoped to find the father I never knew.

I hesitated at the front door of the house. Glanced at my son, a splendid youth on the threshold of discovering more about his grandfather. He smiled at me. We stepped into the house together.

In the sitting room I recognized nothing from my childhood. A TV set, an orderly array of expensively padded furniture, sea-green carpet, a garish velvet mural of the Last Supper; alone on the far wall was a large black and white photograph, framed in gold, of my father as a young man, in a stiff black suit, white shirt and bow-tie, bowler hat in his right hand clasped to his belly. For a moment my breath stuck in my chest: my son was the mirror image of his grandfather, and, suddenly envious of the resemblance, I tried not to accept it. At John's age I had looked like my mother – short, stumpy, fair almost like a European, with brown, blond-tipped hair. Here, beside me, my father was alive again physically in the darkly handsome, very Samoan form of my son.

As we walked up the wooden stairs, I tried to suppress my inexplicable jealousy. Our footsteps rang hollow; the house smelled of the uncanny twists of history. 'How many times have you been here?' I asked my son in English. (In our home, as in my grandparents' home where I was reared, Samoan was spoken only to the servants and those Samoans who couldn't speak English.)

'I used to come on his birthdays, you know that.' My father's birthdays were only for his grandchildren: lavish organized games and presents and unlimited food for the children, while he sipped expensive whisky and observed them.

My father's bedroom was at the end of the dimly lit corridor. 'I've never been in there!' John whispered.

'It's been a long time for me,' I admitted. (Almost a lifetime, I wanted to say.)

'I liked him,' he said. 'I liked him a lot even though I visited him only once a year.' He paused. I wanted him to continue telling me about the man my father had grown into. John knew more about that man than I did. 'He kept telling us about you:

how we, his grandchildren, should behave like you did as a boy. Obedient, hardworking, outstanding at school. How you always used to protect your brothers and friends who were weaker than you . . .'

I didn't want to listen any more. I turned the door-handle and pushed open the bedroom door.

The gloom of the bedroom gaped at us. Out of it seeped my father's smell: the healthy, almost stale odour of hard work, thrift, clean Sunday sermons, and his working khaki shirts and trousers which he insisted on wearing until they were shiny with age and then he cherished them more. Mingled with this, underlying it like a river-bed, was the strong smell of mould and old books and mildewing paper.

Hesitantly I entered the room.

The curtains were drawn. A brilliant slit of light, from a gap in the curtains, cut across the darkness. In it, bright particles of dust were floating.

It was as if I had never left that cluttered room with its stacks, the enormous four-poster bed and its canopy of a tasselled mosquito net, and the oversized kapok mattress covered with a thick white sheet with embroidered lace edges; its wall of cupboards, in which he stored all the presents he received but never used.

'Are you okay?' John asked me. I nodded, straightened up and walked to the stacks, with my back turned firmly to him.

'Open the curtains,' I said.

The zipping of the curtain rings being pulled across the metal rod was like the sharp slashing of a bush-knife through parched grass. For a moment the daylight blinded me but I refused to let my son see me shield my eyes.

'What are we going to do with all this?' he asked, gesturing at the stacks.

It jumped out of the depths of my being before I realized it.

'Burn most of it!' my voice said. Before he could argue with me, I started dragging a box into the middle of the room. 'We'll take them outside and burn whatever we don't want!'

'But . . .' he started insisting.

'Just do what I'm asking you!' I said. His eyes, for an instant, were bright with anger. 'It is of little use to us!' I pleaded, avoiding his eyes. 'Whatever books are in good condition we'll give to the public library.'

He picked up a tattered cardboard box that was bursting with magazines. Fat cockroaches scuttled out of it and vanished into the stacks as John brushed past me.

I stood listening to my only son's footsteps thumping down the corridor and then down the stairs, remembering, with fear and regret, the unforgiving thunder of my father's boots stamping out of our house after quarrelling loudly with my mother whenever he came home drunk and accused her, our family and God of feeding off his blood, every sacrificial ounce of it. To block out such disturbing memories I hugged two small boxes and, as spiders and cockroaches burst out of them and wriggled down my clothes and body, I stumbled out of the room, dripping insects that hit the floor and fled like the boyhood years I didn't want to trap me.

There is a shady stand of fau trees behind the house, at the edge of the stream. The fau were yellow with flowers, their leaves were turning brown, ready to be shed. I found a half forty-four-gallon drum in the garage, rolled it to the middle of the fau trees and, using dry twigs and branches, started a small fire in it. The smoke wafted up into my face.

I refused to allow my thoughts to analyse, dissect or argue with me. Quickly I sorted through my two boxes, mainly files and accounts from his business. I watched my hands flipping through the pages, my mind reading random figures and sentences, then screwing up the pages, I dropped them into the flames. The fire surged up greedily as I fed it.

The papers seemed to be alive as they squirmed and turned

black and crumpled into white ash. At times, bits of black swirled up into the tangled branches of the trees or over to lie on the water like shattered pieces of a black mirror.

John kept bringing the boxes; he refused to look at me.

The next box contained newspapers and magazines. I didn't bother to read any of them. My hands ripped and tore and screwed up the pages.

The fire roared like wind blowing through a small tunnel. I became oblivious of time, caught in the fury of feeding my father's remains into the fire.

All the books that were in good condition I saved in the empty boxes. A random survey of the books' titles revealed that my father had avoided collecting fiction – no poetry, or novels, or plays, or stories. Most were about religion, mainly fundamentalist tracts; there was a large section of biography and autobiography, mainly about religious and business leaders. I counted three about John P. Rockefeller. Travel literature was plentiful too; most of it was about Europe which my father had never visited. Teach-yourself books about construction, architecture, book-keeping, accounting, astronomy, French, Russian, English, carpentry and other subjects featured well too.

I saved none of the magazines or newspapers. The magazines were nearly all religious (the *Watchtower*, the *Light of the Angel* and so on) and practical, related to his business.

Once I glanced up from my work to see the whole tangle of trees aswirl with white smoke that brimmed up fiercely, like a vengeful joy, through the foliage and into the hungry sky.

John kept bringing the boxes.

We were now into business ledgers and account books, filled mainly with his neat figures and handwriting. Thick, bulky well-bound books. To rip them apart I had to open them, hold one side down with my foot, and pull upwards with my hands. The sharp-edged pages cut my hands often, but I didn't notice. Scattering the torn pages over the flames, I watched all the debts he had incurred, all the profits he had worked so diligently to make and all the losses, that had left their wrinkles on his brow and a perpetually complaining peptic ulcer in his disciplined stomach, turn into ash. Like my own orderly life, his had been determined, to a great extent, by the profit and the loss neatly recorded and balanced, year in and year out. Even his family had lived according to that tide.

For a few frightening minutes a set of pictures flicked through my mind as I observed the thick leather cover of a ledger squirming and writhing and shrivelling up in the fire, like human skin. A group of Nazi SS Officers in their black regalia and armbands, their eyes capturing the flames in a mad joy, around a fire in which books were burning; white flame bursting from the mouth of an oven into which a corpse was being pushed; a row of high black chimneys thrusting arrogantly into a grey sky . . .

'Are you all right?' My son saved me. I nodded. Throughout the day he would ask that periodically, and I would notice that he was throwing nothing into the fire: he was leaving the burning, the burial in fire, to me.

At midday, John asked if I wanted to go home for lunch. I shook my head and continued feeding the fire. Soon after, I realized that I hadn't come across any letters, so when I went through the boxes I looked for them. Their absence was a painful puzzle. Letters contained personal revelations but there were none, why?

'Have you come across any of his letters?' I asked John who shook his head. 'How far have we got?'

'About half-way through the mountain!' He chuckled.

We would find no letters to or from him. To me he had bequeathed an inheritance without eyes into his flesh, blood and spirit. Once again a deliberate denial, and I raged, working more intensely to thrust more and more of his corpse into the flames.

A few months after they divorced, my father married a woman

who was almost half his age. We (my mother and two brothers
Max and Henry) shifted to my mother's family, wealthy merchants
who hadn't wanted her to marry 'that poor and uneducated
Samoan' (my grandmother's description). They were half-castes
(part-Europeans is the term in vogue) but considered themselves
'Europeans' superior to 'the Samoans'.

My grandfather's father had been an American trader from
Connecticut who settled in Samoa, marrying my great-grandmother who was the daughter of another American trader and a
Samoan mother. On the other hand, my mother's mother was the
daughter of English missionaries.

My grandparents refused to allow us, their grandchildren, to
see our father again; they did it effectively by sending us to St
Andrews, an Anglican boarding school in Auckland, New Zealand;
and in our presence they never again referred to our father or
mentioned his name.

Even our Samoan surname was changed to our grandparents'
English one. It was as though our father had never existed, that we
had been 'born of a virgin' (Henry's description, later). Our
mother never remarried; she had many suitors but, encouraged by
her parents, she could never again break from the rich, comfortable
bondage of her home.

My grandparents, though they were born and raised in Samoa
and had visited America only once and England twice, modelled
the life of our family on what they believed was that of the English
Victorian gentry. Our lives were governed by the word *proper*.
There was, said my stern and austere grandfather (whom I
respected but couldn't love), a *proper* way of doing everything,
even dying. And the proper way was strict, severe and inflexible.
As boys there was a proper way to dress, which meant long-
sleeved shirts, shorts, socks and shoes, and not a spot of dirt was to
be seen on any of these at any time. In the tropical heat our
uniform was like armour. There was a proper way of talking to
your elders. Speak only when spoken to, and say sir and madam

always. You were to show no pain; no tears were to be seen in public. Every minute of your life was an established routine, a habit predetermined not to offend God, society and Grandfather. Wealth had to be earned properly through dedicated hard work, honest business dealings and faith in the Almighty. Most important of all, we were not to reveal at any time our 'Samoan side' which, according to our grandmother, was 'uncivilized and pagan'.

I loved the strict, orderly world of my grandparents' household. In it I knew where I was, what I had to do, where I was going, and what everyone expected of me. My brothers struggled valiantly to survive within it. Later the always impish, clear-seeing Max described it as 'trying to shape yourself to fit into a rigid mould, like a demon trying to fit into a starched white Sunday suit'.

We started at St Andrews boarding school in 1934. I thrived in it because it was a replica of my grandparents' rigid world.

In 1936, Max graduated and, with our grandfather's proud approval, enlisted in the New Zealand Army; he fought and died in Italy in 1943. With enormous tears sliding down his face – it was the first and last time I would see him cry in public – my grandfather declared, during a memorial service at our church, that his beloved grandson 'had died a glorious death for God, King and Country'. (Our father wasn't invited to the service.)

Henry excelled at every major sport at our school but failed academically. Grandfather's reaction, when Henry returned home to work in the business, was an unforgiving silence. For three painful years Henry tried to be 'the glorified clerk' (his description) Grandfather wanted to turn him into, then he disappeared into the large silence of New Zealand's South Island. The silence ended, in June 1950, with a short note from one of Henry's friends informing us that Henry had died on Mt Cook in a mountain-climbing accident. In full view of his whole family, Grandfather tore the note into neat little pieces, rose slowly to his feet as if he was carrying Mt Cook on his now frail shoulders, and retreated into his study. The next morning, he emerged to tell us that 'in no way is *his* name to be mentioned in my presence!'

I excelled in my studies at high school and university, returning as a qualified accountant with a young wife, daughter of a successful Auckland lawyer, and whom my grandfather approved of wholeheartedly. Soon, after he was satisfied I was running our business efficiently, properly, Grandfather retired from 'active service' (his phrase). He died in 1961, a few months before Samoa became independent, something which he had dreaded and opposed because it meant 'the Samoans, the ignorant forces of anarchy, are going to run and ruin the country'.

He made me his sole heir.

That hot afternoon as I burned my father's treasure, large segments of that history paraded slowly through my mind. It was as if I was re-examining it and feeding it to the fire. My brothers kept returning, insisting on not allowing me to let the fire consume them; and the wonderful, magnificent imagery of our boyhood together eventually pushed all else from my heart. With such beauty came the huge pain of loss, the unhealing wound that bled into an enormous rage when I realized that there could be no profit, no cure, to balance such a loss.

The evening hatched a consoling silence around me as I emptied the contents of the last boxes into the fire. I sat, dirty hands cupped to my cheeks, feeling as if the blood had been sucked out of my every cell.

The fire spluttered and began to die.

'Let's go home!' my son whispered.

Obediently I followed him to our pick-up. Handing me a clean rag and pointing at my face, he said, 'I've loaded all the books you saved on to the truck.'

I got into the truck, looked into the rear-view mirror, then wiped the tears and soot off my face.

I avoided looking at my son as he drove us home. Slowly I

became aware that the smell (more stench than smell) of my father's mouldy, decaying treasure seemed to be smoking out of my pores. Once I brushed my hands through my hair, and they came away covered with soot which, in the thickening darkness, looked like blood.

'You didn't have to, Dad,' John said. It was the first time that day he had called me that, and I tried to clutch on to his forgiveness.

'It was mainly useless paper,' I said.

'You're lucky,' he said. 'You know a lot about him.'

I remained silent as our truck sped through the cicada-voiced evening up to Vailima.

As we got out of the truck in our garage, John said, 'I've saved three of the boxes. I didn't show them to you. One is for you; the other two are mine. I'll put yours in your study.' He was gone before I could protest.

For nearly a week the box sat in the armchair in my study. I avoided it. Finally, my wife sorted through it and informed me she had stored the books in my bookshelves and the folder in one of my desk drawers.

Last Thursday night I opened the folder for the first time. In it is a letter from my father to my mother, and four drawings in coloured crayons: two by Max (as a seven-year-old), one by a six-year-old Henry, and one by me when I was five, all carefully labelled by our father.

My father's florid handwriting in blue ink is now barely visible in his letter to my mother.

As I started reading it, an itchy trembling began in my nose and, within seconds, it had emanated like rippling water throughout my body. I thumped the letter down on to the desk and clutched the desk edge with both hands tightly, until the shaking eased away like a receding tide, leaving me, once again, stranded on the jagged reef of my balloonfish migraine and my father's dismal confession of love for my mother.

Apia
14 June 1933

Dear Margaret,

   *I love you. I will always love you. I will give you a week. If you don't
return with our children by the end of that time, I will consider our
marriage ended. I won't even give your parents the satisfaction of
contesting the custody of our children.*

   God bless you.

I shut the folder and hurried out on to the veranda overlooking
the hills and sharp-edged ravines of Vailima. For a long time I
gazed up into the ocean of stars. Around me, the night breathed
heavily like a jealous lover.

   I refused to look at the drawings that night. I retreated into
our bedroom, stripped off my clothes, slid quietly into bed and,
rolling into a ball against the warm stillness of my wife's side, tried
to sleep.

. . . The cicada has stopped crying. The memory of its sound
lingers in your head like the quivering wings of a monarch
butterfly. You try to hold on to it but, in a brief while, it dissolves
into a regretful whisper. You return to your desk. Finally you take
the folder out of the drawer, pull out the four drawings and spread
them out on your desk. On to the drawings drips the sweat from
your arms. You use a piece of blotting paper to suck up the islands
of sweat.

   You scrutinize Max's first drawing. A scrawny yellow tree
with four branches, like arms without hands, stands in the centre
of the picture, under a strip of navy-blue sky. In the background is
what looks like a line of snow-capped mountains with a red sun
above it. In the right-hand corner of the picture is a tiny creature
with a black, eyeless head and six orange legs extending from both

sides of its body. To the left of the tree, halfway up the page, is a yellow bird with a huge black beak, one pink eye, and scarlet talons.

Across the bottom of the picture your father has printed: THIS IS BY MAX WHO IS SEVEN YEARS OLD. IT TELLS THE STORY OF A PARROT AND A MILLIPEDE WHO GO LOOKING FOR THE MOUNTAIN OF ICE. MAX TELLS ME THAT I AM THE THIN YELLOW TREE.

Max's second picture is in black and red. First you read what your father says about it at the bottom: THIS IS ABOUT A RED FISH IN THE BLACK SEA. You examine the picture from all different angles, trying to find the red fish. You can't. The picture remains a wild tangle of red and black lines, scribbles and whorls.

Henry's picture is an almost blank space inhabited, at the centre, by a round blue creature with two legs extending from its belly, and three toes on each foot. The creature is faceless. HENRY MY SIX YEAR OLD DREW THIS HANDSOME PORTRAIT OF ME, your father jokes at the bottom of the picture.

Your picture, the smallest of the four, is about six inches square. You are trapped utterly in that small space as you confront your five-year-old self. Curled into the prison of that space, like a frightened foetus, is a purple creature which is made up of six barely discernible circles joined together. Two antennae jut from the sides of the top circle, and two pairs of what you assume are legs curve out from the second and last circles. A thick yellow line, the sky, stretches across the top of the space. Right across the bottom edge, like the solid foundation of a house, your father says, THE ARMADILLO IS A MOST STRANGE CREATURE, SO MY FIVE YEAR OLD SON GABRIEL TELLS ME.

You break away from that space, with your father's song – and you admit it is a song – echoing throughout your depths like the bleep bleep bleeping of a satellite piercing the void, the black abyss, searching.

The dictionary is in your trembling hands. You search quickly. You find it:

armadillo (n) small burrowing animal of S. America with a body covered with a shell of bony plates, and the habit of rolling itself up into a ball when attacked.

Once again you find yourself out on the veranda, standing in the night, the cool wind blowing up the steep slopes, weaving and curling around your naked body, bringing with it the inconsolable grief of your parents and grandparents and brothers, your heritage, the profit and the loss no longer in equilibrium; your son, the avenger, is a victim of that terrible history, too.

So high the heavens glowing with a wondrous sheen. So high.

Even your migraine, your kind balloonfish, whose excruciating pain has saved you, always, has deserted you. You know it won't return, ever.

With that acceptance, you watch, fascinated, as your skin transforms itself slowly into a fabulous shell made up of bony plates, and in whose impregnable sanctuary your soul wants to roll up in a ball and die.

Patricia Grace

TOKO *from* POTIKI

I KNOW THE STORY of when I was five. The story has been told to me by my mother Roimata, my father Hemi, my sister Tangimoana, and my brothers James and Manu. But also it is a remembered story. Five is old enough to remember from, and five is not very long ago.

It is a big fish story.

Hemi needed bait for the next day's fishing, and after tea he asked James and Tangimoana to go out on the lagoon with him to catch herrings. James went to the shed to get the little herring lines with their tiny silver hooks. My father cut up little pieces of bacon fat for bait.

I followed James to the shed, climbed up and took a heavy line from the shelf.

'We don't need that one,' James said.

'I need it,' I said.

James didn't argue with me. He never minded and always let me do whatever I wanted to do. I followed him back to the house taking the big line with me.

'That's no good, we don't need that,' Tangimoana said.

'I need it for my big fish,' I told her. She did mind.

'Not in the lagoon. There aren't any big fish in the lagoon, only little ones.'

'There is. There's a big fish for me,' I said.

'Only herrings, and anyway you can't come.'

But I knew there was a big fish for me, and I knew that I would go. That's what I remember very clearly about that night. I remember the sureness that I had. I remember clearly that I *knew*. I knew that I would go. I knew that there would be a big fish for me.

My father Hemi said, 'You can come Boyboy if you sit still in the boat. I'll give you a little line but you be careful.'

'I got my line,' I said, 'For my big fish.'

Hemi did not argue with me, but my sister Tangi stared at my face, and I think she was angry with me. Well I don't really remember Tangimoana staring at my face, but I know that's what she always does. She stares at your face. No one can escape from her.

The day was just changing to be night, and the sea was like chocolate wrapping that you've smoothed with the nail of your thumb. I did not feel small that night the way the sea can make you feel small sometimes. I carried my big line with me. My mother Roimata had taken one of the hooks off to make it safer, but it didn't matter because it was only one big fish that I was going to catch. I only wanted one big hook for my one big fish. She put a piece of paua on my one big hook. The piece of paua was for bait, but it was also to cover the barb so that it would not hook itself into me. I do not remember that, but I've been told.

Tangi and James carried an oar each and I carried only my line, but I did not feel small. I didn't feel small when Tangimoana and James helped Hemi pull the dinghy down to the water. I hurried in my special boots and Hemi lifted me into the bow.

Two pulls and we were out into the middle of the lagoon. Tangi put bread on to the water to bring the herrings. The water was a soft orange colour I remember, and little herrings put their mouths to the water's skin making sharp circles which widened and widened on the surface of the water.

My father and my brother and sister pulled the lines about over the surface of the water and the herrings popped onto them time after time. They wanted me to have a little line so that I could catch herrings too. They were all enjoying themselves I remember — and I've been told — but I did not want to have enjoyment and herrings. I knew why I waited. I was quiet and excited, and I knew. There was a big tin in the dinghy and it was quickly getting filled with herrings.

Soon the light went off the water and then the sea was only a sound — a soft sucking sound and a fish splash sound. When the dark came so did the cold, and I've been told Hemi put a jersey on me. I do not remember the cold but I know it is true that Hemi would have taken a jersey for me, and that he would have put it on me when the sun went down. After dark the sky was white with stars. Tangimoana has told me that. I don't remember the sky of stars, or the whiteness of the stars, my thoughts were in the water. The sky was like a sea full of herrings Tangimoana has told me, but I have no memory of that. My thoughts were not in the sky.

James wanted me to have his line for a little while because he cannot enjoy without sharing. But I waited strongly holding my strong line with its big old hook that had been fixed for deep water, and its heavy sinker bigger than my fist. I don't remember the stars or the cold, or my brother James wanting to share his line with me, or the sinker bigger than my fist, though I've been told. But I remember waiting, and the light going, and the soft splash sounds of the water with all the colour gone.

I remember when the pull came. James, who was sitting by me, grabbed and held onto me so that I wouldn't go over the side. I held on hard to my line. I remember that for a moment there was nothing else, only holding – me holding the line, James holding me. Hemi took the other end of my line, unrolled some of it and tied it to the seat.

'Hold him, Son,' he said to James. Then he said to me, 'Let go now, Boyboy. It's tied.'

I didn't hear him, and I don't remember. I was holding and pulling, and James was holding me. 'My fish, my big fish,' I remember calling.

And then I remember my father Hemi taking my hands and saying, 'Hold it lightly now, Boyboy. The line is tied.' He made me look to where he had tied the line to the seat. 'You'll cut your hands,' he said, 'if you hold the line too tightly.' He stopped me from pulling. 'You'll have us all in the sea. Stop pulling now, let go now and we'll row your big fish into shore.'

I remember that Tangimoana was calling out to my mother Roimata and my mother Mary and my brother Manu and some others who had gathered, and who were sitting on the beach round a little fire they had lit there. 'He got it,' she called. 'Boyboy got it. Toko caught his big fish.'

'Stay there with your line,' Hemi told me when he ran the dinghy up on to the beach. He and Tangi and James got out. My uncles and my cousins helped them to get the dinghy with me in it, on to dry shore. Hemi lifted me out and we could hear my big fish knocking and splashing not far from the edge of the water.

Hemi and I began pulling my big fish in. It was a strong fish, swimming backwards in the shallow water.

'He's swimming backwards!' That's what I remember that Hemi said. Then whoa, we couldn't pull any more. 'He's found a rock,' said Hemi, 'and he's hanging on by his tail. Hold,' he said. 'But don't pull any more. Go and get us a gaff and a torch,' he said to James.

Hemi and I held on while James ran home for a gaff-hook and a torch.

'If we keep on pulling we could break our line, or break the mouth of your big fish and then we'd never land him.' That's what Hemi said.

James was only a little circle of light and a sound of stones sliding as he came running. He gave the torch and gaff to Hemi, then held the line with me.

My father Hemi walked out just a little way into the water with my sister Tangimoana splashing along behind him. He put the little circle of torch light close to the surface of the sea and gaffed my big fish under its head. He swung his arm round and pulled the big fish free of the rock that it had lashed its tail to.

We hauled it out onto dry shore while it barked and barked and smacked at the stones with its long heavy tail. It is in my memory that the big fish was much much bigger than me, and longer than the little dinghy sitting on the shore.

'We got it, we got it,' Tangimoana was shouting, and there was talking and noise from everyone.

'It's a conger Dad,' James said. 'A big conger.'

'It's bigger than he is,' said Hemi, 'Boyboy it's bigger than you.'

We dragged the big eel up further onto the beach and my father Hemi found a heavy piece of wood and whacked my big fish on the head with it. I do remember the sound. My brother Manu was hiding away with Mary's arms round him, and she was saying, 'Never you matter Boy. Mary look after Boy.'

My father Hemi lifted the big eel from under its gills and half-slid half-carried it to the verandah where we could see it in the light. It was half the length of the verandah, or that's what I remember. It was shiny and black, and shiny silver underneath. Its eyes were little dark pips, and you could tell nothing from its eyes – nothing about its life or its death. Its head was the size of my head, or that's what I remember. And I remember that I was both sorry for my fish and glad about it. Also I remember that I was not afraid of it even though you could tell nothing from its eyes.

We pulled out the stomach of my big fish, and the cockabullies and crabs that it had been feeding on. Then Hemi cut off its head that was as big as my own head, or that's how I remember it. He made a long cut down the middle of it, from its head to its tail, then took the long bone out and opened the fish out flat. The whiteness of the inside was a surprise to me.

Hemi sent Tangi for the salt and James for the tub. I helped James to hose out the tub, then we poured the salt into it. The pile of salt was like a little snow mountain and when we put the water in, the little snow mountain melted right away. Hemi and Roimata cut the eel into strips and put the strips into the brine we had made. Hemi scrubbed a heavy board to cover the tub with so that the fish would stay clean, and so that cats would not come and try to take the fish away.

Well we were up late that night helping with my big fish, that's what I remember, and we hadn't even had our baths by then. We had to hurry and not play in the bath, and not be a big eel swimming and splashing.

Manu got into my bed so that he wouldn't call out and cry in the night. We went right under the blankets and we were big conger eels living under the water at the base of the snow mountain. We had little eyes like pips and long fins from head to tail. We had sharp close-together teeth and crabs in our bellies, and we swam and dived and fought and bit and flopped our tails until all the blankets were on the floor.

Then our mother Roimata came in to speak to us and to tidy us, but still we did not go to sleep for a long time after that. I don't remember if Manu cried in the night, and called and kicked and struggled in the dark. I don't remember if that was one of the nights that I woke with his fingers pinching hard into my arm.

There is a lot to remember about that night, and some of it is my own remembering, and some of it is from what I have been told since. But what I remember most of all about then, what I remember truly and really was that I *knew*. I knew that there was a big fish for me. I knew when Hemi said that he was going to get herrings, when I went to the shed for the line, when I was lifted into the dinghy, when the water was soft, orange and bangled, when I let the big, heavy line down, when the night came, and the cold came – but I do not really remember the cold – I knew as I listened to the soft sea sounds, and before the pull came, that there was a big fish for me. And what I have known ever since then is that my knowing, my own knowingness, is different. It is a before, and a now, and an after knowing, and not like the knowing that other people have. It is a now knowing as if everything is now. My mother Roimata knows about me. On that night she said to me, 'You knew didn't you, Toko? You knew.'

We were up early the next day and my father and my uncles did not go out fishing early as they had planned. First of all they buried the head of the fish and the insides of the fish at the roots of the passionfruit vine. Then we all went up back into the bush to get green manuka brush for the smoke fire. Hemi started the sweet-smell fire in the smoke drum and we took the eel pieces out of the brine and dabbed the wetness away from them with a cloth. Then Hemi and Uncle Stan hung the pieces in the drum with all the smoke coming up, and they showed James and all of us how to keep the smoke fire going with the manuka without letting any flames happen.

So then we had work for the rest of the day looking after the smoke. I don't remember, but I know, that it would have been our brother James who did everything and understood it all and knew what to do. He could always do grown-up things. He could always be careful and patient and tidy, like Hemi, that's what our mother Roimata said.

*

When Hemi and our uncles came home they were pleased with James and all of us, and they took the strips of eel from the drum.

The eel flesh was goldy and smelled of the sea and the trees. We wanted to eat some of it right then but Hemi was a little angry with us and told us you didn't eat food until it had been shared, especially if it was from the sea. Ours is a big family he said, which was something to always remember.

★

There is more to the story of when I was five, and it is about when I went to give Granny Tamihana her pieces of fish.

Granny heard me walking on her path. She knew it was me by the special sound of my walking, and she called out, 'Haeremai Tokowaru-i-te-Marama.' I sat down on her doorstep to take my boots off, although that is not a rule for me. I am allowed in houses wearing my special boots as long as I wipe them carefully. But I was pleased to get the big boots off and go into Granny's kitchen. Granny wasn't in the kitchen but I knew where she would be. I went through to the little porch of windows where she was seated on her sheepskin rug preparing strips of flax for her baskets.

I held up the bag of fish for her to see and she said that I was very good and strong. That's what I remember. She said I was a good fisherman and a good little father to her, and a good little father to all my family, and that my fish was myself to give. And she said that she was the one that was going to cook the fish in milk for me, and that she and I were going to eat the fish together, soon, at her own table. Soon when her basket was made.

I put the fish into her fridge so that the little cat would not steal. Then the cat and I watched Granny scraping the flax strips and making the muka at the ends. Then she plaited the muka ends together until her work looked like the long bone that Hemi had taken out of my fish.

While she worked she was telling me and showing me which to lift and which to pull but it was too much to remember. It was just as if she was waving her hands – as if she held the flax strips and did a little green dance with her hands, and then after a while there was a new basket for me.

'I make myself,' she said. 'And give it.'

The sun was coming into the little room of windows. I remember feeling warm and happy on one of Granny's rugs with the garden smell of flax and the sea-sound of her voice, and the shifting sounds of her body and her liney hands.

'Here's your basket nearly finish,' she said. 'Make some handles for your basket when we had our kai.'

Perhaps I went to sleep then, or maybe I followed Granny to the kitchen and watched her heating the fish in a pot of milk, and mixing the dough for the paraoa parai and floating the dough pieces in a pan of fat. I remember the two of us sitting at her table with the fish steaming on our plates and syrup melting and running down the sides of our warm bread. I think I remember Granny putting the very tip of her finger on the knob of her teapot lid as she poured tea for us, or else I know it because it's what she always does. I remember that she talked and talked advising me about everything to do with my whole life. Some of the things she told me were not right out of my understanding, but only sitting on the edge of it. Even so my understanding was more than ordinary for a person who was five. Well that's what I've been told. Given in place of a straight body, and to make up for almost drowning – nobody has told me that but I think it might be so.

And I remember Granny getting up from the table and taking the fire poker from where it was hanging on the wall and swinging the fire door of the wood range down. She stooped, and rattled the burning wood so that the sparks danced, and then she poked more wood in. Fire caught the new wood, and the dry manuka bark lifted and curled and flamed. There was rumbling in the chimney like a storm coming.

Then Granny stood, and I thought that she could have come out of the fire, like a magic fire woman. She stood, in her dark dress, with her old, old face and smoke hair. Her eyes had two dark centres but the whites were lined with red like little fiery pathways. And I tried to walk the fiery pathways but found that they led to places where it was difficult to follow. The way along the pathways was too far, and too magic, too secret and too locked away to follow, or that's what I think now.

We washed and dried our dishes and put them away. I shook the tablecloth outside where the seagulls come, then I followed Granny through to the sitting room with its big brown chairs and flowery cushions and photographs in big wooden frames. The photographs were of long-ago people in best clothes. One was of Granny when she was a girl, standing by her brother who had been dead for seventy years. That's what Granny said. 'That's Tokowaru-i-te-Marama, your great-granduncle, and he's been dead for seventy years. Only me and him, you know,' she said, 'the two of us. And after that, only me.'

Back in the little window room I watched Granny make muka and plait the handles for my basket.

'Riding our horses,' she said. 'Only a little time after that photo there, and the tide down low. Galloping, galloping on our horses on the low-tide sand. Well there is a kehua there that day, on that little rock, and that kehua give my brother's horse a very big fright. Yes, the horse see a very big kehua there on the little rock sticking up in the low water just in front of here. Well. The horse get very wild you see, very wild. The horse get a very big fright. My brother fly out in the air you see, because of the big kehua make his horse very wild. And down, down, and splash in the small water. And bang. His head break on that rock there with a big kehua on it. My poor brother, ka pakaru te upoko.

'Those days I cry and cry for my brother. And smack him too. They make my brother all ready for the people to come, and dress him up nice and put him in our wharenui there. And I look at him, and you know I smack him hard. I throw my flowers down hard, and I kick that pretty box with my brother in very, very hard.

'Well my daddy and my aunties growl at me and hold tight on to me, and I can't smack and kick. I have to be a good girl after that. I have to be good, and all the people from all everywhere come and see my poor brother. I have to be a good girl.

'No more fishing for a long time after,' Granny said. 'No more fishing and no more going in the sea. Just like when you are born, Little Father. All the people have to wait and wait for the water be right again. Just like for you, Little Father.'

She gave me the finished basket which was cool and green-smelling, then she led me back to the photos.

'The time your great-granduncle is born, that's the time all those people die of a bad sickness, tokowaru i te marama. Eight people die in one month here, and eight tupapaku on our marae. Eight in one month. But it's a good name for you Little Father, your great-granduncle's name. And it's your own name now.'

I thought of the other Tokowaru-i-te-Marama galloping along the sand, being thrown from his horse and falling to hit his head on the rock. The dull, hard sound of when my father Hemi whacked my big fish with the heavy stick came back to my mind. And the life of the long-ago Toko and the life of my big fish seemed somehow to come together. There was a big kehua there.

I put on my boots and went home along the beach shouldering the gifts I had been given.

There is something else to do with my five-year-old story and the story of my big fish. It is to do with the passionfruit vine. 'Vine' and 'brine' were both new words to me then, and these words quickly recall that time for me whenever I hear them.

My mother Roimata had taken a passionfruit cutting from

Granny Tamihana's vine. At the time when I caught my big fish the cutting was dry and without life, that's what I've been told. But after we buried the fish head and fish guts there the plant began to grow and grow. The branches began to swim everywhere like a multiplication of eels. It was as if the big eel head with its little seed-eyes was birthing out trail after trail of its young. All the little eels swarmed the shed walls and the trees, whipping their tails and latching them to the walls and branches, still growing and multiplying all the time. And the eel-vines had a thousand hidden eyes, a thousand tails and a thousand hidden hearts.

The hearts are dark and warm and fit in the cup of your hand. You can pull out the hearts without pain, and when you open them you find the thousand dark seed-eyes. The seeds are a new beginning, but started from a death. Well everything is like that – that's what my mother Roimata says. End is always beginning. Death is life.

The goldy seeded fruit is sharp-tasting and stinging, and leaves you with red stained fingers and a smarting, blooded mouth.

And the endless vine going everywhere is like a remembrance of the time, which is really a now-time, of when I was five, and of the big barking fish that I knew was waiting for me on the white sky night in the orange lagoon.

Fiona Kidman

HATS

LIKE TURNING YOUR hand over, things could go either way
with the weather. Six a.m. and the bay is turbulent and green, but
at that hour of the morning anything can happen. Standing at the
window, just listening, the whole house is a heartbeat. Looking at
the bay, the water, the clouds. I think I can hear the busy clink
and chatter of the rigging on the boats parked on the hard at the
bay, but that can't be right, it's too far away. Oh you can hear
anything, see anything on a morning like this, it's the day of the
wedding. Our son's getting married.

There is a stirring in the back rooms; there is so much to do,
I will never get done, it's crazy this, but the wedding's to be here,
not at her place but mine. I am speaking now of the bride's mother
and myself. Well, it's a long story, how the wedding comes to be
here instead of there, but that's the way it is. She's bringing the
food later in the morning, and there'll be crayfish and scallops like
nobody ever had at their wedding before, and mussels of course.
They are mussel farmers from the Sounds. They. Well I mean the
bride's parents.

I love our daughter-in-law-to-be, I really do. You might
think I don't mean that, mothers-in-law rarely do, but it's true.

She's a good person. She's loyal. She's had to put up with a few things. Our son's on a win. I want to see him married.

Perhaps they know that. There are times when I think they haven't been so keen. Perhaps they think she could have done better. I don't know. It hasn't been easy, getting this wedding together. But if you knew him, our son, you'd know she wouldn't settle for anyone else. Anyone *less*. Now there's a mother talking, but I've fallen for it, that same old charm of his, and I'll go on forever, I guess. He puts his arms around me, and says, 'Love ya, Ma,' and I'd forgive him anything.

It's true. He brings out a softness in me. That, and rage. But the anger never lasts for long.

There is no time to go on reflecting about it this morning though. There's the smell of baked meats in the air, I need to open up the house and blow it through, I've got the food warmer to collect from the hire depot, and the tablecloths aren't ready, and I have to set up a place for the presents, and there's his mother, that's my husband's, to be got up, and there's relatives to be greeted, and oh God I am so tired. Why didn't anyone tell me I'd be so tired on our son's wedding day, it doesn't seem fair, because I want to enjoy it. Oh by that I mean, I want it all to be right, of course, and I want to do it graciously. We've been at each other a bit over this wedding. Them and us. But I want to make sure it goes all right today. They're bringing the food and the flagons of beer; we're providing the waiters and waitresses in starched uniforms, and the champagne. You have to cater for everyone at a wedding.

Eleven a.m. The food hasn't come. The flagons haven't come. She hasn't come. That's the bride's mother. The wedding is at two. I am striding around the house. The furniture is minimal. We've cleared everything back. There's hardly going to be standing room. That's if there ever is a wedding. There is nothing more I can do. Nothing and everything. If only we had another day. It would be better if we had held off another month. The weather would have been better. Not that it's bad but the breeze is cold. It'll be draughty in the church.

The church, ah, the church. It looks so beautiful. The flowers. They are just amazing. Carnations and irises, low bowls of stocks . . . there are the cars now, all the relatives bearing trays and pots and dishes, straggling up the stairs. The food looks wonderful. God, those crays, there's dozens of them. I'm glad they've done the food, I could never have done it so well. And the cake. Our daughter-in-law-to-be's auntie has made the cake and it's perfect too.

Everyone's exhausted, it's not just me, they've been up all night. Still, I wish they could have got here a bit sooner and we all have to get dressed yet. It's cutting things fine. I feel faint, even a little nauseous, as if lights are switching on and off inside my brain. She can't be as tired as I am, nobody could be that tired. How am I going to make it through the rest of the day?

'I'd better be getting along,' says the auntie to the bride's mother. 'I've still got to finish off your hat.' The aunt has a knack with things, clothes and cakes, she's the indispensable sort.

Inside me, something freezes. 'Hat,' I say, foolishly, and in a loud voice. 'You're wearing a hat?'

There is a silence in the kitchen.

'Well, it's just a little hat,' she says.

'You said you weren't going to wear a hat.' I hear my voice, without an ounce of grace in it, and I don't seem to be able to stop it. There is ugliness in the air.

The auntie, her sister, says, 'She needed a hat to finish off the outfit. It wouldn't look right without it.'

'But we agreed,' I say. 'You said you couldn't afford a hat, and I said, well if you're not wearing one, I won't.'

The silence extends around the kitchen. She fumbles a lettuce leaf, suddenly awkward at my bench.

'It's all right,' I say, 'it's nothing.' My face is covered with tears. I walk out, leaving them to finish whipping the cream.

'Where are you going?' my husband says, following at my heels.

'Out. Away.'

'You can't go away.'

'I have to. I'm not going to the wedding.'

'No, stop, don't be silly.' He's really alarmed, I'm right on the edge, and he's right, I might go off at any moment and make things too awful for everyone to endure. At the rate I'm going there mightn't be any wedding.

'Come into the shed,' he says, speaking softly, like a huntsman talking down a wild animal. 'Come on, it'll be all right. You're tired, just tired.'

I follow him. Inside the toolshed I start to cry properly. 'I want a hat,' I say. 'I wanted to wear a hat all along, but I promised her. I promised I wouldn't get a hat.'

'I'll get you a hat. Come along, we'll go into town and buy you a hat.'

'It's too late, the shops will be shut.'

'We could just make it to James Smith's,' he says. But it is too late, I can see that. Even if we broke the speed limit I'd only have five minutes, it being Saturday. The shops were due to close in half an hour.

'I can't go without a hat. What'll I do?'

'You'll think of something,' he says. 'You always do. Hey, we can do anything, can't we?' He pulls my fists out of my eyes. 'What can we do? We can . . .' He waits for me to join in the refrain with him.

'We can walk on water if we have to,' I chant.

But I'm not sure how I will.

Back in the kitchen everyone is tiptoeing around. 'It looks wonderful,' I say heartily. 'Just great. Don't you think you should be getting along. I mean, if you're going to get dressed?'

They nod. They are not deceived, but they are glad to be excused. They have been afraid to take their leave in my absence.

They are gone, and our son and his best man are dressed, preening in their three-piece suits. Oh they are so handsome. It calms me, just seeing them. As for him, I want to stroke and stroke him. My boy. In a suit. Oh I'm square. When it all comes down to it. But he's proud of himself too.

'Y'okay, Ma?'

He doesn't know what's been going on, but he sees I'm pale.

'Of course I'm okay,' I say, and for his sake I must be. I must also have a hat.

I ring our daughter. 'What about all those hats you bought when you were into hats?' I ask. I think of the op shops where she has collected feathered toques and funny little cloches. I have a feeling that none of them will suit me. She is so tall and elegant. 'I think they're in the baby's toybox,' she says.

'Have a look,' I command.

'God, I've got to get dressed too.'

'Have a look.'

I hold grimly on to the phone. She comes back. 'There's three, the black one with three feathers, and the sort of burgundy one, and the beige one with the wide brim.'

'That's it, the beige one. I'm sending Dad over for it right now.'

'But Mum.'

'It'll be all right. Well, look I can try it anyway.'

'But Mum.' This time she gets it out. 'The baby's been sick on it.'

'How sick?'

'Really sick.'

No one is going to put me off now. I think she is conspiring with the odds to stop me making a fool of myself. I won't let her save me, though. 'Dad'll be right over,' I say.

But it's true. The baby has been very sick on the hat. I'm sure our daughter shouldn't have put it back in the toybox like that. I resolve to speak to her about it at some later date.

In the meantime there is work to be done. I fill the sink with hot soapy water and get out the scrubbing brush. In a few moments the sick has gone. I have a soggy felt hat dripping in my hands, but at least it is clean.

The husband and wife team, 'available for cocktail, waitressing and barman duties in the privacy of your own home', has arrived. 'Don't worry about a thing,' they say. 'You just enjoy yourselves and we'll take care of everything from now on.'

In the clothes drier, the hat whirls around.

Our son has left for the church. Soon we'll have to go too. My husband is resplendent. He wears his father's watch chain across his waistcoat. His father was a guard on the railways, back in the old days. That watch has started a thousand trains on country railway stations. Sometimes I remonstrate with my husband for wearing it; it doesn't always seem appropriate. Today it is exactly right. The spring in the watch has given up long ago, but the watch will start the wedding on time. Sooner or later.

My hands shake so much he has to do up the pearl buttons on my Georgia Brown silk. 'It's time we were going,' he says tentatively. I know he's thinking about the hat, and wondering if he can get me away without it.

But it's dry. Dry, and softly drooping around the brim, so that it swoops low over my right eye when I put it on. I stare at myself in the mirror, entranced. I feel beautiful. I glow. I love hats. This hat is perfect.

Our son's wife-to-be is late, but then she usually is. Anyone is allowed one failing. I don't mind. It gives me time to relax, breathe deeply, smile and wave around the church. Across the aisle I see her, the mother of the bride. She is not wearing a hat.

Instinctively, I touch the brim of mine. I have shamed her into coming without her hat. I should feel jubilant but I don't. I feel bad, wonder how to take mine off without drawing attention to myself. But it's impossible. At the door to the church the priest has said, first thing when he sees me, 'Oh what a beautiful hat.'

I look away, embarrassed. I tell myself I must not think about it. The wedding is about to happen, and we can't repeat it when I'm feeling better, so I've just got to stop thinking about it, the hat on my head.

And then they're there, coming into the church together, which is what's been arranged, and it's not quite the same old responses, because some of that wouldn't be suitable, but they say some nice things to each other, making promises to do things as well as they can, and they're so young, so very young, and that's all you can expect from anybody, to do their best, isn't it?

The couple are facing the congregation now. This really is very modern. Our daughter stands up at the lectern and reads from the Book of Ecclesiastes, and then some Keats, *O brightest! though too late for antique vows*, and she's pale and self-contained and not showing signs of things turning over inside of her, and so lovely; she and the boy, her brother, look at each other, and it's as if they're the only ones in the church for a moment, *Holy the air, the water, and the fire*, like a conversation just for the two of them, putting aside all their childish grievances, though a few people in the church who haven't done English Lit. look a trifle confused but it doesn't matter, these two know . . . *so let me be thy choir . . . thy voice, thy lute, thy pipe* . . . and then our son and his new wife's baby cries at the back of the church where he's being held by the auntie, and the spell's broken, as the two parents look anxiously after their child. The wind rises in the funnel where the church stands, and a plane roars overhead, and the light shines through the stained glass window onto the same spot where my father's coffin stood last year, and with all the light and the sound I don't hear any more of the service, I just smile and smile.

It's over. We're forming up to leave. She and I look at each other across the church again. Suddenly it's all bustle and go, and what none of us have thought about is the way we get out of the church, but there it is, as old as the service itself, or so it seems, the rituals of teaming up, like finding your partner for a gavotte, step step step an arm offered and accepted she goes with my husband and I go with hers, that's the way it's done. Delicate, light as air, we prepare our entrance to the dance, to the music, but before we do, she and I afford each other one more look, one intimate glance. Hatted and hatless, that's us, blessed are the meek, it's all the same now. We're one, her and me. We're family.

Owen Marshall

A DAY WITH YESTERMAN

CHATTERTON WOKE to the birds. The absence of pain may have been the reason. He moved his legs, sucked in his stomach, but nothing caught; just the squeak of the plastic sheet beneath the cotton one. Chatterton was accustomed to the need to occupy himself much of the night; to sidle and belay from ledge to ledge of darkness, but not all that often did he hear the birds begin. He marvelled at the intensity − a sweet hubbub as a base, and superimposed the longer, individual exclamations of thrush or blackbird. He had the pleasing thought that the birds gathered at his house to inaugurate a special day. Chatterton folded the sheet under his chin, so that the blanket no longer tickled, and he made himself a little wider and longer to pop a few joints and check that he was in good shape.

A mild suffusion of light from behind the curtains strengthened as Chatterton sang 'Danny Boy' and 'The White Cliffs of Dover'. He stopped with a feeling something of value was slipping away, and then it came to him, a recollection of the night's dream in which he had made love to an ample woman beneath an elm tree in Hagley Park. It was to some degree an explanation of his mood. Chatterton was sensible enough to enjoy authentic emotion however it reached the mind. Before the experience quite faded he closed his eyes to breathe again the fragrance of the elm and observe a wisp of auburn hair quiver with the pulse of her neck. He lay listening to his birds as morning came. How young at last I feel, he assured himself.

By the time Chatterton was in the kitchen, he could get by with natural light. He poached himself an egg without boiling off the white, and he watched his yellow feet like flounders on the floor. He would never recognize his feet in a crowd, for they were just any old, yellow feet. Truck rigs passed with a roar on the nearby motorway as they tried to get a clear start to the day. Chatterton rubbed his knee to loosen the joint. The skin seemed to have no attachment to the bones, and slid all ways. Only the young body savours its union.

As the birds wound down, Chatterton finished his third cup of tea, and went back to his bedroom to choose his clothes. 'I'll make a bargain with you.' He addressed a small, familiar god. 'Best clothes for best day.' The trousers were a quality check, but big at his waist and so the band tucked somewhat under his belt. A grey jacket, with a chrome zip, that his daughter had given him for Christmas. Tropic Sands aftershave, which the label exhorted Chatterton to splash on liberally, but which he did not. 'Chatterton,' said Chatterton to his own reflection, 'you are an old dog.' He looked at all the bottles on his drawers, and decided to take no medication at all. Before he left the house Chatterton buffed the toes of his shoes with the socks he was putting out to wash. He should have known better, for the bending sent him dizzy, and he over-balanced and fell on to the smooth lino by the bench. He had a laugh at himself, and felt the cool lino on his cheek as he lay and waited for his head to clear. In the corner was a false cut in the lino: Chatterton could remember clearly the wet day seventeen years before when he had laid the lino and made just that false cut. How difficult it is to fault life's continuity. The rain had caught the window at an angle, and drained like rubber tree striations across its surface.

As Chatterton walked to Associated Motors he calculated a route which would keep him on the sunny side of the streets, and he watched other people on their way to work, disappointed that he couldn't recognize them as friends. He nodded and smiled nevertheless.

Chatterton helped part-time with the accounts at Associated Motors; so very part-time over the last months that Susan was surprised to see him. 'And you're looking so smart today,' she said. Chatterton knew he was. He began to use the computer to calculate GST payments. Chatterton enjoyed the computer, and was impatient with people who claimed they couldn't adapt to them.

'Life is adaptation,' he said.

'Right, Mr Chatterton.'

'How I could run when I was young.'

'Could you?' said Susan.

'I was a small-town champion,' said Chatterton, 'and could have been a large-town one with training.' He was wistful rather than proud.

'I like netball,' said Susan.

'Ah, your knees are wonderfully smooth,' said Chatterton: his fingers nimble on the keys.

The Sales Manager broke up their flirtation. 'How are you feeling?' he asked.

'I am in complete remission today,' said Chatterton. 'I can sense my prime again. I'm growing young again very rapidly.' The Sales Manager laughed, for he thought Chatterton intended a joke.

'How about taking a Cressida down to Dunedin then for me? It's needed there today,' he asked Chatterton.

The mechanics watched in envy as Chatterton took a set of provisional plates and two of his own cassettes. They hoped for such perks themselves. 'Hey, Chatters, you lucky old bastard,' and Chatterton winked and executed a no-fuss manoeuvre before them in the yard.

'I thought the old bastard was dying or something.'

'Dying to get away in that car, all right.'

In fifth gear the Cressida was only loping on the Canterbury Plains. Chatterton fed in his Delius cassette and the quiet interior was sprung with sound. Chatterton wondered why he dreamed so often in old age of hang-gliding. Something he'd never done, yet increasingly his night views were from above, the cold air whistling in a rigging he didn't understand. Progress was relentless, and from landscape and people half-recognized he was borne away. He supposed it might be a side effect of the medication. When he was younger he would have tackled hang-gliding. He had been an athlete hadn't he, and a soldier?

At Karitane Chatterton turned off to take the old road. He could avoid the increasing traffic. He liked that swamp flat: rushes, brown and yellow mosses, mallards, and pukekos with their bookish, striding way. Later there was a stranded man – enquiring face and car bonnet raised. Chatterton stopped, and the man came with grateful haste to meet him. His name was Norman Caan. He began to thank Chatterton, who smiled, but was distracted by the peace as he stood there – the quiet road, the crimped blue light over the sea, the headland beyond with an apron of gorse on the steeper ground. The wind from the sea was wine, and it scented the beachside grass and bore spaciousness inland.

'I do appreciate you stopping. I've got something of a problem as you see, and I've a city appointment at one.' Caan was close to Chatterton; his voice a trifle plaintive. He put out his hand and Chatterton shook it.

'Sorry,' said Chatterton, 'but what a day it is. Isn't it? How things continue to fit newly together, year after year.'

'I suppose it is.' Caan looked at the sky, blown almost clear, and the hills and the inlet and the horizon seaward, as though he had just entered a large building and had its architecture commended to him. The coast curved, and a far cutting bore a drape of pink ice-plant, and the sun shone back from it as if from glass.

As they examined the engine of Caan's Volvo, Chatterton noticed a balding spot at Caan's crown, as if a tidy bird had been scratching a nest there. Chatterton passed a hand over his own stiff, grey hair. A dunny brush he'd heard it called. He had to admit Caan's clothes were better than his own however; an integration of style and texture which Chatterton could recognize, yet not explain.

'There's nothing we can do,' said Chatterton. 'Lock up and come with me. We can have someone out in no time.' But back at his own car, instead of getting inside, Chatterton was drawn to the bank again. 'Will you look at that though,' he said. 'No pain there at all. Will you look at the ripples on the bars as the tide comes in, and the bubbles over the crab holes in the mud.' The single cloud against powder blue made a cameo brooch of the sky; birch leaves tossed as a mane on the back of a macrocarpa hedge. 'You don't mind just for a moment?' asked Chatterton. 'It's just such a day.'

'No, no,' said Caan.

'It's just such a day,' said Chatterton. Caan had no option, but his face had initially a shrug of the shoulders expression as he watched Chatterton move to the edge of the bank above the coast. He was only a few feet above the sea, yet Chatterton sucked several breaths as a diver would on a high cliff. 'I shall become part of it. I see it all as if I'm twenty,' he said.

Despite concern for his situation, Caan was affected by Chatterton's wonder, and something more – something naive in his cheerful age and the trousers belted too large, and his hair bristling. 'It is rather splendid,' said Caan; diffident in praise of his own country.

'You know,' said Chatterton, 'today I keep thinking of when I was young.'

Somewhere between Lake Grasmere and Seddon the black AJS left the road at speed and took an angle into grass standing high as a field of wheat. There was no way of stopping quickly. The bike's metal scything through. He heard only one sound, that of the rushing grass, and he was aware in the clarity of fear how bright the sun shone on that roadside grass like wheat. Yet there was nothing hidden; no snare, no ditch, and fear gave place to exultation as the grass slowed him and he KNEW that nothing there had harm in it: an instant almost too brief to allow him the dangerous conviction that he couldn't die. The black, heavy AJS off the road; the hissing, even fluster of the wheat-grass in the vivid sun. All in a few seconds, he supposed. All happening in a few seconds and in heightened perception. And the bike had stopped and he found himself quite alone in that landscape, stalled high from the road with grass packed around him, the cicadas coming back to chorus, and fine pollens settling on the black tank of the AJS.

'Like riding through a wheat field,' said Chatterton.

'Sorry?'

'I was thinking back,' said Chatterton. 'Other days.'

As they passed over the hills into the city, Chatterton and Caan, together completely by chance they would suppose, talked freely. Chatterton found it easier to be honest as he grew older, and the knowledge that relationships had no necessary continuation ceased to disconcert him. Besides, Caan was prepared to listen as well as talk. Chatterton liked a positive listener; he could be one himself. They covered the decline of state medicine, the loss of flavour in Bluff oysters, the self-serving of the political powerful, and the suicide of Tony Hancock. There is a good deal of satisfaction to be had from free-ranging criticism. 'But then I'm a deal older than you,' said Chatterton.

'Not so much surely; I'm retired.'

'There are two possibilities as you get old,' said Chatterton.

'You become archaic, or you leave the world behind in your progress. Either way increasing isolation is the result.'

'Well, isolated numerically perhaps.'

'And in confidence. It's hard to be confident and old. The opposite of what most people expect I suppose.'

'But you are,' said Caan.

'An act of faith. Besides, superstition and disease have me now, so I indulge myself. There's days sometimes that favour you, you know.'

'Propitious,' said Caan.

'Pardon.'

'Propitious.'

'Yes,' said Chatterton. 'That's it.'

'Anyway today you're welcome to travel back with me, and have lunch with me too. I'm allowed a guest at the Rotary Lunch I'm addressing. I'll have my car delivered, and afterwards we'll pick up my sister who's coming back with me to recuperate for a while.' Caan was pleased to be able to establish the immediate future, and to provide for Chatterton's repayment within it.

The President of Rotary was a splendid host, just one size larger and more glossy than his fellows as befitted his office. 'So much of what service groups do now is taken for granted,' he said. 'Assistance is an expectation now; almost a right.' Chatterton noticed the barman's black reefer jacket, and it produced before Chatterton his grandmother's sewing basket. The fine wickerwork and the embroidered top – black, black, with a country spire perpetually slate blue. The colours were ribbed, and the tranquillity of even execution rather than the subject had made an ache which allowed of no expression. So he had built childlike barricades of pins around the black field's spire in attempts at the protection which his memory was later able to assume.

'We get told who we should be supporting, and how much,' said the President. 'We get told we're not doing enough rather than thanked. Not coughing up sufficiently.' Chatterton enjoyed a free whisky, and watched the last members picking up their badges. The President led the way into the dining room, and they took their places before three slices of ham on each plate. Chatterton rather enjoyed the Rotarian mood; an aura of confidence and good intent that arises from reasonable success in the world and a wisely unexamined life. Chatterton looked with favour on his ham, and waited for the vegetables. Caan talked to the President.

'I ran my own business for twenty-seven years, then it grew too complex and I sold out. That's one of the things I want to mention in my address: the need to understand there's a point at which a business becomes too much for the managerial skills of its founder alone. A lot of concerns go wrong at that stage.'

Chatterton admired the Rotarians across from him, particularly an assured man in his thirties, eating carefully and smiling carefully as he listened to his neighbour. A man well carapaced in a three-piece suit, and trusting the ground beneath his feet. Chatterton wondered if he himself at any age had looked that way; and knew the answer. The man had a sheen almost; the beauty of a live lobster, an exoskeleton creature, any vulnerability safe within. He was all jointed precision of appearance. Chatterton caught his eye.

'Good on you,' said Chatterton, and they lifted their forks in mutual salutation.

'Few business men can make the transition from personal to corporate management,' said Caan. 'And why should it be expected, or easy.' Caan stopped, and looked first at the President and then at Chatterton as if some explanation was expected from them. His face was pale, and he swallowed several times. 'I feel rotten,' he said. 'I think I might be sick.' His head gave a shiver, and he sighed as if lonely.

'Perhaps the cold meat,' said the President. Caan and he left the table and went through the conversations to find a place for

Caan to lie down. Caan walked as if he were carrying a tray of marbles and the loss of any of them would be his death.

Chatterton was offered more vegetables, and accepted all but the peas. Sprouts he had, and potato balls and corn heaped like nuggets of gold. And no pain was swallowed with them; no pain whatsoever. The President returned alone. 'He's lying down,' he said. 'He says he feels a little better.' The President looked searchingly at Chatterton. Chatterton lacked an executive mien, and there was grey hair tufted in his ears. He alone in the dining room had a jacket with a zip. There was a sense of ease though, and good-will and self-will. The President was not a fool. 'Caan suggested you might speak instead,' he said. Chatterton was happy to be of service; he liked to talk to people. And he had his best trousers on, even if they were gathered at the waist somewhat. He had visions to draw upon, his life among them.

When the President's routine business was over and the Serjeant-at-Arms had imposed fines with sufficient humorous innuendo, Chatterton was introduced as a colleague of Norman Caan. As he waited to speak, as the polite applause eddied about the tables, Chatterton was reminded of his last Battalion reunion, and by another step of recollection Birdy Fowler, who died of heatstroke before they came out of the desert. Chatterton hadn't been invited to speak at the reunion, and he thought there was a need for Birdy's name to be heard again. So Chatterton began his talk with several of the stories Birdy used to tell when drinking: the Rotarians laughed at the ribaldry of natural man, and Chatterton laughed in tribute to a friend. Then Chatterton talked about his illness; the prostate and spleen which had been taken, the disaffection of other organs; about how to make it through the nights, the spiritual and practical ingenuities by which it's possible to inch closer to the day. About his wife who had been very beautiful when she was young and he was a coarse, stupid boy. About his dream of steam trains ascending steep tracks through the bush, so that the engine fumed and panted, the white steam like egret's feathers flared against the leaves, wild cattle crashed away, and deep, faded varnish of the inner woodwork still showed a living grain.

The green, sashed curtains quivered at the windows of the hotel. The long tables of Rotary luncheon had flower vases, and pollen beneath some of them was spread like pepper on the white cloth. A waitress with her hair up in gel was at the kitchen swing doors, ready to clear away. She picked her lip, and wondered if she would be through by four. We make the mistake of assuming that our present experience is the world's. The tussock would be blowing on all the crests of Dansey's Pass, glue sniffers sitting with statues of the city fathers, a fine rain flaking on to the pungas of the Ureweras, a sheer excalibur of sunlight from the high window of a panel shop in Papanui transfixing young Marty working there.

The Rotarians were normally uncomfortable with personal revelations, which could easily obscure sound business practices, but as Chatterton was unknown to them they felt none of the embarrassment that acquaintanceship would have brought. They were quite struck by his eccentricity, his passion, and the evident movement of the bones in his thin cheeks as he talked. Chatterton had an innocent pride as he left with the President to find Caan. He was resting on an alcove chair in the foyer. His coat and tie were off, and his head relaxed backwards. 'I think I'm all right now,' he said.

'Well, Mr Chatterton was a considerable success,' said the President.

'That's the second time he's saved the day,' said Caan.

'I just sang for my supper,' said Chatterton. The President's laugh was high-pitched; almost a giggle, and odd from such an imposing man.

Caan's car was delivered as he and Chatterton sat peacefully in the foyer. Caan washed his face with cold water, and then decided that he was recovered. 'You'll understand that Joan's had a hard time of it,' he said when he returned. 'She left her husband to make a mid-life career for herself in physiotherapy and then found she had cancer. The treatment's knocked her pretty badly.' Chatterton knew the treatment, but he didn't think about it as they drove to the nursing home. Instead he enjoyed the dappled shadows on the road through the green belt, the shimmer caused by the breeze on the tops of the trees, and imagined himself joining in with the afternoon joggers – putting his weight well forward on the slope and judging a pace to keep both legs and lungs comfortable. The bellows of the chest in full use; cooling tree air on the damp singlet; hair heavy with sweat patting on the back of his head as he ran.

On the front lawn of the nursing home a badminton court had been marked out. Young people played vigorously there, their bare feet silent on the grass, their voices loud and sudden. Joan was waiting in the lounge with her two cases beside her. 'She'll need a good deal of rest of course, but we're all optimistic,' Caan said as he and Chatterton walked past the lawn. Chatterton watched a brown girl leap forever so that her arms and breast were outlined against the sea. He wondered why God still chose to punish old men. As Caan came closer to the lounge he smiled and raised his hand, but his sister was behind the glass, and nothing could be said. She wore a light dress of floral pattern that would be considered cheerful perhaps – when purchased for someone else. She wore lipstick but her eyebrows were very pale, and to hide her baldness she was topped with a tam-o-shanter, green and red. She had the eyes of the travellers of illness.

'I'm sorry we're a bit late,' said Caan. 'It's been an odd sort of day.' As he told her of it, and Chatterton's part as an explanation for his presence, Joan and Chatterton regarded one another. When Caan finished, Chatterton touched the woollen cap in a friendly way.

'I had a hat, but not as colourful as yours,' he said. He took one of her cases, Caan the other, and they waited at the door while Joan farewelled a nurse. 'Chemotherapy as well as the ray can be pretty much a sapping combination,' said Chatterton when she was back. 'Is your hair all out?'

'All out,' she said.

'So was mine,' said Chatterton, 'but it grows in again. Mine grew back very wiry.'

'Very wiry,' said Joan. Well, frankness could work both ways.

'And you get a good deal of strength back.' To demonstrate, Chatterton stopped by the car and threw the case up, and caught it again in both arms. 'See,' he said eagerly.

'You get used to him,' said Caan.

'Are you so very different?' she asked Chatterton.

'I'm in search of natural man now,' he said.

'Too late, too old,' she said, but Chatterton threw up the case again and capered with it. The badminton players cheered; a nurse stood watching from the office and telling others over her shoulder what was happening.

Caan asked Chatterton to drive. After his illness at lunch Caan wanted a restful trip. Chatterton was obliging once more. As he drove he calculated aloud the unexpected profit he was making on the day – the price of the bus fare to Christchurch, and of a midday meal. Enough for a week's groceries, or for semi-gloss to paint his small porch. 'Do you enjoy painting?' he asked Joan. The triviality of it stimulated Joan; she was tired of weighing up life and death. She began to talk of the renovations she had done years before on her house at Port Chalmers. Although her voice was well back in her throat, and somewhat husky, it increased in tempo and her tam-o-shanter nodded green and red. 'Oh, no, no,' interrupted Chatterton decidedly. 'You should always strip back before repapering for a first rate job.'

'It's not always needed.'

'Shoddy, shoddy,' cried Chatterton.

'What would a man know about making a home,' said Joan. 'What does a man remember.'

Chatterton was in the presence of things which gave an answer. The water in the pink heart of flax, and a monkey puzzle tree to hold up the sky. Sheep coughing out the night, and in a winter drizzle the horses smoking in the dray. His mother standing at the laundry, pushing back her hair with her wrist, smiling at him, and the smell of hot woollens and yellow soap again. Old coats without shoulders on nails there like dried fish, and gulls following his father's plough.

At Timaru they had cream freezes, and turned off from the main road at the Showground Hill to rest and eat. Chatterton leant his arms on the top wire of the fence, and watched the downs and the mountains beyond. He led a game to distinguish as many shades of green as possible. 'Nine different colours. To stand and see nine different colours of green,' said Joan. 'All growing from the same soil; all compatible and with the promise of some use or crop.'

When he looked south, Chatterton sensed a change in the weather, and he told the others to expect a southerly. A fisherman gets to read the elements of his locality. Chatterton encouraged Joan to talk as they went on north. He refused to be deferential just because of her trial. 'You have to be careful illness doesn't make you selfish, you know,' he said. 'And you could do a lot more with your appearance – a young woman like you.' He could say such things because of his own illness, his lack of malice, but mostly because of a special innocence which arises from experience and is the mark of rare and successful old age.

'I was never at all religious before,' said Joan. 'Now I'm an atheist by faith rather than logic. And I've got tired of most of my friends: they almost bored me to death when they came. What you expect rarely happens. You, Norman, you're one of the worst.'

'But I'm a brother. All brothers are boring. They lack sufficient biological variation to be otherwise.'

Eventually release was almost overpowering for Joan. 'It's stuffy,' she said. 'I feel dizzy.'

'It's the closeness before the change,' said Caan, 'and you're not used to travelling yet.' Joan took off her woollen hat, and leant back on the seat. Her naked, bird's head had a little downy hair, and the skull plates joined in apparently clumsy workmanship.

'The treatment can have a long-term effect on your food preferences,' said Chatterton. 'Peas and beans for instance. I can't eat them at all now; the smell disgusts me, while fruit is a positive craving. Nectarines and satsumas: ah, there now.'

The southerly came through late in the afternoon, catching them before Ashburton. The churned cloud, wind that flogged the trees and bore a scattered rain too pressed to set in. The temperature dropped as if a door had been opened. 'Oh, that's much better,' said Joan.

'Let's sing "Danny Boy". You know "Danny Boy"?' said Chatterton.

'Oh Danny Boy, the pipes—'. Three of them together. Chatterton likes to sing, although he has a poor voice. He watched the broad, shingle river bed, the islands of gorse and lupin in the scattered rain. He thought of his nineteen-pound salmon near the mouth of the Waitaki; the gravel unsure beneath his waders as he turned, and the cry going up from his fellow fishermen as they gave way for him. The salmon don't feed: they strike in anger or homecoming exultation perhaps. The river aids its fish against the line, and swans form a necklace above the struggle as they pass to Lake Wainoni.

'We're all a bit high,' said Joan. 'I like the song, but we've all light voices and we need someone deeper. A bass baritone, say.' The southerly was blowing itself out, but the coolness remained. Near Dunsandel they saw a hitchhiker with a giant pack and the legs to make light of it. Chatterton pulled up ahead of him.

'Can you sing "Danny Boy"?' he asked. The hitchhiker was willing, although for a time he was embarrassed by Joan's head.

'Where do you come from?' she said.

'Dubbo, Australia.'

'We've all of us got problems,' said Caan.

There were enough voices for a barbershop quartet. 'Oh Danny Boy, the pipes—'. The Australian sang well. He was out of the weather and travelling in the right direction. Over the sinews of his brown arms were raised a few graceful arteries, and the whites of his eyes glinted in a tanned face. 'The green, green grass of home—' they sang as Caan conducted. Joan and the hitchhiker, who couldn't remember each other's names and would never meet again, combined their voices, and smiled at each other because of Chatterton's caterwauling.

They dropped the Australian baritone at the city overbridge. Chatterton took his pack from the boot, and Joan gave him a bag of seedless grapes she had from the nursing home. 'Goodbye, Danny Boy,' she said. What could he make of them: what could they make of themselves. A hitchhiker's experience is only life accelerated. 'Oh my God,' said Joan as they went on. 'I've had my hat off all that time. What a sight.' She laughed at her own humiliation, and wiped her eyes. She put the tam-o-shanter on once more, for the formality of parting with Chatterton.

The wooden house was like the others that surrounded it; insufficiently individual it seemed to be his. Chatterton stood in the drive as Caan came round to take the driver's seat. The evening was calm, but the evidence of the southerly was there. Leaves stripped by the wind and gathered on the concrete in the lee of the house. Leaves of peach and maple. Leaves of birch with aphids still clustered on the underside. The wind's violence had in its eddy a delicacy of graduated winnowing, and the litter diminished to a whip tail of fragments which included two ladybirds, a length of tooth floss, tuft of cat fur, and ended in a line of most fragile, perfect dust.

'But we'll keep in touch,' Caan was saying. 'You cheer Joan up because you know what she's been through, and she won't have many people to visit her while she's here.'

'If you can be bothered some time,' said Joan. The sheen of her hospital skin wrinkled in a grin.

'You know, right from the very start I had a feeling this was going to be a good day,' said Chatterton. 'It's a sort of Indian summer perhaps.'

'Life is sad though, isn't it?' said Joan. She looked up at him with a terrible openness.

'Oh yes, sad, but not dreary, not lacking purpose. But sad sure enough,' said Chatterton firmly. He went to the protected corner of his small garden and came back with a red rose for Joan; an old English rose, dark and red. 'Old style roses have the true scent,' he said. 'Aren't I right.' She held it to her face. 'Eh?' he said.

'Yes.'

Two white butterflies tumbled in the air above the letter box, and Chatterton smiled, not withdrawing his attention from the car as Caan backed out. 'He's a hard case that one,' said Caan. 'He gave a speech off the cuff at the Rotary meeting you know. Hardly a moment for thought.'

'He's certainly got no singing voice, but he sees through things all right.'

Chatterton waited to see them drive away; not the last-minute shame-faced turning of some people's farewells, as if they feared what might be being said of them. Only his trousers suggested age; crimped at his slender waist and bagging somewhat at the seat the way trousers of old men do. When they were gone Chatterton arched back cautiously, and pressed with the flat of his hand on his stomach. He decided to stay in his garden while he felt so well. Did he tell them he was an athlete once, he wondered. Unthinkingly he kept his arched stance as he tried to remember. All the things he could do then, all the things he could feel. Chatterton could see his dark roses on the fence, and the two ladybirds upside down and closer in the whip tail dust upon the concrete.

The scent of the rose seemed to linger, maybe only in his heart, for he was no longer sure of such distinctions. What would he think of next, he wondered. He would fetch a beer and have it in his garden, because of the extra money and the friends he had made that day. As he turned to go, he had in recollection the sight of the Marlborough hills, and a hawk the colour of a moth against the sea of the sky.

Apirana Taylor

TE TOHUNGA MAKUTU

THIS IS NO FAIRY-TALE, I tell you. Let us remember the ancestors of we Maori were a warrior race who feared nothing but witchcraft. This tale is true. Passed on to me by word of mouth. Perhaps it happened not long ago. To this day, give or take a few years, we Maori have known Christianity for barely a hundred and fifty years.

There lived a tohunga makutu. He was an evil man. And a large man. The largest thing about him was his puku. He lived by slaying people with his magic and eating them. He would then hang the bones of his victims in the trees which surrounded the cave in which he and his wife lived. They'd lived in that cave for a long time and would continue living in that cave for a long time.

Travellers who passed by were first killed by him and then their flesh was cooked and eaten by him and his wife. He had great knowledge of bush lore. He could talk with birds, animals, rivers, the wind, earth and mountains. But his knowledge was deepest in what are known as the black arts. His magic was so powerful none could oppose him.

Villagers who lived in the area hated and feared this tohunga. Not only did he slay passers-by, but he also often demanded that one of the villagers be delivered to him. It was never long before that villager was devoured and the bones hung outside in the trees. Where they would clitter and clatter in the wind.

The villagers reasoned they could ill spare adult life, as this was needed to dig the gardens, catch the fish and protect them from enemies. So it was often the youngest and tenderest of their children who was delivered to the tohunga makutu.

Bones and gristle littered the cave floor. His wife used skulls for her pots. There were bones scattered and strewn about the track that led to his cave. And from every branch on every tree, bones dangled and swayed in the breeze. Click click clicking together. There were so many bones that if you walked there, you'd think you were in a forest of bones.

The villagers tried all they could to rid themselves of this man's reign. They asked tohunga who used their magic and expertise for good to help them. But no one was powerful enough to overcome him. The good tohunga had their own bones cut up and made into flutes and trinkets.

The villagers' champion warriors tried to kill him. They all failed and were never seen again. And at night the villagers were further tormented by the sound of the bones of yet another of their loved ones, clicking in the wind.

Finally a young man decided he must kill this tohunga makutu because all the villagers nearby who were related to the young man were being killed and also the tohunga had recently killed the young man's father.

At night, he decided, I will sneak into the cave and surprise this ngarangara, this insect, with my patu. I'll club his brains out before he can cast a spell. He left for the cave armed only with his taiaha and patu. He was afraid but not of hand-to-hand combat. He was afraid he'd be slain by witchcraft. The desire for utu, revenge, moved him on.

The wind and bones were still and silent as though they waited for something to happen.

As he approached the cave he recognized his father's bones dangling from a branch just above the track. He cut the bones down and could not stop weeping.

'My son,' said the bones. 'Don't stay here. Don't go into the cave. Go away from here. Quickly.' His father's warning made the boy more determined to kill the tohunga. But he didn't get a chance to use his patu.

The tohunga knew he'd come. He used his magic to overpower the boy. When he discovered who his next victim was, he was delighted. For this boy's father had cursed the tohunga with his dying breath, saying, 'My descendants will use your head as a container for their fish hooks.' He therefore took a number of days to skin this boy alive so that in front of the bones of the victim's father he was able to torture the father's spirit beyond the grave.

Then he cut up the boy, bones and all, and fed the pieces to his pet dog. Only after the young warrior stopped screaming did the god of mercy come in the silence and allow the boy death's relief.

Perhaps it is a blessing death comes to us all. But it wasn't a blessing for the tohunga makutu. His power was not strong enough to fight off death. As he aged he was tormented by the fact he knew what would happen to him when he died. His last great act was to slay his wife and eat her.

When the villagers heard the tohunga makutu was dying they rushed to the cave and killed his children and ate them in front of him. The villagers laughed and told the tohunga that they would soon kill him. But first they gathered the bones of their loved ones and wept over them.

As they did this the tohunga saw that soon his brains would be eaten by these people and in time fern would grow from his pito. He began a cursing chant with which he could slay the villagers but they realized what he was doing and they killed him before he finished his song. They crunched up all his bones except his skull, and scattered the bone powder throughout the land. This was done so the bones could never join again and the tohunga return.

The villagers used the dried head of the tohunga makutu as a container for their fish hooks. And for years heaped their anger, hatred and insults on his head. In order to curse the man's memory and torture his soul.

Sue McCauley

from OTHER HALVES

TUG CHOSE TO REMAIN in bed, where he had spent the whole day, and declined to eat. Over the steak Liz told Jim about the homeless boy she had met at Valleyview and now taken in. Sitting across from Jim, watching him scrape aside his mushrooms (of course, she ought to have asked) with a delicacy which proclaimed pedigree, she could believe it was that straightforward. Jim found her story unremarkable. He was accustomed to the dispensing of good deeds. His mother, he told Liz a little wearily, used to do Meals on Wheels.

He showed more enthusiasm over the discovery that she had been a psychiatric inmate. From his questions she realized that the possibility of madness lent, for him, an edge of mystique.

When they had eaten and were sitting in separate chairs in front of the fire, Tug breezed through the room and into the kitchen to slice and butter himself a piece of bread. She had earlier put his grimy clothes to soak and now he was wrapped jauntily in Liz's pink chenille dressing gown. On his return trip she introduced him to Jim who extended his hand with a conspicuously affable hello. Tug paused, glowered and moved on, slamming the bedroom door behind him.

'What did I do?'

'Nothing. I have a feeling that was aimed at me.'

'Are you sure you know what you're doing. I mean, is it safe for you . . .?'

'He's only a child,' she said.

'He looks capable of looking after himself to me.'

'Did you look after yourself at sixteen?'

'That's hardly the point, Liz. How long's he going to stay?'

'I don't know. I suppose until he finds somewhere.' She felt defensive. Good causes ought to manifest themselves as cherubic waifs pale with gratitude.

'You know,' said Jim, conversationally, changing the subject, 'I've never really known any Maoris. Not personally. There just never were any in my particular circle of friends and acquaintances.'

'Then I wouldn't take Tug as representative. They come in all shapes and moods.' She had meant it to sound wry but it came out tart, a rebuke. Jim, she thought, looks at Tug and sees not Tug but a Maori. Tug looks at Jim and sees not Jim but a dick-head. Obviously it simplified things greatly for both of them. Were the complications simply her own invention?

She tried to retrieve the threads of earlier conversations, but an uneasiness remained. It was as if, Liz thought, they were being watched. Then she realized with dismay that this was possibly true. The house was old and the door to Tug's room had a keyhole. As if in defiance of the same possibility Jim moved his chair closer to Liz and took her hand onto his lap.

Tug appeared on cue. He swayed across the room, purposefully nonchalant, and positioned himself in front of the bookcase. Jim's voice tailed off limply in the middle of a memory of boarding-school humiliations. Tug studied the book titles.

'Are you looking for something in particular?' She asked him brightly, a nervous student teacher.

Tug turned to look at them. 'One with screwing in it.'

Liz felt herself, absurdly, blushing. 'Try Henry Miller,' she said, not looking at Jim. 'Second shelf to your left. The black cover.'

He found the book and thumbed through the pages sourly. 'Bet it's slack.' But he took it with him back to the bedroom.

Jim suddenly remembered his need for an early night.

'I'm sorry about . . .' Liz nodded towards Tug's door.

Jim shrugged. 'I just wonder if you know what you're letting yourself in for.'

She walked to the gate with him. He invited her to go with him to an exhibition opening on the following Saturday, and brushed her lips in a dry kiss.

She confronted Tug in his bedroom. 'This is my home and I won't have you being rude to my friends.'

'Whaddid I do?' Looking up at her in injured innocence.

'You know.'

'Aren't I allowed to read your books or something? Is that it? Stink book anyway.' He tossed it onto the floor. She left it where it was.

'You're a toad,' she said, but no longer angry. 'And I don't think you'll make it to a prince.'

'What's that mean?'

'I'm too tired,' she said, 'to explain.'

Tug spent almost all of that week in bed. When Liz left in the mornings he would be asleep and when she got home from work he would still be in bed, listlessly thumbing through a magazine or simply staring up at the ceiling. If he got up for dinner – and he had little appetite – they'd talk in a polite and almost formal fashion. His manner wasn't so much guarded as apathetic. After a few attempts at jollying him Liz let him be, telling herself that such apparently bleak inactivity must be fulfilling some need in him. And, even lying listless and silent in bed, he provided a certain reassurance, was a bulwark against the mindless panic. Someone to come home to.

On the Friday Ken drove her, in her lunch-break, to the lawyer's office where their separation was to be made official. She was allotted a third of the proceeds from the sale of their house if and when it was sold. A generous agreement, the solicitor said, the courts would probably have allowed her less.

'I gather this is an amicable separation? Good. And there is no problem about access? No? Right. If you wish to attempt a reconciliation and renew conjugal relationships but then resume living apart that will not be considered a breach of legal separation.'

So still nothing was final. The game went on. Did she want or didn't she want? This pretence that people had a choice.

She let Ken do the talking, suspecting anyway that he and the solicitor had some kind of prior understanding from which she was excluded. She signed the papers thinking ruefully of the Treaty of Waitangi. How could you ever know the magnitude of what you were signing away?

'Perhaps we've got time for a celebratory drink,' Ken suggested, back in the car.

'I don't exactly feel like celebrating.'

'I still can't understand you.' He edged the car out of its parking space. 'I never did, all those years.'

She was tempted to say sourly, You never tried, but she knew it took two, and how hard had *she* tried? Besides, she felt an absolute need to have the whole marriage parcelled up nicely and prettily.

'I'm not sorry, Ken,' she said. 'I mean I don't regret all those years. I did love you.'

Ken was watching the car ahead. It had a sticker which said JESUS OUR ONLY HOPE. 'I've thought about that quite a lot. The truth is I didn't love you, Liz. I don't think I ever did.' He was still watching the car with the sticker.

Liz felt numbed with the pain of it. Eleven years of her life flushed down a toilet bowl. 'What a pity you didn't think to tell me sooner,' she said limply, looking at the people on the footpath who could not know that she had just been stabbed in the conjugal back.

'I think it's best to be honest about it,' he said.

'Oh yes,' she said, 'much the best.' She thought about people who died laughing.

'I mean what sort of shit is he? Maybe he's just bitter, d'you think? But he really seemed to mean it. It must be true then? All those years. I was just the cook and the cleaner and the bloody laundrymaid. Very convenient. Oh, it must have been more than that. No it probably wasn't. He didn't lose. He's got Michael. He's got his fancy women. But what was the point of saying it? Why couldn't he have just pretended at the end. Oh God.'

Tug jerked her wrist savagely towards him. 'Shut up,' he roared. 'For fucksake shut up. It's over, okay? There's no point in stirring it round and round. You're screwed in the head I reckon.'

Liz tried with her left hand to prise his fingers from her wrist. 'At least,' she said venomously, 'I manage to get out of bed.'

Tug rolled his eyes sardonically, but released her arm. 'If you don't mind leaving the room,' he said, 'I'd like to get dressed.'

She lay on her own bed, afraid that he would leave her, listening to his footsteps. He came to the doorway sniffing at his armpits. 'Even smells clean,' he said of his jersey, pleased. He tossed her wallet onto the bed. 'I've taken some money.'

'Help yourself.' As sarcasm it was indifferent.

'Thanks, I have.'

She heard him slam the back door and pad down the path.

She lay on the bed and thought about mental cruelty and degrees of mental cruelty and whether there was something about her that invited it, and why. Then she heard him come back, knowing it was Tug for who else on these bleak winter nights travelled in bare feet?

He came straight to her bedroom and spread a feast beside

her. Fish and chips steaming, a bottle of sherry, a bottle of whisky. He beamed as he opened the packets.

'Tug,' she protested, 'we couldn't afford whisky.'

'Only paid for the sherry. And the greasies. Here's your change. Go on, count it.'

'We'll take the whisky back. Later. I'll come with you.'

'Fuck off. It's a present. I got it for you.'

'But you didn't pay for it.'

'So what? Maybe I did and maybe I didn't.'

'I know you didn't.'

'If we take it back they'll book me.'

'I don't think so.'

'Jesus. Don't be thick. I got a record. Jus' say thank you and take it.'

She took it. He went for glasses and she prepared a speech.

'Tug, while you live here no more stealing, okay? It's just not on.'

He poured them each a sherry. 'Liz, while I live here no more crying and moaning your arse off, okay?'

'You need some shoes,' she said. 'We'll have to get you some shoes. Your feet must be freezing.' She reached to touch them. 'They are.'

'Last winter I had gumboots. I kept them on all the time so's they wouldn't get nicked and there wasn't nowhere to take a bath and when in the end I took them off I had weedy feet.'

She laughed. 'What do you mean, weedy?'

'There was weeds growing on them. Fungus stuff. True.'

They wrapped themselves in rugs against the cold and kept refilling the glasses until Ken no longer mattered. Raking out memories of his mother Tug said, matter-of-fact, 'Since she died you're the only person who's loved me.'

She was astonished. 'How do you know I love you?'

'But you do, don't you?'

'I suppose so.' Hedging it even then and amazed that anyone

could expose himself so incautiously to rejection. With a certain shame she sifted his words for motive. Were they as innocent and trusting as it seemed? Was he trying to trap her into some kind of emotional obligation?

Later, he asked, 'Why do you stare at me so much?'

She was embarrassed. 'Do I?'

'You're always staring at me.'

She said, truthfully, 'Then it's because I think you're pretty. I mean I like looking at you. I suppose I envy you. Brown skin looks so much better than white skin. That's a fact, whatever people may say. It seems a bit unfair really.' She registered the unintended pun, but it didn't seem worth spelling out.

Tug studied the colour of the back of his hand judiciously. 'Yeah, you're right. That's why I only look at you when I really have to.'

The lady artist wore gold satin pants and high leather boots, her hair was straight, glossy black, her husband wealthy and old. She overshadowed her paintings which were abstracts in blues and purples and splotches of brown. If you joined them all together the paintings would have looked almost identical to the material of a dress Liz had bought from Kirkcaldies when she was nineteen. She had loved that dress, and at nineteen she would also have loved the exhibition opening and the party which followed when a selected few of them adjourned to the home of the lady artist.

At nineteen Liz had been a devoted admirer of the world and its people. She was continuously delighted by her amazing good fortune in knowing and meeting so many entertaining, talented and charming individuals. And here she was, deja-vuing in the same circles. But the familiarity lacked pleasure, she stood awkward in her black dress, remote and disengaged. She was not overlooked; her association with Jim lent her prestige and besides she was a new face and a fresh audience.

A plump little man with fleshy lips proffered a bowl of peanuts.

'I'm a criminal lawyer. You can take that however you like.'

'I believe you,' she said.

He laughed with his teeth protruding like a horse and gave a sweep of his hand. 'Did you ever see so much intellectual wankery?'

She smiled dutifully. He thrust his face towards hers. 'You wouldn't like a quick fumble in the spare bedroom I don't suppose?'

'No thanks.'

'Then you won't mind if I try elsewhere?'

She shook her head. He bowed and moved away.

Jim was in a corner being whispered at by the lady artist. A young woman warned Liz that there was a lot of bad acid being circulated these days, a young reporter boasted that he had never set foot on a rugby field, then a middle-aged man recited a poem about manuka bushes to the whole room. Leonard Cohen gloomed from the stereo speakers, joints passed from hand to hand.

A toothy woman in a caftan complained piercingly about the increasing number of louts in the city square, and Liz wondered if Tug was at home or out louting. The little lawyer was put in mind of a party he was once at where loutish males forced one of their women to lie on the table amid the beer flagons while they removed her knickers and shoved a saveloy up her. Then the men shared the saveloy. It was a most successful story. The toothy woman proclaimed it epitomized the average New Zealander. Someone else asked the lawyer if he liked saveloys and he smiled enigmatically. 'That's nothing compared to their gang initiation rites,' said another.

Liz moved away, less in disgust than anger. She felt, obscurely and drunkenly, defiled on Tug's behalf. She had a picture of herself standing, immobilized, with each foot on a separate iceberg and those icebergs incompatible and drifting apart. At some point, she warned herself, she would have to choose.

Jim was still wedged in the corner with the booted lady. He was tracing shapes on his hand, explaining something, with a frown of concentration. The artist's hand was nestled in Jim's crotch. She was smiling. Liz made her way quietly up the sumptuous passage and rang for a cab.

Tug was in bed. Checking on that, she stumbled against the doorpost.

'You're drunk.'

'A bit. Were you asleep? Shall I put the light on?'

'If you want. How was the party?'

'Awful. Full of stupid people.'

'Dick-head bring you home?'

'No. I got a taxi.'

'You left him there?'

'He seemed quite happy.'

'You left before it finished?'

She wanted to explain that she had chosen her iceberg and that the choosing had opened up another dimension of possibility which had seemed both shocking and inevitable. Coming home in the taxi she had made herself an unthinkable promise. Now she took a deep breath and dragged back the words that were cowardly fleeing from her mind.

'Tug, I'd like to sleep with you.'

He just looked at her, eyes widened.

'Well?' she snapped it out. The waiting was unendurable.

He squirmed beneath the blankets. 'I'm not sure what you mean.'

'Oh God,' she pleaded. 'I mean what you think I mean. Just say yes or no.' Her courage had abandoned her, she wanted to retract, deny, pass out.

He pulled the blankets up to his eyes and said something muffled from beneath them.

'I couldn't hear,' she said helplessly.

He lowered the blankets to chin level. 'No,' he said clearly.

The embarrassment was smothered in relief and a sudden sobriety. 'I'm sorry Tug. I'm really sorry. I should never have said it. You're quite right. We'll forget it. Okay? Everything just like it was.'

He nodded without conviction.

At breakfast Tug was polite and watchful. Liz was polite and regretful.

'Are you hungry?'

'No thank you.'

'There's some bacon?'

'No. Really, I'm not hungry.'

'But you'll have a cup of tea? I'm just making one.'

'A cup of tea. All right. If you're making one.'

'Michael's coming today. I thought he'd be here before now.'

'Might go out for a while. See some of the boys.'

'That's a good idea. You haven't been out for days. Shall I keep dinner for you?'

'Don't worry. I'm not sure what time I'll be back.'

I've frightened him away, she thought. I've betrayed his trust.

In the bathroom mirror she reminded her reflection that she was old. Her gums were receding, her skin was loosening. There were furrows and crow's-feet. She was old enough, as he'd once pointed out, to be his mother.

She wanted her times with Michael to be gentle with shared laughter and affectionate gestures, but there was an awkwardness between them. She wanted to explain, atone, be forgiven, but Michael watched her with veiled eyes remembering (she thought) her weeping past.

She walked with him to the park, aware that Ken had the car and access to more exciting diversions. He told her about the air-force bomber he had under construction at home; his hardest model yet. She listened but did not comprehend. Michael was a small encyclopaedia of weaponry and warfare.

At home again they made gingerbread men and he talked about their plans to move north. 'Won't you miss me?' she pleaded. 'I s'pose so,' he said, looking down at the table. After tea he watched out the window for Ken's car coming to take him home.

At midnight she was woken from a dream about Toothless Neddy in a soldier's uniform crouching injured in a barn. She went to answer the phone. Did she wish, the operator asked, to accept a collect call from a Mr Morton in Dunedin? *Dunedin?*

'Liz?' He sounded anxious. 'Liz, I'm in . . . hangon . . .' She heard him open a door and ask, 'Hey, whassa name of this place?'

'Dunedin,' she said when he returned.

'Yeah, that's right. Always forget names.'

'What are you doing in Dunedin?'

'Nothing much. Standing in a phone box.'

'I meant . . . well how did you get there?'

'Drove down. Me and some of the boys. In this Holden. I drove from Timaru.'

'Whose car is it?'

'One of the boys.'

'He owns it?'

'He found it. Finders keepers doncha know?' He laughed. 'Mightn't be home for a few days so I's ringing to let you know.'

'Like how many days?' Wishing she didn't need to ask, wondering if in Dunedin it emerged as a plea or a threat.

'Not too many.' He was being reassuring, paternal. 'I'll be home by next weekend, okay? You won't give my bed to anyone?'

A whole week.

'I might,' she said off-handedly. 'It depends.'

An instant reaction. 'Go ahead then. I probably won't be coming back anyway.'

'As you like.' But she allowed him the satisfaction of being first to hang up.

'I was really tired so I just thought I'd slip away on the quiet. I didn't want to mess up your evening. It just didn't occur to me that you'd be upset about it.'

Sitting in the Grand Hotel with its red leather upholstery and mahogany-stained tables Liz thought how easy it was to be sophisticated when you didn't really care.

On Monday she had decided there was little point in her continuing to see Jim. But this was Thursday and Tug had not come home and her resolve seemed perhaps a little hasty. Jim had been away attending an Indigenous Culture seminar in Palmerston North. He had told her about it, he said, though she had no recollection and would she have forgotten something as portentous as an Indigenous Culture seminar? Anyway here he was buying her drinks and almost nervously explaining that his association with Elly, painter of blue and purple abstracts, was a matter of ambition on her side and reluctance on his.

'You don't need to explain,' Liz told him. 'I don't own you. I don't want that kind of involvement.'

She could see that he was impressed, that her indifference attracted him. She felt ashamed of herself, yet after he had called at the coffee bar that morning to invite her for drinks she had made a deliberate decision to be encouraging. Jim was politeness, conversation, *normality*. When (if) Tug returned her role would be more clearly defined if Jim was around. No more embarrassing lapses.

She watched him walk across to the bar to refill their glasses. He walked with such confidence. Her mother would like him.

From across the room the plump lawyer caught Liz's eye and waved. Liz waved back, smiling. It was so easy to be acceptable.

She'd been home an hour when the phone went. She ran to answer it. A wrong number. But it was natural to be worried, she thought. He could have been arrested. The car might have crashed. Both seemed more probabilities than possibilities.

If he was dead she wouldn't be notified — they'd track down some next-of-kin. For her he would just have disappeared.

She switched on the radio and waited for the hourly news bulletin and the names of road fatality victims. There were none.

Friday night. A car slowed down on the street; all evening cars had been passing and slowing, but this one had no muffler. Liz went on reading but the words were just words on their own and would not link into sentences. The car stopped. Definitely it had stopped. There were shouts and a slamming of doors, then the car drove off again. She began again at the beginning of the sentence; the street was full of houses expecting visitors.

The door was locked and he hammered on it with unnecessary force. Liz got out of bed and went to open it, remembering how much he could irritate her.

'You was in bed?' He smelt of beer.

'It's quite late.'

She went back to the bedroom, he followed her and stood leaning against the wall.

'You glad I'm back?'

'Well, I'm glad you're still alive anyway.'

'You was worried?'

'I suppose the car was stolen?'

'It was and it wasn't. Fat Boy paid the deposit. Only under another name.'

'What did you do down there?'

'Nothing much. Just mucked about. They wouldn't let us in at the prison.'

'But you had a good time?'

'Not really,' he said. 'I's homesick.'

She was going to laugh, but she saw he meant it. 'Well, you're home now,' she said.

He looked past her at the window with its curtains drawn and she knew in a curdling instant what he was about to say.

'You remember the other night, what you said . . . Did you mean it?'

'I was drunk.' Her cowardliness shamed her. 'Yes, I meant it.'

He was crouching beside the bed holding her hand. The whole of her was a hand being held. His face was hidden against the bedspread; when he raised it his eyes seemed huge. Blue eyes, she thought, were intrusive, they invaded you. Brown eyes looked inward; they went deep, you could float in them. Possibly drown.

At eleven Liz had been religious. She had planned to be a missionary in some dark tropical land tending the sparrow-legged bulbous-bellied children who had eyes like Tug's eyes. She longed for selfless dedication and righteous anger. She wrote to Trevor Huddleston, care of his publishers, but he was no doubt too busy to reply.

Her mother sang in the Anglican church choir on Sundays, but Liz was privately scornful of her mother's style of religion – social introductions, descant harmony and a Sunday spiritual inoculation. The daughter waited to be overcome by some dark, tumultuous force; she longed for surrender and dedication and intensity. The feeling was strong in her that she had been Chosen, yet she hesitated, wanting confirmation; a sign; however small. She created opportunities for this to happen beyond the bounds of coincidence, but when no bushes burned, no telegraph poles split in two and the messages of the clouds remained obscure she finally lost interest.

She committed herself then to Ralph and his various successors – stray cats and broken birds. A few died but most of them recovered. The birds flew away or stayed around the home as semi-pets; the cats she took eventually to the S.P.C.A. where they were probably destroyed. Liz was aware of this likelihood but remained committed to tending her ailing strays.

After a time her spiritual aspirations began to seem nothing more than a childish phase. Watching her battered birds flap off awkwardly into the suburban skies she would tell herself that if there was some infinite truth this was it and it was beyond question or comprehension – just *there* like the hillside, like the sea.

And sometimes when she was alone, out riding Delilah, entranced by the shape of her horse's ears and the fall of her mane, she would get a sensation of pure happiness. Although the feeling itself was beyond description it was accompanied by a vague sensation of thirst. For herself she defined it as rapture. She had no doubt it had something to do with that infinite truth.

And now, absurdly, with Tug's hands and mouth moving over her body she thought of religion. She remembered the sharpness of her longing for intensity and surrender and she recognized that incomparably exquisite thirst. *Of course*, she thought. *Of course*.

He was shameless. He presented his body as a chef might present his finest cuisine, confident that every morsel – every hair, every pucker and crevice – was delicious and desirable. And gradually, as he explored her own body without permission or hesitation she felt three decades of caution and apprehension crumble and fall away. For the first time in her life she felt unreservedly – well, *almost* unreservedly – lovable.

They lay tight in each other's arms.

'What are you thinking?' she whispered, feeling that dull thirstiness all through her.

'I's thinking what a lot of time we wasted.'

'That was your fault; you turned me down.'

'I's scared. I mean you're sort of . . .'

'Like your mother?'

'Not now you're not.'

She laughed. 'So what happens now?'

'We start again.'

'I meant . . . I won't regret it,' she told him. 'Whatever happens I could never regret it.'

She woke at eight, exultant. She felt as she had felt after the birth of her children – permanently, cataclysmically altered. She had looked at the clock before she fell asleep and it said half-past five. Tug had fallen asleep about an hour before her, his arms still tight around her. When she slid a hand down over his buttocks he had thrust against her even in his sleep. Now, remembering that, she grinned to herself wanting him to wake so she could tell him.

He was buried beneath the bedclothes. She pulled them down carefully, wanting to look at his face. Unveiling it like a national treasure. His eyes flickered then opened wide and he grabbed at the bedclothes and pulled them back over his head.

'Tug?'

'I thought it was a dream,' muffled through the blankets.

'It wasn't, and you can't stay under there forever.'

He lowered the blankets slowly, fearfully, to make her laugh.

'What happens now?' he asked when they reached his chin.

'I guess we make the most of it while it lasts.'

'How long d'y' reckon we'll last?'

She thought about it. In her experience euphoria had never been more than momentary. 'Two weeks?' she ventured in wild optimism.

'I'd say nearer two months.'

She shook her head.

'Two months,' he repeated. 'D'you wanna bet? Two dollars, ay?'

'I don't want to bet.'

'Come on,' he urged, grinning already at his own joke. 'Make it a bit interesting.'

She cuffed at his head but he ducked. His face grew solemn. 'You wanna know something?'

'What?' Anxiety welled.

'It wasn't me who had the weedy feet. It was Bones.'

Keri Hulme

TE KAIHAU/THE WINDEATER

Lies and Reflections

THERE IS

a sandbank somewhere at the end of Earth where ocean stops and welkin stops and the winds of the world come to rest. They are chancy beings, like their cousins the Fates, and prone to sudden inhuman boisterousness – which stands to reason; they have never claimed to be human. Indeed, they affect to despise us and almost anything to do with us. Someone got under their guard though, once. They became aunties.

I thought I'd begin like this rather than by saying, I was born and now I'm dying. That's so commonplace, and we know everybody does it. What I want to do is lay before you the unusual and irrational bits from my life because they may make a pattern in retrospect and, besides, they are the only bits that make sense to me right now.

For instance, I made the mistake of asking my granny on *her* deathbed whether her best story was true. Her best story went like this:

'There I was, not quite sixteen and your mother just due to come into the world and all alone, because your grand-dad had gone

across the river with a barefoot horse and the river had flooded
and he couldn't get back. I was greatly in pain and terrified that I
wouldn't be able to help myself and maybe the babe would die
before it lived ... at the worst moment, when it felt like your
mother was going to be jammed in me forever and I could do
nothing about it except sweat and scream, at that moment there
was a light. Now, you must understand that we didn't have the
electricity and it had been early afternoon when I began to labour
and my labour had gone on deep into the night; I had lit no
lamps and the range had long gone out. Today I'd say someone
switched a light on: then, I thought the moon had come to visit.
As well as the light, there was a sweet low voice, a man's voice,
saying "Not to worry, girlie, she'll be right."'

My granny would shake her head in wonder at this point.

'How did he *know*, the man with gentle hands? That it'd be your
mother coming into the world and not some boy-child? Anyway,
my pain all went away and your mother came smiling into life.
And I saw that the light in the room came from the glory round
the man and though he said he was a horse-doctor, I knew him
for one of the Lordly Folk and wasn't this proved when the shawl
he gave the baby for a welcoming gift melted away when she
turned a year old?'

Well, I never had an answer for that question, never having seen
the shawl (or much of my mother for that matter). I grew up
curious about granny's story though, because she never had another
like it – just dour little morals ill-disguised as tales. So, I asked her
on her deathbed, was it true? Lordly Folk and shining faces and
that? And she frowned, and whispered huskily, 'What would you
tell your man when he came home distraught and found you
cleaned and peaceful and the baby wrapped in a silken shawl?

What would you tell anyone? The terrible truth?' Then she sniffed, and died.

That has always been my trouble, you see. I have always asked the wrong questions and I have always got answers. Now I would ask her, Did he have redbrown skin faintly luminous, like the moon shining through a carnelian? Were his eyes so black that you only saw the lightning crackling in them? Was there some small thing malformed about him, a finger too many or a discolouration of skin?

It is four decades too late to ask her anything. You could try a question in the next couple of hours, though.

Behind Every Wayward Action Stands a Wayward Angel

I was a plump happy baby. I smiled at my unsmiling mother and chuckled wetly and merrily when she cried. I smiled at everybody, I smiled at the whole world. I thought life was a whole lot of fun. It was just as well I got smiling over and done with then.

The first thing I remember is something everyone says I shouldn't, because I was too young – eleven months old and just starting to walk. Nobody was keeping an eye on me out in my playpen on the lawn, nobody thought they needed to keep an eye on me. My mother was in the kitchen or wash-house, keening to herself (probably); my Dad was knackering another unfortunate horse (probably), and my granny hadn't come to live with us yet.

Now, the lawn was comfortably warm and I was chewing happily through an earthworm. I remember, vividly, the gritty brownish insides and the moist pink skin and the wriggle. Suddenly, there was a shadow and two cool redbrown hands and a marvellous trustworthy voice (you bet your life eleven-month-old babies know a trustworthy voice when they hear one) saying 'Ka kite te taniwha, e pepe?'

Well, that meant buggerall to me but I drooled earthworm

charmingly and nodded hard, indicating I was all ready to go or whatever. All I recall next is strong gentle dark arms carrying me through the sunshine, bringing me to a waterlit place. 'Titiro!'

Can water both sink and burgeon at the same time? It was waterspout and whirlpool, a great green helix of live water, anaconda parading through its own massive and vibrantly-splendid coils, spooling and rising and falling, spooling and rising and melding.

'He taniwha, ne?'

said the beautiful trustworthy voice, just before the gentle arms opened and dropped me in.

Looking Like a Looking Glass

I don't remember anything else until I was ten or so. The rest of my childhood might as well have never happened. I am told that I stopped smiling. I grew into a large overly-toothy blundering child who lurched through life inviting adult snarls and blows until a teacher discovered I was legally blind.

Whoa back. Legally blind is not at all the same as the real thing. While I was an eye-cripple, unable to recognize people or hills or my own hands at the end of my arms, as soon as I got glasses I could see, more or less; I could make out what adults meant when they maundered on about birds or views (or light-bulbs, for that matter). While it was a nice surprise to discover such things at the age of seven, it had two curious effects on the way I looked at the world. One was, I never quite believed what I saw.

For instance, if I look in a mirror I see someone of average height and twice average weight with cloudy no-colour eyes and pale brown skin. As for my hair:

Granny: 'Your mother had fine silky seal-brown hair and I had fine silky seal-brown hair and your grand-dad

(God rest him) had fine silky seal-brown hair so where did those corkscrew red things come from?'

(Give her her due, she never looked at my father when she said this, who had fine silky coal-black hair anyway.)

But the person in the mirror isn't me as I *know* me. Many people have this feeling. If you look in mirrors, reflections is all you see ... true, but my feeling carries beyond mirrors. I look at a mountain I have looked at a thousand times before and think, Did that peak always look like that? Wasn't it a little sharper last time? And hasn't that bluff shifted slightly to the south?

The second effect of the belated discovery of short-sightedness was this: I know what I see (I think) but I'm quite prepared to acknowledge and believe someone else sees the same thing very differently – and that a third party sees something else again. Seeing is not necessarily believing: seeing is a matter of faith in sight.

If you look in mirrors, you might see someone else.

Moonshickered

The house we lived in (until my granny died there, and my Dad and me moved out) was old. It mumbled to itself on dark nights. There were places on the back verandah that were dangerous for even a child to walk on, and none of the doors would shut because the joists and rafters had sagged. Outside, there was a garden as old as the house, and as well looked after. In fact, telling where the garden ended and the scramble of bush and swamp began was difficult. Two things helped: whoever had planted the garden had loved redhot pokers, and a rough perimeter of them resurfaced each spring; close to the creek, was an orchard, unpruned and lichenous but still producing fruit. A child told not to go into the bush could find helpful patterns of apples and pears, rotten or ripe, defining boundaries. A child was frequently told not to go into the bush. Granny did not like the bush. Maybe it arose from the fact that my grand-dad had wandered away into it and never reappeared. Maybe it was because she had spent most of her life helping to hack farms from the bush, and she thought it resented her, and hers. Whatever the reason, my granny had unpleasant ways of ensuring a child did what it was told, so I was grateful to the orchard and the kniphofia. Particularly to the former one memorable evening.

I was eleven and had been in the bush all day (I'll tell you why later). Come moonrise, I knew I was late getting home and that my granny would have searched the garden. I knew she would be waiting. I knew my Dad wouldn't be home.

Thinking back, from the vantage point of 30 years on, it was an uneasy light. There was the red hugeness of the moon swelling above the trees. There was the rotten-ripe air of the evening. There was my fraught state of mind. So the boy standing in the shadows swishing a stick through the air and matching its whistle with his own may not have necessarily been there (except I saw him plain as in daylight). I remember him as tall, with broad shoulders arrowing down to a slender waist, and I remember thinking it was the hunter's moon that made his hair and eyes both so black and so bright, and his skin so palpably red.

I looked warily at him and he tossed the stick to me and whistled, and tossed an apple to me and whistled, and I frowned at both for a moment until, in some atavistic corner of my brain, a thought formed, an old old thought.

Next moment I was excitedly gathering a skirtful of grub-rich apples, and *next* moment, hurrying home.

Incidentally, 'unthinking' is the only word I know to describe that state of atavistic *knowing*, but 'moonshickered' fits pretty well what happened next.

When my granny said coldly from the back verandah, 'Well madam, where have we been and how are we going to explain it?' I giggled. I sat down ten feet away and fitted an apple to the stick and flicked it and it sped with bruising force to spatter squashily all over granny. Her howl of outrage was matched by my squealing laughter, her movement towards me by two more speedy apples. I kept up a barrage of apples and laughter and she retreated into the house.

O that cider smell fizzing in my nostrils! And laughter rising in pitch to become ululation as twenty thousand wild and battle-happy ancestors rose out of their dark and joined me hurling apples and jigging under the bloody moon.

When Dad came home, there were shattered windows and apple splatters and smears everywhere and his mother-in-law cowering pale-faced and shaking inside and his maenad daughter raging redfaced and shrieking with laughter outside.

My granny and I declared a truce thereafter.

The old old thought I had was called 'atlatl', but that's not as helpful as 'moonshickered' is it?

Jokes of Gods and Whims of Ancestors

My granny finally died when I was 18. She took a long time about it. She had a stroke (unfortunately she was making porridge at the time and dropped onto our coal range) (Dad found her) (I found Dad) that disabled her from doing everything a human does, except talk. There was another question I asked her on her deathbed: Where do you come from? 'I'm a Celt,' she replied with an ancient and unknowable pride.

Well, her accent was odd, could've been Irish or Scots or maybe anything else. All in all, she didn't tell me much at all. (Of course, now I'd know to ask who her mother was, who her father was . . .)

My Dad wasn't much help with the matter of ancestry either. When asked about his mother-in-law to wit his wife to wit my mother, he said, 'Dunno much except the old bloke came from Cornwall.'

It was a bit tender to approach my Dad on the subject as to

where *he* came from, who *his* parents were, because he'd been brought up in an orphanage. He knew he was part-Maori (so did Granny, who made sour snide little comments about that), and at some time during his orphanage years he'd been taught the language. He didn't tell it to me – or rather, he told an infinitesimal amount to me.

Because when as a 13-year-old, newly gone to high school, I finally plucked up courage to ask him, 'Dad um, about your Maori side, our Maori side, *my* Maori side . . .?' he smiled tightly and said, and wrote down for me so I couldn't mistake the answers to my questions Who are You and Where do You come from?

'Ko Pakatewhainau te iwi, no Wheatewhakaawi.'

I made the mistake of saying that out loud out proud at school.

All the Smiling Faces Lonely People Keep on Walls

Photographs make up a large part of some people's lives. They will grin at old photos, weep before portraits, relive days so long ago they are turned sepia and curly at the corners. They keep their friends on the mantelpiece and their relatives in albums that would smell musty, only the leaves are turned so very often they smell of sweat and finger-grease and tears.

They prefer to talk to pictures because you can make the perfect answers back.

That doesn't quite apply to my father.

He is largely a silent man and I think I have conveyed that he couldn't care less about dead family. I think he loved my mother (who left him just after I was rescued from seeing the taniwha). I know he loves *me* which is not as reassuring as it might ordinarily be.

You see, he is a knacker, a horse butcher. Somebody has got to do the job, sure. My father is, I understand (never having seen him at work), gentle and dispassionate and thoroughly efficient. No horse, I understand, ever goes terrified to its death in my father's yard; no owner of a horse has ever made a complaint about the way my father treats the dead horses he sometimes has to collect. In fact, most of them hand him photographs of their beasts in their heyday, ears pricked forward, eyes liquidly ashine and alert.

If the owners of the horses he kills, or retrieves, don't give him a photograph, he takes one himself before the creatures are dead or are seen to be dead. He lives in two rooms above his knackery. The walls of the rooms are covered with many thousand photographs of horses. He is surrounded by horses, equine sad looks, equine glad looks, equine sighs and equine laughs.

My father loves horses much more than he does humans but I rather hope he will put my photo in some small spare space soon.

An Episode of Bagmoths

I spent as much time in the bush as I could as a child because I was looking for rare insects, maybe ones no one had ever found before. O the sadness when I found one . . .

Now, when you're very shortsighted, you only see what is immediately in front of your nose. I early became aware of things that writhed oozily or scuttled away on a fringe of legs. When I learned to read, I read voraciously – but only about insects. They were my fascination and comfort and path to future fame (I thought).

We have many splendid and curious small creatures, from giraffe-weevils to astelia moths. There is such a range with so many bizarrely-beautiful life-cycles, that I should have grown up into a happy-ever-after entomologist.

I was 12. I had a collection of moths that would make a lepidopterist sweat with pleasure but it lacked something that, while not in itself a rarity, was very rare in an undamaged state.

Are you familiar with the work of an Australian cartoonist, Mary Leunig? Her art is generally macabrely, bitterly, funny, but there is one where the humour is relatively gentle. It shows a young male moth with gaudy wings standing by a suitcase and looking at his watch. On the wall behind him is a skinny bagmoth case — his own. There is also a fat wriggling case — the woman, of course, late as usual in getting ready you think, and grin before turning to the next page. The real joke is that the woman in this case will never finish getting dressed because female bagmoths remain forever in their cocoons. They are wingless grub-like creatures: to pull one out of its silken home is to kill it.

Male bagmoths pupate and emerge winged and ready for action. There is one slight problem. Bagmoths tend to live way apart from each other, munching their way through the bush, dragging their cases behind them. As in everything else, the race is to the swift — first come, first serve so to speak — so off flutters the male in feverish haste, battering himself against twigs and branchlets and ruining himself as far as I was concerned. The only thing to do was to make a collection of bagmoths, hope there was a male among them, and anaesthetize it as soon as it came into the world.

I scoured the bush for bagmoths and found a thousand and 33. I converted my wardrobe into a bagmothery and reaped manuka by the armload to feed them. They all reached maturity and *none* of them turned into beings with wings. At least, not the proper Oeceticus omnivorous wings.

I was looking at them disconsolately one afternoon, one thousand and 33 fat bagmoths hauling their homes around as they got stuck into fresh sprays of manuka, or snoozing, the mouths of their cocoons drawn shut. And suddenly, I saw it. One cocoon was contorting into s-shaped bends. It was wriggling frantically. Bagmoths did not do this in my experience, even when attacked by parasitic wasps. A male moth was hatching, late but at last!

I took off my glasses and leaned eagerly close to the switching case. In one hand I had a killing bottle. Any moment now . . . something began to emerge from the bottom of the bagmoth case, very slowly at first but then with awful swiftness. Insect legs, insect abdomen, glorious? red! wings and a tiny head. With teeth. It looked like a human head. With human teeth. It was grinning at me, its minute black eyes viciously bright. The grin lasted a very long second. Then the thing dived powerfully into the air and sped past my goggling eyes out through the door and away.

I didn't touch or look at or even think about an insect in any entomological sense ever again.

Incidentally, if you're wondering how bagmoths female and male get it together in real life, why not keep a couple and see? Hurry, though. There's not much time left.

Never the Same Wind Twice

There's only one thing I've ever discovered since, that I enjoy as much as I enjoyed the world of insects and believe you me, I've tried more than a few things.

It's breathing.

Ordinary day-to-day breathing is fine, having the charm of novelty inasmuch as every lungful is slightly different, and deep breathing all right for some situations, and meditational breathing okay if you like meditation, but what I am talking about is the awareness of breathing.

Some mornings I'd wake up very early and grin with delight as I drew in that first conscious chestful of air. It tasted better in my lungs than wine ever tasted on my tongue. It was ecstasy, it was *sweet*, air soughing in and all my little alveoli singing away with joy and oxygen-energy coursing through every space and particle of me. I could feel my heart in its cardiac sac swell and float, held down only by ropes of veins . . . it flutters against those ties, wanting to soar in free air as a great luminous pulsing living balloon . . . hey! grab another breath! This time'll do it!

You've heard skylarks duelling for space, each pegging his own sky-claim with frantic song, making a chestburst effort to keep every other dueller fenced out as they quest higher and higher into the blue yonder? Sometimes I'd feel like their song on ordinary everyday air.

I *love* breathing. Damn, but am I going to do it hard when I stop.

Granny's Revenge

I cried just after my granny died, not for her though (she was far better dead by that stage, and I hadn't liked her much while she was alive). Remember I said the old lady had spent most of her life helping hack farms from the bush? Well, we had always understood that each new farm had just about paid for the last one, and that when my grandfather was lost to the bush, my granny was left destitute. But no: she had twenty thousand pounds squirrelled away and she left it all to me. My Dad grinned faintly when he learned that. He gave me good advice. 'Buy a small house and invest the rest girl,' and then he shifted quite happily into the loft rooms of his knackery. I did what he said, bought a solid little house on the edge of town, right on the beach, and put the rest away to work for me. If I lived fairly frugally I'd never have to work for it.

Boy, the old lady must have hated me a lot. She'd obviously never forgotten those apples.

The Early Sown Skulls

We were one hell of a gang on the beach.

There was Elias, who lived closest to me, quarter of a mile away, bright and gay and very knowledgeable about drugs. He was discreet but indefatigable in the pursuit of new lovers. There was Pinky and Molly and Chris, an oddly-sexed trio who were indefatigable in pursuit of each other but rather liked others to watch. There was me, independent and alone and indefatigable in pursuit of any boy or man who would help me explore more of myself as a woman.

Don't yawn like that. I'm not going to tell you any of what went on except to say that I learned a lot about myself and others and enjoyed most of the learning very much for the three happy years it went on. At least, I think I did. What with the drink and the smoke and capsules that Elias handed round with gay abandon, I can't remember much of the detail.

I do remember the young pothead who staggered to our bonfire one night, drawn by The Smoke amongst all the other.

'Could smell it a mile away,' he husks, and coughs throatily. He's a stocky youth with an oddly-gaunt face, and raggedy-black hair. The firelight dances on his bare chest and shoulders, on his teeth as the joint passes to him and he smiles slowly, 'maaan, that's so sweet,' cupping his hands round its ember end. He sucks and sucks and sucks, an inhalation into the deeps of his belly down below his belly down past his horny bare soles maybe, and the joint grows ash and shrinks and shrinks to a sickly stickily-yellow roach that he finally takes away from his lamprey suck and looks at admiringly. An nth of an inch left, just nippable by nail, bong fodder only. Without breathing out, not seeming to be breath-holding, not even looking distended round the cheeks or chest or eyes, he passes the thing on. Pinky was next, and dropped it, and we couldn't find it in the sand.

The young pothead smiles his gaunt slow smile at us, and it seems to have too many teeth now. None of us grin too widely back. As I recall, he never did breathe that toke out.

By the by, Elias and Pinky and Molly and Chris lived long happy lives by the standards of a couple of centuries ago.

The Beach Arab

When I didn't know what I know now, I said that the Beach Arab was the pothead's cousin. I was only half-joking, for while he was tall and thin (but full in the face), he had a similar slow smile and the same raggedy-black hair. He never wore anything but denim shorts and his skin was a rich reddish brown. If you were on the beach, you generally heard him before you saw him because he played a fat little flute made of bone whenever he was alone. He came shyly to our bonfires at first, always eating whatever food was handed round with his fingers, even when it was a salmon mousse the fastidious Elias had made one March evening. He came less shyly as time wore on and he came to know Elias, then Chris and Molly, and lastly, me. Soon after that, I left the beach forever – but that's a story to come.

He had a strange sense of humour, the Beach Arab (no, he never told us a name).

There was one afternoon I recall in bright detail: three American tourists had invaded our bonfire and were talking loudly, heartily, amusing themselves with the local natives. We were quiescent under more sherry and smoke than usual, smiling dreamily and politely at them when their words gonged more harshly than ordinarily at us. The Beach Arab trailed in, a little after the voice of his flute.

And presently one of the Yanks said gushily, 'And what do you Mayories eat?' Chris who was Danish from Dannevirke looked at Elias whose parents both came from England, and Elias looked at Pinky, a strident Glaswegian, and Pinky in turn stared in astonishment at Molly who blushed all over her Coast Irish face. She didn't look at me, and while I was thinking out loud 'Uuhhh . . .' (what the hell did my father ever eat that was different, except horse?, and that didn't seem too Maori to me), the Beach Arab smiled and bowed and swept off a rock and away scuttled a small crab and the Beach Arab dived on it and put it in his mouth, chewing and smiling while the Americans gasped and went Mygahd Dan do you *see* that? and the little legs (half of them) tweedled on his lips until he swallowed the first bit and sucked them in.

They deserved it. I mean, did you ever see a brick-red Maori? Okay okay okay, so did I, so have I.

Birds of a Feather

It was a three-quarter moon, waxing, that night. We lay together just beyond the rim of the firelight, listening to the others talk. Later, when they had gone, the Beach Arab played his bone flute: rather, he talked into it and the words came out intelligible music. His round face looked both very dark and very oriental under the moon.

After we had made love, I smiled at that moon. I had a house; I had the kind of life that suited me down to the ground, and I didn't have to work to enjoy it; I had friends who were warm good fun, and here I lay satiate, gently held by a young man's strong arms, gently held by a lover. I went happily to sleep and dreamed of taniwha.

When I awoke at sunrise, he was gone, but not far. There he was, down by the sea's edge, naked, washing himself. I ran gaily down to help.

I remember thinking, I must have something on my contact lenses, he can't have feathers on it.

I remember saying, hesitantly, 'hey that looks like fun?' but then his upright ure wilted and the shining bronze-green feathers tucked themselves down tidily round it.

I remember looking at the flat silver sea, watching the water suddenly shiver under a passing breeze.

I remember his smile, o yes. I had seen that same smile on too many different faces, a whole flock of them.

I remember running home and locking my door and *never* going onto the beach again.

Funny thing though: I don't remember feathers on it under the three-quarter moon.

Home Is Where The Heart Is

My solid little house has four rooms; bedroom, wash-house, kitchen and living-room. For three years I kept it immaculate. For the next ten years I – grew things. Don't get me wrong: it was comfortable enough. I had some pet slime moulds in the wash-house and a live & let live policy with any other agents of decay. There were umbrella toadstools on a dishcloth that I recall fondly, and something phosphorous in a bedroom corner that I never touched. Once a month, when the local liquor store delivered my crate of gin, I gathered up all of the tins I had strewn around, put them neatly into rubbish bags and left them out for whoever takes such things away. Someone did. Just as someone delivered the tinned food I ordered.

I'd've kept on that way until my liver gave out except for a series of accidents.

Dry Horrors

About four one morning I awoke with a throat-aching thirst. This was usual and so was my remedy, stumble out to the kitchen and get water in a glass and gulp it. After the second gulp, I remembered something.

Now, I'd had contact lenses for 12 years, ever since long-ago Elias suggested they'd be a better idea than glasses. He was so right: I had got to love rain, and swimming was fun; steam, whether from showers or just-opened ovens or body-heat, was no longer a blinding hazard, and I never once sat on my lenses.

I'd just swallowed them, though.

Remember breaking your lens-case yesterday? Remember putting your lenses into that glass, just before you stumbled right off to bed? Yeah, you remember all right.

I thought about an emetic.

I thought again.

I whimpered until dawn.

In desperation, I rang my father. He sort of snuffled. 'Um well,' he said, seemingly unsurprised to hear from me for the first time in two years and with such a subject too, 'yeah well. Flax'll make you run, y'know. You can always stop it afterwards with little koromiko leaves.'

I wasn't sure whether he meant to use the koromiko as a cork and I wasn't going to ask.

'I'm not scrabbling round in my own shit,' I said shortly.

'You could always have a good meal of, say, scallops, to make it easier?' He openly snorted.

Conversation between a knacker and a drunkard isn't an easy matter, even when they're father and daughter. He did promise to take me to my optician's however, and three hours later, there he was, spruce and grinning on my doorstep. He sniffed a little at the fungal smell and looked sideways at my puffy face and gin-bloated body. He always did think people should go to hell in their own handbasket however, so made no comment at all, merely guided me into a taxi and out into the optician's and back home again.

'Take care,' he said then, and that was the last I've seen of him. You'll gather we weren't ever close. I should have been born a doomed filly.

Until my new lenses arrived, I lived back in the world of blurs. I couldn't go outside because I couldn't see who or what was coming — and for the first time in a decade, I wanted to go outside. Being returned to a condition of childhood had the odd effect of making me, well, not a child, but in some way renewed. The half-empty crate of gin was left untouched while I engaged in warfare with heat (you ever tried to pour boiling water from a jug you can't see into a cup you can't see?) and retaught myself to see with my fingers.

When the new lenses arrived, I put them in and realized immediately that was a mistake.

They melted into my eyes and I could see perfectly but not only what I wanted to see.

They Have Made the Moon a Skull Who Was my Lady

It is three sober days and nights later. I am walking back to the cleansed house under a thin frail fingernail edge of moon. I am breathing deeply and with joy for the first time for years and frankly don't care if there are creatures with feathered penises in this world.

There are two people swaying together at the bus-stop. She is short and stocky, almost squat, and she is tall and heavily-built and they are twined. The stocky one is muttering, They have made the moon a skull now, walking on it, she is a skull now, while the tall one is singing sadly about some lady lost, some lady gone, and the words run eerily together, mutter and song. As I tiptoe past, they stop singing and muttering and stare at me. Their eyes glow.

I look hastily away and see that the grinning moon really is a skull, the fingernail edge a highlight on her bare jawbone.

They Have Exits and Entrances Galore

Someone or something has started using my print as a getaway route.

It is a reproduction of George O'Brien's *Dunedin Harbour From Flagstaff Hill* and every so often, just as I've stopped looking at it, a particle of intense light swoops into the water past the wharf on the lefthand side of the picture. Three seagulls flying in an isosceles triangle mark the spot.

The oval nineteenth-century print doesn't bat an eyelid at this intrusion, not even when a similar (identical?) light sears *out* of the water (aft of the steam vessel making its way across the harbour).

There! I caught one out of the corner of my eye doing it again!

The Constancy of Roads

I discovered today that, during my ten years' self-immurement, my optician's clinic had burned down and she had shifted to the North Island. I had walked down to the clinic, my courage screwed to breaking point, to have her test my strange new eyes.

Walking back, I can't find the bus-stop.

Denying the Mouse

I can hear it. Every night for the last week.

Clink of chopsticks on foodbowl as it creepytoes across seeking morsels, leftovers, bits I've missed. Everything gets gnawed by its tiny defiling teeth.

I've left out tasty poisons for it, in neat dishes. One night I heard it chuckle over my latest cunning trap.

The experts advise setting baits in its own run. How? Mouse-runs are the most secretive of paths. They go winding in and out of my walls with no sign, not even an exit hole. Entrances in deep shadows, exits elsewhere.

I can't believe I have a mouse problem. For one thing, in all the years of sloth and mould, neither rats nor mice showed up. Why should my bleached clean house draw them? For another, the thing is way too smart, and there was that chuckle. Maybe a mouseman? A minute anthropomorph, complete with basket of pottery droppings to scatter or stick in strategic places – what better way to disguise your predations than under the guise of another pest? and somehow, I can't see him/her/it raising narrow buttocks and squeezing out an instant turd. Nah, a little factory where they manufactured guises in silence.

In my walls.

Come out! I know you're there. If I can only see you once, I won't kill. I won't even try to kill you. I'll stop setting traps and I'll put out little dishes of good food. Come on, play fair.

Tonight there are two of them and I can hear their thin voices singing 'We'll Meet Again'.

Even Barnacles Have a Swimming Phase

I had a choice; stay, and drink myself to death, or, leave and try and find a heart somewhere else.

There was an eager buyer for my house the first day I put it on the market. He was an ordinary-looking fellow, thin and pale with nondescript hair, so I let him have it for five times the price I had paid for it.

His smile lit up his mirrored shades.

Next Time, Leave it Lying There

At first, I spent a lot of time on the Cook Strait ferries. It was soothing, watching the waves from the safety of the deck, and I liked the food. I stayed one night in Picton, the next in Wellington, and I could have gone on living like that for the rest of my time except I got noticed after the first year, and turned into a celebrity after the second.

I gave in and bought a motor-home and set off round the North Island first, never staying more than one night in any place. I had no pictures and the van was mouse-proof and I never looked for bus-stops or at moons.

I did pick up hitch-hikers – I liked to talk and there is something wrong about telling stories to your own ears.

I had been driving around for a year when I picked it up.

There was a young weary man slumped at the side of the road. He lifted his head and gave me a tired one-sided smile when I stopped. He didn't say anything while I talked, just stayed with his head bent, long felted rastafarian dreads swaying as we sped round corners. I thought one side of his head looked . . . odd, as though the skull was slightly dented and the skin darker and oilier there, but he was quiet and tired with none of the jolty energy or lightning smiles that I knew and dreaded. He didn't say a word until I said, 'Taumarunui, mate, I'm stopping here,' when he said 'Ta, mate,' and slipped out the door before I'd pulled to a stop. Tired he might have been, judging by his bent head and the way he sloped in his seat, but he was exceptionally agile. He did a speedy little dance as he hit the road, never a slip or a stumble, and then trudged slowly, heavily, away. The van spun up a small whirlwind as I drove into the town.

It's Better Never than Late

Nemesis shouldn't look like this.

Forearms on the table, head on clenched fists, I study the thing.

It lies in a pool of light, in the one-eyed glare of the lamp.

It looks like a slender rectangular tube.

It is a dull leaden colour, but is partly wrapped in what looks like finely-plaited sennit.

The sennit is darkly gold and ends in a snood as though it were hook.

It is three inches long and half an inch wide and half an inch high.

It weighs nearly forty pounds.

I *know* that is impossible.

When I picked it up off the seat it felt warm. I swung round to look for the young rasta but he wasn't anywhere around of course.

It is now very cold. A thin splay of ice crystals creeps out all round it.

I touch it with a tentative finger. A shining bead leaks out, bleeds out, like freshmelted solder or particularly viscous mercury. It lies there, glaring up at me.

The finger I touched it with aches.

After a while, I pour myself a gin. Then I pour myself another gin.

In the morning, there are little silver words on the table.

WHAT IS RAISED WILL BE SUNK.

And the tube is snugly ensconced in my aching left hand and I cannot let it go.

Mules Are Stubborn Creatures

I caught up with him many many months and miles later, on a marae in the far north.

He was lolling next to a very old woman and he hadn't bothered to change any of his shape. He knew I'd get to him when the time was ripe and he was ready.

I stood cradling my hand which had become inhumanly swollen. He stares openly at me and I stare openly back. For all his illdoing he is utterly beautiful, red and black and white perfection.

He is smiling at me and his smile is without pity.

I ask without words, How do I get rid of it? and he answers without moving a muscle, Go to Rotorua and find the pool that bears my name. It will come off in the pool.

'That will kill me!'

and he shrugs, still smiling.

The elder snuffles round her cigarette, unruly shreds of tobacco leaking out in a fan. She grates, 'It's all for the best, dear' and grins, an eldritch mahogany unsuitable grin.

There's a pigeon beside her with bright black eyes.

'They often come to me dear,' she says hoarsely, 'though they never admit they're lonely,' and a strong wind from the east came up and spun her and the bird away.

★

The Tantalizing Maze

Is there ever a real answer to anything or a true end to any story?

I hope you realize I tried so hard to stay away from the boiling mud of Rotorua but the strongest of people would be daunted by a fortypound weight clenched forever in one hand.

Yes, I tried cutting my hand off. Whatever the sinker is made of, it is impermeable and has grown all through my arm.

Yes, I tried taking my hand to every doctor and quack under the sun, but they couldn't see anything or feel anything.

It all boils down to this: there are things quite outside humanity and we can't do battle with them. We have to leave it to their own kind to bring them to heel.

Doubtless they will, if they feel we and the world are worth it.

Would you like to know the brightest dream I had of the future? (No, you wouldn't like to know the other ones at all.)

Never Trust a Dreamer Who Can Also Tell Stories

'Give me that bottle. This one's gone dry.

I've been out picking cockles. It's spring tide. They dig themselves down to normal level but the water leaves them exposed early. When you walk over the mudflat, you see them clamping shells, squirting water in bepuzzlement. I have two kit of cockles – I know, that don't mean much to you. All I know is that two kit give you a feed and enough left over to swim in apple vinegar, put in the cool place for tomorrow.

I think sometimes of those squirts. A watercry of help. Dismay. Horror. When you pour them out of the kit into the pan, they don't make a noise, not like mussels. They sik and hiss and squeak sometimes. Cockles just lie there and die in the steam. Only some don't. Obstinate. You get this feeling when you finally crack the shells that they hoped their shutness would save them. It doesn't. Of course. Crack them on that stone.

I like my cockles raw. Smack two shells together, like cracking walnuts. The weaker always gives. That's sweet, living meat. Or, just steam them open, the flesh not burnt, just lushly half-cooked. Add a sauce. Vinegar if you're feeling harsh. Or a mix of root-ginger (did you see the big lilies blooming up on the hill as you came through the big swamp?) and garlic and soy. We still get the soy from Dunedin. The people of heaven never quite left there. Just as well, eh? There'd be none left otherwise. Add some sherry – now, that cask I have comes from Nelson, they got a rich crop there. I swap my bulks, for that sherry. And the wine of course. Have some more.

Anyway, you got this sauce, sherry and ginger, garlic and soy, and you dip the nearly-dead not-cooked meat into it, and eat.

O it's sweet.

I almost wouldn't mind someone eating me, like that, did they it with appreciation, like that.

My glass?

O, there's one here can mould glass. Blows it. Makes fires and breath and silica sand to a magic. Containers. Jewellery. A weapon or two. My glass. That's her over there, squatting next to the hunter with the copper earrings. Drift we call her. Lightning we call him. I'm translating, of course.

Anyway, momentarily, and we can eat the cockles I picked. Friend, you'll understand if I say I'm a little surprised to see you here bare? I mean nothing coarse. Yes, that's the old worm ... you'll know that worm eh! Eh, the times the creature has coursed the worm. The last season I saw you was Thunderstorms. Seven cycles ago. Here in the simple seaward hills, we don't take note of more than a year-name. But you know that of course. It's not that we pride ourselves on ignorance. No one but a fool does. Just, our way is working up more bones, lapping our own fat cover, growing our own strength. Eating and growing. Us. Basic.

Yes, bare is maybe a wronging word.

I see in your silence your woundedness showing.

Look, when you walk round in your metal skin someone sooner or later is going to think, Ah hah! Flesh *and* cooking pan. That's the way we are round here and you've been on expeditions enough to learn that. We don't think your armour protection or superiority. We skewer.

Taking that metal hide off isn't trust though. Trade for trade is what every thing is. You didn't leave us that worm, for nothing. Your skin's not off, for nothing.

Well, you know better than to misunderstand the savagery and viciousness of us children, heh?

I'm sorry for all the smoke, the cavern is new and unfiltered yet. Nah, it's no special fire, just a joy-thing for this night. Night comes, we must have shelter. Sometimes a fire too. Smile against it, but you wouldn't be out there either, in your suit or out of it. It's wilder than us, night, and too many things tramping around with a taste for soft meat.

Metalmaster, I can ask you bent questions. You come from Cityrace. Can you answer this? Lately I have these night-thoughts. Whatever the Singers tell, I don't think we've changed. Did we ever love each other? Say the Singers. Me, I think we're just the same as we always were, humans, cockles.

A pity you're bare. It's so nice, cracking shells.

Have that bottle, there's wet enough in it, yet.'

I Mean, It Probably Was a Dream

That's all it was. Ten minutes of talk, our kind of language yet not our talk. Sitting in a dark smoky place, with a lot of people around chatting their not-our-language and gnawing things. Sitting in somebody else's head and knowing they were terribly afraid. Sitting in their head and listening to a skinny old man ramble on about how he liked cockles. Wishing his eyes weren't so shiny, weren't so black, and especially wishing I couldn't see what all the other black-eyed people were chewing on.

If it was a dream, the future is going to be way worse than the past.

I don't like thinking that today is the high crest of humanity; tomorrow, we all fall down.

The Jewelled Frame

It's funny, trying to encapsulate your own life. As I said at the beginning, it's only the peculiar bits that make any kind of sense, but I am disappointed in my hope of them also making a pattern.

What I seem to have created for you is an old spiderweb, the kind that is a gallery of past feasts. Here an emerald shard of manuka beetle, there the plundered silken hold of a wolf spider's egg-case; some delicate purple-blue, powdery blue tussock butterfly wings interspersed between the coarse and glassy remnants of blowflies, and in this broken corner, kept as ruby as in their strident heyday by some nasty arcane skill, the little lights of cicada eyes . . .

What is missing, what is needed to make sense of it all, is the spider.

If You Can Raise Up Islands, You Can Push Them Down Again

I know exactly what is going to happen when I drop the sinker in the boiling pool.

There will be a few indescribable seconds of passing between consciousness and nothingness but that doesn't worry me.

The body will drift down, down, and the snooded sinker will

slide down further and faster. Some time later, it will reach the place where the crustal plate is tender and touchy and then, like a good little bomb, it will shed its protective skin and be what it is, a seed of antimatter.

And just before the fish shatters into an archipelago, the incandescent cloud will roar helterskelter over Auckland and boil all the northern sea to a frenzy. And all along the line, the volcanoes will gout and the wild tsunamis rear up and speed in huge glassy walls over every innocent island there is. And the canoe will rock and most of it slide under the waves.

Unless my Dad is killing a horse at the time, he will probably be looking at a picture of his vanished daughter and wondering why he can't yet decently take it down and leave the room to the laughing horses.

A Question for the Spider at the Heart of Matter

Who made the fatal mistake?

There was a childhood spent fishing up islands and wasting Granny's fiery nails. Snickering over Tuna's dirty jokes and then massacreing Tuna in a dirty-joke way. Putting stutters in the sun's path, battering down a star's pride, because it was a way to make the world happy. But then you wanted to play saviour and there is *no* fury like a saviour scorned.

Your fury was an impotent sputtering for so long; you were reduced to small deadly jokes. Then, I think, you learned to fly from mind to mind and time to time as easily as you formerly flew from man to bird and back again. After that, it was an easy jump into another world altogether where you could play at large again.

There was this troublesome reminder here and now though, a splinter that irked. Maybe you would have been content to let the matter rest, let the Old Lady keep what you had unwisely made available for her to take.

Somebody offended your pride so much that you made a sinker where before you'd made a hook, that you made lucky me over to find it.

Who?

The Windeater

There isn't such a word, eh. There's a lot of us around though. I came across the term as a gift, if you like, a sort of found gift. For instance, you break up a perfectly respectable word, happily married in all its component parts: you know it means several things, like a loafer or a braggart. Or a woman who takes part in certain rites. Or it can mean the acquisition of property without any return being made, as well as a spell that is cast to punish somebody behaving in such an unmannerly fashion. That's when it's a whole unbroken word, but if you split it, a power leaks out and becomes a woman trying to make sense of her self and her living and her world.

Which all goes to show the charming naivety of us humans. Sense of a world indeed!

> Now, ask me anything you like because
> my hand is getting too heavy and
> in another second,
> I'll be gone.

Lloyd Jones

SWIMMING TO AUSTRALIA

WARREN WAS FIRST into the water. He lifted his knees and kicked out over the shallow surf and dived beneath a breaker. Warren made it out beyond the breakers and lay on his back. Any moment he would call out 'Marilyn' as was his wont when underneath a car and needing something from his toolbox. In that way of fat women at public swimming pools, Mum squatted – a slow immersion in the water.

We caught up to Warren – Tess, Bron and myself – and Mum, covering the last few metres underwater, surfaced next to Warren and surprised him with a kiss. Then Warren spoke up and said, 'Australia is out there.' He pointed with his hand and we tried to make out the exact place on the white horizon. Tess began to say how she couldn't see a thing – but lost the confidence to finish the sentence, or say it loud enough for Warren to hear. 'Yep,' said Warren. Australia, he meant. Our mother stared over his shoulder to the horizon with a dreamy smile, as if it had just become clear to her what the rest of us could not make out.

Well, Warren had seen what he wanted to see. Without a word he just swung around and headed for shore, and the rest of us obediently followed. We picked ourselves up out of the shallows and wiped the salt from our eyes, and the first thing we saw was Warren sitting on the wet sand, pulling on the wet ends of his beard. 'Same old place,' he said, and to Mum as she bent down for the towel, 'I'm the abo with the spear. Watch out.'

We drove to McDonald's – Warren ordered nothing for himself which confirmed that he was upset, and at some point, either in the car or in the doorway at home, Mum kissed him on the cheek and said, 'Maybe some day.' But that was Warren, we told ourselves. Like a child when he couldn't get what he wanted.

Other times we drove to the end of the quarry road and watched in silence the sun deliver itself to that place Warren had pointed out, and felt ourselves to be fools for not following.

'Keith says formwork is a hundred-dollar-a-day job there now,' he said.

It grew awfully quiet. We could hear our own breathing. Finally Warren said, 'Yep. I don't know for the life of me why we need to stick around here.'

Then, a week later, 'How would the Musters like to team up with the Gilberts and travel over to Oz?' Warren happened to be cutting his meat, which he kept at as if nothing controversial had been uttered. We exchanged looks but were slow to comment. Then Warren put down his knife and fork, and got up to leave, slamming the door to the kitchen. We heard the car start up, and the spit of gravel as he reversed out to the road, and Mum said Warren had got a bit antsy.

We travelled out to the West Coast beaches this particular afternoon, the last week in February. Warren was in a serious state of mind. There had been some shouting from the bedroom, after which Warren emerged and rounded us into the car. I didn't care one way or the other, but, of course, choice didn't enter into it.

He drove faster than was comfortable. Every other car was an arsehole, and usually Mum would have said something like, 'Warren, better late than dead,' but she didn't and I knew it was killing her not to say anything.

Warren's mood had not improved any when we got to the beach. He pulled off his T-shirt and kicked his slippers inside the car. It was up to each of us to keep up; to get out of the car so he could lock up. He was in no mood to be delayed.

Tess complained of scorched feet so I picked her up and carried her as far as the wet sand. We were all business.

A bunch of kids were playing on a log, and a man wearing goggles swam side-on to the waves with a painfully slow 'crawl' action. Every now and then a wave gently lifted him up, inspected him, and put him gently down again.

Warren dived and smacked his fists. He bullied his way out beyond the breakers. Further out he lay on his back, staring up at variable skies. None of us felt like swimming to his exact whereabouts, but since we were seated at the same table as it were there wasn't much else to do but to look the other way. Mum had a race with the girls to hurry them along. We duly fell abreast of Warren. We were a good distance from shore but none of us gave it a thought. We had hit a warm seam in the current. 'Warm as bathwater isn't it,' said Warren. And once to Bron, 'This way' – as if she had veered off course.

Mum said it wouldn't surprise her if we bumped into an oil tanker way out here. Bron immediately said she wanted to go back.

My mother laughed. 'Just a little further, Bron. You are doing fine. All of you.'

Then she put in a couple of powerful strokes to where Warren was shuffling along on his back. I heard her say, 'We need to talk.'

'I'm all ears,' he said.

'Not out here.' But then she said, 'Supposing we did, what about the children?'

I heard Warren say, 'We've been through that one enough times already, Marilyn.'

'What about Tess – her friends? And Bron? Jimbo just about to start high school . . .'

'New friends. New schools,' he said.

'Fine,' said our mother.

'Fine is what,' he said.

Some spluttering from Tess attracted attention. She had swallowed sea water. So Warren rolled over on his back. He idled there while Mum swam back to Tess. She wiped away a trail of snot for Tess to say she wanted to go back. She was cold.

'Go back to what?' called out Warren.

'We're on an adventure, sweetpod. Yes, we are,' she said, nodding her head, I think to reassure herself of the idea. She called back to Warren, 'I've just told Tess we're on an adventure. Isn't that right?'

'Pretend. Pretend,' he said.

'I hate Warren,' Tess said quietly.

'Warren loves you,' Mum said.

Warren paddled his feet and blew up a spurt of water like a whale.

'That's right. Mollycoddle her, Marilyn. Every time that girl sniffles the entire company has to pack it in.'

'Tessa is fine, aren't you sweet?'

Tess nodded, allowed herself to be placed back in the water under her own power. She put her head down and swam furiously, out past Warren.

'Dawn Fraser,' he said, now sitting in the water. 'That's another thing, Marilyn. We would have new heroes. More of them.' And he began to reel off the names of famous cricketers, tennis and league players. 'The Great White Shark,' he said, because he knew I had done some caddying before Christmas.

'Not to mention climate,' he added, and we stared out to sea.

Back the other way the beach had sunk from view. We seemed to be bobbing above the tops of farm scrub.

Suddenly Mum asked, 'What are we doing out here, Warren?' Her brave smiles had been deceptive after all. And of course. She must be worried. Probably she had been worried the whole time. But Warren pretended innocence.

'I don't know,' he said. 'You tell me. I know what *I'm* doing. Jimbo, what about you?'

I said I did.

'See. Jimbo knows what he's doing. What about you, Marilyn?'

Then Bron piped up that she didn't want to go to Australia. She was young enough to say what she felt, and I for one was pleased she had, even if it was just to say that she didn't want to leave behind her dolls.

'We'll buy more. Better dolls in Australia,' said Warren.

'But I want Hetti.'

'Hetti can come too. Jesus,' he said. 'What a party of sadsacks. Sing a song somebody.'

When nobody did Warren started to sing 'Advance Australia Fair'. He lay on his back as effortlessly as before and sang at the top of his voice. Barely noticeable at all, Mum had started to hum 'God Defend New Zealand'. Why, way out at sea, did I feel so embarrassed? In between Warren's bellows we could hear Mum's fragile tune. I don't think she was particularly aware of what she was doing, at least not until Warren had finished and she was still carrying on.

'Well, well,' said Warren, as Bron joined in with breathless gasps. I could see Bron's feet and arms scrabbling to tread water, to stay afloat, and her face growing red with the struggle of getting out the words. I wished she would stop. It was a stupid thing to be doing way out here, without anything solid underneath us. At the completion of 'Advance Australia Fair' Warren might have turned and stroked for the New South Wales coastline. But when Mum and Bron finished I felt as though we were all about to sink to the bottom, that there was nothing in this world to keep us afloat, other than this old Victorian prayer.

'You silly bugger, Warren,' Mum said then, and swam over to

where Warren floated secure as a log. She was halfway there when Bron said she had had enough. She was tired, and was heading back to shore.

'Bron. Please honey.' But Bron did not appear to hear. She was breaststroking for the beach. Mum turned around to Warren who was singing in a silly voice a few more bars from 'Advance Australia Fair'. He was enjoying himself — anyone could see that. Then Mum turned back to me and Tess. She said she wanted us to stay out here. 'I want us to stay together,' is what she said, but below the waterline I could see her legs quietly propelling her towards Warren. For the first time it occurred to me that her problem had become our problem. She reached Warren, and the two of them smiled back at us. Warren had one of his hands inside Mum's togs and they were looking at us, pretending that there was nothing for us to see that might cause alarm.

Maybe Warren was right after all. Even in late March summer hung on — women and girls wore summery dresses — a fringe of surf stretched to the white cloud, and beyond. There was a lightness here that included all manner of possibility, whereas, at home, everything had seemed anchored to the ground.

Warren's friend, Keith, a man in shorts, long tanned legs and desert boots, was there to collect us. He was pleased to see Warren. Tipped his hat to Mum. But the rest of us caused him to scratch his brow. Mum and Warren squeezed into the front; me, Bron and Tess sat in the back of the ute.

The air was bone dry, and Bron complained her eyeballs were drying out. Soon we were driving away from the city and the air smelt of bark and leaves. And suddenly of hot road mix, where we slowed for a road gang. Then for a long time we were on a highway. Driving to where — none of us knew. A few times Mum looked back over Warren's arm, which was slung along the top of the seat, to see that Tess wasn't hanging off the end of the tray.

Bron woke Tess soon as we hit the sea. We had entered a stream of traffic and were making slow work of it along a beach esplanade in the shadow of tall buildings. We stopped at the big M. Warren ran across for burgers and shakes, and we set off again, heading inland, away from the coast until the tops of the buildings marking the beach had grown small to the point of vanishing.

There were times in the days ahead when each of us thought we could smell the coast. Perhaps it was simply a longing to be where other people were. In the dusty quiet of the country it was a lot to wish for. Sometimes we sat on the porch and followed a red dust cloud across the flat scrubland, which traced the progress of a four-wheel drive. At night Keith put roo bars on his ute and from our beds we heard it smack through the undergrowth; the rip of rifleshot, and the high whine of a vehicle held in low gear.

Warren and Keith went out shooting most nights. Friends from school it turned out. They took it in turns to hold the spotlight and shoot. Another man did the driving, a fellow from the Danish 'steelie' gang with whom Keith and Warren were contracted to help build the retirement village – 'Ocean View' as it was called – in the foothills. Warren sometimes returned home and reported having spotted the sea. On clear days it was possible – as well, it was comforting to know it was there; that there was this edge, that is to say, a limit to this new life of ours.

Our house for the time being was the former headmaster's house in the grounds of an abandoned country school. We were saving ourselves a bundle living here, according to Warren. It was that, or drive to and from the coast each day.

'It doesn't bear thinking about,' Warren said, after a few weeks of our being settled. Although Mum did say that she felt able to chip in were we on the coast, where jobs were to be had cleaning out motel rooms and apartments. 'For that matter,' she said, 'I might even teach piano.'

'Oh I can imagine that,' Warren said. He walked to the fridge, took out two beer cans, and tossed one to Keith.

We were into our second month and everything new had become familiar and practised. Warren couldn't think why Tess had to land awkwardly after all the times she had landed perfectly okay. Most times Warren slapped the side of his door and we jumped clear, like hunting dogs, from the back of the ute outside the school gates. This occasion the ute started to roll away, then stopped. Warren got out angry at the noise Tess was making. She was screaming and it was hard to know which part of her hurt. Warren stroked her hair and pinched her cheek. But it turned out to be her wrist, which he then held and kissed. He babied Tess until Keith called out something like, 'Time!'

But Tess was complaining that her arm hurt. Really hurt. Warren took another look. He gave it a waggle and pronounced it okay. He had done the same thing plenty of times in his younger days on the rugby field – at worst he had sprained his wrist. And there was nothing you could do about sprains other than exercise patience and let nature take its course. At the same time he wandered back to the ute with a troubled look.

I think Bron, as much as myself, was prepared to believe Warren. Tess was prone to over-reaction. And already her tears had dried. She didn't mention it to her teacher and had no further complaint until that evening when she said it was hurting again.

Warren and Keith were watching the league on the box. Warren stretched his bare foot forward to the TV dials and with his big toe turned up the commentary.

But Tess was crying hard. Everything she must have held in all day was coming out. She hated Australia. Her arm hurt. And as much as Warren leant forward to concentrate he wasn't succeeding. Finally he had had enough, and yelled so he could be heard, 'Marilyn, will you shut her up for chrissakes!' Then he shook his head and I heard him mutter to Keith, 'Every time you can bet your bottom dollar that little . . .' He shook his head again and shivered, got up and walked over to Tess. He stroked her hair. 'What did I say this morning, Tess? I said, "It's a sprain."'

Mum wondered aloud whether we had gotten ourselves travel and health insurance, which only further aggravated Warren.

He said to Keith, 'Can you believe this? A small girl falls over and suddenly we're looking at airlifts to hospitals. Tessa. Tess! Listen to me . . .'

But she was crying too hard. Sobbing her eyes out. Mum led her to the room where she and Warren slept, and Tess's sobbing carried on in there, through the doors, in competition with the league.

Warren returned to the sofa and shook his fists before his face.

'What have I done to deserve this?'

'I give up,' said Keith.

Then Warren noticed me lurking, and ordered me to the couch.

'The guy with the ball. See him! There! That's Bella. He's crunched through more bones than you've had hot dinners.'

'That would be true,' said Keith.

Then Warren said to Keith, 'It's still all new to him.'

I heard them shooting later that night. I lay with a sheet over me, listening to the crack of the undergrowth and Keith's ute. It was going on later than usual. Mum came and sat on the end of my bed. 'Still up?' she said, trying to be jolly. A light from the hallway found her face; a full cheekbone of smile that with a little prompting, I felt sure, might turn to something else. 'I suppose it all seems a bit strange. A new school. New country,' she said, and I knew she was waiting for me to say it wasn't that at all. She was daring me to speak her thoughts for her.

'Oh well,' she said. 'Tessa seems to have gone off all right.'

In the morning Tess was very quiet. She had no colouring. It was impossible of course but she appeared to have shrunk, as if each tear she cried had contained a piece of flesh. She sat at the table with her bad wrist in her lap. Warren and Keith were still asleep, so we tiptoed around like shadows. After breakfast Mum told us to get dressed – she had an idea, and hurried us along to brush our teeth. We were leaving the house when Bron allowed the fly screen to snap back on its hinges – and the fright stopped us in our tracks.

Out on the road the plan faltered again. Mum took Tess by the hand and looked to the road behind. There was no traffic for a hundred miles – at least that is the way it felt. 'Has everyone a set of legs?' she asked.

We walked along without making a race of it. The one car that came along, stopped. The farmer was headed a short distance, to the store where we got our groceries. He was surprised to hear we were headed for the coast. Mum told him, 'We have a young lady here with an arm that needs seeing to.'

The farmer scratched his nose. He wished it were tomorrow. Sunday he was taking his family to Southport. Tell you what, he said, if we were still on the road on his return from the store he would drive us to the coast. Otherwise we might as well stay on the road and try our luck.

Luck took the shape of Keith's ute. It crept up behind: its fat wheels sucking up the tar.

Warren sprang out. A light joke on his lips, he said, 'Now where is this lot of nomads headed? Same place we are, I hope.'

Without a word Mum lifted Tess into the back of the ute, among the bits of animal fur and clotted blood from last night's shooting. She hauled herself in – me and Bron followed.

I barely remembered anything of the passing landscape which we must have passed all those weeks earlier. Tess lay in Mum's lap. Her hand flopped on the end of her wrist and she held it up not so much because she wished to show it off, but because it was more comfortable that way. Mum stroked Tessa's hair. Otherwise she was lost in her thoughts.

Soon we entered the outer suburbs. We struck the first set of traffic lights and, after that, the malls. Again there was the sniff of the coast. A light breeze that we never got further inland. Bron said she wanted an ice-cream, but we passed the ice-cream parlour on the green light and drove to a newish building with tinted windows where Keith, I later heard him tell Warren, had been treated for the clap.

The x-ray revealed a clean fracture. Now that it was pointed out, the bend in Tessa's arm seemed obvious and we wondered how we could have missed it. Warren said he could have sworn it was a sprain. The nurses took no notice. If anything they were short with him – and Warren was asked three times by as many nurses how it had happened. Then I heard one of them behind the curtains quietly ask Tessa for her account.

The arm was to be set that afternoon. Mum stayed with Tess. Warren gave me and Bron ten dollars. He pointed out the hotel where he and Keith planned to hole up, and left us to roam.

That evening we drove back towards the foothills it seemed to me that we were driving away from everything that was sensible and sane. There was Warren's work, and home, and no overlap, and no way of anticipating what was to happen next.

It was a week later that the ute pulled up early afternoon. Keith didn't come inside the house. It wasn't worth thinking about at the time; only a clue in hindsight. Warren rough-housed his way through the fly screen, gave each of us a filthy look and made his way to the refrigerator. He took his time in telling, and when he did he stared at the floorboards and jabbed angrily with his hands to make the point that we would hear it told once, and that was all.

The company developing 'Ocean Views' had gone bust – or been placed in the hands of receivers – and for the time being cash was on hold. I didn't like the sound of 'for the time being'.

I heard Mum and Warren, later that night, making plans in

the living room. Mum was doing most of the talking and for once Warren was listening.

'This is no place for children. How much have we saved up?'

'A thousand . . . twelve hundred,' said Warren.

'We will need a car. Not a ute mind you, Warren,' she said. 'My children have travelled in the back of that thing for the last time.'

That was the end of Keith. We didn't see him again.

We bought an early model Holden inside of which the whole family and Warren could sit. Warren changed the points and plugs, rustled up a retread from somewhere – and we were roadworthy, heading back for the coast, where we turned south, stopping along the way at building sites for Warren to go and enquire after formwork or carpentry. We stayed in camping grounds and did our washing in laundromats. Mum got work house-cleaning, so we would stay in a place for a few days – never more than a week – until we had petrol money.

It made no sense. Buildings were going up everywhere, but at every site Warren went to the back of the line. Further south, and men gathered outside the sites; they sat on the fence like a line of still vultures, waiting for a job to come free. We pulled along outside, and Mum sent Warren across to the foreman's office. The men watched without any talk in them; sawing grassblades between their teeth. And they watched Warren's return the same way.

'Guess what? Last month they wanted formworkers,' he said, getting back in the car. Always last month. I wondered how long, how much longer this was going to go on, and why we didn't just pack up and fly home.

Then one night we had to make a choice between somewhere to stay and petrol; Mum just kept driving south through the night, and the new day dawned in Taree.

Me, Bron and Tess untangled ourselves from the back seat, and sat up to find we had arrived in a park or public domain. We were parked on the edge of a field. Near a huge tent were elephants and horses. A man in tights walked along a rope. I looked at the map and found we were in New South Wales. The doors cracked as we tumbled out, and from the front seat Mum stirred.

Then we saw Warren coming towards us from one of the caravans parked in line. An older man in a white singlet and braces followed after Warren, who looked keen and ready with news.

'Wake up your mother,' he said. 'I think I may have something.'

But he did it himself; leant in the driver's door and said, 'Marilyn. Payday.' He shushed up then because the man in braces had drawn near. Mum got out of the car. She tried to smooth out the creases in her dress. There was the matter of her hair too, and as she sneaked a look in the fender mirror, she said, 'Jesus. Heaven help.'

The stranger nodded at her, and took each of us into account. Then he made as if what he had to say gave him no pleasure at all. Turning to Warren he said he had misunderstood their earlier conversation. He had been so long in the circus business he had forgotten what a formworker was.

'I had in mind juggling, the wire, something of that order,' he said. 'But what you are about to tell me is that you're not a circus performer.'

Warren nodded, and studied the ground. He raked his toe back and forth in the grass.

The circus man seemed to be taking stock of the situation. He looked at each of us, again. And nodded.

'Still,' he said. He had a thought. He twirled a finger in his ear, and while he was doing that he gave Warren a good going over. Walked around him twice, before finally he said he might have something. Mum smiled at Warren, and he took her hand.

Many years ago, in Italy, the circus man had seen a useful sort of stunt which he had, for some time, meant to introduce to this hemisphere. Maybe that time had arrived; if Warren, of course, was interested. Warren checked first with Mum. She nodded, and Warren was given the privilege of saying, 'Okay then.'

We were travelling north again, through towns we had passed in a single night – Port Macquarie, Kempsey, Coffs, Ballina.

Warren had his own tent. On its side was a picture of a strong man with curly hair and black moustache, and the words 'Man of Steel'. Kids up to the age of twelve paid two dollars for three punches to Warren's stomach. Clearly the man who hired Warren had not been telling the truth. Bron and I had gotten friendly with one of the acrobats who said the last 'Man of Steel', a Hungarian immigrant, had developed kidney trouble, and the circus had left him in hospital in Scone, New South Wales.

'Light hail on a tin roof,' was how Warren described his day's work. But at night our caravan reeked with the liniment Mum rubbed into his stomach and sides. Slowly he began to soften, like one of Keith's skins after a steady beating. The job was taking it out of him. No sooner were we in a new town than he suffered the runs. And the rest of us had to put up with his irritability.

At such times we left Warren in the caravan, alone, and Mum led us on a walk in a strange town.

'Luckier than most kids your own age to be seeing the world,' she said. We didn't feel lucky, but of course she was trying to put the right spin on things. We knew we should be in school, and in a strange kind of way it was unsettling not to be found out, or even feel as though we faced that risk.

In Ballina Warren said he didn't know for how much longer he could keep this up. We heard him groan at night when he rolled onto his sore ribs. He had become a nervous man. The drop of a pin turned his head. The circus manager came to our caravan to say he was pleased with Warren's work, and to ask whether the kids needed something to occupy their time. Mum herded us under her wing and told the man the children were her concern.

'We want to go home,' Tess blurted, and the man chuckled. He poked his head inside the door and took it all in in a sweeping glance. 'This looks homely enough to me,' he said.

'Excuse Tessa,' Mum said properly, but the man waved a hand at her, and walked away.

'We will be out of here by June, Tess,' Warren said. 'June I feel will be time enough.'

We were prepared to believe it. We had something to look forward to; a means by which to mark progress. It was only three weeks off.

But June arrived, and nothing happened. None of us even had the heart to mention the fact of it being June. Not even Tess. We were in Southport, very close to where we had set out. Some of the terrain I recognized from the times we had ridden in the back of the ute. Not only had we lost our place on the calendar but we appeared to be going around in circles.

We had certain games and rituals to push ourselves on. At night, as we lay on our mattresses, Tess asked Bron to describe her teacher, Mrs Marshall, whose class Tess was to have started this year. Then she asked Bron to describe all the kids in her class, which Bron did, fitting out a name with a set of eyes, hair and skin colouring, and habits, so no two were the same. It ended this night when Warren sat up in bed at the other end of the caravan and sent an empty liniment bottle crashing against the wall above our heads. Mum yelled at him to control himself, and Warren slapped her.

I showed up at Warren's tent the following afternoon. I had to push through a flap and Warren looked up, saw it was me, and went back to reading his newspaper.

'Jimbo. What do you want?'

What I wanted was not easily put into words. A short while passed before Warren glanced up again and cottoned on.

'Chrissakes,' he said.

'I paid.'

'So you paid, Jimbo. That's a dollar to the circus, and a dollar to me.'

It didn't make any difference, and he shook his head. He was leaning against a table, rolling back and forth a small pebble underfoot. Then he said, 'Never. Not in my wildest dreams did I ever think it would come to this. Your mother and I, Jimbo . . .'

He looked up then, and said, 'What the hell. Let's get it over with. Three shots.'

He stepped onto a small raised platform, the kind a conductor might use. I tried to see him in the same light another visitor to the tent might, but I couldn't get past the fact it was Warren.

'Do you want the full works?'

I said I did, and Warren said, 'Okay then.' He folded up his newspaper and slapped it on the table. Steadying himself he closed his eyes and concentrated for a moment. Then he started to recite with a strange accent, 'My name is Saffrez, last of the desert tribe of Assyrian strongmen . . .' I noticed his hands bowling into fists at his sides, and was concerned that he might be forgetting who had paid here. But he collected himself and carried on. 'Hit me, the great Saffrez. And watch your sickly knuckles turn to dust . . .'

Warren's elbows fanned out from his sides and he tensed his stomach muscles. He waited with his eyes closed for the punch, for me to get my money's worth. Perhaps all along I had known I wouldn't throw a punch, but what surprised me was my total lack of desire. And at some point when Warren realized that nothing was going to happen, that he had tensed himself up for nothing, he sat down where he had stood. 'Chrissakes,' he said, dropping his face into his hands. Then he shoved his hand out. 'Go away Jimbo. Don't look at me. Leave me please. Go to the beach with your mother.'

I nodded, and said, 'Okay.' In a sense still listening to Warren. On the other hand I think we were all glad to be walking away from it all, the yawns of the sedated lions, the pink candyfloss and the alcoholic clowns.

The shadows from the buildings had almost reached the line of dried foam above the wet sand. A knot of swimmers looking for excitement kept between the flags but well shy of the heavier waves. Me, Bron, Tess with her cast wrapped in plastic, and Mum, stuck together in the same channel, bobbing like corks, taking it in turns to check the arrival of the next breaker. There was no way out beyond the waves. No calm for a horizon to sit along like a painted line. Nothing but movement and foam as far as the eye could see.

And then, without warning it seemed, we were being dragged along a channel parallel to the beach; fighting it at first, then not bothering. None of us was unduly concerned. 'Look, Egmont,' Bron said, of the spit of sand jutting out from the beach, where we might scramble ashore. Meanwhile we did just enough to keep afloat. There was no question of us getting cold.

In time Warren showed. Mum was first to spot him by the parking meters above the beach. I think we had all expected Warren and were nervous at the prospect of his trying to wave us back between the flags, to where he imagined safety lay. He was still in his circus outfit, and we watched this wild figure try to stay abreast, burning his feet on the hot sand as he stepped gingerly between the tidy Japanese sunbathers. None of us said a word. We were comfortable for the moment to just tread water. We were waiting to see if Warren would join us.

Shonagh Koea

MRS PRATT GOES TO CHINA

AFTER ARNOLD'S FUNERAL some of them came back to the house to say their piece or have their say, depending on which was longer.

His sisters all said that Arnold had not looked well for years.

'Whenever we saw poor Arn we said, "Arn's not looking so hot," we said, didn't we?'

A cousin chimed in.

'I saw Arnie last Tuesday. No, I tell a lie. Wednesday it must of been because Wednesday was the day Mavis said to me, she said, "Ron, that car's making a funny noise, a sort of pop in the motor, Ron," she said, and on the way to the garage I stopped at Vi's and who should I see there but Arn. "Arn's not looking well," I said. And that was the last time I saw poor old Arn alive.'

Mrs Pratt's father-in-law, or Arnold's father as she preferred to call him because it cut her out of the connection, had to be led away after this. Clinging to a thread of life at ninety-one, he had been senile for the last eleven years and incontinent for longer. Mrs Pratt thought how lucky it was that she had sat him on a wooden chair.

'Why was it Arn that was taken?' said old Mr Pratt.

According to his late mother Arnold had been one of the most delightful children ever born. He had been the wonder of the nursing home, the pride of the street, brilliant like all Pratts from the moment of birth which took place after a short labour of only an hour and a half, yet another mark of his consideration and brilliance.

He shot out of the world more quickly but with less warning the previous Thursday, felled by an aneurism in front of the refrigerator. He was holding a chicken sandwich in one hand and a glass of beer in the other and had been in the middle of saying, 'Haven't you collected my dry-cleaning yet, Louise?'

'Did he say anything?' A Pratt aunt's voice trailed away into her handkerchief.

'Before he died? Oh yes,' said Mrs Pratt. 'He said, "Haven't you collected my dry-cleaning yet, Louise?"'

'And you hadn't.' The reproof was unmistakable.

Her cheerful tone was an error and would be added, she knew, to her list of crimes – disliking boiled lollies, saying 'Isn't it a beautiful day' at Arnold's mother's funeral, saying Gloria's husband was too good for her and suggesting as a gift for Aunty Vi's golden wedding a sharp tap on the head with a hammer.

Wasn't it just like Arnold to think of his dry-cleaning? they said, at a time like that? Arn was that tidy.

Mrs Pratt stared at her shoes. All she could think about was how Arnold sorted through the rubbish bin to see what she had thrown out. How when she had two dishes of eggs in the refrigerator, one fresh and the other hard-boiled, he used to put them all in one large bowl because it looked tidier. How, thought Mrs Pratt, do you tell a fresh egg from an unshelled hard-boiled one?

His detailed neatness and his relatives had nearly driven her crazy. She thought of the time she lay on the carpet crying and saying she wished they had poison in the house so she could drink it and die.

Arnold had said, 'I'll just hang up your coat,' and after that she got up and cooked lunch. Arnold liked a cooked lunch and he liked coats to be hung up.

When they were newly married she begged to be taken away. This would have solved the problem of the relatives, but not the neatness. Arnold, obdurate, would not move.

'But I was born here,' he said. 'What would Mum say, and Aunty Vi, and what about Uncle Colin?'

In a fit of cold wildness Mrs Pratt packed some things and went on the bus, all one day and part of the night in a bitter frost, to see her mother.

'I hope you don't want anything,' her mother said. 'Buggalugs hasn't left much. I've been trying to keep it quiet but you might as well know he's gone off with some woman from up Nelson way. He's booked up stuff all over town and took my best clock. Just put the kettle on, will you? And get some wood in. Don't use any of the good stuff, that's for visitors. Get that mucky barky stuff. Good job you come really. The place hasn't had a good do through since you left.'

Mrs Pratt returned to Arnold and in time there came to her an obscure philosophy which she possessed secretly like the thorny shell of a crepuscular sea creature placed in an inner pocket.

Gradually she learned to snatch a little of what she called life within the framework that Arnold's obsession with neatness imposed, and learned to wear the yoke of his requirements with grace. She avoided his relatives when she could.

Only once did Mrs Pratt reveal this to Arnold and that was the afternoon a Pratt approached her in the library.

'How dare they,' she shrieked at Arnold the moment he stepped in the door that evening. 'They've got everywhere else. The library is mine.'

It was ridiculous. The library was a public place. As for relatives – she knew that when you married a person you had to bother with his family. It was simply that Arnold was all she could cope with.

Big Arnold, that plump and pouting puffin, had taken a step or two back at this belligerent stating of her territory by his uncaged canary.

In time quietness came upon them but never peace and that difference between quietness and peace is what their ease cost. Meticulous neatness was what he required and meticulous neatness was what he received. That was the bargain. Affection, interest and animation she saved for the cat, the birds in the garden and successive spiders named Albert who lived by the bathroom door.

'Why did you marry me, Arnold?' she asked him once.

'Don't ask silly questions.'

'Do you love me, though?'

'Not now,' said Arnold. 'Later.'

She supposed they meant different things by love and her spiky shadow on the wall that day seemed to lengthen, to assume the characteristics of a number in a sociology text dealing with the children of disturbed homes who seek what they lack in any marriage, and do not find it.

So ran Mrs Pratt's thoughts after Arnold's funeral.

'He was a wonderful man,' said Arnold's Uncle Colin, jammy bun in hand. 'Only sixty-four. Hardly more than a boy. He was a prince among men.' He thrust forward his cup. 'Fill her up again, there's a good girl, Myra, and give me a bit of that cake over there.'

Someone gave Mrs Pratt a cup of tea with milk and sugar added — she disliked milk and sugar in tea — and a large ragged piece of cake on a saucer. Arnold would not have liked that, she thought. Arnold would have liked a proper plate.

It was time now to do a particular job that had weighed upon her all day, had weighed upon her heavily since Arnold sank down in front of the refrigerator.

'It'd do her good to have a good cry,' said one of the cousins. 'Have you had a good cry?'

This last remark was addressed towards Mrs Pratt in a louder voice than was necessary as though Arnold's death had deafened her.

'Have a good cry,' they urged. 'Go on.'

Mrs Pratt did not care to reveal herself to the Pratts. If there was anything to cry about it was the wasted years and she had wept over those as she wasted them. If tears were to be shed now she would shed them for her lack of grief, for the invasion of her kitchen by the Pratts, the inspection of her dishcloths and for the fact that an unknown woman in an orange coat had looked in her wardrobe.

'He certainly done you proud,' she had said, fingering Mrs Pratt's grey fur jacket with the lucky sixpence in the upper left-hand pocket. 'He'll have left you a bob or two. You'll be sitting pretty.'

Mrs Pratt stood up. She must do the job.

'Goodbye,' she said. 'I am going to say goodbye to you all now.'

Goodbye? They turned questioning faces towards her.

'Goodbye. Permanently,' said Mrs Pratt. Her arms lay by her sides, the thumb and index finger on each hand linked to form a circle to induce calmness. This idea had come from a book. Mrs Pratt read a lot of books.

'We'll say goodbye now and we'll come back again tomorrow, first thing.'

'No, thank you,' said Mrs Pratt. 'I am going to say goodbye to you all now permanently. Now that Arnold is no longer here my link with you is severed.' How carefully she had mouthed the words as the clock in the hall struck one in the morning, then two, three.

'This's Arnold's house. We'll come if we like. We've got a right.'

'Goodbye,' said Mrs Pratt, the cracked record approach according to the book but like all instruction books it did not mention the party getting rough, the soufflé sinking or still being unpopular after reading *How To Be Popular*.

They said they knew what was best, she was upset and did not know what she was saying.

'Goodbye,' said Mrs Pratt.

She had never liked them.

Arnold's mother's wedding cry of 'So my son's married a nothing' was replaced in time by 'I've got no time for her' and 'She hasn't got our sort of appetite.'

If her dislike had been a seesaw it would have rocked on their gargantuan eating habits. It would have bounced on their custom of never saying thank you, of never congratulating a living soul on good fortune. It would have rested on their collective stupidity which was such that they regarded as lovably quotable an aged Pratt's habit of saying 'Everything have its season' as if this were a vividly Confucian remark instead of the ungrammatical corner-stone of Mrs Pratt's dislike.

In her life their season had come and now it could go.

'We've really got to be quite fond of you, sort of,' said one of them now. 'In our own way, over the years. You're quite a dag, that way you've got of talking.'

'Goodbye,' said Mrs Pratt.

As they crushed underfoot the golden leaves of autumn all down the front path they said what she needed was nourishment.

'If she was a needle,' said Myra Pratt, 'you couldn't thread her.'

They said they would be back in the morning to go through Arnold's things and when would Arnie's house be going on the market because Uncle Charlie was quite a good land agent and could do with the commission.

'Don't forget that Uncle Colin's the same size as Arnie in most things,' they said. 'Except shoes.'

They thought Arnold's footwear might fit Gloria's husband.

'Not that he's much chop,' they added, Pratt-fashion.

On a westering wind their voices came, dully now, through the trees.

'She shouldn't of cut back Arnie's roses so hard.'

'Look what she's done to his Lisbon lemon.'

'What about Arnie's new raincoat?'

'Did you ask her about his golf clubs? The new ones.' She supposed that was from a thinner, sporting Pratt nephew.

They jammed themselves behind the wheels of bottle-green or chocolate-brown motorcars and revved the engines with glutinous throbs, children like dumplings spilling over the back seats and the exhaust pipes giving off a brownish haze which could have been vaporized treacle.

It was strange, thought Mrs Pratt, that they reminded her constantly of food. Even their clothes were often patterned with currant buns or peppermint sticks, or had foreign writing on which said 'Le Fromage', 'Déjeuner, s'il vous plaît' or, for variety, 'Champs Elysées' which they thought meant being good at sport.

Mrs Pratt shut the front door and went to telephone the builder who had always done any alterations to the house.

'I would like you to come as soon as you can,' she said in the pedantic little voice that had been her arcane refuge from Pratt encroachments. 'I want you to make the front fence higher.'

How high did she want it? he asked.

'I don't really know,' said Mrs Pratt. 'But it must be higher than a person.'

They agreed on six feet.

'And I require a new front gate,' said Mrs Pratt. 'A gate like a door, with a doorknob and a lock so that when my friends are coming I can unlock it and otherwise I can lock people out.'

After that she meticulously cleared away all signs of occupation by strangers in what was now her house – it was easy as it just meant sweeping up drifts of sausage roll crumbs – and then she went to bed.

In the ensuing days the Pratts called often with that particular brand of persistent inexorability often possessed by the thick-headed. She did not answer the door.

A voracious reader, she gave up her usual diet of novels which for the most part dealt with the implications of life and death, public and private responsibility in satirical but wickedly funny vein. She waded through murder mysteries at the rate of two a day because they presented death, waste, spite, destruction and misery in cheerful guise within bright covers and they warmed her.

Spreading herself a little through the house now, she ate her meals off a tray where she could watch the birds. Often she ate only an apple or a banana. Arnold had liked all meals to be large and cooked, served at the table.

She used Arnold's garden twine and began to keep it in the kitchen instead of the garden shed. Her coat was rarely hung up.

Occasionally she would open Arnold's wardrobe which still contained all his clothes and she would say, 'Good morning, Arnold. Wind from the north today, always a bad quarter,' or 'Well, goodnight, Arnold, I'm off to bed now.'

Irreligious and unspiritual, an unbeliever in most things except the unquenchability of the human spirit, she nevertheless clung to the idea that it was a trifle rude to toss out all Arnold's things. What if some essence of Arnold remained?

Mrs Pratt gave up trying to explain to her friends that she left Arnold's possessions in their usual places out of politeness, not morbidity.

'Now you promise that next time we come you'll have done something about those things,' her friends would say and Mrs

Pratt, gently promising, would chide herself the next minute for mendacity.

Arnold had, after all, fed and clothed her all those years and she was used to him. A sort of affection came to her for Arnold when she realized that he took refuge in the minor details of life to avoid greater issues like triumph, aspiration and glory.

'Oh,' he had said when she told him this. Just 'Oh,' and he went off through the house holding a broken black shoelace and never said another word about the lack of spares in the shoe cupboard.

Her friends thought she should go away for a holiday.

'To forget,' they said, though she did not wish to forget her life. It was the only one she had had, and she had done her own odd best to ornament it.

'I might go on some sort of a trip,' she said experimentally to the builder who had by now begun work on the fence and the gate.

The builder nodded, and handed to her the day's offering, a 1900 sovereign in mint condition.

He collected coins and often brought one from his collection for her to see.

'And what would you think of this?' he would say, handing her a spade guinea or a Georgian penny. She often thought he presented the coins in lieu of conversation for he was an exceptionally silent man. She actually preferred them to greetings and remarks which were always over so quickly. The coins could be looked at, mulled over, put away and got out again, looked up in books, rather like a constantly revised conversation and more satisfying.

'Very interesting,' she used to say at the end of the day and he would pop the coin back in his pocket. That was all, but she sensed he knew she had looked it up in books and had found out its history in the course of the day like wonderfully satisfying silent chit-chat.

'I wouldn't mind going somewhere,' she told the builder, 'that reminds me of nothing. Where the people are not like people I have ever known and where nothing is at all familiar.'

The builder drank his tea and the day's coin felt warm and heavy in her hand, friendly even.

'I think I might try China.'

'There's an interesting place, now,' said the builder. 'China.'

Her friends stoutly maintained that the Sunshine Club tour of the world would be better.

'You'd see everything,' they said. 'Seventeen countries in thirty-eight days, and a cooked breakfast supplied throughout. You couldn't even read the notices in China.'

Notices did not interest her, she said. No language was necessary to see butterflies and animals or to look for the plaited nest of the hummingbird.

What she wanted to do, people said, was do Honolulu, have a look at Paris, mow through the Continent and have a peep at Greece for a couple of days.

'And don't forget the Dark Continent,' said readers of geographical magazines. 'Don't forget Mother Africa.'

'What I'd like to do with you,' said a large woman at a cocktail party, 'is to dump you down in the middle of Renaissance Italy.'

Mrs Pratt gave an imitation of pretended interest, but in her own mind her purpose became clear. She wished to go to China, and she would go there.

Her packing was accomplished behind closed doors and with the velvet curtains drawn so it would never be known that all she did was toss a few bits and pieces in a little bag. Arnold would have made her pack again with more things in case of this or that.

Addressing Arnold's wardrobe for the last time before her departure she said, 'Au revoir, Arnold. I am going for a little holiday in China. I will not lose my traveller's cheques. I will watch my handbag like a hawk and I will not overspend.' That was the sort of thing Arnold liked to hear.

A peculiar blitheness came over her as she tripped, like a forty-seven-year-old child of five summers, out over the tarmac to the aeroplane. She feared her radiant joy would scorch the steps to the cabin.

An image of the myriad towers of a fabled land glittered and trembled in her mind like a brilliant mirage as she was borne through the starry sky towards China.

It seemed that her whole life, which had been made up of chaos with flashes of joy, was now being weighed down on the side of joy.

Elizabeth Knox

from **POMARE**

LEX SCRAMBLED BACK DOWN the home side of the stopbank. It was tea time and the street was quiet. The Keenes ate closer to – as Frank complained – society hours, so Lex knew she wasn't yet missed. As she passed Sands' she heard her name called and looked about. A window was open into the narrow gap between the side of the house and the neighbours' fence. Thomas was hooking his hand at her. She came on to the edge of the property then was barred by a low hedge.

'Push through it,' Thomas whispered.

The hedge grazed her legs, but she was quick and it scarcely stung. She stopped beneath his window and put her hand on the wall where the weatherboards were still warm from a glancing sun.

Thomas folded his arms on the sill. In this light his skin looked dark, congested with the colour behind him – not a dim room but purple curtains, unlined. 'I've been sent to bed; not for being bad but "too seedy", Dad says. What do you think of that?'

'Seedy is short for going to seed,' Lex said. This was what passed for an opinion with her. 'Are you in bed?'

'My feet are.'

Lex could recall being sent to bed, in the afternoon, sick with the English measles, and how she woke at evening to a borderline light and the curtains open. 'Once when I was sick in bed I woke up—' Lex began, the recollection flat against her face like cold glass. 'The sun was going like—' she ran her hand along the weatherboards, '—*now*. It was the same window in our house. This window on this side.' Their houses were identical, but that the Keenes' was asbestos clad. 'The edges of the window were all yellow and the sky was blue. So blue—'

'Because you were shut in when everyone else had gone down to the river for a swim.' Thomas tried to help her out, this younger child who, as she spoke, blew up in his face, as gradual and fierce as a *Mount Vesuvius*, *Fairy Rain*, or *Flower Pot*.

'No, not fine, blue. Blue you can't breathe. Like, suppose there wasn't any air on the other side of the window. Or not much. Like on top of mountains. Like Sir Edmund Hillary and the oxygen tanks.'

'I've had oxygen.'

'Isn't it just another word for air?'

'No. It's special rich air.'

'Is it nice?'

'Yes.' Thomas seemed tired, he laid his head on his arms.

Lex looked at him with her mouth open – trying to imagine the different taste of oxygen to air, like cream to milk, then she went on: 'Suppose you are on top of a high mountain, without oxygen tanks—' she made a swift search of her father's mountain stories and found, '—the summit. You're on the summit and it's like a desert island. The air below you is the sea, the air above is the sky, freezing cold but not frozen and all blue. That was my blue.'

Thomas simply looked at her, quiet, his eyes cleared of colour by the dusk and curiously doll-like between their unfringed lids. Then he asked, with effort, 'Was it real?'

'I don't know.'

'Were you scared?'

'Not that something would happen, but I shut my eyes.'

Thomas moved his head to look along the gap between the house and neighbour's fence. At, perhaps, some kin of Lex Keene's blue. The spindly hawthorn, each branch, twig, spine and blossom black against the sky, looked like the template of all flowering trees. There again was the other world that seemed, often now, to pull up and park beside his own.

Thomas felt four icy pressure points on his forehead and when he opened his eyes – they had been closed – he saw the palm of Lex's hand, a shallow rosy cave. She drew back. 'You went to sleep,' she said.

Pain ran a comb through Thomas's bones and he came apart, slid back without a word on to his bed leaving the window unlatched. Lex called his name and listened. Silence made an emphatic reply. The room's darkness seemed organic, and the furry mildew that dotted the windowsill spores dropped of that darkness.

Frank caught his train well before the six o'clock swill. But it was still packed. He hefted his satchel into the luggage rack – already bulging, an overstuffed string bag – and stood holding on to a chrome knob on the end of a seat. The doors shut, the unit chirruped and set out from the shelter of Platform Five. The commuters flipped up the corner of their newspaper or narrowed their eyes against the glare from the platform of polished patches of old chewing gum, then the dazzle of broken glass between browned stones.

Frank stood facing a newspaper ad, a picture of Holyoake rising above a ripped-out headline: BRITAIN'S NEW MOVES TO ENTER EUROPEAN COMMON MARKET. The slogan read, 'More Than Ever Leadership Counts.' Frank inaudibly advised leadership not to count its chickens but its days, then looked around for something better to read.

It was near dark when Frank got off the train. And when he turned the corner where Taita Drive curved to follow the river there was more light from the street lamps than the sky – and from kitchens, domestic yellow electricity. No house had yet drawn its blinds, so Frank could see into every kitchen (repetitiously, kids at kitchen tables, mothers at sinks) at the front left corner of each house – State houses – the street a strip of film spooling between the shops at Pomare and those at Taita.

Frank saw Lex in her school clothes and pinafore coverall. She ran towards him – all sprint, no skip – as if in fright. But she hadn't seen him and he watched her turn down the path to the house and pause, as he planned to, to look for people in their kitchen.

'Less', she had called herself when she was younger and lisping still. Less. No parent is as intimate with a second child as a first. Frank had no notebooks of Lex's odd, childish remarks, or folders of scribbles. He had misfiled the curl from her first haircut, and his camera had broken shortly before her second birthday and hadn't been replaced. Jo was odd and, as the IQ test confirmed, highly intelligent. It was Jo he played pieces of music and lectured on the composers' lives. Jo he read bits of Tolstoy and Proust. He hoped Jo would grow up able to appreciate the achievements of great men. He hoped she'd be a like mind – perhaps write him letters about concerts or museum visits from the great cities of the world.

But Lex – Lex was born by emergency caesarean. Hester was white and depleted and weaned the baby at six weeks. Lex was colicky and, while Hester slept, Frank would walk the baby – curled up around her gripe and crying in long, exhausted screams – walk her up and down the kitchen. Since then she would always at least pause to reassess her distress if he asked her, 'Don't cry, Curly.' It made him feel able, and he loved her. He had no plans for his second daughter but her happiness.

Frank's daughters were in the lounge, sitting in the cool animated light of the television. This was a recent shift in the polarity of half the houses in the street. At evening previously unused front rooms – polished pianos and wedding photos or, in the Keenes' case, the bookcases and radiogram in its oak cabinet – were now full of kitchen chairs, still children and the demons of these broached Pandora's boxes: *The Adventures of Rin Tin Tin, Travellers' Tales, Cameras on the Campus*.

Frank remembered standing hand-in-hand with Lex on the footpath outside a neighbour's house, at dusk, watching through a window the first television on the street. There was something wrong with the vertical hold and the image scrolled up and up. He had to explain to Lex that this wasn't how TV told its stories – like those toy televisions in vogue with children; made with a box, two sticks, and a roll of paper on which pictures were drawn – a scroll of comic panels (Lex: 'And they find a Martian hiding in a tree . . .').

Steph was picking her nose. Frank tapped on the window and all three girls started, then laughed.

The book Glenda had chosen for the week was about dreams. It was bedtime and Thomas was in bed, and dreamy. The people in the book – Marianne and Mark – their tiredness was catching. Thomas made to yawn, tried to gulp down sleepiness. But he was tired rather than sleepy – and frying in discomfort, hot, curling up at the edges.

'And sure enough,' Glenda read, and her voice waned like a radio slipping off the station, 'she had hardly lain down for the night before she was asleep, and asleep was dreaming.'

Glenda had saved a life; Thomas was there and saw it. The previous summer, on perhaps his last long walk – he was tired then, but undiagnosed – Thomas had trailed along the river bank after Glenda and her boyfriend. The teenagers picked a spot by the rail bridge where the river was too swift for swimming, away from all the other picnickers, locals, the kids adrift on patched inner tubes. Glenda and her boyfriend laid their towels among the boulders, edge to edge on a mat of gravel. Glenda unfastened the back strap of her bikini and held its stiffened cups carefully against her breasts as she lay down. Her boyfriend smoothed Coppertone on to her back. 'Go away, droopy,' Glenda said to her brother, 'but not near the water.'

Thomas went the other way, clambered over progressively larger boulders, deposited by remote floods in the years before the city began to milk the Hutt's white headwaters. Under the rail bridge Thomas found Jo and Lex Keene, and Hayley Moynihan. They stood by the first cement pile, on a shelf hacked from the river bank. There was enough room for a tall man to stand upright, his head touching the steel girders of the bridge, or for children ten and under to stand on tiptoe reaching, without being able to touch. The shelf was completely dry and littered with broken glass (brown beer bottles) and charred wood from camp-fires. The piles themselves were sticky and stank of urine.

The girls were waiting for a train, for the clamour of a train passing at speed above their heads. They had been swimming and were still damp, wet cotton togs gathered to their bodies by row after row of shirring elastic. They were grubby, uncomfortable, expectant.

The wind shifted and the children were warned by a gust of noise, the bells at the crossing on Taita Drive. The rails sizzled. Hayley began to shout; she covered her ears. The ground trembled. The noise bore down on them, full spate, and swept everything away. They yelled, Thomas too, and danced in terror, in exaltation.

Then it had passed; the bridge shivered into solidity and only the rails telegraphed back the sound of wheels dropping across each join – clank-clank, clank-clank – a quarter, then a half mile up the line.

'Let's wait for the next one,' Thomas said.

'Clickity-click, clickity-click,' Hayley chanted, 'sixty-six, clickity-click!'

Lex picked up a charred stick and began to draw on the pile – a cupboard and crockery; a rack with dangling kitchen forks, spoons, fish-slice, potato masher; then, against the right angle of earth, a cat of snowman simplicity, two circles, ears, tail, whiskers.

Hayley had another blackened stick and was drawing, blasphemously, holes in her own hands while singing the peanut song:

> A peanut sat on the railroad track
> his heart was all a-flutter
> along came a train, the nine-fifteen
> toot toot, peanut butter!

As they waited someone walked by, overhead, limped from tie to tie – all the children recognized the wheezing hinge of David Hough's callipers. A minute after David passed the rails sizzled again, and Thomas and Jo's eyes met, alarmed. They ran out from under the bridge to see that – No! – David was only halfway across and had come to a halt looking up the line. He turned and began a hopping run back the way he'd come.

The children could see the train, a rattler, carriages drawn by a diesel engine – a big blunt front with a cow-catcher ploughing the air before it. Thomas and Jo began to shout encouragement to the limping boy. The train gave a blast of its horn, a megaphonic groan. Hayley stood gaping. The train horn sounded again, then the train began to brake. Lex ran back under the bridge and pressed her face into her imaginary kitchen cabinet; charcoal smeared her forehead and cheeks.

The train was on the bridge. David looked back over his shoulder and lunged forward, his shirt-tail flapped and the brace on his leg flashed in the sun. Then Thomas saw Glenda and her boyfriend stand up from among the boulders. The boyfriend put his hands to his head and pressed his skull; his eyes seemed to move farther apart, as if he was searching for an aperture through which an idea might make its way. Glenda had forgotten to hold herself together and Thomas stared at his sister's breasts. His eyes, in expectation of blood and violence, had never seen anything so tender and lovely. Glenda waved her arms and shrieked, 'Hang over the side!' She yelled this over and over, till David Hough, the train nearly upon him, veered to the edge of the bridge, caught hold of a protruding tie and dropped. The train crossed the place he had stood. He swung, shuddering with the bridge.

The train slowed to a stop, half of one carriage still on the bridge. The driver climbed out on to the footplate of the engine and looked back along the track. Glenda's boyfriend had scrambled up the embankment and on to the bridge to haul David to his feet. The driver began to shout, something about the police, prosecution. Glenda sat down on a rock and fastened her bikini; shook herself into it. The driver had a radio telephone – he shouted – that cretin had better stay put, the police would want to speak to him. Commuters had pushed their windows up and were peering out. 'You see to it!' the driver bawled. Glenda's boyfriend waved. David Hough sobbed and gasped, there were candlesticks of snot on his top lip and Glenda's boyfriend held him by the shirt – had done touching him for the moment.

'He'll get the belt, I bet,' Hayley said.

'Perhaps he'll be fined or sent to prison,' Thomas said.

'Borstal. Boys go to borstal.' Jo knew these things.

'His daddy will give him a good hiding.' Hayley relished the idea.

Thomas looked around. 'Where's Lex?'

Lex crouched halfway up the stopbank wiping her hands back and forth across the grass. Her hands were grey, reeking, and there was a streak of oil on her face, blacker than the charcoal. 'It came from the train,' she explained. 'It dripped down on me. I thought it was his blood.'

Glenda sat at the end of Thomas's bed. As she read she squeezed his foot through the covers – the counterpane. *Peter Pan*. She said he should try to put his pain into his shadow. But his shadow was a patch of mist, a warm breath shrinking on a cold windowpane. Was he confused? Hadn't they finished *Peter Pan* last week? Tonight it was *Marianne Dreams*. The book was face down on the bedspread. Glenda was at the door, calling, 'Mum! He's bad!'

This time the pain followed as the fever let go and left him settling slowly into a boy-shaped print of sweat, his pyjamas wet beneath him. He was like a piece of toast not put into a rack to cool but laid flat, left softening in its own steam. The fever relented but the pain followed, feeding still.

He wept – dry, weak, persistent – then slept for a short while. There was no gloss left in his young skin and his eyelids looked loose, crepey. The usual marvellous variations in colouring – blush, freckle, subterranean blues of venous blood – he had none of it, nothing but liverish yellow, contusions and pallor.

Thomas's mother folded the sheet back firmly, away from his face. He whined. If she could manage tonight, she thought. Only. If only she could manage only tonight—

The year had gone down in manageable pieces, and she had kept it down, days, nights, hospital visits. It was not an ordeal, it was – only – a dish she had not calculated was so burning hot, a dish containing tonight's dinner that she must not drop till she reached the bench. Not an ordeal – just one of her babies at three a.m. *Just necessary.*

*

Thomas's mother saw him to the lavatory in the early hours of the morning. When he had finished he wouldn't wipe himself, couldn't get up again. He slumped against the wall with his head hung. When she tried to move him he cried out – a piteous, angry, mindless complaint – as if he didn't know she meant the best for him; or didn't know her at all.

Fiona Farrell

A STORY ABOUT SKINNY LOUIE

THE SETTING

IMAGINE A SMALL TOWN: along its edges, chaos.

To the east, clinking shelves of shingle and a tearing sea, surging in from South America across thousands of gull-studded, white-capped heaving miles.

To the south, the worn hump of a volcano crewcut with pines dark and silent, but dimpled still on the crest where melted rock and fire have spilled to the sea, where they have hissed and set into solid bubbles, black threaded with red.

To the west, a border of hilly terraces, built up from layer upon layer of shells which rose once, dripping, from the sea and could as easily shudder like the fish it is in legend, and dive.

To the north, flat paddocks pockmarked with stone and the river which made them shifting restlessly from channel to channel in its broad braided bed.

Nothing is sure.

The town pretends, of course, settled rump-down on the coastal plain with its back to the sea, which creeps up yearly a nibble here a bite there, until a whole football field has gone at the boys' high school and the cliff walkway crumbles and the sea demands propitiation, truckloads of rubble and concrete blocks.

And the town inches away in neat rectangular steps up the flanks of the volcano which the council names after an early mayor, a lardy mutton-chop of a man, hoping to tame it as the Greeks thought they'd fool the Furies by calling them the Kindly Ones; inches away across shingle bar and flax swamp to the shell terraces and over where order frays at last into unpaved roads, creeks flowing like black oil beneath willows tangled in convolvulus, and old villa houses, gap-toothed, teetering on saggy piles, with an infestation of hens in the yard and a yellow-toothed dog chained to the water tank.

At the centre, things seem under control. The Post Office is a white wedding cake, scalloped and frilled, and across the road are the banks putting on a responsible Greek front (though ramshackle corrugated iron behind). At each end of the main street the town mourns its glorious dead with a grieving soldier in puttees to the north and a defiant lion to the south, and in between a cohort of memorial elms was drawn up respectfully until 1952 when it was discovered that down in the dark the trees had broken ranks and were rootling around under the road tearing crevices in the tarmac, and the Council was forced to be stern: tore out the lot and replaced them with plots of more compliant African marigolds. There are shops and petrol stations and churches and flowering cherries for beautification and a little harbour with a tea kiosk in the lee of the volcano. It's as sweet as a nut, as neat as a pie, as a pin.

Imagine it.

Imagine it at night, a print composed of shapes and shadows. Early morning, January 24, 1954. The frilly hands on the Post Office clock show 3.30 so it's 3.25am, GMT, as everyone knows. (Time is no more thoroughly dependable here than the earth beneath one's feet.) It's unseasonably cold. A breeze noses in over the breakwater in the harbour and in amongst the bottles and wrappers by the tea kiosk, tickling the horses on the merry-go-round in the playground so they tittup tittup and squeak, fingering the bristles on the Cape pines and sighing down their branches into a dark pit of silence. Flower boxes have been hung along the main street and as the wind passes they swing and spill petals, fuchsias and carnations. There are coloured lights and bunting which, if it were only daylight, could be seen to be red white and blue because tomorrow, the Queen is coming. At 3.05pm the Royal express, a Ja class locomotive (No. 1276) drawing half a dozen refurbished carriages, will arrive at the railway crossing on the main street. Here, Her Majesty Queen Elizabeth II and His Royal Highness Prince Philip will step into a limousine which will carry them up the main street past the Post Office, the banks and the shops which have all had their fronts painted for the occasion (their backs remain as ever, patchy and rusted). By the grieving soldier the Royal couple will turn left towards the park where they will be formally welcomed at 3.20pm by the Mayor and Mayoress and shake hands with 45 prominent citizens. They will be presented with some token of the town's affection. At 3.25pm they will commence their walk to the train and at 3.40pm they will depart for the south. The moves are all set out in the Royal Tour Handbook, the stage is set, the lines rehearsed, and the citizens, prominent and otherwise, are tucked under blanket and eiderdown, secure in the knowledge that everything has been properly organized. If they stir a little it is because the wind tugs at curtains, or because through the fog of dreaming they hear some foreign noise outside the windows where their cats and dogs have sloughed off their daytime selves and stalk, predatory, the jungles of rhubarb and blackcurrant. The sea breathes. Whooshaaah. Whooshaaah.

BRIAN BATTERSBY WITNESSES A CURIOUS PHENOMENON

Midway up Hull Street on the flanks of the volcano there is one citizen who is not asleep. Brian Battersby is sitting on his garage roof. His legs are wrapped in a tartan rug, his thermos is full of vege soup, and with stiff fingers he is trying to adjust the focus on his new 4-inch Cook refractor. Thousands of miles above his head a civilization more advanced than any on Earth is constructing a canal and by muffled red torchlight Brian is tracing the line of it: from the Nodus Gordii SE in the direction of the Mare Sirenum, at mind-boggling speed: a hundred miles a day? Two hundred perhaps? What machines they must have, what power! Above the Cape a meteor flares, green and white, and Brian pauses, waiting for the shower that will follow, but the meteor grows in brightness. Brighter than Mars. Bigger. A fireball as large as the full moon! For a moment the whole town is caught in brilliant silhouette and Brian sits motionless on the garage roof, vaguely aware of music, an odd percussive ticktocking. He cannot identify it, but the fact is that every hen in the town is singing. Necks stretched, tiny eyes like amber beads shining in the warm darkness of their fowlruns, they chorus: Wa-a-a-chet auf, ruft uns di-e Stim-mm-e, Awake! Awake! Out on the Awamoa Road a Hereford cow more sensitive than her sisters is levitating above a hedge and cats and dogs have forgotten the jungle, and kneel paws tucked to soft belly. The meteor explodes at last into a sequined fall of shining particles and the town recovers: hens tuck heads beneath wings, the cow descends with a soft thud and cats and dogs stretch and look uneasily about them into the night, ears flattened. Up on the garage roof Brian is shaking. He knows suddenly and with absolute clarity that those canals are not the work of superior beings who might offer solutions to fallible humanity but are mere ripples of dust blown this way and that by howling wind, and he knows that he, Brian, is a small rather pompous accounts clerk who will spend the next 30 years in the offices of the Power Board, and that his wife wishes now that she'd married Don Barton, former All Black and successful stock and station agent, when he'd asked as a promising junior back in 1948. She stays for the kids and takes out her disappointment in housewifely perfection. It's too much truth to handle all at once. Best not confronted. Brian reaches for his notebook. 'January 24, 1954. 0357 UT.,' he writes with trembling hand. 'Mag. – ?? fireball in clear sky. Green and white.' What amazing luck! What a coup! He peers up into the darkness, eyes still dazzled and sparkling and attempts accurate estimation. 'Travelled 30°–35° start 25° altitude 140° azimuth. Approx. 1 min. 58 sec. duration.' What a note it will make for *Meteor News*! 'Accompanying sonic phenomena,' he adds and reaches for his thermos and a shot of hot soup.

Two miles from his garage roof in the Begonia House at the Public Gardens, Louie Symonds, Skinny Louie, aged 15, is giving birth.

SKINNY LOUIE HAS A BABY

The Begonia House is warm, steamy, sticky with primeval trickling and the sweet-sour smell of rampant growth. Louie has managed to drag some coconut matting into a corner and squats there, full-bellied and bursting, hands clamped to a water pipe while her body tears in pieces. No one can hear her groan. The Gardens are empty. Only beds of pansies and petunias wheeling away from the glass house along the edges of gravel paths, circling the Peter Pan statue and the Gallipoli fountain and the specimen trees with their identity labels tacked to their trunks. Louie is on her own.

Far away to the south is the dark little warren where she lives with her mum Lill. Lill isn't in tonight either, as it happens. She's been off for three weeks or so on a Korean boat and she won't be back till it leaves for the north with its cargo of snapper and squid, and the girls are put ashore. Lill says she's got a thing for the chinks: she likes them small and smooth and she likes the way they pay her no trouble and she likes the presents: whisky, stockings, a nice jacket. It's better than hanging around the Robbie Burns anyway taking your chances with any poxy John who fancies a bit between jugs. Louie came with her once or twice down the boats, but she gave them all the pip, got on people's nerves being so quiet, hanging around like a fart at a funeral, so Louie stayed home after that while Lill with her Joan Crawford lips and her hair curled went into Port. At this moment she's bobbing about two miles off Kaikoura wondering if she's got enough to go eight no trumps and Louie is in pain. She has walked for days to this place, travelling by night, and by day when the sun slammed down like a pot lid, she has curled round her belly and slept under a bush or a bridge.

She has often done this: got the jumpies, set off walking till she's quiet again, then turned for home. This time she's had them bad. She has walked and slept for days, sucking a stone for spit, following the road up from the city to the hills, past the white rock where she lay once months before to warm herself in the sun. She'd been sprawled, dozing, light tangled in her lashes in tiny scarlet stars, when a shadow fell upon her like a stone. Louie looked up and there was a hawk hovering. She lay very still. The hawk flew closer, settled. She took the weight of him, gasping as his talons drove tiny holes in her breast. He dipped his tail feathers in her open mouth. She smelled the dry bird scent of him. Then he rose wings beating into the sun and she lost him in the glare.

She passed the rock two nights ago. Yesterday morning she stopped near a country store where she got a whole Vienna slipping it quick as winking under her coat while the man was lifting trays from a truck. She'd sat under a hedge in early morning half-light and picked out a hole, chewing slowly, and a plump grey mare had come to her from the mist and stood while she squeezed its titties and took the milk, licking it from her fingers, glutinous, sticky, Highlander Condensed. When the sun was up, she slept. It was wise to hide by day. She didn't trust cars. When she was little, cars came to their house, crawling like grey beetles round the road from Port and when they saw them they'd run away, her and Alamein and Yvonne, because the cars meant questions and picking at their hair for cooties and icecream sticks forcing their tongues back and where? And why? And how often? And Lill in a paddy, though she was as nice as pie to the lady clearing a space and saying would she care for a cup of tea? But as soon as the car had gone it was bloody cow and why the hell couldn't Louie learn to smile instead of standing there like some mental case because if she didn't they'd have her out to Seacliff, she looked that daft. Lill slammed around them savage, so they learned to scatter when cars came, hiding like the cats in the smooth places beneath the hedge or the washhouse. But once Ally and Yvonne weren't quick enough and the lady got them, took them away somewhere and they were never seen again. So Louie hid from cars. You couldn't trust them.

Tonight, Louie has crossed some paddocks sniffing for the sea and found herself on a hill above a railway line which curved down into a crisscross pattern of light. Her body was heavy and her back ached. She'd been picking at the bread rolling doughballs when she went to the lav suddenly, no warning, right there in her pants, so she peeled them off and stuffed them steaming into a bush. Cough said a sheep. Louie began to walk along the railway towards the town. The pain in her back was growing and another tiny nut of it pressed at the base of her skull.

Clump clump clump sleeper by sleeper careful not to fall between and have bad luck. Around her everything was coming alive: trees tapped her shoulder, fence posts skittered by on the blind side and the grass lined up and waved. The weight in her belly heaved and she had to stop at the bottom of the hill for everything to settle. The railway line crossed a street. Louie stepped from the sleepers onto tarmac and ahead was an arch of flowers, framing black shadow.

Then the pain came up from behind and grabbed her so that she had to cry out as she used to at school when Wayne Norris chinese-burned her arms or stuck her with a pen nib saying cowardy custard cry baby cry only this was worse and she tried to run away through the archway into the dark. The pain lost her there for a bit so Louie took her chance, stumbling across a lawn to the shelter of trees and a cage where a bird asked her who was a pretty cocky, along paths frilled with grey rows of flowers to a glass house gleaming when the moon came from behind cloud where Louie hid, sneaking into a corner. But this pain was too smart. It had slipped in beside her already and was squeezing sly, cowardy cowardy custard, driving her into a black hole where there was nothing but a voice groaning over and over and her body ripping and suddenly silence. A slither. And silence.

On the coconut matting between her legs lay a sticky black thing, wriggling in the sweet stench of blood. Louie crouched waiting for the pain to jump her again but it had gone, sidled off shutting the door silently. Louie wiped some jelly from the black thing and it mewed under her hand.

They lay quiet together. Slowly the glass about them turned to grey squares then white and Louie felt her legs twitch. The warm air here settled round her head like a thick blanket and she needed out. She took her cardie, and wrapped it round the thing then stood carefully, wobbling a little, and went outside where the grass was shiny and her feet left dark prints as she walked on water past the bird and the flowers to the archway and the street. She moved slowly past houses with their curtains drawn still and the cats coming home to sleep, down a long street to the shore. The sea was stretching and waking too and the clouds as she walked up the beach were golden bars with the sun slipping between. She stopped from time to time to wash blood from her legs. She ate the last of the bread. In a cleft in the low clay cliff were a wheelless Ford, some mattresses stained and spitting fluff, broken boxes, a pile of rotting plums. Louie was tired. She dragged a mattress into the car, and curled up to sleep. On the gearshift a nursery spider had spun its web. Baby spiders jittered under the membrane, hundreds of them. Louie prodded gently at their opaque shell and they scattered at her touch but she was careful not to tear a hole because then the cold could come in and kill them all.

That's the story of how Louie Symonds, daughter of Lilleas

Symonds popularly known as Shanghai Lill, gave birth. The paternity of the child is in some doubt. It is possible that the father is Wayne Norris, an acned youth who, since primary school, has paid Louie in bags of lollies for a quick poke in the cemetery on the way home. She's particularly fond of gob-stoppers. She likes lying back in the long grass beside the stone IN L VING MORY of Isabella Grant 18 blank blank OH D TH WH   IS THY   NG while Wayne wiggles his dicky about prodding hopefully, and when she's had enough of that she can say get off, roll over and see how the lolly has changed from red to yellow to blue.

Wayne is a definite possibility.

It is equally probable that the father is a hawk.

THE QUEEN COMES BY TRAIN

The Queen was coming. Maura stood with her mother and father and Shona down by the railway crossing at the very end of the route. She would have preferred to be in the park suffering torments of jealousy while some other little girl with perfect curls and a perfect dress handed the Queen a posy while performing a perfect curtsey, but they'd been late and this was the closest they could get.

Dad hadn't wanted to come at all. 'Load of poppycock,' he'd said. 'Mrs Windsor and that chinless cretin she married riding along waving at the peasants and mad Sid and the rest of them bringing up the rear kowtowing for all they're worth. Lot of nonsense.' 'I think she's pretty,' said Maura who had a gold Visit medal pinned to her best frock and a scrapbook of pictures cut from *Sunny Stories* in her bedroom: The Little Princesses at Play with the Royal Corgis on the Lawn at Balmoral, The Little Princesses in Their Playhouse which had a proper upstairs and wasn't just a made-over pig pen with ripped sheets for curtains. 'Mrs Barnett says the Queen has a peaches and cream complexion.'

'Peaches and bloody cream!' said their father, thumping the table so his tea spilt. 'There weren't too many peaches around back in 1848 when her lot were gorging themselves in London while our lot ate grass, and don't forget it.' Dad hated the Queen, Oliver Cromwell and Winston Churchill because of the Troubles and the Famine and because they-came-across-and-tried-to-teach-us-their-ways. 'That's years ago,' said Mum. 'Now turn around Maura so I can brush out the other side.' Maura turned, glad to be relieved of the tight ringlet sausages which had dug into her scalp all night. 'And what about during the war?' said their mother, who was pink-cheeked today and ready for a fight. 'They stayed in London didn't they? They stayed with the people in the East End right through the Blitz and the Queen Mother even said she was glad the Palace got bombed because then she could feel they were sharing the suffering.' 'Suffering?' said Marty. 'What did she know about suffering, one of the richest families in the world and you know how they got there don't you? Murder and betrayal and half of them illegitimate into the bargain, born the wrong side of the . . .' 'Shh,' said their mother, her mouth tight-lipped round a blue satin ribbon. 'The children . . . Hold still, Maura, for pity's sake.' Marty drank his tea morosely. 'Eating grass,' he said. 'Eating dirt, so some English bugger could go in velvet.' A final tug at the ribbon and Maura was released. 'Well, are you coming or not?' said Mum driving a hat pin into her pink church hat, and Dad said he supposed he would, if she was that set on it, but he was damned if he was going to get dressed up. The Queen would have to take him in his gardening clothes or not at all, and Mum said nonsense, you're not leaving the house in that jersey, so go and get changed, there was still time, but of course there wasn't and they could hear the crowd roar like a wave breaking before they were halfway down the hill and they had to run and push even to find the place to stand by the Gardens gate.

The pipe band was wheezing and wailing a few yards away and Maura would have liked to go and stand up close to watch the men's cheeks puff and the rhythmic flap of their white duck feet and to feel her ears buzz with drum roll and drone. But they were inaccessible through a dense forest of legs and bottoms: fat, skinny, trousered, floralled and striped, milling about so that she felt as frightened and inconsequential as she had when she'd opened the gate at Uncle Roy's and the cows had pressed through before she'd been able to jump to one side, buffeting her in their eagerness to get to the paddock. She'd have liked a ride on her father's shoulders, but Shona was already in place looking goofy with her paper flag and her bottle teat clenched between her teeth. Maura tugged at her mother's hand but knew she was too heavy and that her mother couldn't lift her, not now with the baby inside. Mum looked down and said don't fuss poppet and hang on tight because there's such a crowd. Maura needed no instruction. Around her the huge bodies pressed and she took sticky hold of her mother's skirt. The crowd noise was like static which tuned in snatches into God Save the Queen and cheering. (The Mayor's wife was presenting Her Majesty with a white begonia in a silver casket, Mrs Barnett told them next morning, and the Mayor was giving the Prince a photo of the Begonia House to hang on the wall at Buckingham Palace.) Then the roar built like rain drumming and Mum stood tiptoe saying, 'Oh she's coming! Maura, you must see her properly, this is a Once-in-a-Lifetime Opportunity!' And before Maura could protest she had scooped her up, and was tapping a man's shoulder and asking, 'Could my daughter get down to the front please? She can't see.' Handing her over like a parcel, passed from person to person till she stood at the very edge of the crowd where there was no coach and no horses but an ordinary man and woman walking along the road past the baths, talking sometimes to the crowd or waving, and the woman's face was a bit like the Queen's but not peaches and cream and topped with an ordinary hat, not a crown. People were calling hurrah hurrah and the pipe band shrilled so Maura waved her flag uncertainly as the man and woman passed by and in a very ordinary way, exactly as anyone might, climbed up the stairs onto the train, turned and waved, and the train chugged (whooshaaah whoosh-aaah) away down the track.

Then the crowd broke. Maura stood with her paper flag but no hand came down out of the press of bodies and no voice said, 'Ah, there you are Maura,' lifting her up to safety ... She was pushed and prodded, spun and stepped about until she found herself up against a floral arch and beyond it lay a smooth and empty lawn, so she went there, and once she was there she remembered the parrot and then Peter Pan and then the Begonia House where you could pick up fuchsias from the floor and wear them for earrings, and that was how she found the baby.

It was like finding the kittens mewing blind and wriggling in the long grass by the sand pit, except that the baby's eyes were open and it waved its hands sticky and streaked with cream but perfect just the same with proper nails. Maura took her hankie and spat on it as her mother did for a lick and a promise and wiped at the baby's dirty cheek. The baby turned instantly to her finger, opened its pink toothless mouth and sucked. Maura was entranced. She gathered the baby up as she had gathered the kittens, tucked firmly inside the dirty cardigan, and carried her discovery out into the sun.

PEG AND MARTY ARE GRANTED UNDERSTANDING

They stood by the gate, frantic, pale. 'Bloody irresponsible,' Marty was saying. 'Sending a child her age off on her own in a crowd like this.' He hadn't realized till this minute how much Peg's impulsive optimism, which he loved, also infuriated him and how much he longed to attack and destroy it. Predictably she was refusing to recognize how appalling this situation was. He knew. He'd seen the worst happen. He'd seen a man step on a patch of desert dust and his legs sever, the trunk falling after in a torn and heavy arc. He went to Mass, but knew it was useless, that this was simply habit, and that you could pray as Donovan prayed on the truck coming out at Sidi Rezegh and die mouthing Hail Mary in bubbles of blood. He voted Labour, argued with Jansen in the tea room who said that the unions were full of bloody commies and they'd been dead right to send in the troops in '51, but knew that this faith too was illusion, that there was no common cause, that the reality was each man alone, bleating, as the blow fell. And here was Peg with a daft bright desperate smile saying the swings, she'll have gone to play on the swings. And Peg is avoiding Marty's eye but knowing him there beside her, the heavy dark weight of him and his despair which she can't touch, ever, or relieve. She can make him laugh, she can love him, but when they lie together a bleak and faceless nothing sprawls between them grasping at her throat so she wakes, heart beating, night after night. She fights against it in Marty, suppressing panic as she does now, refusing to share his vision (Maura face down on the duckpond, dragged into the water lilies by the swans, hand in hand with some enticing nameless terror . . .). But at this moment she knows suddenly that she won't be able to struggle for ever, that her optimism is a frail thing and that in time she will have to choose: leave or give up the fight, let the blackness take her. Love and survival are in opposition. It's appalling. Too big a truth to face all at once. Better encountered bit by bit. But look, there is Maura now, safe and sound after all ('You see?'), her blue nylon dress stained and carrying a grubby bundle. And 'Mum,' Maura is saying, 'I've found us a baby.'

They take the baby along the street to Dr Orbell's surgery and as they pass people draw back on either side like waves parting and quiet for a second with curiosity. But when the family with its grubby bundle has passed, an extraordinary thing happens. People turn to one another and in a sudden rush, earnest and eager, they confess those things that have most oppressed them. They tell one another truths, pleasant and unpleasant. So McLean, most prominent of the prominent citizens, tells Davis the Town Clerk that he bought land on the northern river flats six months before development on a tip-off from a cousin on the Council. Jameson, junior partner in Lowe, Stout and Jameson, seeks out Lowe and tells him he has invested £5,000 of clients' money in a salmon hatchery which appears certain now to fail. Partner reveals that he has swindled partner, parent has coerced child, friend has failed friend. So the day of the Queen's visit ends for some in scuffling and recrimination, for others in forgiveness and pity. We make what we can of the truth.

WHAT HAPPENED TO LOUIE

When it grew dark Louie walked along the shingle to the river's mouth. Her legs still ran with blood and her breasts tingled so that she had to lie face down on the cold river sand to soothe their swelling. She followed the bank inland through dank grass willow and blackberry feeling her body lighten, her feet finding their accustomed rhythm and visible again across the sack of her vacated belly. That night she ate a pie she found in a safe hanging from a tree. Yellow pastry, gravy, meat. On the third night she ate only a handful of leaves so that her mouth ran with a green cud. The nor'-wester blew down the valley, burning the grass to brown crackle and a butter-moon slid across the sky. The river was loud with the sound of stones being dragged to sea. She came to a hall, brightly lit within its ring of cars, and climbed the smooth shoulder of the hill behind. Scraps of music, thump of dancing, laughter, the rattle of sheep running off into tussock and matagouri. Louie stands alone on the crest looking out over the valley. The power lines loop from hill to hill and Louie reaches out to swing down and away with them. Like in the movies. Like Tarzan.

She dazzles in a moment and rises splendid into the night sky.

*

THE YOUNG FARMERS' CLUB EXPERIENCES A BLACKOUT

In the valley the Young Farmers' Club summer dance is inter-rupted by a blackout halfway through the Military Two. Couples stand arm in arm in the dark while Mort Coker tries the switches and the fuse box in the kitchen. Someone has a look outside and shouts that the whole place is black, it must be bird strike or a line down up the valley. In the darkness body blunders against body, giggling. Then Ethne Moran finds a torch and the beam of it squiggles over faces caught wide-eyed like rabbits on a road. Someone brings in a tilly lamp. The band attempts a few bars, deee dum dee dum who'syerladyfren, but stops because no one seems interested. They stand about instead talking, and a few couples are edging away to the dimly lit corners. Then Ethne, who has organized the supper, claps her hands and jumps up onto the stage. 'Come on,' she says, lit by the tilly lamp and holding in her outstretched hands a strawberry cream sponge. 'No point in letting good food go to waste! Give us a hand, Margie.' Margie Pringle brings out the sausage rolls and finds a bread knife and Ethne kneels by the lamp to cut the cake into triangles, cream spurting beneath the blade. Side on her white dress is transparent and Ross Meikle watching thinks she's a cracker. Big breasts, curving stomach, long in the leg, and good teeth nice and even, with that little gap at the front. Ethne looks up. She hands him a piece of cake, then leans towards him and bites his ear lobe very gently leaving her uneven imprint in soft flesh. 'You do something to me,' she sings in a buzzing whisper, 'that electrifies me.' So they go outside into the warm night where it turns out that she isn't that struck on Bevan Waters after all, that she'd fancied Ross all along. On the back seat of the Holden she proves moreover to be astonishingly inventive, so that together they execute with ease a whole series of manoeuvres which Ross had previously discounted as possibly risky, definitely foreign and perilously close to deviance.

Ross thinks as a result that it might be worth dropping Margie Pringle who was getting on his nerves anyway with her lisping sweetness and that he'd be better off with Ethne who was bossy god knows but had a few clues.

Meanwhile, within the hall, Warren Baty is confessing that it was his ram that had got in among the Coopers' Corriedale-Romney flock last winter and Jim Cooper, a whole season lost, is saying, never mind, no lasting harm done. And Alasdair McLeod is telling the Paterson brothers that it was him who nicked their chain-saw; he'd come over one afternoon when they were out and borrowed it and he'd meant to give it back but they'd made such a fuss calling the police and all that he hadn't felt he could face it and he'd be around next day just to get the bloody thing off his conscience. Miria Love is telling Joan Shaw that she doesn't like the way she conducts Women's Division meetings and Pie Fowler is telling anyone who'll listen that she can't stick the valley, they're a bunch of snobs who've never let her forget for one minute that she's a townie and she'll be off back to the city just as soon as she can settle things with Bill.

Around the walls hang the valley teams since 1919, lined up for the photographer, thighs spread, fists clenched, unamused by the extraordinary goings-on in the darkened hall: under the influence of the night, sausage roll in one hand, beer in the other, the young farmers appear to have been overwhelmed by truth. The room is buzzing with honesty and for some the accompaniment is love and forgiveness, for others bitter recrimination. There seems to have been a sudden rise in the temperature. 'Remember the morning after,' the valley teams counsel, stonily. 'In the morning will come the accounting.'

A Power Board gang went up to check the lines next day. They found nothing out of place and the power had come back on, of its own accord, at dawn. There was a pair of footprints burned deep in a rock by the pylon; about a size five, they reckoned. That was all.

So, that's the story of how Skinny Louie, daughter of Lilleas Symonds popularly known as Shanghai Lill, gave birth, and walked up the valley and vanished in splendour.

Her baby was taken in care by Marty and Peg Conlan. She'll be grown by now, ready to come into her territory. Any day we could hear of her, storming in from the desert, swooping down from the eye of the sun, casting truth about her like a bright shadow.

And won't we scatter.

Gregory O'Brien

THE VERGE OF LOSING SOMEBODY

from DIESEL MYSTIC

CAN YOU SEE the town from here? asks Johnny Ruatara. On the far side of the river, the far side of six empty milk bottles and a dead pukeko.

Dargaville rising in a vapour. He watches vessels shuffle up the harbour, reads their names and counts them – five vessels on the fingers of one hand:

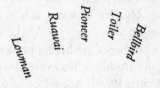

We are sitting on swings in a park beside the Northern Wairoa River. It is late afternoon when the swings are at the lowest point of their trajectory and it is early afternoon when the swings reach the highest point.

I tell him I am on the verge of losing something. But he tells me not to worry. He lost a lake once.

The park is located on the verge of the highway south and on the verge of losing somebody.

Can I tell you a story a diesel mechanic from Ruatoria once told me? Johnny Ruatara asks.

I know the story, I reply. I know that man.

Johnny Ruatara was once responsible for a number of trees and one, to be exact, lake. These he was devoted to. And would march among the rows of seeds-to-become-trees, speaking words of encouragement.

Grow, gentlemen, grow!

Wandering about the newly irrigated land.

Grow, lads, grow!

Then, one night, his lake walked off. Under cover of storm clouds, the lake burst its bank and travelled as far as the Northern Wairoa River, taking a pumpshed and family car with it.

His telephone rang in the early hours of the following morning. It was the Forestry Service and they wanted to know what had happened to their lake, which now amounted to only a few acres of mud with a curious wooden artifact protruding (this they later identified as the prow of a Maori canoe). By the time Johnny Ruatara arrived at the scene, three men were surveying the breach. One suggested it had happened before, that lakes come and go. Another believed the lake could be *reinstated*, talked of the height of a river, the elevation of water, a lake going down (or is it up) in the history of clouds.

Hands knotted in disbelief, umbrellas prodding at the sky, the men stood viewing the landscape between Lower Lake Rototuna and the Northern Wairoa River. According to what laws of nature or chance, they wondered, did the lake rearrange the cattle in their fields as it made its way off.

Johnny Ruatara mentions uncovering seashells in the mud at the bottom of the lake, skeletons of saltwater crabs miles from the coast, their brains intact, still ticking over.

And he mentions the artificial raising of the lake level four years earlier, more than the surrounding embankment could stand. And that season's unseasonal rain.

The previous afternoon he had seen a man in red trousers on a red field. A presage of a storm beyond the weather.

And how were they now going to water the trees? It appeared to be up to the three white clouds in the sky above the lake and the three men in white shirts who were now busily eating an orange, split three ways.

What do you make of that? asks Johnny Ruatara. A lake come to rest, gone off into the ocean somewhere by way of the Northern Wairoa River, which must have, some time during that night, swelled for a moment, twitched and proceeded. A lake harvesting half-grown crops, the newly planted kauri, gone down among mud-barges and burnt-out wrecks. And they are still talking of repairing the breach, plugging the abyss . . .

Now it is night-time at the lowest point of the swing's trajectory and late afternoon at the highest point.

One day you'll get your lake back, I assure him while walking back to the car. But it won't be those three men in white who will be responsible.

Driving away from the verge of leaving somebody, it occurs to me that the lake must be hiding somewhere near the bottom of the river. And Johnny Ruatara knows where it is, as he sways backwards and forwards. And, from the highest point of his swinging, he can now see the first rays of morning light crossing the waters.

My eyes travel great distances to reach these tears. And reflected in each tear I find the face of a woman. Her eyes survey a particular longing and her hair rises and falls as the wind inside each tear rises and falls.

Anne Kennedy

THE ROAD TO DAMASCUS

MY GREATGRANDMOTHER who couldn't suck eggs. Oh she was hopeless, a mope and a malcontent. She was tardy and truculent, vague and vain, but her main failing was — she could NOT budget.

She could scour she could starch she could sew she could knit, she could stew up the meat and boil fat to make soap. But could she behave? Could she be thrifty? Could Greatgrandmother be satisfied with *anything* in this *world*? Oh no she was chronically covetous spendthrift and shiftless.

What was the matter? they asked on the Coast. (That's where they lived, there was only one Coast.) She had a husband a house nine children to fill it, a cat and a dog and a goat and some geese. Chooks — bits of fluff that blew round in the yard — rabbits to boil, turnips to bake. What, what more could she possibly want?

Her husband's employment was not of the ilk of the typical man on the job on the Coast. He wasn't a shoveller he wasn't a groveller he didn't get black and take baths in the yard. He earned more than most he took home more than most. But Greatgrandmother said she didn't see more than most.

He said *she* couldn't budget.

Her husband (Greatgrandfather, 'Kennedy' to her) was not an unreasonable man he was not a bullying man. He adored his wife. But from the very day they were wed he saw he'd have to keep a tight rein on Greatgrandmother. And he did.

Each week there was the ceremony of the breadwinnings. Greatgrandmother received on her tongue what Greatgrandfather deemed necessary for food clothes bills and unforeseen, and she blessed herself. The rest – one of the great mysteries – went into a fund for the education of a son at a seminary in Sydney.

There was James there was John there were Frank and Vince. There was poor little Joe who drowned one grey day. And there were Molly and Annie and – then they lost count – till they came out at the end with nine mouths to feed nine bodies to clothe. School shorts to be bought woollen stockings and socks sturdy shoes for the boys pinafores for the girls. Nightshirts and night-gowns, longjohns and petticoats. And two suits of clothes for the man of the house, one workaday grey, one black for the sabbath, with white winged-collar shirts and gold cuff-linked cuffs and a soft-knotted tie of funereal silk.

On Sundays Greatgrandmother laid out this suit. She laid it out as if it were dead with a reverence reserved for not-of-this-world. She had laundered the shirt on Monday mended on Tuesday starched and ironed on Wednesday and brushed and aired the whole outfit on Saturday ready for reincarnation on Sunday.

On this day, the seventh day, she also put away her husband's weekday clay pipe and replaced it with his Sunday birchwood.

Then Greatgrandmother made the beds aired the rooms stoked the range laid out the breakfast prepared the joint for dinner put the vegetables in to soak and mixed the dry ingredients for the pudding. She fed the chooks fed the cat fed the dog fed the youngest. She got the children ready got herself ready by flinging on her coat and pinning on her battered flat black straw hat, and the whole family went off to Mass.

Greatgrandmother couldn't behave. She could not would not

pray. She'd sit in church and look along the pew filled with her children all clean and shiny and pressed and she would feel proud. She'd kneel down and look at her husband all clean and dull and pressed and feel – fond. She'd stand up and look at the other people in the church, the boys with their sailor collars, the girls with their sashes, the men in their grave suits and the women in their coats. At last she would pray.

It was the year of Our Lord 1894. The fashion was for cape collars big sleeves caught in at the wrist and Mary-Mother-of-God a bell-shaped fall from a tapered waist. There were some beautiful coats Amen-Amen oh there were, some magnificent specimens among the worshippers. Linen mohair camelhair wool. And the furs in that church! Not just lapin, sinners, but real furs, lynx and skunk and Russian fox, sable seal marmot goat. There were furs among the faithful.

Greatgrandmother's coat didn't have much of a pile. It was a thin greenishgrey gaberdine with a shine and it hung on her back like a streak of slime. The hem had been altered so many times it was now puffed up with a fat false pride. She'd bought it as part of her wedding trousseau – a married woman must have a serviceable coat, one that can take the good with the bad – and there'd been little to spend on frivolities since, what with nine mouths to feed nine bodies to clothe and a son to send to seminary school.

But all the same she was ashamed of the coat.

After Mass she would scuttle away from the throng and walk quickly home with her flat black straw bowed and there would be glad to unspike her old hat and shake off the hideous green gaberdine, to be safe in the kitchen and warm near the range and clean shiny and pressed in her work overall. She blew up the fire sliced up the bread dished up the porridge brewed up the tea. She was here she was home and away from the world who would jeer at the state of her gaberdine coat. Her husband updated himself with the news.

Her husband (Greatgrandfather, Kennedy, the same) stayed in

his Sundaysuit all the day through. The boys wore their longs their best shirts and their ties, and in order to keep their velvet frocks clean the girls played outside in their smocked petticoats. If there were visitors that afternoon the family of course would want to look neat.

Greatgrandmother cleared the breakfast dishes away. She put the joint and the potatoes in the oven. She boiled the pudding in a muslin cloth. She stewed some plums she made sweet sauce she made Yorkshire. She turned the potatoes. She steamed the greens. She reset the table and made the gravy. Finally she dished up the dinner.

But typically the meat was tough and as usual the potatoes were underdone and the silverbeet lukewarm, the pudding was gluggy and the sweet sauce – sticky. Oh she was hopeless. Look at her sitting down to Sunday dinner and still in her apron! But they all ate and they all worshipped the ground she walked on.

Now Greatgrandmother was not a working woman. She didn't earn money for her labours like any common drudge. Why should she with a husband to keep her? Greatgrandfather certainly wouldn't approve of his wife selling herself. No wife of mine will work! No wife was Greatgrandmother.

She deceived her husband, not because she wanted to but because she had to. She hid from him, in full knowledge of her wrongdoing, the fact that she was operating a little business.

Each week day she would go down to the gate to meet the children as they came from school. Hordes of children running shrieking like locusts ravenous children her own seven youngest amongst them, and her own would rush up to the house and into the kitchen, seven curses, and ravage the bread bin the cake tins the cheese cooler and milk pail.

One afternoon Greatgrandmother baked a tray of her mother's cupcakes. She baked in her sleep, in her childhood, she dreamed and sang as she baked. She dreamed of things fuzzy and snuggly and tapering ever so slightly at the wrist and she dreamed of herself as adored. Greatgrandmother took her tray of cakes down to the gate where she set them on a table and put up a sign: Cupcakes ½d each.

Soon a plague of children arrived. Some of them had ha'pennies and they bought cakes and the other children stood on tiptoe to watch with currant eyes and to beg for a taste just a nibble *please* and then they ran home to ask for ha'pennies ha'pennies Mum can I have a ha'penny for a cupcake tomorrow they're bosker cupcakes.

Tomorrow Greatgrandmother baked two trays of cakes. She dreamed and she sang, she sang *Mama's little boy* and *O Bread of Heaven*. More children had ha'pennies and she sold all the cakes. The next day Greatgrandmother baked *three* trays of cakes and mothers had given their children sixpences to buy cakes for the whole family a round dozen Betty get me a round dozen of Mrs Kennedy's cupcakes. Greatgrandmother put up a new sign: Cupcakes ½d each, 6d a baker's dozen. They were famous cupcakes.

All the same Greatgrandmother was ashamed. She was ashamed of her peddling her greed and her wile. Wasn't she already vague and vain? Now she was voracious as well. Great-grandmother was nothing but trash. She hid the evidence. By the time Kennedy came home in the evenings all trace of the cakes – the table the sign the baking's takings – had been whisked away and the children sworn to secrecy with threats of no cupcakes and rewards of – of course – cupcakes, and although Mrs Kennedy's cupcakes were known all over the valley and although her husband must have known he could not *but* have known, he never mentioned the matter. Perhaps he too was ashamed, deeply ashamed that his wife was a known woman.

Though she was half-tramp half-man being gainfully employed Greatgrandmother after a few years had a respectable sum. Not a large sum but a tidy one. Greatgrandmother at last had a pile.

It was the late 1890s. She had been laundering and starching and airing and laying out all the while. She had been preparing and stoking and cooking and baking and sweeping and keeping the sabbath holy. But Greatgrandmother wasn't quite as hopeless as she had once been. The girls now washed up and peeled and scrubbed. The boys gardened and chopped. Kennedy had once heated the water for a bath but for this last Greatgrandmother was remorseful. She may have turned into a tartar a shrew a vixen, but there were limits.

Greatgrandmother kept her cache in a crock that was supposedly full of cucumbers in brine. One morning she flew through her chores, she washed and she cleaned, she cooked and swept, then she went to the crock and unplugged the cork and emptied the contents into a drawstring purse. She put on her green gaberdine. She skewered her black straw hat. Greatgrandmother walked into town. She went straight to the bank and changed the ha'pennies and sixpences into notes and suddenly she was light-as-air and heady and girlish and she tripped across the street to the furriers where the window was full of dancing bears. She went in.

Madam, said the furrier appearing, You require a fur?

Oh there were furs! There were furs upon furs the whole shop muffled and stuffed with fur. Greatgrandmother was overwhelmed she was stifled and pushed back by a million a billion waving shafts of hair. She prayed briefly Lead us not into temptation Oh Lord deliver it. And she pointed, bending her finger in an unaccustomed arc, to the most delicate of the bears a creature with a coat the colour of her three-fruit marmalade.

Yes, I think I require . . . And immediately it was before her. It was as if she wore red leggings and brass buttons and cut the air with a whip and cried out Marmalade bear! and the ludicrous animal lumbered away from its companions and reeled for her pleasure. It was as if she had power, Yes I require.

Greatgrandmother peeled off her cold gaberdine. The furrier took it and ran it up a pole like a flag for all to see, then he invited her to slide into the garment she had chosen. Compare

compare! and Greatgrandmother did, breathlessly. The fur was cool inside it was warm. It was heavy and buoyant at the same moment prickly to the touch and silken to stroke. It was sensuous and skinlike.

As if it were made for Madam, said the furrier, as if she were Madam.

Greatgrandmother turned seductively as if she were naked in front of the large oval mirror. The coat had an angry collar, petulant sloping shoulders, determined catches and an arrogant swagger below the waist. Oh she was vain wanton wasteful avaricious.

I'll take her thank you and I'll wear her, said Greatgrandmother and it was like a land transaction. She handed over 14,000 cupcakes her labour her childhood her sleep and her small ruth voice. The furrier swept them all away and counted them. Then he took the gaberdine down and folded it reverently in tissue paper and placed it in a great box for Greatgrandmother to carry home.

She didn't go straight home she walked about the streets. She walked because she bore a weight on her shoulders and she liked the feeling of it, a little woman with a large weight. She walked because she enjoyed the sensation of creatures swishing about her legs, animals and children, and she walked because it was a marmalade coat and the autumn day was of marmalade light.

As she walked she told herself You're a vain woman you're a wanton wasteful avaricious woman and you're a virago. But she didn't really believe it. She believed the fur coat was all these things and the fur coat was the sweet fruit of her secret labours. (No wife of mine will work!)

I don't work, she told herself. I don't work I only carry bricks. *I don't work I only carry bricks*. The idea of a little woman carrying bricks was more than she could bear and for some reason she cried. She walked along in the marmalade coat and her funny battered black straw hat, happy, crying.

As she was nearing home a man appeared on the road ahead of her and she was startled because you didn't see many people out walking in the middle of the day and she felt conspicuous wearing a fur, a fur coat indeed in this neighbourhood. She felt herself to be glowing in an aura of fur and she feared the man might see her from the distance as brilliant and daunting and as if it were Saint Paul he saw and this the road to Damascus might fall down before her struck and adoring. Hail hail! The adorned!

Greatgrandmother shrank a little, she shrank inside the marmalade fur but she walked on and she and the man drew nearer and nearer and presently she saw that he smoked a pipe and the smoke brushed his cheeks. They came together closer and closer and Greatgrandmother saw that it was indeed Greatgrandfather, her husband, Kennedy.

Oh she was afraid aghast and adither! Shesheshe — leapt through the nearest gap in the roadside hedge and crouched down behind it trembling like a small ginger animal caught in a trap. She stayed low until she had heard Kennedy draw level pause and continue on his way. Then she shuddered, a long enduring shudder that worked its way around her shoulders down her spine and her legs and out through her toes sweeping before it greed vanity wastefulness ambition — sins, sins. When the shudder had left her she tore off the marmalade fur. Fool thing, vacuous shallow and worldly! And straight away a new peace came over her, a goodness she had not known before when she had desired to be eminently desirable in ermine or fox or sable or seal. She wrapped the fur with veneration as if this were a dead child and leaving the box under the hedge went home clasping her gaberdine coat about her.

Greatgrandmother didn't bake any cupcakes that afternoon nor did she dream nor did she sing. Wearing the green gaberdine and the flat black straw she combed the length of the hedge on the way into town thinking to retrieve the fur and return it to the furrier. (I'm so sorry, I made a mistake. I'd like you to take the coat back if you will ... Madam, I ...) But there was no box. There was no marmalade fur.

In later years Greatgrandmother's daughter-in-law, my grand-mother, acquired a grey squirrel necklet. She went into Kirk's one autumn day and put it on her husband's account, never thinking to mention it to him and when the bill came he paid it. My other grandmother had a silver fox fur, a gift from her husband. It had piercing glass eyes and hard little paws that trailed pitifully down her back and her grandchildren thought that because it had eyes and paws it also had a soul.

Her daughter, my mother, wore a 1950s-length swirling musquash coat that drew the hands of children hungry for tactility and the admiration of her husband, my father, who paid a hundred pounds for it. Three furs. Three women. Not one cupcake did they bake.

Greatgrandmother got it all wrong. It's the men who buy the fur coats.

Barbara Anderson

MISS HOBBS THINKS ABOUT THE PEONIES AT THE KAMIKAZE PILOTS' MEMORIAL AT ETAJIMA

MARCIA HOBBS STARES across the kauri table at the new Art man's hair and swallows. It is the wrong colour, not the blue-black sheen of Senri's but it has the same springing strength: each hair seems to leap from the scalp. The parting is definite, a white track on the left-hand side. Mr Marden turns his head and Marcia sees that it begins from a similar whorl of hair on the back of the head. At the base of the man's stomach where the hair begins, Marcia knows, individual hairs tough as wire will lie against the curve of his white belly.

Before she went to Japan Marcia had always been conscious that she had not done enough with her life. She thought of it flowing back over thirty years to dolls' tea parties beneath the flowering currant, her finger anchoring the lid of the teapot in imitation of Granny's. Her flowered teaset had a red 'Japan' stamped on the underside of each piece. There had not been a lot of action in Marcia's life since those days. Not a lot of endeavour, thrust you might say. It had all just as it were happened, as though she had fallen into a stream and drifted along like Ophelia with weeds in her hair and a faint smile on her lips. She had not taken her life by the scruff of its neck, moulded and hacked it, knocked it into a shape she could visualize – of which she could think, Marcia Hobbs: This is Your Life.

She was astonished at the vigour with which the younger members of the staff, Margot, Carmen, Susan, to say nothing of Jenni, attacked life, flinging two or more lives into each day as they dashed about after school kicking life into motor bikes, snatching up babies, attending seminars to keep up to date. And still taught well, cared, had relationships.

And not only the young. Look at Miss Franklin for goodness sake.

Perhaps it was because she had never learnt to rush. There had never been any need. There had always been plenty of time. No man or woman ran yelling out the door each morning scrambling for a bus, a slice of bitten toast clutched in one hand. Granny went to her room to change, to prepare a face to face the world an hour before she left the house, which was seldom. Her hair alone took half an hour to coil and sweep into a French roll, to anchor and stab with pins.

Marcia's father, a top dressing pilot, had been killed in an air crash in the Rimutakas when Marcia was two. The Cessna just fell out of the sky according to a farmer who happened to be watching. The wreckage lay hidden in deep bush (rugged terrain the papers called it) for months before it was found. Her mother sold up in Tawa and went back to her widowed mother and Aunty Pat over the harbour at Eastbourne. Aunty Pat worked for a local accountant; she just had to pop round the corner. Granny worked in the garden. Marcia's mother knitted. The sun shone.

And you certainly couldn't rush with music and Marcia was musical from infancy, hanging on her mother's every hum, lisping the names of the great composers familiar as household words. All the family were musical. Very musical. Good music surged through the house. Bad music was rigorously excluded. They all played. Marcia began piano at five. They listened to good music on the Concert Programme and their stereo, which was the most precious thing in the house. —If there's a fire, said Granny, settling herself on the sofa for a Brandenburg, remember. The stereo first. Aunty Pat drove them in to all the concerts, sweeping around the harbour in her Escort in plenty of time for a good park.

Marcia had an excellent start and all the encouragement possible, except that her mother wouldn't let her play in the Comps though Miss Engelbretsen thought it would be good for her. Mrs Hobbs tied back Marcia's pale fluffy hair. —There's too much pressure, dear. Pushy mothers and pert little girls and that sort of thing. You wouldn't like it.

It became obvious that Marcia was not concert platform material. —She plays beautifully, said Miss Engelbretsen rubbing her knobbled fingers together. —But . . . There was some thought of private pupils. —But then with private pupils there'd be all the financial side. I mean think of it. Bills and everything. You know how hopeless you are at Maths. And dealing with ambitious parents. Just think.

Marcia decided on a private school in Mount Eden. It did mean moving to Auckland which was probably one of the few non-drifting decisions she had ever made. It worked out all right though and she loved Mount Eden, she liked the girls, she enjoyed teaching even, except for the ones with talent who wouldn't try, wouldn't practise, wouldn't damn well *care* about their precious gift.

In her second teaching term Marcia attended a course in Asian ceramics at the Museum. It was very good. Excellent in fact. After the first lecture the class moved *en bloc* to the Asian Hall to look at examples. Marcia stared at the thick creamy surface of the early Imari bowls. The cobalt underglaze grasses were a few vivid brushstrokes. Her eyes swam with tears of pleasure.

—I'd like two like that, said a woman behind her. —One for cream and one for icing sugar. Marcia turned, her eyes blinking. The pleasant face smiled.

The unlabelled saucer in the next case had been been mended with clamps. A line of gold divided its surface. The larger side was translucent white except for a small spray of plum blossom; charcoal flower, terracotta buds, leaves of turquoise and greenish gold. On the smaller side exuberant patterns of fine black lines covered the turquoise glaze which was splashed with deep violet peonies. That is the most satisfying man-made object I have ever seen, thought Marcia. I shall go to Japan.

She sat on the steps of the museum and stared across the harbour to North Head, then walked around the monolith of the Cenotaph. It was inscribed 'Our Glorious Dead'. 1914–1918 was carved on two sides; 1939–1945 on the others. 'This is consecrated ground' said the bronze notice.

I'll go quite soon. It appeals to me.

But then Granny died in her sleep and Aunty Pat said she couldn't stand it another minute and went to Nelson. Marcia came home to Eastbourne because Mother was nervous on her own quite naturally. She was lucky to get a job at Girls High in the middle of the year. The previous music teacher had left, just like that. Una Benchley said she would be happy to come to some arrangement about lifts from Eastbourne but Marcia had to learn to drive because of the concerts and taking Mother. She hadn't enjoyed the driving lessons. Especially stopping and starting on hills with her heart in her mouth and the ABC instructor smoking his head off. But it was lovely walking out to the carpark after the last lesson to find her Mini waiting instead of being dependent and fitting in. Marcia felt like stroking it.

She took over the garden at Eastbourne. —It's growing on

me, she told her mother, once she had mastered the need for mulch in sandy soil and the role of compost in the production of deep rich friable loam. She spent hours on her knees among the peppery-scented leaves of the geraniums attending to the paths of broken shells which were such a thing to weed, Mahler tapes blasting from her cassette recorder.

Life flowed on until suddenly Mother died. Her head dropped forward during Beethoven's Fifth and she was gone.

—She went just as she would have wanted, sobbed Marcia to Aunty Pat who had come over for the funeral. Aunty Pat picked a piece of apple peel from between her two front teeth. She stared at the yachts lilting and tossing on the harbour and ate the scrap. —Mnn, she said. —I'd better cook a tongue. And a chicken.

—Go for God's sake. Go! Get out, cried Aunty Pat at the airport tightening the strap around her old green suitcase and giving it a quick kick before handing it over to the young woman behind the Check-In counter. The airport was packed. It had been closed by fog for two days. Slack-faced men in track suits and dirty running shoes milled around shouting at each other. A child submerged beneath an orange anorak howled, banging its head against a distraught young woman's thighs. The woman dropped onto her three-inch heels. —Shut up or I'll belt you, she screamed at the streaming face.

Aunty Pat gave the suitcase its final heave and turned to Marcia, her face pink with effort, her forehead puckered. —Look, she said. You've always wanted to go, God knows why. When I think of what they did to our boys . . . Look! If you don't go now you never will. She paused, her tongue flicked her top lip. —The money's there. And go on your own!

But *Japan*, pleaded Marcia. —It's so . . . She couldn't say foreign.

—You know a bit of the language don't you?

—A bit. Years and years of University extension courses, for this very moment.

—Perhaps a tour, said Marcia, her top teeth resting on her lower lip.

—Go on your own, shouted Aunty Pat as her flight number crackled above their heads, almost indecipherable in the uproar. —It's the only way to go. She hugged Marcia, her eyes on the man at the desk behind the doors leading to the departure gate. She nodded at him slightly as though to indicate she was just coming, she wouldn't be a moment.

—Travel, she cried as she charged forward, —is an intellectual Outward Bound. She turned at the doors and waved. —A challenge! she yelled.

The aircraft was full but she did have a window seat. The man beside Marcia was large and informative. He leant forward in his distressed-leather jacket, his stomach expansive above the safety belt. —It's my mother. She's far from well. Terminal.

—Oh dear, said Marcia, her eyes on the flickering figure of the well-groomed man demonstrating emergency procedures on the TV screen. He adjusted a yellow oxygen mask and smoothed his hair back. He was followed by a black man and a white woman who crossed their arms and leapt onto an escape chute. They hurtled down stiff-legged, their smiles bright. Into some ocean presumably.

She dragged her eyes from the screen. —I'm sorry. The pores of his nose were huge.

—In Japan? she murmured.

—Good God no. The nose retreated. —In Manchester.

Her scalp tightened. —But we're going to Japan!

—Sure. Sure. I'm doing some business on the way. I'm in Plexiglass.

—Oh. Gratitude to this beautiful blue-jowled man flowed through her. —The announcing thing quacks so doesn't it. Though of course they wouldn't let me on if I'd got on the wrong one would they. Her voice trailed away.

He understood perfectly. A hand patted her knee.

—Tell me about Plexiglass, said Marcia.

He told her. Eventually he clutched the back of the seat in front of him, heaved himself up and backed into the aisle. —Toilet, he said.

Marcia dipped her head in consent and leaned back. Someone was kicking the back of her seat. Chestnut curls appeared above the seat in front of her. The small face beneath had the dark eyelashes and hooded eyes of the born vamp. The little girl removed her thumb from her mouth and pouted. Marcia sat very still. Smile and you've got them for the duration. —Hullo, said the child. Marcia stuck out the tip of her tongue, rolling it like her childhood friend Bernice whom Mrs Hobbs had declared *persona non grata* after the problem with the rhubarb. The head disappeared.

Her fellow traveller reappeared and eased himself into his seat. — If you'll excuse me, he said, —I think I'll get a bit of shut-eye. It's a long way to Manchester. The plane bucked briefly. —Clear air turbulence, he said, closing his eyes. —No problem.

Marcia shared a taxi with him from the airport. —Thank you, she told the departing back, but he was gone, leaping sideways onto an island swept by streams of hooting traffic.

Miss Franklin had told her to print the name of her hotel on some cards. —It's the only way, she said. —There are no street signs or numbers or anything as I suppose you know.

—Yes, said Marcia, her pile of School Certificate theory books flattened against her chest.

—They smile and nod and you think they understand but

believe me they're only smiling and nodding and anyway nodding means No in Japanese. Or so I understand, continued Miss Franklin. —You can always get back somehow to the hotel if you have a card, even if it's not in Japanese. Or that was Jean's and my experience. She banged a wet strength tissue against her nose and sniffed. —For what it's worth. And when you get to the hotel take one of their matchbooks with you whenever you go out. That's even better.

Marcia had drawn the name of the hotel in Japanese characters as well. The driver nodded and smiled and they continued on their way to her hotel. Each step was a minor adventure. Checking in, the money, tipping the bowing taxi driver, all were simplicity itself. They could understand her halting phrases, or appeared to. Marcia could scarcely believe it. I can do it all. I can do anything. I am a traveller in Japan which is the land where I wish to be. I am completely at home. Escorted by a diminutive porter who with smiling insistence shouldered her hand luggage as well, she marched across the gilded foyer with her room key. The child porter pressed the arrow pointing upwards.

The lift door opened and Marcia was face to face with a man in ceremonial dress. He wore a wide pleated and divided skirt of black and white striped silk tied at the waist, a short black coat with two circular white crests covered what Marcia knew to be a black and white under kimono. He stood very still, his head high, his face unsmiling. He was magnificent, Marcia could see that.

The man's head moved fractionally.

—Are you coming up? he said.

Marcia shook her head. —No.

I am a traveller in an antique land.

The doors shut.

The porter stared up at her, puzzled. —Madam up next time?

★

She inspected the cluster of unsolicited mini-gifts in the bathroom, a shower cap, a shampoo, a sachet For Removal of the Stain. A blue and white *yucata* in a plastic bag hung on the door. The lavatory flush water had a most disconcerting swirl. Marcia bathed, changed, and went downstairs in search of food.

Near the reception desk stood a cavern of glass and light labelled *Sushi Bar*. A large sign on one wall displayed coloured photographs of delights within; boiled shrimp *sushi*, cooked egg *sushi*, raw fish *sushi*. A good idea. A solution. Better than waiters and a formal dining room, and anyway *sushi* was real Japan. Marcia hoisted herself on to a high stool at the bar and watched the slim young chefs dance before her, their knives flashing as they chopped vegetables, seaweed and raw fish with life-threatening speed. She ordered, pointing and smiling, made confident by attentive courtesy. The young man smiled back and whipped a small celadon-green bowl in front of her. It was filled with steaming liquid on which floated one dark unrecognizable leaf.

Soup? A finger bowl? Her stomach clenched, she blushed with shame at not knowing, at shame at caring about not knowing.

—It's a finger bowl, said the man on the stool beside her. —*Sushi* can be eaten with the fingers.

—You've changed, she said. Banal beyond banal.

He smiled. —So have you.

—Your . . . your clothes, were so beautiful.

—Uniform. He smiled. —I was returning from my niece's wedding.

—Oh.

—Do you know about Japanese weddings?

—No.

—I will tell you.

—Thank you. She shifted slightly on her stool.

—The main thing about Japanese weddings is the expense. He looked at her, his face concerned. —The money. You know?

She nodded.

—The kimono my niece wore cost two hundred and ninety-six thousand yen to hire. That would be . . . His fingers moved, a quick strumming of air as he worked it out. —Something like a thousand American dollars. Marcia shook her head. —Ttt, she said.

—The bride and groom must give presents to all the guests which should be equal in value to those they receive. It is not easy you know. It is extremely expensive. Nowadays many couples are married outside Japan. His hand gestured. —Your food.

—Thank you, said Marcia gazing at the plate of edible art as though he had given it to her.

—We Japanese eat with our eyes.

—Yes. She turned to eat. There were mirrors everywhere: the dancing chefs, the food, glass, the shimmering steel, all were reflected endlessly. Amongst it all, incongruous as an uncooked bun in a fish factory, a small pale face looked back at her. She could stare at the man more easily though.

—Some of them come to New Zealand, she said with the quick stabbing pride of the native abroad. —To be married, I mean.

—New Zealand? Ah! Sheep. He glanced again at her plate. —You pick each piece up you see. He indicated a small saucer of dark sauce. —Then dip one side in that then . . . His hand gestured towards his mouth.

The For Removal of the Stain might be necessary. —Chopsticks would be easier, said Marcia.

Chopsticks appeared.

The pale bun face smiled. —Thank you.

He tried again.

—Many sheep.

She had managed chopsticks for years but the *sushi* parcels were not easy.

—That's right. Millions of sheep.

—It is a very beautiful country.

—Yes, she said, chasing an egg *sushi* around the curve. Any moment soon he'll mention the Milford Track. But what a face, what pared down beauty of line and form. —Especially the South Island, said Marcia.

—There is a walk, a very beautiful walk through mountains.

—Yes. 'The finest walk in the world.' The Milford Track.

—*Track*, he said, one palm slapping the mahogany formica counter.

—People come from all over the world to walk it.

—So I have heard. His *sushi* plate and round bowl were placed in front of him.

His hand was beside hers. The fingers were long, tapered, almost transparent when seen against the light. —Why have you come to Japan?

—I have always wanted to. It's such an interesting culture, she babbled. —So many beautiful things.

—And pollution. His right hand moved with speed, seeking, dipping, despatching. He rinsed the fingers in the finger bowl. Traces of soya sauce swirled in the warm water. —I am free at the moment, he said, picking up a rice-paper napkin. —I could show you things.

—Thank you, said Marcia to her startled face, the dancing lights, the acrobatic young men leaping behind the *sushi* bar.

As Marcia notes the exact way Cliff Marden's hair springs from his scalp she remembers surprise, amazement, but no regrets. For it is better, is it not, to have loved and lost than never to have known at all. And anyway she didn't lose, not in that sense. She was not ditched like Carmen, who told the Staff Room so last year in as many words. —I've been ditched, she said. She has no shame, Carmen, she wears her heart on her sleeve for all to see which Marcia knows is a sad mistake and never did, nor does. Not of course that there was anyone there to watch Marcia's sleeve for squealing tell-tale hearts. That was part of it, probably, her complete anonymity. Otherwise how could she possibly have had the sense, the wit to accept the Outward Bound challenge of Senri. She kept nothing from him. Her passion, her astonishing abandonment, her willingness to try anything once and usually again and again and again. Is it better? Is it better? Marcia's slightly bandy legs are crossed beneath the staff-room table. They move slightly, the top one presses down. Carmen smiles at her. Carmen smiles too much. Cliff Marden can't take his eyes off her. Anyone can see that. Marcia rocks back and forward a couple of times. Senri's body was also compact and beautiful beyond words.

He was home on leave from the Japanese Embassy in Washington he told her next day. —I am a minor functionary, he said, pleased with the phrase. —We can travel together. I can show you things.

—All right, said Marcia.

The bullet train's speed was 180 kilometres per hour according to a speedometer attached to the wall of the carriage. They stared out of the window, searching through the mist for the perfect cone of Mount Fujiyama. —There it is, said Senri. Marcia turned to laugh at him in an attempt to hide her disappointment at the unconvincing glimpse. Behind his head an arrogant young Japanese with a crewcut and a lasso glared at her from an advertisement for Marlboro cigarettes.

—Why do so many Japanese men smoke?

—They think it's macho. He paused, his eyes on the advertisement. —I gave it up when my wife died. In Washington.

—I'm sorry.

He bowed, then picked up her hand and kissed the palm. —Don't talk, he said. He looked out the window at the clouded landscape spinning by.

—Did he tell you about *wabi* at your classes? Your teacher? Did he tell you? He turned again to the window.

—Melancholy restraint?

He nodded. —That view has *wabi*.

He kissed her palm again and lay back, silent and still.

It is good to know nothing. To wish to know nothing. *Wabi* discarded, she leant back, hand in hand with the surprise of her life.

—I'd like to stay in a Japanese inn, she said in bed that night.

He opened his eyes slowly. The solemn beauty of his face, the angle of his cheekbones moved her almost to tears.

—A *ryokan*? I don't think you'd like it, he said.

—But why?

He leapt up from the crumpled bed and strode around the room. His body was hard, smooth as pale jade.

—You would feel like a cow in a china shop, he said.

She snorted with laughter.

He stood on his toes, his arms above his head. —I am tall for a Japanese. *Ryokans* are designed for small ladies and gentlemen. He patted the air three feet from the ground. —Everything is the size for dolls. And your room lady comes in always, to unroll the futon, to roll the futon, to serve the food, to help with your kimono. It is a bowl for goldfish. There is no privacy.

—Oh, said Marcia.

He cupped one of her breasts in each hand, weighing them. —Exactly. They rolled back on the bed.

—I like teets, he said later.

She leant on one elbow, startled. Did he mean tits?

Marcia had not heard either word since the educational whirl of Eastbourne Primary.

His hand reached up to stroke the nape of her neck. —Japanese men like this area also. That's why Utamaro's courtesans all have low necklines at the back. Their kimonos. His hand sketched a sweeping curve. —Very seductive.

—A reverse décolletage? But she had to explain it. Every difference pleased them, they rejoiced in each discovery, each small gem of language or custom mined and ferried from a foreign land.

—Your legs are bandy and you walk pigeon-toed. He demonstrated, fingers closed, as he flapped the strong hands one in front of the other. —That's very beautiful. But you can't walk like a Japanese woman, you see, because your teets are too big. He glanced at her face. —I am telling you this, so that you will understand.

—I don't want to walk like a Japanese woman. I am not, said Marcia, dismissing thousands of scuttling females from her mind, —a Japanese woman.

He was on his knees, the sheet dragged tight around his thighs.

—You are wonderful. More wonderful than any. My golden lady.

Please choice carefully, said the sign above the mini-bar.

—Anyhow, he said thoughtfully. —I have never stayed in a *ryokan* with an English lady.

—And I am not an English lady.

His hand stroked her stomach.

I am here. I will stay here. I will leave Girls High. I will go to Washington but first we must go to Eastbourne to settle things. Walk along the beach. She saw his footprints beside hers, their line very straight, the toes turned out.

His parents are dead, which is a good thing.

—Haydn, he said one night lying flat on his back in Nagoya. —Haydn is for happiness. For when life is good. We should have Haydn. The Kaiser Quartet.

She took his hand.

He was a perfect guide. He knew everything, he understood everything, he never told her too much. Marcia walked pigeon-toed beside him, incandescent with happiness as he explained the ritual of the tea ceremony, the structure of an Edo screen. They climbed hand in hand to a small temple. It was empty except for two young women who danced the foxtrot in silence, their bodies moving in unison, a Walkman clamped to each impassive head. Senri smiled. —Technology, he said.

They followed Marcia's travel plan; from Tokyo to Nagoya to Kyoto. He insisted on paying for meals. Her room was pre-booked and every bed was vast, his supply of condoms inexhaustible. It was all very simple. It could not have been better planned.

They were surrounded, mobbed almost in the gardens of Mijojo castle by schoolboys in black uniforms and peaked caps. —English, they cried. —English rady. Please to speak English. Where you from, rady? Senri barked one word and they fell back, their arms hanging, their faces blank beside the scarlet maples.

—What did you say? asked Marcia.

—I asked them to stop, said Senri. He took her hand. —Come. I'll show you the nightingale floor.

The sprung wooden floor squeaked at every step, singing to warn a sixteenth-century shogun against surprise attack. Nearby were panels and painted screens on which butterflies hovered above shimmering silver grasses; high-stepping roosters, their tails plumes of gold and red, strutted beneath branches of plum blossom.

An identical rooster skittered in front of them later in the afternoon as it chased a recalcitrant hen back to the fold behind a Heian shrine. Senri bowed low before the altar, clapped his hands together once and bowed again. He signed the book. She watched him as he drew the strokes of his signature, enchanted with every move he made, each aspect of his different being.

She heard her mother's voice answering an unheard comment from Granny on the sunporch. —Marcia is simply not interested in men, mother. I've told you that before.

—The Shinto religion is a very agreeable one, said Senri later, opening his lunch box with careful fingers. —It has no sin. He picked up a small red crab from its compartment with the chopsticks provided and put it in his mouth, gazing across the grey lake beside the bench on which they sat. —We've just missed the cherry blossom. It is always more sad when you have just missed something.

—I like the way it doesn't last long. Ephemeral, said Marcia, eyeing her red crab with doubtful eyes.

He stared at her. —Would you do something for me?

She smiled. After all, she didn't have to eat it. —Of course.

—Would you come with me to Etajima? His mouth puckered. —It is not an idle request.

She smiled at his pride in the idiom. —I'd like to very much.

—Yes. The Inland Sea is not too far away. The pollution is very sad. But there is a memorial to the Kamikaze pilots.

The lake was very still. —Oh, said Marcia.

—There were over two thousand of them. They chose forty to represent all the others. For photographs, displays. One from each province. There were too many you see, otherwise.

—Yes, I see.

—My mother's brother was one of them.

—Oh, she said again.

—My parents were very proud, my family. Especially as he is one of the forty as it were. One of the ones chosen.

—Yes. They would be. (Of course they would be. They would have to be, wouldn't they.) Did they . . .? I mean . . .

—But I have never seen it. The memorial. I must do that.

—Yes, of course. A sharp breeze swarmed across the lake, scurrying the surface into miniature waves.

He bowed. —Thank you.

The main thing was their youth. Large photographs showed boys in pilot's uniforms, some serious, some smiling into the eye of the camera. One or two were laughing.

—They were so young, said Senri. —Expert pilots who volunteered as of course many did, were rejected. They were needed, you see, as teachers and escort pilots.

Marcia said nothing.

—My uncle was twenty. He indicated a proud face above a white scarf tucked into the neck of a uniform. The eyes stared straight through her.

—He looks like you.

—I look like him. His name was Senri.

Forty large display cases contained articles of uniform, a sword, books. Some attempt had been made to indicate an individual life. A group of laughing young men lounged against a training aircraft. They sang around a piano. They swam naked. A smiling Kamikaze tied his comrade's white headband as he sat in his cockpit. It was all beautifully done.

—His *hachimaki*, said Senri pointing. —They were worn by samurai warriors. A symbol of coolness and courage. They all wore them on their last missions.

There were poems. Extracts of letters. 'May our death be as sudden and clean as the shattering of crystal.'

'I shall fall like a blossom from a radiant cherry tree.'

A giant photograph of the final ceremony before take-off covered an end wall. A young man in an old-fashioned flying helmet, his face calm, drank his final toast to the Emperor. Both hands were raised to lift a small pale saucer to his lips. The man beside him waited his turn.

She felt ill, sick with rage. Rage for all victims of war, willing and unwilling, rose in her throat.

—The last toast, said Senri, —is always drunk in water.

Marcia put out her hand to the cool marble wall. The heels of her sandals clattered on the tiled floor. —I'm going outside. She turned to grope her way to the door.

His face was contrite. —I have upset you.

She looked at him in astonishment. —*Upset* me? She lurched

across the high entrance hall in her silly clacking sandals and went outside. Clouds of smog covered the beautiful harbour, misty islands rose from the shadowed sea. Unheeded boundless destruction. Waste waste and more waste. Marcia's hands were clutched tight against her chest, she was panting with rage.

A line of small children led by a slim young teacher trailed across the courtyard chattering and calling to each other, bright parakeet schoolbags on their backs. They swept around the corner and disappeared. She could still hear them, but only faintly.

Senri was at her side. —It was a long time ago, he said. —Come. Look at these.

The tree peonies stretched down one side of the memorial. Hundreds of varieties, few of which Marcia had seen before, had burst from their tight buds into a blowsy profusion of pinks and white; white with strong gold stamens, maiden's blush to fat-lady rose, deep crimson to dark wine, the flowers swayed above or hung their heads from exuberant grey-green bushes.

Several of the blooms had small paper umbrellas above them.

Marcia stared at one, speechless.

Senri smiled, his hand on her arm. —For protection, he said. —You can understand that. They are very fragile, you see.

John Cranna

MY GRANDFATHER was a large man with a strong laugh who grew pomegranates for pleasure, but for reasons that only gradually became clear to me, and certainly were not clear to him, it was felt necessary from time to time to strap him to a bed and apply electric shocks to his head.

When I saw him after his treatment he had difficulty in recognizing me, so I stood at his side for a while, repeating my name until the dullness had gone from his china-blue eyes. Although I was only fifteen, I was careful to arrange my face into a mask of apologetic innocence, in fear that he would begin to link my appearance with the treatment he was receiving. When the Pale Suits had gone away he would get up slowly and go out into the garden, where he would walk for a time, occasionally stopping at one of his fruit trees to touch the skin of a pomegranate that had hung there all summer, as though extracting its smooth permanence from the wreckage that had been made of his immediate past.

My grandfather had travelled in the time when this was still possible, and had collected musical instruments from around the Pacific. They stood in the dim corners of the house, or hung on the walls, a great Javanese gamelan in the hallway, and a Chilean lute on a shelf above. In the long afternoons when our visitors worked on my grandfather in the front room, I could hear the instruments in their other lives singing to me. The gamelan I knew well; it sat on the edge of a clearing in the jungles of Java, played by smooth-faced boys, its heavy sound mingling with the trees and the soil. The sound was very clear to me; it lodged in my chest as a kind of ecstasy, and it would only fade when the surge of voices from the front of the house told me that the men had finished with my grandfather. They went then to the kitchen and spoke to my mother, although I could never hear what they said to her. I watched from a window as they walked down the drive, two men in pale suits, one of them carrying an aluminium case, which was laid carefully in the back of the waiting vehicle.

The house and the garden were too large for the three of us who lived there, we had unused rooms, some still locked and containing the possessions of members of the family whose whereabouts were no longer discussed. On one side of the long hall that ran through the house my grandfather and I had our rooms, and on the other, at the furthest end of the hall, was my mother's room, a sanctum that no one was allowed to enter. My mother was a graceful person who moved about the house without ever seeming to touch it, and who each afternoon following lunch would brush my cheek with the lightest of kisses, before retiring to her room for the remainder of the day. After she had gone the long hall held a trace of her perfume, lingering there amongst the instruments, as though the house was reluctant to concede her departure.

At the edge of the orchard my grandfather sat and watched his pomegranates ripen, indifferent to passing showers. In a murmur that carried across the lawn to the house, he spoke endlessly of his years travelling the Pacific in search of instruments for his collection, struggling to prevent the treatment he was receiving from unravelling the thread of his memory for ever. I sat beside him on the grass and tried to follow the path of his reminiscences. From Java and the jungles of Indochina it would lead suddenly east to Mexico, then south to the deserts of Chile, before veering west again to the island chains of Micronesia. A story that began in Djakarta might end in Santiago without his being aware that the location had changed, and fragments and characters from one tale would find their way into others, so that his monologues were jigsaws of confusion that held me entranced for hours, but which I could never fully understand.

Some things, however, were clear to me. He had always stayed among the ordinary people, whether it was in the shanty towns of the great cities or in the small, poor towns of the interior. He was obviously welcome in these places, and because of his enthusiasm for the music of the people, instruments would be produced and impromptu concerts arranged. He was often invited to join in the music-making and in this way he became a competent performer on dozens of the instruments he had collected. I could only dimly recall the times from my childhood when he performed for the family in the front room, but I have a clear memory of his large figure stooped forward slightly, playing a lute made from the shell of an armadillo, and holding it so carefully in his arms that he might have been cradling the shell of a massive rare egg. The lute, which was from Chile, now rested in the hallway, where it had remained untouched for many years.

One of my grandfather's remaining clear memories was of his time in Chile and he told me of the year he had spent there in the northern deserts, studying the ancient music of the Atacameno Indians. The language of their songs, he said, was so old that the performers did not understand it themselves, and he described the strange sound of the great side-blown trumpets that accompanied the performance. He had lived in the home of one of these musicians and he spoke of the stark beauty of the deserts and of the resilience of the people who had lived there since the dawn of time. One day, as we sat in the orchard, he told me with surprise in his voice that he had never been happier than when he was with the Atacameno, but when I asked him why he had left, his eyes dulled and his story slid off once more into confusion.

The men in pale suits were visiting twice a week now, and as I sat there beneath the fruit trees, I heard the quiet sound of their vehicle pulling up at the bottom of the drive. My grandfather fell silent at their footsteps on the gravel, and was suddenly very still in his chair. We could hear the Pale Suits talking with my mother, and then her breathless voice calling to us across the lawn. My grandfather got up and walked slowly towards the house, where our visitors would now be waiting for him in the front room. I waited for a while, then went into the hall and sat there in the gloom amongst the dead instruments. I concentrated very hard, until the loudest sound I could hear was the steady beat of the blood in my ears, then softly, across a great distance, I heard the strains of the lute singing in an Atacameno village, and the music grew stronger and more clear, until I was there among the scatter of low huts, listening to the lute as it cut the thin air of the desert. I saw my grandfather, dressed in the clothes of the Indians, working with them in their carefully irrigated fields on the desert's edge, and returning each night to study their ancient music in the household of a master musician. I saw him crouched by an oil lamp, taking down the music of an evening performance in his notebook, and writing out the unknown language that was used in the ritual songs of fertility and death. And then the lute began to sing of strange Indian tribes my grandfather had never mentioned, the Aymara and the Pehuenche; it sang of their languages, of their music, of the rich collection of myth that held together their pasts, and it sang of their struggle against the lethal promises of a new order that had come recently to their land. I was so absorbed by the tales of the lute that I almost missed the babble of voices from the front of the house that signalled the end of my grandfather's session, but the moment the Pale Suits opened the door into the hall, the lute fell silent again.

When the men were in the kitchen, speaking in their sing-song voices with my mother, I went in to see my grandfather. He lay on the bed, the straps loosened at his sides, staring up at the ceiling with unblinking eyes. An acrid smell hung in the room, and a circular stain lay around him on the sheet. I stood there for a while, listening as the kitchen door closed and our visitors' footsteps receded on the drive. I watched the stain spread out across the bed, and thought, They've embalmed him and the fluid is already beginning to leak out. His body seemed a long way off, as though it was withdrawing into the angles of the room, and I felt a sensation of falling. I put a hand out to the wall, and as I did so my grandfather turned his head to look at me, his face blank and his eyes empty of all life. He made a weak gesture with one hand. 'They're very kind to take so much trouble with me. I feel I should be more grateful . . .' I had never spoken to him about his treatment before, and now, hesitantly, I asked what they had decided was wrong. He frowned, as though trying to remember a complicated diagnosis that had once been fully explained, but eventually he shook his head and lay back, his eyes fixed once more on the ceiling. Behind me the door opened and my mother came into the room in a cloud of perfume. She opened the curtains with one hand while holding a handkerchief against her face with the other. 'What have you done, Father?' she said. 'You know you really can't behave like this in front of our visitors.'

That evening, as though in protest at my grandfather's lack of discretion, she failed to appear for dinner, so the two of us ate alone. Although he had bathed and changed his clothes, a faint odour still hung about him, and when I sat down to eat I found my appetite had gone and I could not bring myself to finish my meal.

It had been six years since my sisters and my father had gone away to the mountains. I was too young to understand at the time, but soon after that the schools closed down and before long the Pale Suits called at our house for the first time. My mother would not allow me to go into the city, so the only Pale Suits I saw on foot were the pair who came to visit my grandfather. At other times I saw them passing the house in their long vehicles, and always they were on the wrong side of the road, driving very fast. When I asked my grandfather about the Pale Suits in their vehicles, he was unable to tell me anything. He was fully occupied, it seemed, with his dissolving past, and the only energy he had left for the present was expended on his orchard. There his pomegranates hung thickly on the trees, the best crop there had been in years, he told me, and the fruit were at the point of cracking from within with their own ripeness.

My grandfather spent many hours in the orchard, inspecting the bark of the trees for disease and the leaves for the first signs of summer blight. Often he would stop and stare at a ripening fruit for a time, touching it with his open palm, before moving on to the next laden tree. The longer his treatment continued, the more important the orchard became to him and sometimes he would call me over to a tree and explain his methods of soil preparation and pruning. It was important, he said, that there was someone to take over the orchard when he could no longer manage it. From the bottom of the orchard I could see the outline of the distant mountains, and I began to watch them more closely, thinking of my sisters and my father, trying to imagine them eating and sleeping somewhere among that jumble of pale shadows.

On the next occasion that the Pale Suits visited, the gamelan sang to me, and it sang from a shanty town on the edge of the great city of Djakarta, the music of its gongs shimmering and dancing in the Javanese dusk. Behind the knot of musicians the shanty town stretched away until it disappeared in the haze of cooking fires. The music of the ensemble was very solemn; it spoke of the land the people had struggled for and lost, of their flight to the city, and of the new poverty they had found there.

The steady chime of the gongs reached into the corners of the furthest houses, so that it seemed in the end that the entire shanty town echoed with sadness for a time when better things had been promised, and the promises had come to nothing. As night fell, the music faded into silence, and I saw a small boy, asleep on the dirt floor of a hut, clutching in his arms a perfectly made model of the great gongs my grandfather had spoken of. Although he was fast asleep, he held the gong so tightly to his chest that it was possible to believe it was his only possession in the world. But now that the gamelan had ceased, the shanty town was slipping into shadow, and before long I was back in the gloom of the hall, waiting again for our visitors to emerge, the instruments lifeless shapes around me.

I no longer had the courage to visit my grandfather in his room, so I went out and waited for him by the orchard. Eventually he came across the lawn, moving like a blind man, groping his way to his chair beneath the trees. I watched as he tried to speak, his tongue lolling between thickened lips, and I knew then that if his treatment continued in this way it would eventually silence him altogether. I never thought of discussing any of this with my mother. For some years now she had been so detached that her presence in the house seemed almost accidental. We did not discuss the Pale Suits and my grandfather's treatment because we did not discuss anything of importance. It seemed that some part of her had become too fragile to exist in the world of the Pale Suits, so that she had retreated to the sanctuary of her bedroom, a room whose only concrete reality for me was as the source of the mysterious scents and beautiful clothes she wore.

Then something happened which changed the course of the summer. One evening I looked from my window and saw a glow on the horizon, a glow which flared gradually brighter until it lit up a great section of the central city. At one point I thought I heard the distant sound of explosions. It was nearly dawn before the glow subsided to a dull red. The next day there was increased activity on the road outside, with the long cars of the Pale Suits travelling faster and in greater numbers than I had ever seen. In mid-afternoon there was almost an accident, when a driver approached our bend too fast and had to struggle to keep his vehicle under control. I saw a momentary look of fear on the face of the Pale Suit at the wheel, a look that stayed with me for long afterwards. It had never occurred to me that Pale Suits might be able to experience fear. The activity on the road outside continued into the next day, which was a treatment day for my grandfather, and the two of us sat in the orchard and listened to the steady sound of the passing vehicles. My grandfather was slumped in his chair, watching the drive in silence. Even the most halting reminiscence now seemed beyond him. Flies from the orchard settled on his face and arms and he did not seem to have the strength to wave them away. The hot afternoon stretched out for an age, and to pass the time I counted the vehicles as they took the corner. By dusk I had counted 142 and yet the Pale Suits had still not arrived, so at last we went inside to eat. There was a feeling of unreality about the meal that night, I could not recall the Pale Suits having ever missed a treatment day before.

This feeling continued into the rest of the week as the Pale Suits still failed to call. Outside the vehicles came and went on the road, sometimes alone, sometimes in great convoys, but none of them pulled up in the drive, and by the end of the following week the Pale Suits had missed five treatment days in all. By now I had begun to notice small changes in my grandfather. He moved among the trees in the orchard more freely, his shoulders were straighter and he no longer trailed the faint smell of urine that once had followed him about the house. Before long his reminiscences began again, and now they were a little easier to follow. Tales that had once baffled me with their shifting locations and broken plots started to hang together, as though a fragile thread had begun to run among the scattered pieces of his memory. Some of his stories stirred in me a strange feeling of recognition, as though I had heard them before but when too young to remember or to properly understand. He spoke of his voyages among the endless atoll chains of Micronesia; he told me of the time he had contracted a rare strain of malaria in the Mariana Islands and of being paralysed by village liquor in Guam. The liquor had been drunk at a celebration to mark his mastery of the rare stomach bow after months of apprenticeship to the leading musician on the island. He had lain in a coma for ten days, and, on coming to, had been presented with one of the oldest bows on the island, cut from hibiscus wood and strung with finest pineapple fibre. Through some special reasoning that was never explained to him, his coma had been taken as a sign of exceptional suitability for the instrument.

My grandfather told his stories with a new vigour now. There was no stopping him once he had begun on a tale, as though the long months of his treatment had diverted his memories into a dammed lake of the imagination, and the obstruction that had been holding them back had now been cleared away. Instruments which had lain in dusty corners of the house for years and whose origins had been a mystery to me became suddenly recognizable – I identified the stomach bow from Guam at once. The instrument hung in one of the unused rooms, a length of curved wood with a split gourd halfway down its length. My grandfather explained that the gourd was placed against the musician's stomach to amplify the vibrations of the fibre string. From his tales I also identified a shawm from Guatemala, a nose flute from Truk and a log drum from the Philippines.

We would sit in the orchard until after dusk, the trees turning to dim shapes around us, the line of distant mountains catching the last of the light, as my grandfather exercised his returning memory and the fruit flies gathered in clouds above our heads. It was very peaceful there in the orchard, the vehicles on the road outside were another world away, and I began to believe that the Pale Suits had bypassed us, that we no longer had any place in their scheme of things. We had come to a silent agreement not to discuss this, however, for fear that we might alter some delicate balance of invisible forces that was keeping them away.

My mother was unaffected by the absence of the Pale Suits. She came and went in the house in the way that she had always done, appearing in the morning and for meals and retiring to her room for the rest of the day. The house, however, had changed. The windows now let in more light, the dust on the floor did not seem so thick, and the doorways of the unused rooms no longer gaped like mouths onto the hallway. The house was breathing again. I could sense the sweeter air moving among the rooms and, although the instruments were no longer singing to me, they rested more easily in their corners and on their shelves. I felt sometimes that the instruments were beginning to replace my sisters and my father, and I thought of them as more real in some ways than those distant members of my family who had gone away to the mountains so many years before.

In the orchard my grandfather's pomegranates had reached their full maturity, and the branches of the trees bent almost to the ground with the weight of the fruit. The days had come to taste the first of the fruit and we decided to hold a small celebration to mark the occasion. We set up a table under the trees and spread it with a white cloth. My grandfather laid out two plates and a cutting-board, and I hunted through the drawers until I found the sharpest knife in the kitchen. We knew which of the pomegranates we would choose; we had been watching it for weeks. It hung on a tree near the bottom of the orchard, perfectly formed and with an unmarked skin of deep crimson. My grandfather took the fruit from the tree, placed it in the middle of the cutting-board, and we sat down facing each other across the table. We had agreed that I would carve the pomegranate and he would be the first to taste its flesh. When I cut into the fruit I thought that I had never seen a brighter splash of red, and the juice ran in rivulets across the board and stained the white of the tablecloth. My grandfather lifted the pomegranate to his mouth and bit into the flesh, his hands trembling a little as they always did when he ate. I was watching the pleasure spread across his face, when a movement in the direction of the house caught my eye. At the edge of the orchard, standing very still and watching us intently, was a Pale Suit. My grandfather was so engrossed in the fruit that he did not see the expression on my face, he went on eating the pomegranate until he had finished it, while I sat there across the table from him, unable to take my eyes from the stain of the juice on the white tablecloth.

When they had gone inside with my grandfather, I dragged the table around the house and placed it under the windows of the front room. By standing on the table I could reach the level of the window, and although the curtains were drawn, I found that by positioning the table carefully I was able to see a part of the room. At first I could not pick out any details, but as my eyes began to adjust I made out my grandfather's feet on the end of the bed, shoeless and still. Beyond his feet something winked in the gloom of the room, and after a while I realized that it was the light catching the turning reels of a tape machine. I stood there, mesmerized by the reels, my face against the window, and I might still have been there when the curtains were thrown back, if a pale shape had not moved between the machine and the window and broken into my trance.

I carried the table back to the orchard, and set out the cloth and plates as we had left them. Then I went inside to where the stomach bow hung on the wall. I concentrated on the instrument, listening for the hum of its fibre string. Nothing disturbed the quiet of the room. I tried again, straining into the silence, searching for the echo of the distant atolls, and knowing now that it was more important than ever to communicate with the instruments. But the bow would not sing to me; it remained mute and still on its hook on the wall, and I realized then that in my weeks away from the instruments I had lost my old intimacy with them, and I did not know how I was going to close the gap that now separated us. I thought of the pale shapes moving in the gloom, of the turning reels of the tape machine, of the other, unseen contents of the aluminium case that our visitors always brought with them. And I thought about the change that had come over them while they had been away. The Pale Suits had been impassive before; they had come and gone without showing any sign of emotion in their work. But there was something different about them now, a new tension, as though a deep anger lay behind their bland faces. Our visitors were in the front room for longer than I could ever recall, and eventually, exhausted by the knowledge of their return and by my attempts to rouse the instruments, I fell asleep on the floor of the unused room. Much later I seemed to hear the sound of my mother calling, and because she was calling something that was strange to me I could not decide whether I was dreaming. I lay still, and after a long pause I heard her voice again and realized that I was awake and that she was calling to my grandfather in the orchard. I got up and went outside to where the evening light had begun to illuminate the back garden. When I saw the orchard I stopped. Not a single pomegranate remained on the trees. In the middle of the orchard, swaying slightly on his feet, was my grandfather, and around him in all directions lay the remains of the crop of pomegranates. In his hands he held a heavy stick, and his shoes were crusted and stained from trampling the fruit as they lay on the ground. He was squinting into the trees, inspecting each in turn to make sure that he had not missed any of the fruit, and then he threw down the stick and walked past me towards the drive. He stumbled a little, regained his balance and went off down the drive like a blind man, leaving behind him in the gravel a trail of seeds and red pulp. I saw my mother, pale and motionless, watching us from the porch. She seemed to be looking past the wreckage of the orchard to the mountains beyond, and I knew then that she was thinking of the others, but I could not tell from her face whether she believed we would ever see them again. Then she turned and went back into the house. My grandfather was nearly at the road now and I ran after him down the drive. Although the traffic had fallen off a little in recent days, the road was busy, and the great vehicles of the Pale Suits still came and went at speed. I had almost reached the bottom of the drive when my grandfather crossed the pavement and went out on to the road. A vehicle that had just rounded the corner made a wide arc to avoid him, its horn blaring and its tyres crabbing on the asphalt. My grandfather followed it with vacant eyes as it pulled to a halt further down the road. The driver looked back at us through his rear window. By now I had my grandfather by the elbow and was leading him to the pavement. I raised an arm to the driver in the hope that he would drive on. As I led my grandfather back up the drive, I heard the vehicle pulling away into the stream of traffic. Back at the house my grandfather sat in the kitchen looking into space. He did not move or speak for several hours, and eventually I had to lead him like a sleepwalker to his bed.

As though making up for lost time the Pale Suits returned the next day and on this occasion they brought their vehicle to the top of the drive. When they got out I saw why. On the back seat, in place of the usual case, there was a much larger case made of the same bright aluminium and heavy enough to need both of the men to lift it. They were too concerned with getting the case into the house to notice the condition of the orchard. They carried the case down the passage and past the gamelan to the front room, and as they did so I imagined I heard the low chime of a gong, as though the instrument had been brushed in passing. My grandfather sat in the kitchen, watching the Pale Suits come and go, his blue eyes sharp and feverish. When the front room was ready the Pale Suits came into the kitchen and waited for my grandfather to get up. He remained in his chair, his arms limp before him on the table. The three of them seemed to be there an age, the men standing silent by the door and my grandfather motionless in his chair.

At last he got to his feet and went out into the hall, and I knew then that his resistance was over, that his last defence lay in the wreckage of the orchard and that the Pale Suits would now be able to do with him what they wished. When the door to the front room had closed behind them the house became very quiet and I tasted the stale air moving once more through the unused rooms, ebbing and flowing among the inert instruments. Then from the hallway I heard the chime of the gamelan, and as I listened it came once more, a low echo on the dead air. The instruments were waking again, and they had not waited for me to try to reach them first. The chime of the gamelan was solemn and regular now, welling up through the house like a heartbeat, until I could feel it through the soles of my feet and sense its heavy pulse in the pit of my belly. I saw again the shanty towns of Djakarta, the smoke haze low over the huts, and my grandfather sitting cross-legged in the circle of gamelan players; and then through the sound of the gamelan like a sharpened blade came the pure tone of the lute, singing from the deserts of Chile, telling of the ancient music that anchored the past of the people against the shifting sands of the desert. And now other instruments were waking and crowding in on the lute; I heard the sigh of the Guatemalan shawm and the rapid beat of the Filipino log drum. Instruments that had never sung before were breaking their years of silence, emerging from their dusty corners of the house for the first time in order to jostle for place in a chaotic rising choir. The air around me was alive with rhythms that broke in on other rhythms, with melodies that surfaced briefly before being drowned by the surge of some new voice joining the chorus, as instruments struggled to find their true voices after years of disuse. Slowly the milling sounds began to take on some order, the instruments were beginning to complement each other, as though fumbling their way towards a common voice. And then they began to sing in concert, sometimes one taking the lead, sometimes another. They sang of the howl of the typhoon in the tin roofs of the great shanty towns of the East, of the blinding rains and steaming heat; they sang of the harsh lives of the shanty town dwellers and of the peasant farmers on their meagre plots of land. I heard then of the hopes of the people for another life, of their struggle to make a new, better order from the old ... and suddenly the music of the instruments grew dark and discordant, and the gamelan sang of blood on the grass of the teak forests of Java, the lute spoke of burning huts in the Chilean deserts, and the drum beat out the rap of midnight fists on the doors of Filipino slums.

And like shadows appearing in the cities and in the country-side, I saw men in pale clothing who emerged from the dusk, who stood on street corners and listened in market-places, who went quietly among the people with their soft, sing-song voices, watching and waiting, and who moved when they were ready with deadly swiftness to still the struggles of the poor. I knew then as the dark chords of the music swirled around me that my grandfather had been touched by these things, that his life of travel among the peoples of the Pacific, the secrets he had learnt from them, the music he loved and its sacred place at the heart of their cultures – all this had eventually led him to the dim front room of his own house, where the pale figures of our visitors attended him on a urine-soaked bed, while a lifetime's knowledge slipped through his mind like water through sand.

At that moment the chorus of instruments stopped abruptly and I heard the door of the front room burst open and the sound of feet in the hall. The Pale Suits stood in the doorway, looking about them at the silent instruments. One of the men wore gloves of pale rubber that came halfway up to his elbows. The Pale Suit with the gloves went over to the stomach bow and gently plucked its fibre string. The instrument gave out a low, dull sound, as though it had hung there untuned and unplayed for twenty years. He listened as the note faded into the corners of the room, watching me closely as he did so. 'A young musician,' he said. 'Following in the footsteps of his grandfather.' The Pale Suit walked among the instruments, sometimes running a gloved finger across a dusty body or plucking a slack string. When he had finished his inspection he stood once more in the doorway with the other man, gazing thoughtfully around the room. Then he turned and the two of them went back down the hall to the front room.

Later I sat in the chair at the edge of the ruined orchard and watched the Pale Suits load the instruments into their vehicle. First they packed the gamelan, after dismantling it into its various pieces, and then added the stomach bow, the lute, and the Filipino log drum. When they had stripped the house of the last of its instruments they climbed into the vehicle, backed slowly down the drive and moved off in the direction of the city.

I set off for the mountains that night; travelling only by darkness and avoiding the roads, I estimated that it would take me ten days to reach them. I did not know how I would find my sisters and my father when I got there, or even whether they were still alive, but I knew that I could not stay to watch the final decline of the house. I saw it then as the Pale Suits would eventually leave it, gutted and open to the weather. I saw the wind lifting the iron of the roof, the rain beating through open windows onto the floor . . . I saw my grandfather wandering through its empty rooms and I saw him going out to sit by a blackened orchard overgrown with weeds, freed at last of the intolerable burden of his memories.

Ngahuia Te Awekotuku

THE BASKETBALL GIRLS

TIHI LOOKED AT HERSELF in the mirror. Closely, critically. Decided she was ready to go out into the kitchen and show herself off to the family – Koro and the kids, maybe an auntie or two or three, having a cup of tea and warming their feet by the coal range.

Everyone – everything – stopped as she came through the door. Tall, fair, and slim. She let them all inspect her; she was proud of her long shapely legs in the sheer black stockings (two and eleven from Matthias, what a bargain eh), her firm supple knees (she was too quick to fall, and much too vain to graze them on the knotty asphalt court); and her flexibly fine ankles cased in the black canvas boots. Tihi was a Basketball Girl. And she was one of the best.

And oh, how I loved to look at her. Saturday afternoons that winter, off I'd rush next door, straight after breakfast, quick as whitebait, into Koro's kitchen to ogle and admire. Staring at Tihi was a treat. And following her from a safe distance was even more of a treat, as long as we didn't 'cramp my style, you kids'.

She'd meet her mates at the Hindu shop. Two of them, Cindy and Pera. And they'd buy soft drinks in slender glass bottles, with

long wax pink straws. Green River, they'd say. Matching the
colour of our girdles and ties. Green River – for luck.

Meanwhile, we'd all be hanging back – if there was a gang of
us – and we'd wait for the bottles, which were dropped more or
less in the same place every time. One with a chewed straw (Pera),
one with the straw rammed and buckled in the bottle (Cindy), and
one still neat and whole (Tihi). Each bottle was worth fourpence.
Three made a shilling. Wow, that was a fortune!

Which I never made, for I was too busy watching Tihi. She
walked like a princess. Very straight, yet there was a ripple in there
too. Maybe like a panther, with her long black legs. Her gym was
always pressed and almost sharp at the edges of every one of her six
box pleats – three in front, and three at the back, that made twelve
edges. Done early every Saturday morning, with the iron hot from
the range, and a well-scrubbed, damp, worn-out flour bag with the
edges picked out. Every pleat was just right; so that the gym hung
from her shoulders like a straight black box, with big sections in it,
like panels. Over a snowy white long-sleeved blouse, with a
specially stiffened collar. And a carefully knotted emerald green tie.
Koro himself taught Tihi how to do the tie up 'tika' – properly; and
he was truly pleased with himself that day, folding the green silk
fabric in his barky old fingers, chuckling at his attentive mokopuna.
Tihi. Te Tihi Teitei o Kahukura. The highest arch of Kahukura;
Rainbow's End. She was well named. And she showed how well
she'd learned to do the tie, by skilfully knotting the girdle as well.
The colour of new spring grass, woven into a length of narrow
wool, two yards long, cutting the box pleats in half, nipping into
her waist, lifting the hem even shorter! This always interested me –
the gym no longer looked like a big black box; it pulled out very
slightly over Tihi's chest, while still going straight down the back,
though all the pleats gathered and crimped, just a little way over the
girdle, and fell in a skirt to the middle of her thighs.

Underneath the hem were other things too; they popped and
snapped and kept the black stockings up, pulling taut an inky black

line that ran from her heel all the way up the back of her leg. Cindy, Pera, and Tihi spent a lot of time worrying about these lines – those damn seams they were called, as the three twirled and danced and twisted, craning their necks over their shoulders, peering down at the back of their knees. Pera had the most trouble; she was shorter, but somehow much fuller, and though she ironed her gym just like Tihi, it just flared and flounced, swelling out in the front at the top, and jutting like a shelf from the back of her bum. So her hem was sort of even.

Tihi always made sure her damn seams were straight. 'Cos that's a *rule*', Pera would roll the words out, husky and rich, and they'd laugh and laugh. Even Cindy, who seemed a bit sour, she'd laugh in a gravelly, raw-voiced way. Her knees were always grazed, her eyes were always there, on Tihi. They would shine like dark embers from her strong face; though not the prettiest, she was the tallest in their trio. And she starred on the basketball court, shot after shot after shot.

Off down the street they'd stride, arms linked. Tihi in the middle, Pera on the right, Cindy on the left, all in rhythm. The Basketball Girls. Pleased with the world, and with each other. Going to meet their mates. Going to play the game. Going to win.

Saturday after Saturday, I followed them, and I wondered at their pride, and their grace, and their beauty. Even on wet days, when the rain lashed the asphalt like acid, and their boots would slide and slip, their pony tails flop and straggle. Even on days when they got 'cleaned up', usually by a visiting team from a bigger town – because at home, they knew they were the best. They had the trophies to prove it. And Auntie Lily, with her green lapels lined with a brazen glitter of badges, she said so. She was the coach, and a ref, and the selector, and she knew. That was that.

*

So spring came, and all the skinny willow trees turned the colour of the river, and the season was over. No more basketball till next year. No more following Tihi and her mates down the street on a Saturday afternoon. No more till next year.

And eventually, next year, winter, arrived. After a summer of blinding white softball pants and Tihi with a sunburned nose and cracked mouth and peroxide streak in her hair. Which was still in a ponytail, with the same green ribbon.

Winter arrived. And with it came Ahi. In a gleaming two-toned Zephyr Six, with bright red stars that flashed like rubies on the fenders. Ahi turned up to take Tihi to basketball, every Saturday. Just Tihi, because Pera had moved to the coast to look after her Kuia, and Cindy – well, she had just sort of vanished. Dropped out of sight. Who knew where.

Still young, still nosey, I'd hang around next door while Tihi got ready for the game. She still had that magic for me, even though she didn't meet her two mates any more at the Hindu shop; and with no Green River bottles to fight over, the other kids weren't interested in staying around. Tihi would meet Ahi instead; Ahi, who pulled up in the gateway in that amazing car. Ahi, with thick, jet-black hair cut like Elvis but a little longer at the back, like a fat duckbum. And dark glasses, green green glass in thick plastic frames. Ahi, who never smiled . . . and never got out of the car to go in and meet Koro either. Just waited, quietly, then revved the motor as Tihi gaily pranced out, flipped open the passenger door, kissed Ahi on the cheek, and then with a filmstar wave at her greatest fan (me) was off. Down the road with Ahi, who somehow felt familiar to me. Somehow.

Then it happened. Koro had a turn one Saturday morning, just as Tihi was ironing the sleeves of her blouse. She rushed out the door and was back in five minutes with Auntie Nel who had a car and worked at the hospital. They took Koro up there, where he was to stay and get fussed over for a couple of weeks.

And I was told to wait, and tell Ahi.

Oh, I thought, my eleven-year-old brain buzzing with the responsibility, my face a smear of tears. What was I going to say?

The car pulled up, all polished and shining. Ahi was checking the dark glasses in the rear-vision mirror. Slowly, I walked over, carefully arranging my story. It still came out all garbled though, but Ahi got the message, while I blubbered on pitifully.

The car door opened, and Ahi got out, kneeled down, still not saying a word. One strong arm went around me. I stopped snivelling, leaned into the black satin shirt of Tihi's hero, Ahi. Who took off the dark glasses, and looked at me. Smiling, talking softly in a voice I *knew*!

'Don't worry, Huri girl, Koro will be fine, you'll see.'

It was Cindy. Ahi had Cindy's eyes, and Cindy's voice. Cindy had come back as Ahi. Wow! It felt like a secret — it felt neat, though! I was dying to run away and tell someone.

But I didn't. I just went to church and to youth club and to school and waited for Saturday mornings. And the magic of Tihi, getting ready for the game, getting ready for Ahi.

Getting ready for us.

Alan Duff

THE HOUSE OF ANGRY BELONGING

from ONCE WERE WARRIORS

YA GOT THAT! YA FUCKIN *GOT* THAT CLEAR IN YA MUTHFUCKA HEADS, YA *GODDIT*!!

Yeow, Jimmy. Have, man. Nig Heke shuffling on his feet, head goin from side to side, dunno where ta fuckin look. On the floor'll do. (The filthy floor.) What the other pros was doin, who cared. I mean this is heavy as, man. Waiting for Jimmy Bad Horse to bellow his squeaky high voice at a fulla and thinkin: All I want is in, man. Nuthin else maddas. Nuthin.

Then Bad Horse sayin to the others all around: *Whassa* FIRS' RULE, bruthas and sistas? Whassa *firs'* rule in this family? A roar erupting: BROWN FIST-SSZZ FIRS'!! BROWNFISZZ!! BROWN FISZZ!! BROWN FISZZ!! (Oh, man, juss, you know, overwhelming. Kid c'd hardly think.) Yet Nig desperate for a break, an opportunity to ask Jimmy Bad Horse sumpthin, Sumpthin really urgent, Jimmy'd understand. But the big leader with the funny high voice walkin up and down and Nig despairing of getting his question asked. And the fuckin time marchin on. Any other day but this, man.

Even yesterday, when Jimmy Bad Horse'd turned up and tole Nig he could be in, but that don't mean a patch member, just, you know, takin the first step through them big black-painted gates. Like gettin an invite ta heaven, eh Nig? Bad Horse chucklin away in his evil style. Tell Nig he had a dude arranged to rumble with. It was outta him and this other pros from town sumwhere. Man, just point me to im. Even though Nig'd been just about to go to the tangi, Grace's funeral, when Bad Horse showed up.

The rumble turned out a breeze. (Freaked out to start off with till I connected with that left. Then I was right. Wasted the cunt. Man, I moved like I was a boxing champ. God, I was good. Though I didn't like it Jimmy telling me to carry on, kick the poor fucka's head in. But I did. And now look where I am: I'm standing smack in the middle of the Brown Fists' house, man, thas where it got me.)

Bad Horse had em all chanting about Brown Fists coming before even ya own family. That this is your family now, to Nig and another pros, Warren Grady, who Nig'd grown up with, and wanting the same membership for as long as he could remember. Now here they were.

About two dozen ofem; two dozen crazy mad heavy dudes, bout half a dozen ofem sheilas. Who-are-we?! Who-are-we?! Jimmy hadem goin. Had Nig all astir inside except for that feeling of Grace, her funeral. (She's gettin buried today.) Made him wanna piss himself with the urgency. Yet overcome by this sight, this noise-force in front of him: everyone wearin a scowl (I practised my own for years) and those shades, man: cool. I mean cool. Wraparounds. Make ya look meaner'n a snake. And tats, man, everywhere tats. On faces, arms, hands, you name it. Got my own share ofem. Done em myself. Dint make a sound neither when I was putting em on. The cutaway woollen gloves – brown for Browns. Man, make ya hands look like clubs, or like chain mail what ya see in comics. Heavy as. (Oh my old lady, she can't stand Browns. I told her and told her they're only trying to look tough, thassa whole idea to look tough, to look mean. But they're not bad when ya get to know em. And when you're in withem, as a member, then it's heaven. Nig convinced of this.)

But Grace, her face, nagging away in Nig's mind.

Then Bad Horse was right beside Nig and hissin in his ear: We let ya in, man and *this* is your family. Nig nodding, I know that, Jimmy. I accept that. Bad Horse stepping round in front of Nig: Ya bedda. Bad Horse resumed his pacing. Nig sorta sussed that Bad Horse hadn't said the same message to Warren.

The leader'd walk all the way through where the wall'd had a big hole knocked out of it into what used to be a next-door neighbour; from kitchen to kitchen. Then he'd pivot on his heavy (kicking) boots and come back. And the bros and sistas standing there waitin on his next move; a stereo goin in the background but quiet because he, Bad Horse, had said turn it down till he'd finished. The leader'd come right past near a kid's nose on his return: stridin out, his big bulk massive, man (And yet a Heke boy wondering why his old man'd told him this fulla Jimmy Bad Horse had no guts. Didn't he look like he didn't.), and them fuckin arms like tree trunks. Man a fuckin alive, who'd be crazy enough to mess with him?

The picture of Grace grew more urgent in Nig's mind; so he took a deep breath and got Jimmy his next time past: Uh, Jimmy? I, uh, have to go to – My sister, she's, uh – but Jimmy cut him short by stopping dead in front of Nig and turning his vast, Brown Fist emblazoned, back. And Nig heardim in a sorta whisper: Wha' sista's this? Uh, you know, my – Grace. (Hasn't he heard about it?) The big frizzy head with its blue and white headband going from side to (worrying) side, Nope. I ain't heard a no sista called Grace in this family. Then he turned.

And he was looking up at Nig's several inches taller face. What sista called Grace, man? Man, I didn't mean – But the leader turning his back again, and pointing. You mean her? At this skinny bitch, Nig'd seen her around, mean as. Hidden behind her shades she looked meaner'n some a the dudes. Her name ain't Grace. (I never said she was.) And she's a sista. Nig twigging at that. (Oh man.) The half-gloved hand swung to another: Thas Mullah. She ain't called Grace. And *she's* a sista. The head going slowly round at all the faces. Nope, Nope, at each sheila. No Grace here, man. Sorry. But Nig wanting to go see his sister off. Uh, just the way she . . . you know, how she, uh (Can't say it, man. Can't say: died. I can't.)

The face again. Big beard. Big fat face. Big explosion of wild hair. Shades not giving a kid a chance to know how he was goin, where he now stood, now that he'd seemingly broken some code or sumpthin. Oh man, we *know* bout your *sis-ter*, Nig. Clicking his tongue. (No eyes a kid can read. For a clue.) Hers was a, you know, a *hea-vee* trip, man. It was. Then — (shit! the fuck's happenin?) at chairs scraping, fallin over, boots stomping towards him it felt like the fuckin world was comin to an end. Yet a voice in Nig's head tellin him: Keep ya eyes open, man. And keep ya head straight. Don't madda *what* they do to ya, just don't show fear.

But the banging and crashing and stomping and wide arc of denim and eye-shaded advance hard to stand fast against. Nig wanted to piss — nah, *shit*. Just let his bowels open and let the fear flood out. Felt his mind shut off.

. . . Bad Horse saying how he, all ofus, brutha, were with Nig on Grace . . . (this a trick?) man, we know who she is — uh, was. Eh, family? And murmurings of yeah, they knew who she was. Seen her around, you know? . . . I mean, man, her age, eh, she was only, what, thirteen? That right what they say her only thirteen? Oh man, we can dig the heavy trip she musta been on . . . Looking up at Nig after shoving his shades upwards on his head. First time Nig'd ever seen the man's eyes; Nig surprised at how sorta ordinary they looked: just bloodshot brown eyes, nuthin special, nuthin evil *bad* about em. But then Nig's blood ran cold at Bad Horse sayin: Ole man like you got, man . . . Sorta shruggin with his lips how they do. Chuckling. I think anyone'd wanna commit, you know, sideways, they had ta live withim.

Nig not sure if he felt defensive or hatred for his old man. Maybe both. Jimmy still talking: Yeah, we seen her around, knew she was your lil sis. But she weren't one of us, eh. I mean not like we thought you were one of us . . . y'know, hanging out as a pros all that time. But had to learn to trust you, eh Nig. You know, ya mighta turned out sumpthin we, uh, didn't like. I mean, we ain't what you'd call geniuses. Eh Nig? Laughing. Hahaha! geniuses. Man, we ain't even *average*. We're just a packa dumb Maori fullas – oh, and a few sistas – got together. But we got sumpthin most people ain't, Nig. Know what that is, man?

Staunchness, Jimmy. *Staunchness*, Nig. You got it, bro. He's got it, eh bruthas an sistas? YEOW! Their affirming cry lifted Nig's spirits.

Staunchness, Nig Heke. For each other, man, we'd . . . we'd die. (Oh I'd die, Brutha. You just gimme the fuckin word, man: I'd die for a fellow Brown.) We might – Jimmy cocked his head to one side, acting funny – we might even – HAHAHAHA! – even – HAHAHAHA! – you know, loooove each utha. And laughing so hard it made his shades drop back down to near exactly their right position. Man. Tongue licking out over the mo part of his beard, Well . . . Dunno whether we'd go *that* far. Laughin again. And everyone laughin withim; and that word: loooove, echoing over and over from em, the mass, The Gang, as they said it in a dozen different ways: you know, tiptoeing it out, lettin the word sorta plop out, or teasin it out, or spittin it. Like it was some kinda bad-tastin medicine, sumpthin like that, they knew'd cure em. But damned if they were gonna take it, fucked if they were. And Nig could hear the change when their leader yelled: More like *belonging*! Eh people!

Next Jimmy was shakin Nig's hand, tellin im, Welcome, brutha. Welcome. And a boy's heart filled with that sense of the word Jimmy'd used before: *belonging*.

Somehow, with all the members comin up to Nig shakin his hand in the Brown Fist way of receiver holding the right thumb up to be taken in the full hand of the giver, releasing and giving each other a light tickling touch on the palm, somehow Jimmy Bad Horse managed to find Nig's ear tellim: *This* is your fuckin family. From now on, *this* is where you're at. So I'll leave it up to you. Melting back into the crowded room. (God in heaven, but I can't go.) But no time to think. Party time, bruthas and sistas! Jimmy announcing. (I'm sorry, Grace. But what can I do?)

Clink of beer bottles rattling in their wooden crates, a kid – every kid and adult in the room – had heard it all his life. It'd become the music he wanted to hear himself when he was old enough to play it. Crates and crates of the fuckin sweet stuff bein lugged in dumped on the floor, hands grabbing at the contents; decapping with teeth, a ring, cap to cap, on the edges of anything sharp, a belt buckle, a knuckle-duster, a fuckin big knife, man, bigger'n Crocodile Dundee's, and one mad dude just smashing the top clean off and guzzling from the broken neck. Oh, man, Heavee. (Grace . . . Grace, Grace, they're burying you. I'm so sorry . . .) Can't think bout that. Not any more. Too much happenin here.

The stereo turned right up. Can't hear myself think. Drink up, Nig. Drinking up. Marley and the Wailers. Oh man. SOUNDS, bruthas! Sounds. And just the hint of things in the movements of hips, hands, groovin bodies. But too soon yet. Too soon.

Smoke got passed around. Big fat joints half a fuckin yard long. Heads. Sins, man. None a ya fuckin weed for the Browns we *deal* in it.

Smokin, guzzlin, faggin, rappin, bigtimin, hate-talkin, smokin and guzzlin some more. And the music, man, expanding to ya ear . . . hearin it so clear ya felt ya'd composed it yaself, or so clear ya understood the, you know, the creative whatsit behind makin the recording. Oh you know. Smokin, ahhh, but that is *gooood* shet, man. Guzzlin. Like our olds, eh? Haha, finding it funny now, after all this time, your olds boozin their lives away and now you doing the same. Man.

The SOUNDS, keep on callin to a man, tellin im sumpthin, I dunno. Sumpthin about himself, I dunno . . . Like the art, man: I c'n dig the *art* went into this music-making. Why they started looking at each other with that mutual recognition goin snap in their minds: Hey, we're at the same place, man!

Guzzlin, smokin, rappin, *listnin* – (So much potential . . .) – startin to groove in time to it, or move to the offbeats; unnerstandin, mirrorin each other's movements with sly smiles; flowin *flooowin* to this whole new unnerstandin in their heads. Then suddenly droppin it.

Talkin tough and rough, we ain't groovin to no sensitivity, whatever ya call it, it *sucks*. So then their sentences had little length. Short spurts. More like grunts. And curses. Fucks. Cunts. Wankah. That sorta thing. (Yet inside all this unspokenness like some uncoiled spring of beauty, unnerstandin, just achin to unleash itself.)

Eyes hardly stayed in contact with each other – those that weren't hidden or lurking behind the shades – just a flicker, a stolen glance, a shy dart of vision that they, none of em, could hold. But things started expanding again.

The music did it: brought em out, flowered the little buds in their funny little brains, had blossoms bloom in their dirty little ears. The music, man. It loosened em. And when a bad dude gets loose he releases sumpthin.

All that Pine Block growin-up bottled all them years, havin to act tough and only tough or ya die, man, I'm tellin ya; all them years of learnin to be a supposed Maori, man, what it must do to ya, you know, ya actual *potential*. Ah, fuck the potential. Only joking. Only joking. But no sooner said than a dude got taken by the SOUNDS again, or else it was whatever it was in his head been set free; so he was walkin down main street of Kingston,

Jam-ay-kah, with Bob at his side, and the other cats really thinkin he was hot shet.

Then the collective mind shifted again: Volume. We want more VOLUME. And *fuck* the neighbourhood, makin it out as an act of stroppiness, or gang-power display, when truth was (any kid could see) they wanted to hide in the volume of music like they were always hidin behind their shades or in the dope and the booze and the fags; they juss wanna drown out the, you know, the upbringing. The stain of growin up a Pine Blocker. Of growin up havin to fit a role, a race role, man, and thassa fuckin truth you know it and so do I: havin to turn yaself into sympthin ya mightn't be. Yeah, thas what bein a Maori is for a Pine Block Maori. Gimme more smoke.

Passed around again. And again. It'd stone a fuckin elafint, man! Music vibrating the whole fuckin house, all two storeys and two full homes of it. And the truth out in the open now: gonna strut my stuff, man, an I don't care *who's* lookin.

Dancin. Movin this way – that way – cut this way – hey-hey – spin – *hooold*it – now turn. Yeow! Turnitup! Turnitup! Gimme a beer, gimme a beer!

Movin with mah groovin this is a *cinch*, man, a breeze, a doddle – *Lookit* me. (Yet weighted, I dunno, hard ta explain when ya jussa Pine Block nobody who only went ta school to beat up the honkies and feel their sheilas' twats up. Childhood. I think it's to do with childhood this weight thing.) Why so many were doin their thing with eyes closed, as if they were scared of the discouraging adults, the arsehole parents who were always tellin em ya gotta be this, ya can't be this, don't be that, juss a wantin to shut out the voices of authority in ya head, the mystery of ya mind tellin ya ya ain't nuthin but a little cunt no madda *how* hard ya try not ta be – Oh gimme another beer.

Swallowing some more courage, see if tha'll do the trick, shut out that fuckin *voice*'t stays in my head. Nother one. Ahhh, that feels bedda.

Swaggerin, staggerin, actin up, actin out, showin up, playin who cares just don't let the Voice come down a bummer on my, you know, my expression. Juss wanna dance . . . (with my darling, to the Tennessee Waltz – !?) Oh fuck that, man, thaz a *oldie* numba. Member em doin that, man? Our fuckin olds, man, they *love* that wankoff song. Another shift.

Rumblin, man. LOVE IT. Rumblin. Talkin about it – interrupting each other, climbing all over each other in their haste to get the password in. And havin this unnerstandin of sumpthin else about rumblin, the rhythm of it. Rumble in the jungle, member that dude? who was he again? Ali. *Ali*, man! What a fidah! Oh yea, what about Sugar Ray then? *Sugar Ray?* O far out! but he's the – And that dude foughtim that time wouldn't fight no more, what's his name ag – Duran. Roberto Duran, man. Know what they callim in his, you know, wherever the fuck he comes from, language? Hands a Stone. Howzat?! Oh wow. Call me that, man, I'd love it. I seen tha scrap on my brutha's video; man, what a fuckin rumble. He ain't no wankah neither that Duran fulla. No? No, man. Well how come Sugar Ray wasted the cunt? Sugar Ray'd waste any cunt. I mean, he's the *ulti*mit rumblin machine.

Actin out their fistic hero's movies: Hey-hey, watch me, watch me, this is Sugar Ray's Bolo punch . . . ooooooo! ca-boom! HAHAHAHA! In stitches. In an uproar. At the act bein so, uh, so *true*. Hey, what about this: *ba-boom-boom-daka-duk-duk-kapow*! A Leonard combination, pictured in their minds with all the exclamation marks, the *sounds*, juss like out of a comic.

Watch me, watchme: a blurring combination – a pause of posy arrogance – nigger cheek; flickin out a lazy left and kapow! comin over with a big right. Bobbin, weavin, bouncin, Ali-shufflin, Bolo-punchin, shoulders goin whiff-whiff-whiff! like *oil*, man . . . (I) he moves like he's got oil in his joints. Eyes goin all poppy: chin juttin out, shoulders going yahyahyah – kapow! Gotcha! Laughin. Like this, like this:. . . Oh just mirrors, man, of what they'd seen of the world, the creative world, the achieved world doin its stuff, struttin its stuff, on the TV, and every right to, man, cause others'd TRIUMPHED ovah the, you know, the odds. (Juss one fuckin win is all a kid, a man ever wanted. One single victory ovah sumpthin, someone.)

But then a lull comin down onem. This slowly descending lull. And with it: Truth.

Truth. Zingin, pingin, a crackle, a sparkle of electric zaps. Man, is it the dope doin this . . .? Truth about what? Truth about us, that's what. Why, what we done? Nuthin. It's jussa, you know, a process ya go thru. Didn't last long though. Truth doesn't. Truth ain't a continual process; it ain't a game that has a set time length. It's just a zap. A milli–sec buzz. A (uninvited, unwanted) disturb-ance of ya thoughts, like God or sumpthin has stuck a mirror in front of ya when ya weren't expectin it. Nah, it's just a small-time, short-moment hurt that goes, man. Promise ya. Here, drink up. Drink and be happy. A shift again.

Fulla went out back to the kennels, came back with a trio a dogs. More like tanks, ya mean. Bull terriers. Built like fuckin tanks. Black and white tanks. HAHAHAHA! And everyone pattin em, strokin, ear-ticklin, sweet-talkin, or steerin clear ofem. The bro bringin em over to Nig to take a sniff atim, the bro tellin his tanks. Is alright, he's one of us. Pat em, Nig. Nig patting the dogs in turn.

Air thick with smoke. Dope and fags. The music loud but the ear adjusted to it. The other music of more beer arriving in crates, brought in by more gang members and hanger-on associates, the ones with a bit more bread. Man, must be fifty ofem in here now. (Grace.) Can't hear myself think. (But sorry, Grace. I'm thinkin of ya, honest. Gonna make a special trip to your grave. Gonna buy a big buncha flow – no, a wreath. I'll buy her a wreath. It's dole day tamorrow. Tomowwow, as Mum'd say.) Nig having a private little giggle to himself and this sheila comin up to him and askin: Whatcha laughin about, man? And not a bad looker neither. (Man, I might be in here.) Oh this an that.

Nother fulla came in with two more dogs. Rotties. And he wasn't wearin a Brown Fist patch either. Other bro with the three tanks goes up to the associate asksim: Ya reckon your dogs c'n beat bulls? And everyone goin, ooooooo! And the dogs started barkin at each other, and straining on their leashes. Dunno, man. Mine're mean fuckahs. So're mine, man. Nah, I like my rotties. Don't wannem, you know, damaged or nuthin. The Brown lookin at the dude, Okay, man. Spose I'll have ta damage you then.

Real casual, eh. Like tellin the fulla his name.

Fear on the associate's face. Real fear. Like he'd walked into a nightmare and only just realized it. Nig feeling sorry for him, Okay, lettem fight, the scared fulla agreein. The Brown givinim a wicked smile: Thas cool, man. Make it in half a hour; give my boys time ta warm up. Chuckling at the scared dude. C'mon, boys. Pulling his three dogs away. Y'c'n have ya suppa in half a hour. Laughing.

Whaddid you say your name was? Nig to the sheila who'd come up to him. Tania. The sheila givin Nig the Brown Fist handshake. And Nig thinking he might be in here.

Damien Wilkins

CABLE *from* THE MISERABLES

IN HEALEY'S MIND, the character of the Wellington cable
car had always owed less to the steep incline of its tracks and the
harbour views it afforded than to the stern Eastern European
demeanour of the men who took the tickets and drove the car
dourly up the hill to Kelburn. These were faces lacking not only
the inclination towards lightness, but also, Healey believed, the
ability to show anything more than a vague annoyance at handling
the fares, answering inquiries, waiting for the passengers, sounding
the warning bell, until even the act of opening the doors seemed
to be done begrudgingly. It often appeared they would have far
preferred to lock the terminal gates and sit together in the dark,
muttering punch lines to the jokes which occasionally made them
bark alarmingly behind the glass of the booth. For some reason,
Healey found himself attracted to these bleak figures and he often
wondered about the paths they had taken which had led them to
their positions in the glass boxes where they now spent their
working lives.

Of course he saw that the good humour of these men was not
improved by the fact that each day they had to ride the same half-
mile of straight track again and again, watching people enter and

exit and make the same gestures, the same mistakes, the same noises repeating themselves – the sound of the cable spinning, the bell, the doors closing, the shoes skidding across the tiled floor and the helpless cries of 'Wait!' – so that perhaps it was not surprising that there was often the feeling among those who had managed to secure a seat that a team of sour and mildly hypnotized drivers had control of the machines, which moved in odd patterns of jerkiness at an angle of almost forty-five degrees. Nor should it have surprised him, as always it did, that this team regularly engineered it so that the cable car was out of service due to some mechanical fault every third or fourth time Healey went to take the shortcut from town to the campus.

On several occasions as a student, Healey had been forced to join the other passengers in a climb up the tracks, their car having come to a halt halfway up the hill. In such cases, the driver would refuse to give out any information about why they had been stationary for the previous ten minutes. Instead he would slide shut the door to his compartment and engage in difficult discussions over the radio with the Eastern European driver of the car which sat ahead of them. Sometimes the car would suddenly start moving again, and again this would happen without explanation or apology. Or else the doors would open after a suitable time had elapsed, by which the driver gave the passengers to understand that he wasn't going anywhere in a hurry, and if they wanted to get some place they would have to help each other down on to the tracks and walk the rest of the way. He would only utter the words 'Cable! Cable!' which immediately took on the significance of a curse.

As those who could began the trek up the hill – the students and the commuters, the housewives, and the doctors who had their rooms on Upland Road, the elderly residents of Kelburn and the bemused, hysterical tourists – moving through the ill-lit tunnels and slipping on the loose stones between the tracks, careful to avoid the cable, which might at any moment return to life, Healey imagined a slight look of triumph crossing the driver's face as he spread open the newspaper on the control panel in his compartment and began on the emergency sandwich that always made the journey up and down and was employed to stave off hunger until the engineers should arrive to rescue him.

After Claire left him on Willis Street, Healey had turned into Lambton Quay and then, while passing Cable Car Lane, although he had no desire to return yet to his parents' house, where several sets of relations still lingered, and believing anyway that the cable car would be out of service, he found himself paying his money to a man he recognized from years before as one of the drivers who had sat alone in his cable car halfway up the hill and who had caused Healey to be late for a tutorial in which American attitudes towards issues of censorship and sexuality in the 1950s and 1960s were being discussed. On that afternoon, the long climb up the loose stones of the track had filled his mind, not with the questions raised by the essays he was supposed to have prepared for the tutorial, but with the memory of another climb which had seemed endless.

After the holiday house-swap network had been exhausted, Healey's father began taking the family on camping trips. Remoteness and hardship became the twin indices by which he measured the success of each summer. He would say that it was necessary to get away from Wellington, that a man bound to his desk was half a man, and that the blood never reached the brain without a fellow moving his legs. Circulation and ascension, these were guarantees of both physical and mental freshness. In vigorous climbing there was also a kind of moral exercise. Healey's father had always loved a good stiff tramp, although now something other than personal gratification was driving him. A clique had formed at work to get the Department shifted into more suitable premises. The present location was archaic, hopelessly outmoded. According to Healey's father, the extent of this claim lay in the fact that certain people didn't like walking up a few flights of stairs. It was the smokers' lobby and nothing more. Blaming the building for the state of their own lungs. The strength of his opposition, however, seemed more apparent and operated with greater force in the manoeuvres he encouraged in his own family than those he tried among his colleagues. They, at least – his children – would set an example.

One summer they ended up in a tent on the grounds of a disused chalet on the western side of Mount Egmont. The chalet was open only in winter, which, of course, was the only time people came to that part of the country. Still, there was some excitement, though it was not acknowledged by the children, in approaching the chalet from the tree-lined sweep of drive and imagining for a moment that this many-windowed place was their summer residence. Whereas, in fact, the father had turned off the engine so as not to attract attention and the car had silently coasted around the grounds, stopping perhaps twenty yards short of a group of trees and making it necessary for the family to get out and push the car under the branches. Then they had pitched their tent behind the generously proportioned buildings, so as to be hidden from the road and from the owners or management who might have misconstrued the little settlement at the rear of their property. The chalet, indeed, quickly became a kind of elaborately constructed torment for the children, especially when it rained and they were forced to spend the night in the car while dreaming of being inside the cosy rooms which waited empty beside them by the hundreds. How cruel the gleaming bathrooms seemed while they were squatting down in the bushes, holding the roll of toilet paper above the prickling, dewy grass. Yet there was the mountain rising directly above them and, at over eight thousand feet, it was, as the brother said 'a real mountain'. In the winter, when the chalet was full, the snow-covered peak would kill several people per season. In the summer, all but the snow in the summit crater was gone, and Healey's father said they would one day go up it for the view.

At this time, Healey's sister had developed what her parents called 'a mind of her own' and she now simply refused to ascend to eight thousand feet to look out on Taranaki, a region which could only be a painful reminder of all that lay beyond the mountains to the south – notably, her circle of friends. There was also the shadowy figure of a boyfriend, although it would not be for several months after they returned home that Healey learned that, while they were up the mountain, the sister had been absent for the night from the chalet grounds and had been picked up at the end of the drive and taken twenty miles to the north, to the city of New Plymouth.

Having dropped law and while gradually moving to the almost exclusive study of literature, Healey had continued with history, believing it to be a more solid back-up than either classics or one of the social sciences, though the latter had seemed attractive from a distance, if only for the number of women students who gathered in the library to talk, often tearfully, sometimes excitedly, about their experiments with mice. If he, too, joined the psych lab, Healey imagined he might be able to console these women students and weaken the attachments they had formed to the pitiful animals inside their mazes and light chambers.

In his second year, at the time of the cable car breakdown, he was taking a course in American social history. The lecturer was a bearded man in his late thirties who had taken part in anti-war marches while studying in America in the 1960s. For this and for his comparative youthfulness and easy-going teaching style, he was universally admired among the students. Part of the way through the course, the lecturer, who was also Healey's tutor, shaved off his beard, causing the students in the large lecture hall to burst into spontaneous applause. 'With a chin,' someone beside Healey said, 'he looks even younger!'

On the day he had to climb most of the way up the cable car tracks, Healey entered the tutorial room ten minutes late. The room was on one of the upper floors of the library building and it always seemed overly bright under the fluorescent tubes, and too warm. At first, as he found a place and began taking out his books with exaggerated care, Healey had thought the lecturer was talking to the tutorial about an historical character, or speaking in the voice of one of the authors of an essay which had been set for class. Then he realized that the lecturer was talking about himself. He was saying that when his sex life was good, other areas went well also, and these were areas, he said, which we'd normally think had perhaps nothing to do with sex. 'I find I can drive my car better,' he said. 'My parallel parking is suddenly astonishing!' The lecturer looked at the students. 'But when things in the bedroom are not so hot,' he said, 'I notice a corresponding falling-off in other areas.'

He said he was interested, then, in the relationship between sex and our so-called public lives, since the essays he had set for that week's reading were also, in effect, talking about the places where sex and society meet.

The lecturer spoke so naturally it was impossible to believe that he was even listening to himself and certainly, Healey believed, he was not listening to the way his words had settled in the room, since they had effected a quite unnatural silence. The other students were either looking directly at the lecturer while he spoke, as if in an attempt to outstare him and to suggest that they could handle this type of approach, or studying their notes with heads down, hoping not to be called on to respond. Healey found himself looking from the course notes on the table in front of him to the lecturer and then back again. Now the lecturer was talking more about his wife's responses to these same issues, saying that he didn't think this was necessarily a male thing and wondering whether there were people in the group who felt similarly about their own sex lives. And again Healey had the impression, when the lecturer used the word *wife* or *group*, that he was referring to purely historical figures whom he had perhaps come across in the course of some research.

It then struck Healey that the quiet in the room was, in fact, natural. After all, the lecturer's questions had provoked in him not an inquiry into his own 'sex life' but a kind of rightful stubborn silence which gripped the entire tutorial. It was fitting that silence should meet the lecturer's 'frankness', his prurience, and, Healey thought as a student of history, his *goading*. Yet he knew that at this moment of defiance someone was preparing to speak, one of the older students, the so-called mature students, a man in his late-thirties who often hijacked the tutorial by demonstrating a certain long-windedness and obtuseness which masqueraded as 'experience', speaking as a contemporary of the lecturer's, and always beginning any statement, no matter what the historical context, with the words *In my experience*. Everyone knew when the mature student was about to say something, since he always moved his chair back away from the table, as if putting a distance between himself and what was being said at the time.

'In my experience,' the man said, with a scrape of his chair, 'sometimes, yes, good sex equals good life. A confidence thing, I can see that working. But other times, say I've been separated from my partner for a while, when I'm away or she's off somewhere, and it's happened to me quite recently, I feel I can channel those energies, those sexual energies into other areas. Into history essays, or whatever you like. I'm not distracted by the one, so I can think about the other in greater depth. If I don't have a sex life, sometimes I discover I have a better *other life* – no sex, better results – isn't that what the sports coaches say? Anyway I'd like to feed that into the group, perhaps other people—'

The tutorial then erupted, as it often did after the mature

student had spoken, and several students began speaking at the same time, some in prim defence, others in heated attack, while the lecturer moved his chair a little away from the tutorial table.

Healey did not speak. He was thinking of the girl in the previous year with whom he had sometimes slept. He counted three or four times, four if lying down beside her until it was morning was to be included under the phrase 'sleeping with'. And he thought of his dream of involving her in a criminal scheme.

For several months of the year, as a law student, he would regularly go downtown at lunchtimes and steal one or two or sometimes three books from a large bookshop on Lambton Quay. He never thought at the time of stealing about the consequences of getting caught. Once he was inside the bookshop, he thought only of the books which were now on the shelves on Lambton Quay and of the inches they would soon occupy on the shelves in the bedroom of his Aro Valley flat. The only moments he thought about getting caught were those in which he approached the exit of the bookshop with his one or two or, if they were small volumes, his three books – he always carried the books in one hand low at his side – and even in these most exciting moments, he never considered the consequences exactly but simply imagined the feel of the hand on his shoulder, or the sound of a raised voice, or, out on the street, footsteps running behind him. Just as years later on the poop deck, when he had been weighing up the American's proposition of perjuring himself for monetary gain, Healey felt curiously distanced from the notion of 'consequence' and thought only of how this particular piece might be fitted to what had gone before.

In the newspaper there were, periodically, reports of law students convicted of petty crimes. He remembered, in particular, the case of one female student who was said to be in her fourth year and one of the most promising students in her class. She was found guilty of shoplifting, despite a psychiatric profile which identified contributory and extenuating causes. The judge, in handing down the small fine, which would nevertheless debar her from her chosen profession, had spoken of the defendant 'throwing away four years of her life with a few rash acts'. He'd used the word *rash* even though during the hearing it had come out that, since the time of an unspecified family tragedy, the student had compulsively shoplifted items for which she had no possible use nor even desire, since it was also admitted in her defence that she immediately threw away everything she stole, sometimes dropping the merchandise into rubbish tins directly outside the shop. Nor did she have any memory of these incidents, except when prompted under therapy. The case had become something of a scandal among law students and their professors, but the lesson for anyone who broke the law, one senior lecturer said, was there for all to see.

When he read of this case, Healey imagined himself in court on similar charges and unable to name any contributory or extenuating causes, speaking only in breathless stabs, of those places on his bedroom shelves in whose empty inches he had imagined the spines of certain essential books. 'I didn't pinch just anything, your honour,' he heard himself saying. First he stole Russian literature from the nineteenth century, then twentieth-century French; in one go he stole the three books that Katherine Mansfield published in her lifetime; he stole American poetry and the selected letters of German writers; he stole the black-coloured Penguin paperback editions of Greek and Roman authors; he stole anthologies; he walked out with folktales, journals, and autobiographies, he stole several feet of the pale lime colour in which the Penguin Modern Classics were wrapped. And as the collection took shape, sometimes he was excited with the find of an essential book in a red jacket, which he pictured nicely breaking up the line of black, or with a white-spined classic to interrupt the run of green.

The girl who had constituted his sex life of the previous year was called Joanna. She was an English student. When finally Joanna had agreed to visit his flat, a few weeks after they had slept beside each other for several hours, she had immediately begun rearranging his shelves, so that they might appear as in a bookshop or library. Healey had never followed alphabetical order or any order except that of colour and occasionally he would put beside a certain author another author in whose company he believed there might be some mutual pleasure. But he had never been systematic in any of this and, as he allowed Joanna to alter the look of these precious inches, he grew more determined to finally bring it about that they would have sex together, if not that very night, then the next or the one after that – but soon, he promised himself.

It was a miracle, he thought, that Joanna had appeared at the door of his flat alone, since she was usually accompanied by a group of girlfriends and whenever he spoke to her, surrounded like this, Healey was forced to think not only of his image in her eyes but also of his image, or images, in the eyes of all her girlfriends, under whose appraising look the business of trying to bring it about that one night they might have sex together had to be conducted as if in committee. Now they were finally alone; did this mean the committee had okayed the deal?

'This is completely hopeless,' Joanna said, taking two books by one of the Russians from the space which had existed as a block of black and was now occupied by the various shades of the Cs, and letting them hang low by her side as she faced Healey. 'You need a librarian or someone.'

This was the moment – he remembered in the American social history tutorial, which he was remembering as he went up in the cable car – that he dreamed of involving Joanna in his shoplifting scheme. The way she held the books! But then he decided that they would first need to have sex fully and properly for a whole night and be lying naked side-by-side before he could begin to tell her how the books she had touched in his bedroom had come to be there. To tell her now, he thought, would have risked ruining for ever his chances. He would have thrown away many hours, he told imself, with one rash act.

They set out up Egmont after lunch one fine day and by late afternoon reached the hut at five thousand feet. This first stage was on well-maintained paths through sparse bush, and only once had they become disoriented before another tramper put them right. After a dinner of baked beans, followed by tinned peaches for dessert, Healey and the brother went to bed while the father carried on talking to some fellow climbers about routes to the summit, the weather patterns of the mountain, and the number of lives which had been claimed the previous winter.

The sleeping room, which they shared with four or five others, consisted of a joined bunk arrangement, with an upper and lower level stretching from one wall to another. There were no separate beds and during the night, Healey, on the bottom level, was occasionally woken by a neighbour's foot or by the sounds of trampers snoring and coughing. He heard his father above him cry out in his sleep and thought of him falling on to the floor in the middle of the night.

In the morning they rejoined the same path, though after a while the father led them off to one side, saying that he'd been put on to a good thing by a bloke in the hut and this route would save them time. Now, instead of solid ground, they were walking on loose rock, which the father said would soon give way to something firmer a little higher up. After an hour, the rock had become soft shingle into which they sank up to a foot before they could move off. Now there was little vegetation, and as the sun came around they found themselves on a bare and exposed face of the mountain, forced to track sideways rather than upwards just to escape this short cut. It then struck Healey that, just as they had traced the circumference of Mount Edgeware a few summers before, so they were now circling the summit of Mount Egmont, never appearing to come any closer and, in fact, sometimes moving further away.

Just as he had become almost mute in the law tutorial and spoken only rarely in the English tutorial and then never as he wished to be heard, so in the history tutorial he could only bring himself occasionally to read aloud a sentence or two from one of the required readings in answering the lecturer's questions. He could never trust himself to formulate a sentence of his own without running out of breath.

When researching a topic in the library by using the books which were deemed 'essential' and which were invariably put on closed reserve so that every student might have the opportunity to refer to them, Healey was often weighted down by the history of the book itself. He would become ridiculously distracted by its appearance – by how it had suffered and been through so many students' hands over the years that its cover was in a state of disrepair and its original text almost completely buried beneath the notational markings, doodlings, and crossings-out of years of history students attempting to find what was essential in its pages. In his allotted two hours with the book, he found he could read only those paragraphs which had remained relatively intact and from which the essence had not been removed again and again, as the juice is squeezed from a lemon. And such passages, of course, were more or less useless for his purposes.

While slipping about on the exposed face of Mount Egmont, Healey thought that they would become the first father-and-sons team to lose their lives to the mountain in summertime. When they rested, there was nowhere to sit except in the soft shingle they had been struggling through for hours. The sun was shining in a clear blue sky and yet at five thousand feet they had to put on their jackets. At 'base camp', Healey knew his mother would be removing her shoulder straps while sitting on the sunny verandah of the empty chalet reading her book.

His father now seemed concerned and gave up the lead to walk behind the boys, making sure they got up when they fell by supporting them with his arm. And this supporting was not done hurriedly, but gently, the father waiting with patience until everyone felt like going on. He kept speaking about the bloke at the hut the night before who'd put them wrong, and he seemed hurt, not that they were suffering, but that another climber could offer such bad information to *one of his own kind*, as if it were only a matter of protocol; Healey kept thinking, through the tears which now came freely to his eyes, that they were to become summer's first victims.

The brother, who was in the lead, then gave a shout and pointed ahead. Twenty yards away, a line of tourists, with cameras swinging from their necks, were sauntering up the side of the mountain. The party was moving swiftly up the same track which they themselves had abandoned hours before. At first his father acted as if he hadn't seen the tourists and their jaunty flight. Then, as Healey began shouting to them, he was silenced, his father telling him in almost a whisper to conserve his energy, though the boy saw in the father's face, mixed with relief, a momentary flush of shame. Finally reaching the track, stepping up on to its firm surface, Healey had the sensation of being plucked from the water. Quietly, almost sheepishly, they tagged on to the end of the line of tourists.

At the end of the social history course, Healey failed a 'conversation' with the lecturer on the early history of the American film industry. This had been the topic of his essay, which the lecturer, in awarding an average mark, had described as 'a literate precis of the source material'. The so-called conversation was worth ten per cent of the final grade, and Healey had been awarded four per cent. Since then, when 'talking' to the lecturer – a situation Healey did everything to avoid – he felt that each sentence he uttered was worth a little less than half its possible value. Whereas, with other people, he believed he sometimes had conversations which might rate an eight or even nine and that many hovered around the six or seven mark, he knew that he would never reach such a standard with the lecturer.

On meeting him at a social engagement several years after the film conversation, when Healey was sure the lecturer did not remember him, he listened to him talk of his days in America in the 1960s, just as when he was a student he had listened to him lecture on the 1960s peace movement. It was a luncheon, a few weeks before Healey was to leave for America. The lecturer had been a consultant on the board which had given Healey a travel grant for his studies. He listened to the lecturer talk of the time when he had simply left his books behind, in those first few weeks of fall and gone up to Vermont to watch the leaves turn. 'This,' he said, 'is something everyone just has to do.' As he spoke, Healey could not help but think of the lecturer's sex life and whether he and his wife gave each other marks out of ten, and also whether the turning trees in the Vermont fall might not be worth *a perfect score*. And he began to understand, even as he tried to picture the fall leaves of Vermont and rid himself of these old thoughts, how he had feared this man with whom he had once tried to have a 'little chat' about film in that office on whose wall was a large poster of the Marx brothers. He remembered that even as the lecturer talked about Harpo in a certain favourite scene, and Healey, recognizing that this was supposedly the icebreaker, had smiled back at him, he could not help thinking *How am I doing? I should say something now; there's a gap for me* and all the time busily trying to lift a cup of coffee to his lips without the whole thing flying out of his tense grip and ending up against the walls of the office.

One winter night several weeks after he had promised himself that he would wait no longer for Joanna, Healey found himself again surrounded by her girlfriends in the cold, dank living-room of the flat where she lived, seemingly with all the girlfriends, on the side of a ridge high up in Kelburn. He had already had perhaps five or six cups of tea, and when he protested that he didn't want to drink the house dry, one of the girlfriends assured him that it was okay, since every cup had been brewed *from the same tea bag*. 'Our record,' she told him, 'is thirteen cups from one bag – it's criminal how people throw them away after just one!' (Years later, when he came across one of Louise's used tea bags waiting in a cup for a second dunking, he would remember the face of the girlfriend with its look of boastfulness and he would take inordinate delight in throwing the bag away.)

He was now feeling bloated and slightly ill from the milky water, which, for want of conversation, he had heard himself repeatedly agreeing to. Earlier in the evening, the bottle of wine he'd brought had been divided up among the girlfriends and, when equal shares had been poured, the alcohol, with which he had hoped to induce a certain receptivity in Joanna as well as a degree of boldness in himself, scarcely reached the halfway mark in the teacup that he was forced to share with another of the girlfriends, since Joanna had taken up her position in a chair on the other side of the room.

The girlfriends were all 'alternative' types of varying convictions and while describing the course of his study, Healey let it be known that books were really his thing and that as a law student he had quietly seized the opportunity to act as a kind of *irritant to the system*. Joanna did little to confirm this status, but agreed that he had a lot of books, perhaps even too many, a comment which made the girlfriends nod their heads, as if *they had all had dealings with the sort of boy who had too many books*. She said that she doubted whether he was the type of person who took easily to organizing material and that this probably accounted for what she called his 'problems with law'. As Healey suffered a moment when he firmly believed he was in the wrong room and began summoning the effort needed to explain in his now constricted breathing that it was not just a case of organizing material, but rather that he was profoundly opposed to certain tenets of the profession and especially to its methods of deciding membership, one of the girlfriends cut him off by saying that she, too, like Healey, couldn't handle 'all those weekly assignments'.

The tea had begun to press painfully against his bladder, yet the toilet was right beside the living-room and had periodically, through the loudness of its reports, given the impression of actually being inside the room. He couldn't bear to imagine the sound of his urinating into the bowl filling the living-room and being appraised by the girlfriends, though equally unbearable was the thought of contriving his relief so that there was no noise, by which they might think him, somehow, prudish or unnatural. It was only when a group of clearly drunk male students arrived, 'friends of the flat', as Joanna announced them, two of whom Healey recognized as law students whose names the lecturer did not have to look up in the seating plan and who now caused the girlfriends and Joanna to become quite lively, that he finally went to the bathroom. By this stage, he no longer cared how he sounded and purposefully neglected to lift the seat, nor did he bother to wash his hands afterwards, but spent some time scouting around in the medicine cabinet, examining all the bottles and prescribed lotions that bore the names of the girlfriends who were sitting behind the paper-thin walls, shrieking at the lawyers' jokes.

When he had become almost speechless in the cold living-room and was imagining the walk home down the steep streets in the rain, Joanna led him, unexpectedly, since she had been engaged in earnest conversation for some time with one of the law students, to her bedroom where she said she was now tired and had to lie down. She kicked off her shoes. 'Everybody wants me,' she told him, closing her eyes. 'Before, no one wanted me and now there's you and—' Drunk with the tea and the crushing success of the young lawyers in the living-room, Healey fell against her. He could not bear to hear about all these others. He had her now, and that was what mattered. He wanted her mouth. 'My neck,' she sighed. 'My neck's the place.' He bit into the skin beneath her ear. 'Don't mark me,' she told him. He pressed his open mouth hard against her throat. 'I don't know who I am,' she said. 'They always go for the neck.' Healey continued to nuzzle. He could taste the tea in his breath. 'Don't suck,' she said. 'Sucking marks.'

They collapsed on to the bed, a mattress on the floor beneath a window facing the 'wrong' direction since it looked away from the harbour and caught, full on, the force of the southerly storm which had come up quickly in the evening and was causing the window to rattle so fiercely that it was difficult to hear without speaking in a normal voice, whereas Healey had imagined lying beside her and speaking only in *the voice of shadowy bedrooms*. This window was to blame. She pushed him off her and lay still. She wanted one sentence. Words were what she wanted, all strung together in the right order and accompanied by a kind of music in whose rhythm they could be joined. But with the window banging he grew more fearful that, speaking in his normal voice to make himself heard, he would lose everything.

He lay beside her for a time. 'So,' he started finally, 'how do you know those guys?' And it struck him then, in the time it took those terrible words to form in his sour-tasting mouth, that the moment in which he might have told Joanna about the criminal lunch-hours of her bookish law student and his dream of the two of them becoming a double act in the aisles of the downtown bookshops was gone for ever.

When he was rising above the city in the cable car, moving away from Lambton Quay, the scene of his life as a petty thief – a thief hardly resembling those who, driven by social necessity, ran through the books of his grandfather's favourite New Zealand author with such giddy energy, yet connected to these soiled figures all the same – he realized that he had never told anyone, not even Louise, about these most exciting moments in the year he had entered the wrong field. When he had phoned Louise the previous night and woken her up with his senseless rambling about the Russkies, had he not been moving towards such a confession? But of course he had chosen the wrong forum. Nothing was possible on the telephone. He should have known that. It was only when their heads were close together, when their elbows were almost touching on the table, when they were separated by only two small bottles of beer, he thought to himself – was it only then that he could truly say something? Only in Wellington, he said to himself. We always say the timing is wrong, he told himself in the cable car, the conditions, the location, something in the atmosphere, the height of a ceiling, there's always something. What hope we place in these poor incidentals! How lovingly we contrive these small setbacks to keep us from that real failure which at any time might take us by the elbow.

When the tourist party reached the end of the easy path and there began a period of moderate rock climbing, which involved finding a way up some large, rounded boulders, Healey's father signalled that their team should now make its move. Excusing themselves, they pushed through the tourists and hurried up the boulders, as if they had been kept back for a time by the slow crowd ahead and were now taking things into their own hands. As they passed the guide who was leading the party, Healey saw his father give the man a commiserating look as if to say, 'You poor bugger, having this lot on your hands!'

In the sunlight, the untouched snow of the empty crater hurt their eyes, but they clambered to the topmost ridge of the bowl-shaped summit and then, while their father urged them to take in the views, Healey and his brother crouched on their haunches and tobogganed down the icy curve, using the ice-axes, which Healey had thought ridiculous on the way up, like rudders to steer themselves. Then they climbed back up and repeated it. Now the father, tired of pointing with his arm to various landmarks visible in the distance, joined them, and they let themselves go faster, shrieking as they careered almost out of control, so that when the tourists appeared on the summit, they, too, believing it to be, Healey supposed, a local custom, wanted to slide down the sides of the crater. Soon the formerly deserted place they had discovered as if for the first time was swamped with the bodies of inexpert tobogganers rolling about the crater like marbles on a saucer, causing Healey to feel that the experience of Mount Egmont was now over and that they should return to the tent by the chalet.

Healey's sister said she had gone to a nightclub in New Plymouth. While the rest of them had been in their long bunk at five thousand feet, smelling each other, she said she was at sea level, drinking and dancing. This was the year in which the sister 'emerged'. She had left school and started working as a receptionist and dogsbody at a graphic design studio, earning the money with which she could afford to refuse offers to walk for hours without getting anywhere on the exposed sides of mountains. The work had also allowed her, after a few years, to give up on New Zealand, as she put it, and go to London where she was still living. On the rare occasions that Healey had heard her voice on the phone, she apologized for sounding 'like a real pom' before adding that she couldn't get over how bad *his* accent sounded.

Inside the nightclub, she said, there had been a large fish tank stocked with tropical fish. It was not enclosed but open at the top. 'Can you believe that,' she said. 'An open fish tank in the middle of a nightclub!' Nor was the fish tank set in a corner away from danger; it occupied pride of place, being close to the dance floor and to the booth of the deejay, who, between songs, kept alerting patrons to the fact of the tank and warning certain 'wild' dancers over the sound system that they were getting a little close. Apparently the tank was a recent addition to the club, a novelty item to entice outsiders. However, the locals, the sister said, had grown protective of it and were policing the area around the tank. Some bitter words had been exchanged between outsiders who had been tapping on the glass and what she called 'the fish-patrol'. While the outsiders danced and tried to have a good time, she said, the locals watched closely from the sides.

As the evening went on, one of the sister's party – though she would not specify who constituted this group – had become a little drunk and, while dancing, had thrown an empty beer bottle into the fish tank. People had rushed from all sides, she said, to rescue the bottle; dozens of pairs of hands had been thrust into the water, even reaching it before it settled on the bottom. Meanwhile, the bottle-tosser had been quickly escorted from the club, almost for his own safety, the sister said, such was the hostility aroused by his offence. Now, when any member of their party tried to order a drink he was refused, so that after a short time they were all forced to leave. Outside the nightclub, they were chased down the main street by some locals and only escaped, the sister said, when one of their pursuers twisted his ankle, the others stopping to gather around him. Afterwards, she said, running over the phrase as if it meant nothing, she had 'spent the night' with a

member of her party. Around this time she was fond of telling
Healey's brother at a particularly vicious moment in any argument
that all his problems would come into perspective once he was no
longer a virgin.

Years later, as he was climbing the cable car tracks towards
the tutorial, and ever since then, whenever Healey thought of the
city of New Plymouth, it was as if he were recalling a purely
historical city which the sister had once come across in the course
of some research she was doing on the places where sex and society
meet.

As Healey went up in the cable car and could hear the inevitable
conversations about the old cable car and its superiority over the
present model, since passengers had formerly been able to sit on
the outside and jump on and off as they pleased instead of bruising
their shoulders on doors which closed inopportunely – instead of
sitting in this malevolent little box, as he'd once heard a woman
tell her companion – he remembered that there had been one set
of circumstances under which the sternness of the drivers lightened
sufficiently for even a smile to enter those small compartments. It
took a child of a certain age, perhaps between the years of three
and seven, and a certain child's face, not too open, but guarded, a
little suspicious. This certain child, he pictured, knows that the
man sitting by himself in the front of the car, fingering the lighted
buttons, has a kind of secret life, is involved in some deeply private
game with another man, dressed in the same manner, who, even
as the child watches, is approaching from above them in his own
cable car. The child swings casually on the door and the moment
he catches the man's eye, the child has looked away up the hill in
the direction of the other man. Soon the driver will take the child
on his knee, from which vantage point the child may cast a brief
conquering look over one shoulder at the ordinary, seated passengers, and when the other car passes them on the only part of the

track where there are suddenly two lines instead of one, the passengers travelling down to the city will see transposed onto those dour Eastern European features in the driver's compartment the smiling face of a child.

Towards the end of the funeral reception, a family friend, who had contracted polio as a child and now walked with difficulty, each step throwing her body to one side, had said that she would be leaving but that she was not looking forward to the steps down to the road from Healey's parents' house. 'I might have to be carried down!' she said. Everyone had laughed at this remark and agreed that in ten years or so the only way that the Healeys would be able to eat would be to have food delivered *by air*, and that the sooner they installed that hydraulic lift they'd been talking about, the better their social life would be. What good was a view, someone said, if it killed you getting it.

Then Healey's father, whose pride in the house could be pricked by the smallest remark, had begun to speak earnestly, although everyone was laughing, about reaching certain summits and of 'effort rewarded', grabbing Healey and setting his hands on his son's shoulders while pushing him in front of the group. 'Brett here will tell you,' he said. 'Mount Edgeware! Mount Egmont! Oh, this house is nothing to the Healeys. This is only a mound. A mole-hill. This keeps us fit. It's only a ridge but it might just be our lifeline. You can feel your heart going by the time you reach our front door. That pounding is music to my ears!' He went on like this until he, too, began to laugh.

Meanwhile, the family friend had not, as expected, moved towards the door but was standing up and looking pained and slightly guilty. It became clear that because of the glasses of wine she'd had, which, she joked earlier in the afternoon, had gone straight to her legs, the family friend would indeed require assistance in reaching her car on the road below. Healey's father was then first to move, offering her his arm in helping her down the flight of steps to the lower level of the house.

The father and the friend, making their way with difficulty down the stairs, found themselves at the head of a long procession of mourners who had all been drinking for several hours and now wished to offer their advice and assistance to the family friend on the best way to proceed down to the road and what sort of grip the father should be using, since it was also now clear that Healey's father had drunk several glasses of beer and wine and was showing signs of an unsteadiness of his own.

'Careful! Careful with her!' Lillian was calling out.

The organist was saying that he could pick out something on the piano to accompany them on their way down, maybe a little Mendelssohn, though he didn't have his music with him.

'Keep back!' the father was shouting behind him. 'Everybody back or there's going to be an accident.'

'Well at least we're dressed for it,' someone shouted.

'Maybe the priest does discounts for group bookings!'

'Blasphemy!'

'Business!'

On reaching the front door, Healey found that the hysterical note he had heard in its various stages since the graveside – of thirst, expansiveness, fun – had now, evidently, reached a kind of apex in the crowd gathered at the top of the steps. When he arrived at the scene, having had to push through to find out what was happening, he saw that a rope had been wrapped around the woman's waist and, while several uncles prepared themselves to take the strain at the top, the father, assisted by a group of cousins, was half carrying her and half letting her fall down each step. On everyone's face was a look of intense concentration and seriousness, occasionally broken by fits of giggling and the odd voice of dissent, which was immediately shouted down, since what had been finally settled on was the idea of teamwork.

The woman herself, who appeared at times to be abseiling,

was giving slight cries each time she left the earth and blowing her cheeks out with huge satisfaction each time she returned, so that it was not certain whether it was terror that finally got her down or the ingenious management of the father's pulley system.

Peter Wells

'WHY IS FATE always so fucking inscrutable?' queried Perrin McDougal as Eric knelt at his feet, guiding his dead toes into his shoes.

'I suspect,' said Eric rather too tartly, because he hadn't actually thought he'd be acting as nursemaid, 'it means, that way, the old fraud is never quite caught out.'

They were in Perrin's exquisitely muted bedroom, with its frosty Viennese chandelier reflected in perpetuity in the floor-to-ceiling mirror. This now returned an image of themselves, ironically, in poses of almost biblical simplicity. Though Eric thought he caught a faint ammoniacal pong from Perrin's socks. 'Isn't it time, darling, these putrescent articles were, well,' Eric tried to sound noncommittal, '*substituted* for something more savoury?'

They used the telegraphese of old friends, accentuated by the frequently sharp, sometimes hilarious, even acid appendage of '*dear.*' Though in the present situation, with Perrin so ill, the *dears* had taken on a warmer, more amber hue.

'Can you find me my walking-stick?'

Perrin had phoned up that afternoon and commanded Eric – the tone was properly regal and brooked no contradiction – to take him off to the Remuera Garden Centre. Eric thought ironically — though fondly too, because in the contradiction lay the quintessence of his character — that here was Eric almost certainly going to be absent in the flooding spring yet he, Perrin, was planning a lavish bouquet for his 'spring' garden.

'What I see,' Perrin had announced over the phone in that way that had the faint edge of the visionary to it, 'is a mixture of marigolds, blue violas and delphiniums. Don't you remember . . .?'

Eric didn't, but it didn't matter.

'Don't you remember how Aunt Priscilla down in Te Awamutu always had a daphne bush by her front steps and the way it always used to *invite* you — yes, *invite* is the right word' — Perrin kept his legal precision intact, a careful weapon against the unknown, 'so that as you ascended the stairs into her hall, the scent was *incroyable*!'

Perrin now rose to his feet unsteadily. His once fleshy form had been stripped by the disease to a frightening gauntness. His stylish garments — once bought in Melbourne or 'inexpensively' run up in distant Bangkok — clothed his skeleton in a simulacrum of 'health'. To the outside world — that crowd of on-lookers who instantly became extras in the cinema reel of Perrin's declining life — he probably looked only frail, possibly suffering from cancer.

Eric clung to these illusions as he handed Perrin his elegant malacca cane. He was still getting used to the shock of being seen with Perrin in public.

He had told himself as he drove over to Perrin's Epsom bungalow (a clever pastiche of Frank Lloyd Wright, via his Napier disciple, Louis Hay) that the public gaze simply didn't matter, that it was more important to simply help Perrin, that this accompanying him a little along the road was the very least he could do. But the truth was he had gone into a state of near shock when he thought he'd left his sunglasses behind.

He realized when his fingers touched bakelite — they connected with the impact of a lodestone — that he was sweating uncomfortably, not even watching the road. His heart was banging away, in a mocking Judas dance.

'Give us your arm, dear.' Perrin now stood at the brow of his front steps whose very sweep and height had once signalled power. Now they simply spoke danger: Perrin's grasp of Eric's arm was surprisingly tight. Eric registered Perrin's frailty as he leant into him.

He watched the almost random – yet hesitant, hesitant – fall of Perrin's numbed feet.

Suddenly Perrin lurched to a halt. 'This!' he cried in a voice full of emotion.

Shit, thought Eric, stopping back his alarm, *the bugger's going to cry*.

'This is where I want to have a whole *flowery mecca*.' Perrin waved his wand towards a dug circle of dirt. Even though he was facing financial ruin he'd hired a student to create a new flowerbed. 'When people come to see me, I want them – to feel *welcomed*.' The last in a breathless rush. Then Perrin took off suddenly, as if blown along on the coat-tails of his inspiration. Eric hurriedly shadowed his movement, getting ready to catch, hold, balance. But Perrin had miraculously connected with gravity.

'The scent of marigolds!' he cried out in something like rage.

This is the whole fucking trouble, Eric said to himself in an aggrieved way. You can never tell with Perrin what tangent he's going to hare off on next. He thought of the long somnolent telephone conversations they had each night while Perrin waited for his sleeping pills to take effect. Eric would sit in his armchair, armed with a glass of gin, half watching the televisual fantasy of reality while Perrin's voice purred away in his ear – sometimes thin as cellophane, occasionally close as a voice in a dream: his needs, emotional, physical, his dreams; his plans for the future. To sell the house and go to Venice. A week later to offer the house to people with the disease. Another week and he is planning to repaint the hall a Polynesian shade of blue. 'Sea-blue, just that shade of light at dusk – the moment before the sun sinks.'

Shit, and I'm only one of his friends, Eric often said to himself. Not even his oldest. What about his *family*? But Perrin's family in faraway Te Awamutu were in disarray. They were busy tending to their own emotional wounds: they would leave Perrin alone to attend to his actual torment.

Yet, if Eric were honest with himself – and he occasionally was, by dint of necessity rather than pleasure (he was old enough now to realize that honesty, though cruel, was the best policy in the end) – Eric's truth was, silently and subtly, he himself had come almost to depend on Perrin's presence: his closeness. The fact of the matter was Perrin's reality had become the ballast in Eric's somewhat unsteady life.

Ahead of them, as if a testimony, lay Eric's blue, shockingly dented Renault.

Eric's boyfriend was 14 years younger than him. He was a student of architecture who had never heard, thankfully, of aversion therapy as a 'cure' for homosexuality. He could not imagine a city in which there were no bars, saunas or nightclubs. Matthew, handsome, athletic like a basketball player, with an engaging sweep of hair that never quite managed to stay down, had pranged Eric's car in fury one night because, as he yelled out for the whole street to hear, 'You care more about Perrin's dying than *loving* me.'

It was unfair, it was emotional blackmail: it was true.

Eric needed Matthew, his beautiful boyfriend, for the warmth of his flesh, the passion of his kisses: the way he connected him back to life. In the middle of the night he could reach out and let his hand just roll down Matthew's flank and find that softly sweating crease in his knee. This soothed away the phantoms which hid in the dark: Matthew's body was so tangibly real.

Yet for Eric his experiences with Perrin – Perrin sick, Perrin dying – were almost like a pre-vision into the future, a kind of warding off of evil spells so that he would at least know the path of the disease if it should ever strike near him. This was his private truth. And Perrin, who never for one moment doubted Eric's presence by his side, communicated the full phalanx of his illness to him so that Eric's daily equanimity was conditioned by Perrin's. They moved in uneasy duality, two friends linked like horses on a circus merry-go-round, ceaselessly rising and falling together till that final moment when one horse would rise alone.

'Now my funeral,' Perrin took up as the car moved along the streets.

This is what is so odd, thought Eric, as he drove along. When he was with Perrin it was as if that became the centre of reality in the world. Even driving along it was as if the streets of Epsom outside, with their casual realities – a father pushing his babycart into the drycleaners, a woman ducking into the wineshop in broad daylight – became like a moving cyclorama which streamed past them: Eric and Perrin were at the storm-centre, stilled.

'For my funeral,' Perrin was saying in the matter-of-fact, 'now take note of this' voice he used for the important formality of his funeral. He was planning it as he had planned his famous dinner parties, with the exquisite silver, linen and flowers acting as courtiers, nervously anticipating the throwing back of the gilded doors, the regal entrance of the food. Now the unpalatable truth was that Perrin's body would be the main course: and Eric, as a friend who had come forward – and for who came forward and who fell back there were no rules – was to act as courtier, arbiter of Perrin's final feast.

'I only want flowers picked from people's gardens. I don't want *one – one!*' Perrin tapped the floor with his stick vehemently, 'of those embalmed creations dreamt up by florists! And fruit should be whatever is freshest in the shops. Vegetables of the season – organic. And definitely kai moana. That shop in K Road, you know the one. Only the freshest. Can I rely on you for that?'

'You can rely on me for that.'

A slight pause. Eric turned and looked at his old friend. 'Your Celestial Highness,' he said.

Perrin smiled but did not laugh.

Going through the Domain, they were suddenly accompanied by a flock of graceful runners. Eric slowed down in appreciation. There was one man, sweating in the silent chiaroscuro of sport which echoes so closely the fury of sex. They both watched him silently.

Suddenly Perrin wound down his window. 'You beautiful man!' he yelled out in the voice of a healthy male. 'You're the most beautiful flower in the whole fucking Domain today!'

Eric blessed the presence of his sunglasses while inwardly shrieking.

Fortunately the runner turned towards them and, in his endorphin bliss, showered an appreciative smile at them. The other men pulled away. They passed in a blur of sequined sweat on muscular flesh, with frolicsome cocks beating to and fro like agitated metronomes inside their tiny shorts.

Swiftly the runners became manikins in the rear vision mirror.

'Thanks, darling,' said Perrin in a small voice of exhaustion. 'I really appreciated that.'

Eric felt a surge of exhilaration as he moved closely behind Perrin through the gates of the garden centre. Already queues were forming, with well-heeled Aucklanders guarding trundlers full of merchandise. Eric realized he hadn't felt so good – dangerous would be the wrong word to use – since the very early days of

Gay Liberation, when to hold hands in public with another man was a consummate – if inevitably provocative – act.

Now time had shifted the emphasis somewhat – but Eric felt a shiver of pride at Perrin who, once so socially nuanced and named, could now lurch – almost like a toddler in reverse, Eric thought with a saving sense of hilarity. He was completely oblivious to the reactions of people around him. Indeed, as he stopped to pass a cheery word with the middle-aged housewife acting as a trundler-guard, he was actively engaging everyone in his act of dying.

Behind his shades, Eric was aware of people staring. They looked on silently, hit by the stilled impact of thought.

'Perrin!' Eric called out, because it suddenly seemed imperative to keep up contact, 'it's marigolds you're looking for, isn't it?'

He moved over to Perrin and, in a movement he himself had not contemplated, hooked his arm through Perrin's frail, bird-like bones and clung on. That was the mystery: it was he who was clinging to Perrin, not the other way round. But Perrin was off, putting all his suddenly furious energy into pushing the cart along. He was calling out the names of the plants as he went, voice full of glee: 'Pittosporum! Helleborus! Antirrhinum! Cotoneaster!'

Now people *were* staring.

But Perrin was unstoppable. It was as if he were gathering in energy from the presence of so many plant forms which, embedded in earth, nourished, watered and weeded, would continue the chain of life: just as his dust would one day, soon, oh soon, too soon, be added to the earth, composting.

Eric felt an uneasy yet piercing sense of happiness, a lyrical rapture in which he conceived the reality of how much he loved Perrin: of how Perrin was, at that very moment, leading him on a voyage of discovery so that they were, as in the dream, two circus horses together rising, leaping wonderfully high, almost far enough above the world, so that for one moment it was as if Perrin and he were experiencing in advance that exhilarating blast of freedom as they surged away from the globe on which all of life was contained, and beyond which there lay nothing – at least nothing known.

The plants were loaded into the boot. Eric had, at the last moment, tried to modulate Perrin's buying frenzy but, as if in testimony to his mood-swing, Perrin had impetuously bought too much, ordered Eric to shut up, and had sailed past the cash register issuing a cheque which Eric felt sure, with a lowering degree of certainty, would bounce. But Perrin, like a small child now, exhausted, almost turning nasty, threatened to throw a tantrum in front of the entire queue. 'I must have what I want,' he had cried. 'You don't *understand. I must!*'

And now, thankfully safe inside the car, Eric began breathing a little easier. He shook off his sunglasses, which now weighed heavy on his nose. He felt the beginning pincers of a headache. Perrin was saying to him that he wanted – he *needed* – to take Eric's car for a drive. He needed to be on his own. He could drive still. Did Eric doubt him? Why was Eric always doubting him?

'Trust me,' said Perrin in a small voice, like a caress.

Eric looked at his old friend. How much longer would he have him with him, to trust, not to trust, to doubt – to be astonished by. He did not know. So, doubting everything, doubting his own instincts to be firm, to say no, Eric allowed himself to be dropped off outside a mutual friend's townhouse, a refugee, and, standing on the pavement, about to go in, he watched Perrin drive away in his car, faltering out into the middle of the road, hugging the centre line. And seeing Perrin move off, odd, slow and cumbersome, trying so hard to control his own fate, Eric watched his dear love, his friend, turn the corner, with as much grace as possible, attempting to execute his own exit.

Forbes Williams

FROM MOTEL VIEW

. . . SLOWING DOWN FROM the highway as you cross the town's only bridge, you might note the abundance of neon as you first enter Main Street, but all too soon you'll be through all that and back out on to the dark highway. There are three sets of traffic lights in Motel View, but they are traffic lights without purpose – Main Street is the only street – and they are always green. Don't bother slowing down.

You'll continue out along the coast for about another five miles until the road rises sharply and to the left: Hunter's Garage corner. It's actually the second of three nasty bends, but it seems to be the one that does the damage, so watch it. In the winter it can be icy and very treacherous.

Once you're past Hunter's Garage you'll be travelling inland, leaving the bay behind you. You'll wind up the hillsides for about another five miles, till you reach the top of View Rise. At the View Rise lookout you'll probably get out of your car and look back down into the brown silted bay, the steep treeless hills that rise out of its sides, the small but distinct mudflats extending back from the tidal reaches. If it's night, though, all you'll really see will be the flashing coloured dots of Motel View. If you've got a good camera (like John) you may well want to try and take a photograph of all that darkness with the little spots of colour. Put your camera just a bit out of focus and the light blots on the photograph like drops of bright paint. It's like Christmas.

Once over View Rise you'll wind down out of the hills. There's a larger town on the inland plain, and it's only a couple of miles down from the Rise that it first blinks into view, the reassuring sight of a town worth stopping in. As your mind shifts to hamburgers and milkshakes you'll quickly forget the wide round bay, the hills, that odd little amusement park place with the wrong name on the map.

Unless you decide to stay. In which case you'll drive gently once down Main Street till you come to the last motel – The View Inn – realizing with a mixture of surprise and annoyance that there are no takeaway bars, no dairies, no pubs, and no vacancy at any of the motels. If you're like us (John is driving), you'll probably do a slow careful U-turn, crawl back along Main Street, 'just to check', turn back round again at the bridge, speed up through all the traffic lights, and head on to the next town, which on our map is a thin circle round a fattish dot: symbol, I suppose, of hope. You'll speed out along the coast, and the rest you already know.

Unless you have a flat tyre. Then you'll have to stop. This need not take more than ten irritated minutes of your time, but perhaps you'll light a cigarette (as I do) and wander up the road a bit first, intrigued by this strange, quiet town. If you do, you'll almost immediately get a strong feeling of emptiness, even desolation, as if Motel View is in reality a bizarre ghost town. There'll be no cars, no people, no bicycles, toys, trees, or pets. No life but for a few small shrubs set sparsely upon flat, broad mown lawns advancing to low brick fences, no noise but for the soft bay. Set back on their lawns the low single-storey buildings of motel units, long buildings full of dark windows – like a school really, or a mental institution – and no sign of activity inside them. Just those faithfully flashing lights, giant electric words against the sky, each sign its own distinct style of lettering. It's as if the town is no more than an advertisement.

Once you've walked the length of Main Street, you'll probably begin to notice how cold you are – no breeze, just a still, sharp chill.

Christ it's cold, you'll probably say (as I do), rubbing each arm with the opposite hand. Let's just fix the wheel.

You'll walk quickly back to the car, head down over your crossed arms, trying to remember where your jersey is.

My jersey's in my bag. We'll have to open the boot.

We'll have to open the boot anyway. My mind drifts across the vagaries of changing wheels.

True, I say at last. We will.

If you're travelling with John (as I am) you'll just have to put up with the cold, because even with your jersey on the chill gets in, and he'll want to set up the camera to take long-exposure views of the neon signs. Not having a tripod, he'll use the car roof as a solid base, so you won't be able to change the tyre while he mucks about. I'm not bitter, of course, but we are always stopping in the middle of nowhere so John can take photographs of broken fences, abandoned barns and dead cattle.

I'll go in this place here and see if they've got any food, I say, lighting another cigarette. John struggles with a knob on his camera.

Do you want any food? John's forehead is wrinkled in intense concentration. When he concentrates he grunts, and it takes him nearly thirty seconds of periodic grunting to answer.

What?

I said, do you want any food? Will I buy you some?

Do they sell any?

I don't know! Christ!

Okay, okay, don't get shitty. Something breaks off in his hand. Get me some fruit.

Have you broken your camera? I can hardly disguise my hope.

I don't know. I can't see properly.

Well sit in the car with the door open. It's too dark for a photograph anyway. Aren't you cold?

Red deco letters flash on and off above the car. View Towers. And – a smaller, squarer blue – No Vacancy, flashing less frequently and staying on longer. John won't tell me if he's cold or not, so I shrug and begin walking up the drive. The gravel crunches under my feet.

Like all the other motels, View Towers is set well back on its lawn. It has the same tidy shrubs squatting like gnomes, and the grass smells freshly mown. Everyone I know has a fondness for that smell, as if some primeval instinct deep within our evolutionary past was actually preparing us for the arrival of lawnmowers. The motel itself is also like the others, a low dark building full of windows. As I near it I cut across the lawn, quiet as a cat, to spy in one, see if I can see inside. It certainly does not look like a full motel. The windows are tinted, and the building set far enough back from the road that the flashing signs only reflect back at me. All I can see are a few indistinct shadows, nothing certain. I look into several more windows. It is the same in each one.

A sudden schoolboy panic possesses me, and I run back to the drive. I realize once more how cold I am and walk briskly round the back, following the drive, to the motel office.

The office is weatherboard, seems to hang off its new brick motel as an afterthought, even though it is almost certainly the older building. A bare bulb, sitting over a single step, lights the outside. Hundreds of insects dart round the light, as if an insect world war has at last ended.

Hey, you guys, one imagines insects saying to their families. Hey, you guys! The war's over! Let's go down to the light!

A pale yellow wooden door with a frosted glass window leans unhinged in the doorway. One vertical board has been kicked in at its base, and the glass is cracked in several places. Someone has painted in rough handwriting on the door:

View Towers – Moteliers
                        – Colour Television
                        – Bed and Breakfast
                        – 4 Star Service
                        – Credit Cards Accepted
                        – No Vacancy

Standing on the step, I take the door with both hands and lift it with care out of the doorway. I carry it before me into the small office and lean it against the wall. The insects follow me in. Their small wings whisper.

The decor is strictly linoleum. The floor, the top and sides of the high counter, all are linoleum-covered; even the wallpaper looks like linoleum. There's a sign on the wall behind the counter that repeats the painted words on the door.

There's nobody in the office, but another doorway behind the counter opens into a smallish living-room. A small colour TV is going, with some kind of sports programme blaring out, and in front of it – with his back to me – is a short man with short curly hair and a sunburnt neck. He is shadow-boxing, swinging from side to side, and growling out an intermittent commentary on some game which seems to be a mixture of the one on TV and his own private boxing match.

Go get him! he shouts, pummelling the aerial with a brutal left haymaker. There! That'll show you, little runt! Get him! Go get him! He struggles to the floor, perhaps retrieving the aerial, though it could be he has it in a headlock.

I stop for a second, unsure what to do. He seems too violently engrossed for me to consider stopping him. There's a buzzer on the counter with 'Press On Arrival' scrawled alongside, and after a moment's hesitation I decide to risk it. I press. There is no noise. I press again, this time holding it down for maybe fifteen seconds.

Finally another man appears in the living-room. He is fatter than the boxer, but shorter. He stops for a few seconds to look at the TV, then turns to me, stepping into the office. He is rolling up one sleeve, and he looks at me with narrow eyes.

Wha'd'ya want? he says. We're full. Can't you read English?

Maim the bastard! shouts the other man, back on his feet and waving his arms.

We've got a flat. Is there some food we could buy?

He begins on the other sleeve. There's no garage in Motel View. Nearest garage is Hunter's, few miles down the road.

Have you got any food? You know, a restaurant or something.

Grind his head! Grind his fucking head!

This is a motel sonny. Only meal here is breakfast.

Well can we stay?

Jesus Christ! What the hell are you? Kill him!

We're full. I told you we're full. Can't you hear either?

But there's no one here. I looked in your rooms. The place is empty.

He leans forward, pudgy hands gripping the counter.

Kill him! Kill him! Fucking kill him!

Can't you see we're busy? He has begun on the first sleeve again. Already the second one is unpeeling. It occurs to me he possibly spends his entire life rolling up his sleeves.

Have you honestly got no food?

His face reddens. He is the perfect cartoon bulldog.

You better get out of here, sonny, or there ain't gonna be too much of you left.

KILL HIM!

I back out of the office, my hands up.

Okay, I say, okay. I'm going.

Out in the drive I can feel my heart pounding. Some motel. I realize we'd better get the tyre changed and out of here.

At the car John has given up on his photograph. The ground round the boot is strewn with bags.

You just wouldn't believe the people in there! I say as soon as I get close. No food, that's for sure.

I can't find the jack.

God, I thought the guy was going to do me in! Bloody crazy. There was this other guy fighting the air, and just bloody screaming at the television. I reckon we should get the hell out as fast as we can.

I can't find the jack. It's not in the boot.

Yes it is. Eager to upstage I push past him, start rummaging around in the dark boot. It's in here somewhere.

Could it be in the back seat?

I fumble around. I'm sure it's in here. Haven't we got a torch?

The batteries are flat. I don't think the jack's here.

Of course it's here. Where the hell else would it be? Listen, you should have seen these guys. They were off the edge.

Can you find it?

Not yet, but it's in here. I'm sure it is.

Another five minutes weakens my confidence. The jack isn't in the boot. It isn't in the back seat. Finally I accept reality. We can't change the tyre.

John looks at me seriously. His face is alternately red, blue and purple.

What about the guys in there?

Look, honestly, they were going to beat me up.

Well what about somewhere else?

We look up the street. Vista View. No Vacancy. Lake View. No Vacancy. Every one is the same. No Vacancy.

But they're all empty. I just don't understand it.

Well, I don't see that we have much choice. And I tell you, it's too cold to sleep in the car.

I start to shiver. The chill is like a hand down my back.

But we have no choice. Like it or not, we're staying in Motel View.

Emily Perkins

NOT HER REAL NAME

MUD IN YOUR PRETTY EYE

NINE YEARS LATER, you're leaving a bar with a friend and you see him across the wet road, getting on to a bus. From then, from the restaurant.

Francis

You always thought, Francis, rhymes with answers. Which it doesn't, really. But you'd change the s of answers to be soft like his name. Francis, Francis, there's no answers. It was a walking rhyme. A home from the bus-stop rhyme. The rhyme of a fifteen-year-old girl who could feel sad every time she thought of that soft s.

Hands in gloves in the hot water in the sink, you'd turn around and be surprised again, every time, when you saw his face. His eyes crinkled up and were almost lost when he laughed. His laugh was nearly silent and you tried to match it. You and your friend Thea had developed the habit of snorting whenever you laughed. You tried desperately to curb this around him. At the restaurant. You never thought of it as going to work, you thought of it as going to see Francis. You barely remembered that you were a dishwasher.

Brideshead Revisited was on television at the time.

You were not your usual self around Francis. None of the cackle, the shrieking, the tough-girl acts that you and Thea lurched around school and town with. You shrank, you backed off, you revealed nothing. If you smiled it was anxiously, if you spoke it was so softly that people said What? Eh? Speak louder. You were in love with this feeling of self-consciousness. You wanted so much that the constant holding of breath could bring tears to your eyes. The only freedom you allowed yourself was imaginary. Elaborate fantasies you dared yourself to get lost in while Francis banged in and out of the kitchen, carrying plates, scraping them, arguing with the chef. You thought maybe your daydreams would be strong enough that he could read your mind, would look at you, know, love you. Or maybe your body would reach out, involuntarily, necessarily, and save itself on his thin arms. This never happened, of course. You were fifteen. Nothing ever did.

Very thin, with wispy kind of no-colour hair, not tall, pale, dark circled eyes, cheekbones. Cheekbones. Every angle you yourself did not possess was there in his cheekbones. You can't even remember the colour of his eyes. Probably blue, some cold colour. He dressed like he knew nothing about fashion and cared even less. You loved this gap in his knowledge, this laziness, this flaw. You thought nobody else could see how beautiful he was.

What happened was entirely predictable, though you never predicted it. After you'd been at the restaurant for four months, Francis left. He had exams at university and he quit his waitering job. You didn't even know it was going to happen until he said Last fucking time I have to serve up this shit. What? you asked but nobody heard you. Why? and you felt your eyes get hot and you felt dizzy and you felt like running out, now, or saying You're wrong, making a mistake, it's me I'm here, you can't, no. But the same thing happened, nothing. Nothing at all. And he left, he smiled your way and left, and you stayed on through the summer until March when your family moved to Auckland.

ART CLASS

Hey Cody

How are you? I miss you. How's Auckland? Things here are OK. I want to leave school but not allowed. Mum's spazzing out because I told her I quit smoking – stupid – then she found a packet in my room. I miss you. Julie's OK but she never wants to wag school to watch *Prisoner*. There was a drug raid last week and Robert Stone got caught with an ounce in his locker. His dad is really pissed off because he's a cop and he caught Robert once before. Sucked. I can't wait for the August holidays. When are you coming to stay? Are there any OK guys at your school? GROSS the art teacher Mr O'Donnell just came over to see what I was doing, we call him Stiff O'Donnell because he gawks at the girls all the time he is so disgusting, plus he says Far Out all the time like he thinks he's really cool or something What A Dick. Anyway, the mid-year dance is on next week, I'm gonna go. I asked Celia Fox if she wants to go with me. I really like her. Is that weird? I mean, I don't think it is, well I do a bit, but – does it weird you out? I don't really want to be a Lesbian or anything, god I hate that word, but I never felt anything the whole time I went out with Paul, I mean he was a useless kisser but I think even if he wasn't I still would have felt nothing. I guess I like girls more than boys. Well that's OK, I'm not gonna get too freaked out, write back soon and tell me what you think. I've got this great dress to wear, it's purple kind of plasticky stuff, quite short, Mum'll spew. Yuck Stiff O'Donnell is perving I better go. Tell me what you think.

love Thea

PS she said yes

*

It took Cody two weeks to answer Thea's letter. She started about four before she made it sound all right. What really worried her, though, was something she couldn't say in a letter. In the August holidays, she went down to stay with Thea, who was going out with Celia Fox by now, and looking forward to term three starting so they could be the scandal of the school. Cody and Thea got Celia, a seventh former, to buy them some wine one night and they went and drank it in the park. Celia went home for dinner and Cody and Thea sat on the swings, talking. Thea told Cody that just because she liked girls, it didn't mean she was attracted to her. Cody was hugely relieved. Then Thea said not to assume that she wasn't, either, and started laughing so hard she nearly fell off her swing, which did big loopy curves out over the grass. Cody laughed too and swung her swing higher and they spent the rest of the evening there winding each other up and enjoying it more than they ever had before.

This is years ago now. Cody remembers it when Thea rings her up to tell her she's met a new woman. Her name is Thea too. Cody thinks this is very bizarre and one of the hazards of having same-sex relationships. She doesn't want to say this though in case Thea thinks she's been uptight about the whole thing all along.

—Imagine a couple both called Thea, says Thea. —Isn't it awful? One of the hazards of same-sex relationships, I suppose.

—Do you and Thea want to come for dinner this week? asks Cody.

THEA & CODY ON AUGUST HOLIDAYS

It was the boat sheds
in winter
& we ran out of
that terrible play

the invitation read
danger
no climbing
on roof

we'd have slept there
we said, passing
a joint
between us

before the rain started
dreaming California

WHAT HAPPENS NEXT

The Saturday after Cody sees Francis at the bus-stop, she goes to a
party with Thea and Thea. It's a long time since Cody's been to a
party. This one is in a warehouse off Cuba Street. There is a DJ
playing reggae music and a lot of white people dancing to it. Cody
is glad she brought her whisky.

—Something something KITCHEN something, shouts Thea
at Cody.

—WHAT, shouts Cody, —WHERE?

She follows Thea into a small, brightly lit converted office.
There is a bench, a sink and a stove-top element thing over which
knives are heating. Thea helps herself to a bottle of wine left by
somebody. Three people leave, shutting the door. It is much
quieter.

—Thank fuck, says Thea, —I've got to talk to you. I think
Thea's having an affair with a cycle courier.

—Oh no, says Cody. She lights a cigarette. —Male or female?

—Female, says Thea. —Which is worse, I think.

—Are you sure it's happening? asks Cody.

—No, well I am, I haven't asked her, but you know she'll

only lie anyway, I'm pretty sure oh shit Code I'll really miss her if we break up.

—Now hang on, hang on, says Cody. She passes Thea a paper napkin to wipe her face. She goes round the corner of the table to hug Thea and as she does the door opens and Francis walks into the room.

—Sorry, says Francis. —Bad timing. Hi.

It's a question really, he's not sure that he knows her, or if he does, from where. A lot of people are looking familiar to him these days. But he's interrupted something so he's just going to grab a plastic cup and leave.

—Wasn't that— starts Thea, wiping her nose on the lining of her suede jacket.

—Mm? says Cody. —Who? Do you want to go now?

—No, says Thea. —I don't want to leave Thea here. That cycle bitch might show. Can I have some lipstick? They spend a minute putting Thea back together again and then walk out to the party. Thea finds Thea and they dance while Cody walks over to the window not looking for Francis.

He finds her anyway, and this is what he says.

—Leo Tolstoy and his brother believed anything they wished would come true if they could stand in a corner and not think of a white bear.

Cody feels her rib cage expand, contract, expand, contract. She lights another cigarette off the butt of the one she's just smoked. She has a mouthful of whisky, making sure not to spill any down her chin. Her hands shake. She tightens her grip on the windowsill.

—I know you from somewhere, he says.

—Um, says Cody, —I think we might have worked in the same restaurant once, ages ago now, about ten years ago or something, is your name Francis?

—Yeah. He smiles. —What's yours again?

—Cody, says Cody.

—What? says Francis.

—Cody, she says again, hating this. —C-O-D-Y.

—Cody? he says.

—Yeah. She's feeling sick now even without the whisky, wondering where her personality's gone. She could have sworn she had it on her when she left the house.

—Visions of Cody, he smiles.

—Yeah, says Cody. —I never read it yet.

For a while they stand there at the window next to each other not saying anything. Cody looks around the room at the other women there. They all look completely gorgeous. She glances carefully over at Francis. He's looking straight ahead, sucking the rim of his plastic cup with red wine in it. Cody realizes with relief that she is bored, and walks away.

But here she is now at the end of the party and there's only a handful of people left. Thea and Thea have gone home. The cycle courier never showed up. Cody is talking to a red-haired woman about Virginia Woolf and trying to sound informed but not pretentious while keeping Francis in her peripheral vision. She got Thea to make some inquiries for her earlier on and found out he's not with anyone, he just got back from overseas. Which potentially places him in a high-risk category but at least he's available. Cody can't get over how he looks exactly the same. She's not sure whether this is good or bad.

—Ugh, said Thea, —He looks like he crawled out from under a rock. I thought you'd gotten over that Brideshead cheekbone thing.

—I did, said Cody. —I did get over it.

Cody sees him going for his coat and manages to look as if she got up to leave first. There is an art to this manoeuvre and she has to concentrate hard, which is not easy after three and a half hours of whisky and forty-five minutes of leftover beer.

She hears him behind her on the stairs. Once she's outside she stops and looks up at the stars. The night is clear and very cold. She is wide awake. She looks at him, surprised. She smiles.

—Hi, he says.

—Hi.

They walk together down the street, hands in pockets, ears ringing from the music. Everything else is still. They reach the taxi stand.

In the taxi he asks her if she wants to go back to his place. She can't believe it's been this easy. She says OK, still looking surprised, smiling a small smile.

Actually it's not his place, it's his brother's who's away for the weekend. This is a further stroke of luck. Cody does not like to encounter strange flatmates in the morning. The mornings are awkward enough as it is. Francis pours them each a glass of wine and puts a record on. He touches Cody's face. He says, —I remember you.

They go to bed.

—Well, says Thea the next day, —how was it?

—Good, says Cody. —I think. I can't remember much.

—So, says Thea, —what happens next?

SWIMMING BACK UPSTREAM

but here's a
new mark

on my
white flesh

fingers
or mouth

have
bruised it fresh

and I want
to laugh

and I want
to run

and I want to
show you

what you
have done

IN CASE INTERVIEW EVER WANTS TO KNOW

Because there are at least eight other things she should be doing, Cody spends the afternoon compiling the guest list for her Ideal Dinner Party. She has a strong sense that, although she's only a waitress right now, some day magazines will want to know this kind of information from her. Her Desert Island Discs; Night-Table Reading; Who Is The Sexiest Man In Politics, etc.

She decides to limit herself to six guests, three of each sex. She starts with Susan Sarandon. Susan is one of Cody's favourite actresses and it's apparent that not only is she talented and beautiful, she's also a smart political thinker. Plus she's played a lot of waitresses. Cody feels Susan will be an excellent contributor to dinner-party conversation.

Susan Sarandon
Al Gore

Al Gore? He *is* the Sexiest Man In Politics, but maybe a little earnest. Cody's unsure how his environmental stance will suit the style of evening she wants – sharp, funny, an element of risk. Leave him in for the time being. But no Tipper.

That couple the film *Lorenzo's Oil* was about. Real people who changed the world through love and determination. Whoa, then Susan will be at dinner with the woman she played in a movie. Does it matter? Are there too many Americans so far?

Mother Teresa? – maybe not.

It disturbs Cody how hard she's having to think about this. You'd imagine it would be easy enough to rattle off six heroes from the top of your head. But it involves more than that. It involves balance, precision, a successful dynamic. Cody's disappointed she can't think of more famous people in Science, or Classical Music. What about Anita Hill? She's another American, true, but she'd definitely get on well with Susan. Maybe Al could do something nasty to Clarence Thomas on her behalf. Does Al have anything to do with the Supreme Court? Surely he's got some influence.

> Susan Sarandon
> Al Gore
> *Lorenzo's Oil* couple
> ~~Mother Teresa~~
> Anita Hill

The couple from *Lorenzo's Oil* are standing on shaky ground. What Cody needs now is a man. Someone older perhaps, erudite, charming, powerful. Someone witty and wise who can offer the benefit of experience. Someone Al could learn from, and the others could be grateful to have had the opportunity to meet. In literature? Politics? Prince Rainier? Gore Vidal? Gielgud?

On the other hand, Cody does need someone to help with the dishes. And there's always the possibility of one last drink, a walk by the sea, an undeniable electric attraction that demands to be fulfilled—

> Susan Sarandon
> Al Gore
> ~~*Lorenzo's Oil* couple~~

~~Mother Teresa~~
Anita Hill
Daniel Day-Lewis
Brad Pitt
Johnny Depp

The weekend after Francis, Cody and Thea go to breakfast. They try and figure out which of the couples surrounding them just met the night before. Cody needs to talk about Francis.

—I can't stop thinking about him, she says.

—That's bad, says Thea.

—I know.

—You need to fuck someone else.

—Who? says Cody, looking around the room.

—Anyone, Thea says. —There are other guys. Anyone. Just don't obsess about thingy.

—Francis.

—Francis. What kind of a name is that for a guy?

—I am obsessing, aren't I? Cody slops her coffee into the saucer.

—Yes, says Thea.

—I'm enjoying it. I can't help it. I'm out of control.

—Crap, says Thea.

Their food arrives. Cody wonders if the waiter is attractive enough to sleep with. She decides that he isn't.

—And, she says, —I keep remembering things.

Thea sighs. —Spare me the details.

—No, but, like the mascara.

—What?

—Well, says Cody, —There was this mascara on his bedside table. Do you think he's a cross-dresser?

—Were there any feather boas lying around?

—No. Um, I don't think so.

—Cody you moron. He's not a cross-dresser, he's got a fucking girlfriend.

—But you said he was single, Cody says, feeling a tantrum coming on.

—Well I don't know for sure. But make-up is a sure sign of a girlfriend.

—Oh.

—Either that or he's a New Romantic.

—I'd rather he had a girlfriend.

—What are you going to do tonight?

—Get drunk.

—And?

—And fuck someone else.

—Good girl.

REGARDING FRANCIS

I sit in my room
thinking & smoking
thinking & smoking &
whisky all day

I want to write a story
about a man I met
met & went to bed with
went to bed with & left

But it's raining & cold
& the sky is all grey
the words are too hard
the memories not old

there's something there's something
it's too hard to say

*

HOW DO I LOVE THEE?

It's coming up to Thea and Thea's four-year anniversary. Cody goes shopping on Saturday morning for a present. She looks at matching bath robes, matching latte bowls, matching photograph frames. All these are too expensive. She settles for bath oil. As she watches the shop assistant wrapping it, she feels a fist of envy clench in her stomach. She snatches the parcel from across the counter and shoves it deep into her bag. She forgets about it until Thea comes around that night. There's been a fight.

It goes like this.

Thea and Thea are having breakfast. Thea wants to go for a walk to Cody's place. She rings and gets the answerphone but decides to go anyway. She needs to get out of the house.

—I'm going for a walk, she tells Thea.

Thea looks up from her toast. —Do you love me?

—I love you darling, says Thea, putting on her sunglasses.

—Good.

—*Were* you seeing that cycle courier? asks Thea, smiling.

—Thea. Please.

—Were you? she asks, standing in the kitchen doorway now, leaning against the doorframe, casual.

—No. Of course not. God.

—OK, says Thea, —I'm going for a walk now.

She doesn't move from the doorway.

Thea gets up and starts clearing the table. —I love you, Thee, she says.

—Thee, thou, thine, says Thea from the doorway.

Thea giggles. —With all my worldly goods I Thee endow.

—Were you? asks Thea again.

—What? says Thea, scrubbing bacon grease off the grill.

—You did, didn't you, says Thea, clinging to the doorframe now, her fingernails picking at the paint. —You did fuck her. I'm not stupid.

—Thea, says Thea, warning.

—She's a bimbo, you know that?

—Leave it alone, says Thea, pushing past Thea to the living-room.

—I'm going for a walk now, Thea calls after her.

She and Cody go to a movie that night. Thea cries loudly through most of it. When the lights go on at the end her face is red and puffy.

—Can I stay at your place tonight? she asks Cody.

—No, says Cody, —go and make up with Thea. Here, she remembers, fishing in her bag, —give her this. I bought it for both of you.

—Are you sure? says Thea. —She might not want to talk to me.

—One way to find out, says Cody.

She leaves Thea at a taxi stand and walks home alone as the rain starts to spit under the streetlights.

CODY MAKES SURE

There's nothing more boring than people telling you their dreams. God, no. Anyone'll tell you that. And everyone thinks their dreams must be the most interesting, the most symbolic, the best evidence of their inner complexity. Jesus, the number of people who would never tell you about their sex lives but go on about their dreams all day long. It's daytime, for Christ's sake! Wake up! Nobody cares! Besides, there's only about seven dreams really, that just slip from head to head in the night. Tramps.

I'm having a baby
My teeth are crumbling
Wow, I can fly

I'm having sex with
   a) person you find repulsive
   b) person you're related to
   c) person you thought you'd gotten over by now
I'm having sex with
   a) man of your dreams
   b) woman of your dreams
   c) animal of your dreams (surely not)
I'm driving a car and it's out of control
I'm on stage naked, late, and I don't know my lines.

So, dreams are something I've vowed never to talk about. I'm not going to bore you stupid with my extended nightly soap opera. There's just one thing I want to be clear about, though: I have never, *ever* dreamed about Francis. Ever.

THE DITCH

It's been a rocky week. On Tuesday, Thea announced to Cody that she and Thea are splitting up. She's worried that they're becoming co-dependent – whatever *that* means.

   —It's that four-year thing, said Thea.

   —Um, said Cody, who can't remember having a relationship that's lasted more than four weeks.

And then Thea said she was going to Sydney in a month.

   —To live?

   —Yup.

   —You're fucking joking.

   —Nup.

Thea will stay with her cousin until she can get a job and a place of her own. She's serious about leaving. Cody does not welcome this piece of news.

—How fantastic. I'm so jealous, you'll have such a great time.
—Yeah, I'm a bit nervous.
—Oh you'll be fine. I better start saving so I can visit.

Cody spends that evening going over her bank statements and crying. She has fifty-four dollars and the rent's due this week. She doesn't understand why she's a waitress. She doesn't understand anything anymore. She goes to the bottle store and buys a twenty-eight dollar bottle of vodka.

Wednesday, Thursday and Friday Cody says she's busy whenever Thea calls. On Saturday morning Thea turns up with a bunch of grapes.
—I'm not sick, says Cody.
—Why are you avoiding me? asks Thea.
—I'm not.
—Cody.
—What? What? There's nothing going on.
—You're mad at me.
—I'm not.
The kettle whistles and overflows.
—Fucking screaming noise, says Cody.
Thea turns the kettle off and makes tea.
—OK, says Cody, —I hate you. You're leaving.
—I'll miss you, says Thea. —Just don't ruin this last bit.
—Christ Thea. Why is it so hard for me to let people go?
—I don't know, darling. But you'd better get over it.

That night Cody dreams she is a little girl again.

TENDER CALLUS

talked all night
drank till four

> taxi to somewhere
> clothes hit the floor
>
> sighing & laughing
> ten years isn't much
> again & again &
> touch touch touch
>
> so tender he says
> like sirloin she smiles
> sun too bright to sleep
> is callousness guile
>
> yes Francis Francis
> there's no words to say
> just take me to somewhere
> I'd better not stay

Cody shows Gene, the cook where she works, the ad she's put in the paper.

> Flatmate wanted
> 7b Hunter St
> Sat-Sun
> $50pw No pets

—You're mad, says Gene. —You're going to have to stay home all weekend and you could get any kind of freak coming round. You should've just put your phone number.

—Been cut off, says Cody. —Where's the pepper grinder?

—Are you looking for a male or female? asks Gene.

—Don't care really, says Cody. —I just need the money. It'll probably be a disaster whatever sex they are.

—That's the spirit, says Gene. —Take that soup now and the fish'll be ready when you come back.

★

Cody knows she shouldn't be so negative about sharing her flat. She's taken her desk and an armchair out of the sunroom. There's just enough room for a double bed and a small chest of drawers. She vacuumed for the first time in about a month and scrubbed the bath. The *Woman's Weekly*s are hidden under her bed and a couple of Kundera books are lying casually on the kitchen table. She wonders what she's trying to prove. She feels her misplaced pride dragging her around the house trying to create an image of a fabulous self-sufficient working woman. She buys fresh flowers. This is exhausting.

—See you Monday, she says to Gene at the end of the night.

   —Good luck, says Gene. —Hope you don't get any psychos.

THE GENTLEMAN CALLER

All Saturday Cody waits at home for prospective flatmates to call around. It rains, and she plays patience and looks at the dead telephone. No one comes.

   On Sunday she wakes up in the afternoon with a hangover. She thinks, fuck this. She leaves a note on the door and goes to the market. Coming back up her path as dark is falling, she sees someone standing in her doorway trying to read the note. She calls out, —Hi. She runs up the steps to the door. It's Francis.

   She feels her tongue dry in her mouth. She can't swallow. She doesn't trust herself to speak. He looks terrified. He speaks.

   —I'm sorry I didn't call you.

   —I didn't give you my phone number.

   —Um.

   —Uh—

   Cody can't find her key. She considers running back down the path, leaving Francis on the doorstep in the dark.

   —Should I come in?

   —Uh. Sure, I'll just – here it is – uh—

She follows him inside, turning on the lights. They stand stuck in the narrow hallway. Cody doesn't want to squeeze past Francis and he's not going anywhere on his own.

—Have you had many people through? he asks, and she realizes he is here for the flat, there's no mistake, he hasn't tracked her down, sought her out, found her. He's looking for somewhere to live.

—No, she says. —None, I mean, so far. You're the first.

—Oh. Really?

—Yeah, well, it's been raining, so—

—Right. Um, it seems really nice. Is this, um, the room here? He gestures to the sunroom door on his right.

—Yeah that's it, Cody says, not opening the door. —I've been here on my own, you know, I much prefer it. But um, I need the money, I'm trying to save.

—Oh yeah? How much is the room again?

—Fifty a week.

—That's really good for so central. I mean, I haven't got a lot of money, fifty's really good.

—Do you work? asks Cody.

—Yeah, at a second-hand bookshop in town.

—Oh.

—You're a waitress, right?

—Yeah. Uh, so this is the bathroom—

Cody shows Francis around her flat, surreptitiously checking herself in every reflective surface. How can this be happening? A second-hand bookshop? Jesus Christ almighty. Jesus Christ alfuckingmighty.

—Oh and that's my room, she says, flicking her hand in the direction of her closed bedroom door. —And this is the kitchen.

—Gas oven, great. Oh, Kundera. You like him?

—Mm.

—Can I see the room that's going?

—Oh sure, sorry, here—

They stand in the empty sunroom, looking out at the night. Cody is struggling to find an etiquette for this situation. Why is he still here? Why hasn't she just said, Look I'm sorry what a silly mistake, I don't need a flatmate anymore, I'm moving in with my boyfriend, we're in love you know, he's asked me to marry him . . . Shit. Shit fuck.

—Well look, says Francis, —I really like this place. So, um—

—Right.

—Do you need someone in a hurry?

—Yeah I do really, the phone's been cut off, and—

—Oh.

Well that was clever, Cody tells herself. Bang goes your escape route. And now you look like an idiot who can't manage money. You *are* an idiot who can't manage money. Gross financial mismanagement, that's what got you into this mess.

—Um, well I need somewhere straight away, Francis is saying. —My brother's fed up with me sleeping on his couch.

—So that wasn't your— Cody immediately regrets the reference to that night.

—Um no, it was my brother's um room.

—Oh right.

The image Cody has been carrying around with her of Francis's girlfriend putting on mascara while Francis watches from the bed vanishes.

—Look, she says, —Do you think—

—I guess it does look like a fairly foolish idea.

—Foolish. Mm.

—Well, says Francis, —you're desperate for a flatmate—

I'm not desperate for anything thanks very much, thinks Cody.

—And, he continues, —I really need somewhere cheap and central—

—That's me, thinks Cody, cheap and central.

—Also, he says, —I am the only person who's come to look.

—Well, says Cody, —I'm working nights at the moment.

—And I work days, so we wouldn't even need to see each other.

—Yeah . . . says Cody.

—Oh, says Francis, —do you smoke?

—I've just given up, says Cody. —I can't really afford it.

—Well I'm asthmatic.

—Oh right, says Cody, trying not to smirk.

—Well I'm willing to forget what happened between us, says Francis. —I think we could be mature about this, don't you?

—Oh of course, says Cody. —Absolutely. No, it wouldn't be an issue.

—So what do you think?

Cody hates being asked this question.

—Um, she says, —sure. I mean, if you like the room – sure.

—I could move my stuff in tomorrow while you're at work.

—OK, fine.

—Could you leave a key in the letterbox?

—OK, sure.

—Great, says Francis, heading for the door. —Great, I'll see you tomorrow then, probably.

—OK, says Cody, —uh, see you.

She closes the door behind him, feeling dazed and a bit giddy. She waits to make sure he's got down the road and gets her coat and some money and goes to a phone box to call Thea.

—Code, says Thea, —are you sure you know what you're doing? You sound dangerously excited. Are you smiling?

—No, says Cody, —I'm not, I'm quite rational about this, it'll be fine.

—You *are* smiling, says Thea. —I can hear it. And you're smoking. I thought you gave up.

—Just one, says Cody. —I bludged it off the guy at the bottle store. Do you think I'm crazy?

—Yes, says Thea, —I think you're an idiot.

—I am, aren't I? says Cody. —But I don't care.

—Just don't have sex with him again, says Thea.

—Of course not, says Cody. —Of course not. I'm not that stupid.

—Oh Jesus, says Thea, —would you just stop smiling?

Cutting Francis's hair. We sat on the steps out the front of the house. It was the first sunny weekend in a couple of weeks. I had a comb, a bowl of water, and the kitchen snips. Francis had a towel around his neck. There was music playing and the front door was open and I thought, This is it. This is it. Francis's skull was warm under my hands. He was telling some funny story about the bookshop and I was laughing and I snorted and I didn't care. He leant back against my knees and I must have lost concentration because I cut his ear. He kind of yelped and there was a lot of blood, more than seemed natural, and I couldn't stop laughing. This was the wrong thing to do. He jumped up and knocked over the bowl of water and it ran down the steps looking dark and red in the sun. He ran into the house to get a sticking plaster and tripped over because the dark inside was such a contrast to the winter brightness and he couldn't see. I stayed on the steps, squinting, feeling guilty for not feeling guilty. Francis came blinking back outside and I apologized. He wouldn't let me near him again with the scissors. I didn't point out that I'd only finished cutting one side.

★

FLOOD

In the third week after Francis moved in, there is a terrible rainstorm. It starts on Wednesday night and keeps coming all day Thursday. When Francis gets home from work on Thursday evening he discovers that the sunroom roof is leaking and his bedroom's flooded.

—Bloody hell, he says, standing in the middle of his damp rug. —Bloody hell. His voice gets louder. —Bloody bloody *bloody*.

—You sound like my father, Cody says, coming into Francis's room.

—It's bloody soaked, says Francis, his voice under control again. —It's leaking all over the bloody place. Look.

—Oh shit, says Cody. —Whoops.

—What do you mean? says Francis. —Did you know about this?

—No, says Cody, —Of course not. I just mean, you know, bummer.

—Bummer, says Francis. —Bummer? Look at this. Bummer? It's fucked. It's soaked. My bed— He goes to his bed and wrings out a corner of the sheet, —my bed is fucking soaking. Where am I going to sleep?

As soon as the question is out there they both avoid looking at each other. Cody backs out of Francis's room and down the hall.

—Well, she calls from the kitchen, opening and closing cupboard doors, not looking for anything, just needing the covering noise, —You could always stay in my room. I won't be home till late.

—Uh, calls Francis from his room, pulling his bed out from the wet wall, —yeah. Well I might have to.

—That's fine, calls Cody. —I'm going to work now – um, see you later.

—Bye, Francis mutters. —Bloody, *bloody* hell.

Francis drags his mattress on to its side and turns the heater towards it. He checks it every fifteen minutes. It's getting drier, but not dry enough.

Cody stays after work for a special coffee with Gene.
    —Go easy on the brandy, says Gene. —Cigarette?
    —Love one, says Cody. —Thanks.

When Cody gets home the lights are all out. She opens her bedroom door quietly. Francis is in the bed, on his side, asleep. She gets her T-shirt and goes to change in the bathroom.
    Francis opens his eyes. He hears Cody brushing her teeth. He moves further towards the edge of the bed. Cody gets into bed very carefully. She lies on her back as far to the other side of the bed as she can go, her hands crossed over her chest. She tries to regulate her breathing.
    Neither of them moves a muscle all night. Neither of them gets much sleep. Francis gets out of bed at 7 am. Cody stretches out at last. She swaps her pillow for his. The rain stops.

LOOK, FRANCIS

she wants it &
she wants it now
she wants it
& she'll tell you how

she wants it in
the afternoon
she wants it slow
& quick & soon

she wants it soft
she wants it rough
she wants it
till she's had enough

she wants it loud
& silenced too
but more than it
she must have you

Three weekends after the flood, Francis and Cody spend the evening at home together. It is very windy outside and every now and then the house shudders. There is a bottle of wine nearly empty on the floor between them. Francis is berating Cody for having enjoyed a recently fashionable book which is not only sentimental, falsely optimistic and clumsily written—

—But face it, it's also fundamentally morally flawed.

—*You're* morally flawed.

—Don't be so facile.

—Don't be so anal.

—Jargon-monger.

—Pedant.

—Fashion victim.

—Bore.

They glare at each other across the room. Francis clears his throat.

Look, he says, —We could sit here hurling insults at each other all night but I'd much rather go to bed with you.

—I'd much rather eat my own vomit.

—I find *that* hard to believe.

—I find *you* hard to believe.

—Stop it.

Cody pours herself some more wine, finishing the bottle. She is desperate for a cigarette. She sighs. The sigh goes on longer than she expected and she is suddenly afraid she might cry. She stands up. Francis stands up. He looks out the window.

—I'm sorry.

—For what, says Cody.

—That was a particularly charmless proposal. I didn't mean to assume.

Cody goes to the window and stands behind Francis. She strokes the back of his head, down to his neck. She sees Francis's reflection in the window. He has closed his eyes.

—Don't assume anything, she tells him. —And don't talk.

She leads him carefully to his bedroom. He opens his eyes.

An aerial photograph of a city at night-time.

> *Dear Cody*
> *How are you darling? I miss you. I miss Thea too, more than I expected, I might have a job! — details later if it works out. When are you coming over? I miss you*
>
> > *Thea*
>
> > *PS I love Sydney*
> > *PPS Are you being careful?*

BONFIRE

In the dream there is a field. Francis is in the field. She gets closer and she can see the food, the fruit and leaves and meats spilling out of the horn. The Horn of Plenty from her childhood books. A large cream shell lying on the dark grass. *Viands*, she thinks, *nectar*. Francis is back, crouching by the horn, eating everything that comes out. He's wearing his yellow raincoat. He's eating and he's not getting any bigger.

> I got plenty of nothing
> Nothing's plenty for me

Cody sings these lines all day after she remembers the dream.

She doesn't imagine Francis to be the kind of guy who feels sexual frustration. He doesn't seem to be driven by anything like that. She wishes that he was.

I'm the guy here, she decides. It makes sense the more she thinks about it. The two times they've had sex, she's fallen straight to sleep after while Francis has lain awake. She can tell by the darker than usual circles under his eyes in the mornings. Also, she can drink more than him. Which is not to say she can hold it better, but she can keep going long after he's had enough. She knows this is not her most attractive feature.

She's not the guy. She knows that too. She doesn't even know what a guy is, other than Guy Fawkes. She wishes she was more politically active.

She goes to bed at night determined not to dream about Francis. She doesn't. She doesn't. She does.

AND HAD NOTHING TO DO WITH THE SEA

Francis comes home from the bookshop. From the path he can hear that Cody is playing her Kurt Weill record. Again. Christ, he thinks, if I have to listen to 'Surabaya Johnny' one more time I'll smash something.

—Hi, Cody calls from her room. She's getting ready to go to work.

Francis goes into his room and shuts the door. He feels like slamming it but restrains himself. Control, he thinks, calm.

> —I was young, God I'd just turned sixteen—

He can hear Cody singing along, loudly and not very well. He gets the shoe polish from under his bed and starts working on his shoes. He is rubbing furiously when Cody sticks her lipsticked face around the door. He starts, flushes, tries for some reason to cover the shoes with the rag. He feels as if he's been caught masturbating.

—I'm off, Cody says. —Have a good night.

—Yeah, he says. —See you.

He sees her out his window walking down the path, still singing. She's waving her arms in time.

> —You said a lot, Johnny
> All one big lie, Johnny
> You cheated me blind, Johnny
> From the minute we . . .

Her voice trails after her as she disappears around the corner. He should never have slept with her. He should never have moved in. What a stupid mistake. He doesn't even know her. He hates this messy complication of his life. Bloody mess. At least she's clean.

He goes to her room and stands outside the door. It would be easy to open it, walk in, look in drawers, the wardrobe, the desk. Under the bed. Get to know her that way. Cheat. This is ridiculous, he thinks, looking at himself in the hall mirror on his way back to his room. He looks tired. Older? Probably.

He falls on to his bed. The tin of shoe polish gets him directly between the shoulder blades. Twisting around, he knocks it upside down. There is a thick black streak on his blanket. He throws the shoe polish on the floor. It wheels around leaving fainter black traces before it settles. Francis gets under the blankets with his clothes still on. He counts to a hundred. His breathing slows.

When he wakes up it is dark and the room is cold. He feels a moment of lurching panic. He thinks about going into town. He could have a coffee at Cody's cafe. Sit, talk, walk home together.

He has a bath.
He reads a book.

A painting of a bowl of fruit.

> *Dearest Code*
> *Thea says she saw you in a jeweller's shop with some weedy looking*
> *guy.* Tell me she's joking. *I'm working for one of Sydney's top*
> *production companies! — as a script editor. Scares me shitless. I love it. I*
> *miss you, write.*
>
> > *love Thea*

THE CROWDED EMPTY BAR

inside Cody
small & still
sits & waits
an act of will

outwardly, she
runs the race
spins around
for each new face

mantra chants
the inside child
hums her hymn
is meek & mild

the hurricane
outside the eye
shows no sign
does not know why

Francis is a thumb
I want to suck

Cody gets home from work to find Francis and a friend drinking coffee in the living-room. The friend's name is Marc. Marc with a c. Cody's seen it written down by the telephone. Not for the first time, she wonders if Francis might be gay.

—How was work? asks Francis.

—Fine, says Cody. She doesn't really hear him. She can't take her eyes off the back of Marc's head. Marc, Marc. There's something disturbing about the name. Like Jon without an h. Or Shayne with a y. Marc. Spelt backwards, it makes cram. A real word. This makes it seem like code. Code for what? Cram, cram. Trying to break the Code. OK, so her own name is enough of a liability. She shouldn't laugh at other people's. But *Marc* – it's like biting tinfoil.

—Um, I'm going to have a bath, says Cody.

—Fine, says Francis.

From the bath she can hear them talking. About what? She has no idea what guys talk about when they're alone. Sport? Sex? Not those two. Dungeons and dragons maybe. Or the relative merits of MMP and STV. Her? Doubt it.

—Night, she calls on her way to bed.

—Night, Francis and Marc call after her.

It is three o'clock before she hears the front door close.

—I'm pregnant, says Gene at work on Monday night.

—Oh boy, says Cody. —Is that a good thing or a bad thing?

—Both I guess, says Gene, slapping a steak down on the grill.

Cody looks at her closely to see if she's changed. She's read that during pregnancy your hair is at its glossy best and your skin is glowing. But Gene's ponytail is as limp as ever and she always glows at work anyway, from the heat in the kitchen.

—Are you throwing up yet, asks Cody.

—Nah, says Gene. —Soon maybe. Hey— she looks at Cody, worried, —does it show?

She stands side-on to Cody. She's wearing her T-shirt that says *do i look as if i care* on the front, and leggings.

—No, says Cody. —Don't worry about it.

—Good, says Gene. —That means I don't have to tell him yet. He'll do a runner as soon as he finds out.

—So what are you going to do? asks Cody.

—Go ahead with it and pretend he might change, says Gene. —I want to have the baby. Even if I'm on my own.

—You're brave, says Cody.

—And stupid, says Gene.

—Yeah, says Cody, —and stupid.

Cody spends the next day at the library reading international magazines. She mostly skims through the articles, but reads the short stories in *Buzz* magazine and *The New Yorker*. She is relieved to discover that many of these deal with the same sort of man trouble problems as she has got. There's a whole bunch of American women out there writing about stuff she can relate to. The No-Good-Men Genre. Cody feels reassured, part of a global sorority of single women. Things can't be so bad if they have the same situations in San Francisco and Chicago as they do in Wellington. At least they're all in it together.

No. Wait a minute. Cody stops cold. It is not in fact a good thing if man trouble is an international phenomenon. It is in fact a disaster. The one thing she's been relying on is the fantasy of a different breed of man overseas. Every Antipodean girl's dream – Mr Europe! – Mr Africa! – Mr Mediterranean! – take your places please. Now Cody knows that this will never be a reality. Even if she could ever save enough money to go to New York, she'd still be scouring the streets for a halfway decent man. Shit. Looks like she's going to have to ditch romance and hold out for the fast-track, power-dressing career.

She leaves the magazines on the floor and scuffs her feet all the way down the street to the cafe.

WHICH FACE

thirteen at a table
Francis the last
no–one to kiss
left with the glass

port passed round
not immune
towards the star
right through moon

here Francis
have this mask
heart sees face
this your task

have an answer
have some air
from this distance
you're so fair

Francis has woken up too early. He pulls a jersey on over his pyjamas and shivers. The sky is milky blue. He traces a line curving up and around in the condensation on the window. He worries that the shape he's drawn is too phallic. He worries that he worries too much.

In the kitchen he tries to make coffee without disturbing Cody. She'd probably sleep through a siren anyway, he thinks as the percolator hisses over on to the gas flame. He searches the bench for a teaspoon. Old teabags, dirty knives, crumbs. Standards are slipping. On the table he finds a teaspoon under a piece of paper with writing on it.

Mark called twice
sorry forgot to tell you
We need soap!
C.

He wonders how long the note's been there. He thinks about what he has to do at work today. He's trying to make some changes to the bookshop. Get rid of some of the trash and concentrate on the upmarket, cerebral and quirky. He has a sudden vision of himself as a turn-of-the-century shop clerk, tight collar and pinched brow, pushing pieces of paper around on a desk. He wishes he were back overseas. Maybe he'll get drunk tonight.

He stops outside Cody's door. Without thinking, he opens it and slowly steps into her room. She's almost hidden underneath her blankets, face buried in a pillow. He can't see her breathing. He imagines going to shake her, giving her a fright, seeing her uncomposed morning face open in alarm. He doesn't do it. He doesn't do that sort of thing. But he thinks it, which makes him feel guilty enough.

He sits gently on the end of Cody's bed and watches her sleep. She moves her feet a little bit. Nothing much happens. He leaves her room, forgetting on purpose to close the door. On his way to work, he smiles when he imagines her waking up.

A black and white photograph of two schoolgirls on a road.

Cody
Anyone would think you'd disappeared off the face of the earth. I called your machine, your voice is still on the tape. Is that guy hiding you under the floorboards? or boiling you up on the stove? 99% of women are murdered in their own homes. Or something like that.
   Thea.

I'M GIVING YOU A LONGING LOOK

Cody wakes from a late morning dream. The room is hot. She's still heavy and slow from sleep, but her mind is clear. She knows there's something she has to do. Francis, she thinks, which is nothing new. There is something different now though. She feels a pulse somewhere which tells her she's going to do something. She doesn't want to think what it is. She just wants to get there.

She has a bath and gets dressed to music she and Thea used to listen to at school.

> Here's some mud in your pretty eye
> But please drop in if you're passing by
> I'll tell you how much I hate you girl
> Perhaps it isn't true, perhaps it isn't true

She brushes her hair, humming, smiling at herself in the mirror. Tears come into her eyes. She misses Thea. She'll write to her, after she's done this.

Walking into town she wonders if she's been kidnapped by the FBI and brainwashed as a sleeper. I must kill John Lennon, I must kill John Lennon, she mutters, then laughs out loud. She feels hysteria welling up and breathes down to control it. She realizes she's heading straight for Francis's bookshop. What's she doing? This is stupid – she's about to turn back but she gets rid of the thought, she doesn't think anything, the song runs through her head.

> To those who look snide
> And those who connive
> I say love cannot be contrived
> Love cannot be denied

She's scaring herself now, and walking still, getting closer and closer. It's a mistake, it's wrong. No. Just get there.

And if you ask me to explain
The rules of the game
I'll say you missed the point again

She walks into the bookshop and up to the desk where Francis is sitting. There's no one else there.

—Hi Cody, he says.

—Hi Francis, she says. She squeezes in past the desk and stands behind his chair. For seven seconds she doesn't touch him. Then her hands reach over his shoulders and down his chest. Her mouth is very close to his right ear. One hand finds its way up inside his jersey. The other feels the worn leather of his belt. She kisses his throat. He turns and stands and the chair falls over and her back is against the wall and they are kissing each other. She twists him around and she holds him to the wall, holds his hands to the wall, kisses him and hears someone behind her. She lets him go. He is confused.

—Sorry, he says to the customer.

She isn't sorry. She laughs and says goodbye and leaves the shop.

Francis reaches in his desk drawer and pulls out his inhaler. He gulps mouthfuls of Ventolin. The customer asks him if he's got anything by Julian Barnes and he says Never heard of him, when of course he has, he's read everything he's written, but the only one he can remember right now is *Talking It Over*, and he decides that's what they've got to do.

When Cody gets home from work that night Francis is in the living-room smoking a cigarette.

—What about your asthma, says Cody.

—I don't care, says Francis.

—OK, says Cody.

—I'm going to move out, says Francis.

—OK, says Cody.

—It's not healthy, says Francis.

—OK, says Cody.

They look at each other. Cody lights a cigarette off the end of Francis's and steps away again.

—I want you, says Francis.

—Do you, says Cody.

—Yes, says Francis.

—Really, says Cody.

—Yes, says Francis.

—I suppose you want to consume me, says Cody.

—Yes, says Francis.

—Well, says Cody, —you can try.

Later, you can't sleep. You don't care. You reach over Cody for a cigarette. You light it and cough. You lie on your back blowing smoke into the dark above you. Cody wakes up. You pass her the cigarette. You smile at her.

—Cody, you say.

She smiles back. —What? she says.

— Cody, you say. —C-O-D-Y.

—Visions of Cody, she says, handing you back the cigarette.

—Yeah, you say, still smiling, —Every day I write the book.

Biographical Notes

BARBARA ANDERSON was born in Hawke's Bay in 1926. She studied science at Otago University and, thirty years later, English literature at Victoria University of Wellington. She began writing in the 1980s and her first book, the collection of stories *I think we should go into the jungle*, was an immediate success in 1989. It has been followed by the novels *Girls High* (1990), *Portrait of the Artist's Wife* (1991), which won New Zealand's premier literary award, *All the Nice Girls* (1993) and *The House Guest* (1995).

JOHN CRANNA was born in Te Aroha in 1954 and grew up in the Waikato. After living for some years in London, he returned to Auckland and published his collection of stories *Visitors* (1989), which won the New Zealand Book Award for Fiction, and a novel, *Arena* (1991).

ALAN DUFF was born in 1950 of Ngati Rangitihi and Ngati Tuwharetoa descent. His first novel, *Once Were Warriors* (1990), was a major, controversial success, and has been filmed. He has since become prominent as a media commentator and newspaper columnist, and has also published a second novel, *One*

Night Out Stealing (1992), a novella, *State Ward* (1994), and non-fiction.

FIONA FARRELL was born in Oamaru in 1947. After Otago University she studied drama at Toronto University, and has written for theatre and taught drama. 'The Skinny Louie Story' was published in the NZ *Listener* in 1989, and became the nucleus of her novel *The Skinny Louie Book* (1992), which won the New Zealand Book Award for Fiction. She has published collections of short stories, *The Rock Garden* (1989) and poems, *Cutting Out* (1987).

JANET FRAME was born in Dunedin in 1924. New Zealand's most acclaimed writer, she has told the story of the first half of her life in her three-volume autobiography *An Angel at My Table*. Her first book was *The Lagoon and Other Stories* (1951), and she has published a dozen novels, from *Owls Do Cry* (1957) to *The Carpathians* (1988), as well as further collections of short fiction and one of poems. 'Insulation' was published in the NZ *Listener* in 1979 and in her selected stories, *You Are Now Entering the Human Heart* (1983).

MAURICE GEE was born in Whakatane in 1931 and grew up in Henderson. After an MA in English from Auckland University he worked as a teacher and librarian, and has been a full-time writer for thirty years. His first novel, *The Big Season* (1962), has been followed by another ten, including one of the major achievements in New Zealand fiction, the trilogy comprising *Plumb* (1978), *Meg* (1981) and *Sole Survivor* (1983), and *Prowlers* (1987), *The Burning Boy* (1990), *Going West* (1993) and *Crime Story* (1994). He has also published a collection of short stories and novels for children, and written for film and television.

PATRICIA GRACE was born in Wellington in 1937 and is of

Ngati Raukawa, Ngati Toa and Te Ati Awa descent. Her first book, *Waiariki* (1975), was the first collection of stories by a Maori woman. *Collected Stories* (1994) gathers her first three books of stories, while *The Sky People* (1994) contains new stories. Her three novels include *Potiki* (1986) and *Cousins* (1992), and she has written children's stories in Maori and English.

RUSSELL HALEY was born in Dewsbury in 1934 and emigrated to Australia in 1961 and then New Zealand in 1966. His first book, a collection of poems titled *The Walled Garden* (1972), was followed by another, and then three collections of short fiction, *The Sauna Bath Mysteries* (1978), *Real Illusions* (1984) and *The Transfer Station* (1989), and two novels. He has also written a study of the painter Pat Hanly and was co-editor of *The Penguin Book of Contemporary New Zealand Short Stories* (1989).

KERI HULME was born in Christchurch in 1947 of Kai Tahu, Orkney Scots and English descent, and now lives at Okarito on the West Coast of the South Island. Her novel *The Bone People* (1984) won the Booker Prize and is the most widely read and celebrated New Zealand novel. She has also published a collection of short stories, *Te Kaihau/The Windeater* (1986), a novella and poetry and non-fiction. A second novel, *Bait*, is expected soon.

WITI IHIMAERA was born in Gisborne in 1944 of Te Aitanga a Mahaki descent. He studied at Victoria University of Wellington and for some years worked for the New Zealand diplomatic service in Australia and the United States. *Pounamu, Pounamu* (1972) was the first collection of stories by a Maori writer to be published. He has since published two more collections of stories and six novels, including *The Matriarch* (1986), *Bulibasha, King of the Gypsies* (1994) and *Nights in the Gardens of Spain* (1995). He was also general editor of the groundbreaking anthologies of Maori writing *Into the World of Light* (1982) and *Te Ao Marama* (5 volumes, 1992–1995).

LLOYD JONES was born in 1955 in Wellington, where he lives now. Since attending Victoria University he has given most of his time to writing. He has published two novels, the collection of short stories *Swimming to Australia* (1991), and *Biografi: An Albanian Quest* (1993).

ANNE KENNEDY was born in Wellington in 1959 and studied music at Victoria University. After several years in Australia, she now lives in Auckland. She writes for film and television, and has published two novels, *100 Traditional Smiles* (1988) and *Musica Ficta* (1993). Her short fiction is as yet uncollected; 'The Road to Damascus' first appeared in *Islands*.

FIONA KIDMAN was born in 1940. She grew up in Northland and Rotorua and now lives in Wellington. Trained as a librarian, she has worked mainly as a writer. She has written extensively for radio and television, and published seven novels, including *A Breed of Women* (1979) and *The Book of Secrets* (1987), three volumes of short stories, *Mrs Dixon and Friend* (1982), *Unsuitable Friends* (1988) and *The Foreign Woman* (1994), and poetry and drama. Her nonfiction is gathered in *Palm Prints* (1994), a quasi-autobiography.

ELIZABETH KNOX was born in Wellington in 1959. She studied at Victoria University and has been a full-time writer since 1986. She has published two novels, *After Z-Hour* (1987) and *Treasure* (1992), and the first two parts of a trilogy of short novels about growing up in Wellington's northern suburbs, *Paremata* (1989) and *Pomare* (1994).

SHONAGH KOEA was born in Taranaki in 1943 and educated in

Hawke's Bay and Auckland. She has worked as a journalist and teacher. She has published two collections of short stories, *The Woman Who Never Went Home* (1987) and *Fifteen Rubies by Candlelight* (1993) and three novels, including *Staying Home and Being Rotten* (1992) and *Sing to Me, Dreamer* (1994).

SUE MCCAULEY was born in 1941 and lives in Christchurch. She is the author of three novels, *Other Halves* (1982), *Then Again* (1988) and *Bad Music* (1990), and has also worked as a journalist and screenwriter.

MARGARET MAHY was born in 1936 and lives at Governor's Bay on Banks Peninsula. She is an internationally acclaimed children's writer. One of the first of her more than 100 books was *A Lion in the Meadow* (1969), and her novels for young adults include *The Haunting* (1982), *The Changeover* (1984), *The Catalogue of the Universe* (1985), *Tricksters* (1986), *Memory* (1987) and *Dangerous Spaces* (1990). Her collection of short stories is *The Door in the Air* (1988). She has also written for television, and published a number of essays on writing and imagination.

BILL MANHIRE was born in Invercargill in 1946 and educated at Otago University and University College, London. For the past twenty years he has lived in Wellington and taught at Victoria University. He is best known as a poet, and his collections include *Zoetropes: Poems 1972–82* (1984) and *Milky Way Bar* (1992), both of which won the New Zealand Book Award. His collection of short stories *South Pacific* (1994) incorporates his earlier collection *The New Land: A Picture Book* (1990), the choose-your-own-adventure story *The Brain of Katherine Mansfield* (1988) and more recent stories. He has also been an influential teacher of creative writing and edited with Marion McLeod the anthology *Some Other Country: New Zealand's Best Short Stories* (1984 and 1992).

OWEN MARSHALL was born in 1941. After an M.A. at Canterbury University he taught in several secondary schools in the South Island, and now lives in Timaru. His first collection of short stories, *Supper Waltz Wilson*, was published in 1979, and he has now published eight, including *The Divided World: Selected Stories* (1989), *Tomorrow We Save the Orphans* (1992) and *Coming Home in the Dark* (1995). His first novel, *A Many Coated Man*, was also published in 1995.

GREGORY O'BRIEN was born in Matamata in 1961, educated in Auckland, and now lives in Wellington. A prolific and versatile writer and painter, he is best known as a poet, author of six collections and book-length poems. He has also published a novel, *Diesel Mystic* (1988), books of interviews with New Zealand writers and painters, and a study of the painter Nigel Brown.

VINCENT O'SULLIVAN was born in Auckland in 1937. Educated at Auckland and Oxford Universities, he is now Professor of English at Victoria University of Wellington. His oeuvre to date features five collections of short stories, including *Palms and Minarets: Selected Stories* (1992), two novels, including *Let the River Stand* (1993), winner of the Montana Book of the Year Award, and numerous plays and collections of poetry. He has also edited a number of anthologies and is joint editor of Katherine Mansfield's letters.

EMILY PERKINS was born in Wellington in 1970. She is a graduate of the New Zealand Drama School and has worked as an actor, and studied at Victoria University of Wellington. 'Not Her Real Name', her first story, was published in *Sport* in 1993; her first collection of short stories, *Not Her Real Name*, will appear in 1996.

MAURICE SHADBOLT was born in 1932 in Auckland, where he lives now. His first collection of short stories, *The New*

Zealanders (1959), began a prolific career which now boasts over twenty volumes. He is most acclaimed for his trilogy of historical novels, *Season of the Jew* (1986), *Monday's Warriors* (1990) and *The House of Strife* (1993). He has also written a volume of autobiography, *One of Ben's* (1993), and a considerable amount of non-fiction and journalism.

C.K. STEAD was born in Auckland in 1932. After degrees at Auckland and Bristol Universities, he taught for twenty years at Auckland University before becoming a full-time writer in 1986. He has published six novels, including *All Visitors Ashore* (1984), *The Death of the Body* (1986) and *The Singing Whakapapa* (1994), nine volumes of poetry and one of short stories, *Five for the Symbol* (1981). An important and controversial critic of New Zealand writing, his essays can be found in *In the Glass Case* (1981) and *Answering to the Language* (1989).

APIRANA TAYLOR was born in Wellington in 1955 of Te Whanau-a-Apanui, Ngati Porou and Taranaki descent and educated at Te Aute College. He has published two collections of short stories, *He Rau Aroha: A Hundred Leaves of Love* (1986) and *Ki Te Ao* (1990), a novel, *He Tangi Aroha (A Cry of Love)* (1994), and several collections of poetry and plays.

NGAHUIA TE AWEKOTUKU was born in 1949 of Te Arawa, Tuhoe and Waikato descent. She grew up in Ohinemutu and now teaches art history and women's studies at Auckland University. She has published a collection of short stories, *Tahuri* (1989) as well as writing on art and politics.

IAN WEDDE was born in Wellington in 1946, attended Victoria University, travelled extensively and now lives in Wellington. He has published three novels, *Dick Seddon's Great Dive* (1976), *Symmes Hole* (1986) and *Survival Arts* (1988), *The Shirt Factory and*

Other Stories (1981), and eleven books of poems, including *Driving into the Storm: Selected Poems* (1987) and *The Drummer* (1993), and was co-editor of *The Penguin Book of Contemporary New Zealand Poetry*. A selection of his critical writing on art and literature can be found in *How to Be Nowhere, Essays and Texts 1971–1994* (1995).

PETER WELLS was born in 1953 and lives in Auckland. He is an acclaimed filmmaker, whose work includes *A Death in the Family* (1986) and *Desperate Remedies* (1993). His two collections of short stories are *Dangerous Desires* (1991), winner of the New Zealand Book Award for Fiction, and *The Duration of a Kiss* (1994).

ALBERT WENDT was born in Samoa in 1939, graduated from Victoria University, and for many years taught at the University of the South Pacific before taking up a Chair in English at Auckland University. His first novel, *Sons for the Return Home* (1973), was followed by four more, including *Leaves of the Banyan Tree* (1979) and *Ola* (1991), two collections of short stories, *Flying-Fox in a Freedom Tree* (1974) and *The Birth and Death of the Miracle Man* (1986), and three of poetry. He also edited the anthologies of Pacific writing *Lali* (1980) and *Nuanua* (1995).

DAMIEN WILKINS was born in Lower Hutt in 1963. He studied at Victoria University, worked in publishing in London and Wellington, studied writing at Washington University, St Louis for two years, and settled in Wellington in 1992. He is the author of a book of short stories, *The Veteran Perils* (1990), a book of poems, *The Idles* (1993), and a novel, *The Miserables* (1993), which won the New Zealand Book Award for Fiction.

FORBES WILLIAMS was born in Melbourne in 1960. Since moving to New Zealand in the mid-1970s he has lived mainly in Dunedin. A qualified doctor, he teaches at Otago Medical School. His first collection of short stories is *Motel View* (1992).

Acknowledgements

Every effort has been made by the publishers to contact the copyright holders of the material published in this book but any omissions will be restituted at the earliest opportunity.

BARBARA ANDERSON. 'Miss Hobbs thinks about the peonies at the Kamikaze Pilots' Memorial at Etajima' from *Girls High*. First published by Victoria University Press 1990 and Martin Secker & Warburg Ltd 1990. Copyright © Barbara Anderson 1990. Reprinted with permission.

JOHN CRANNA. 'Visitors' from *Visitors*. First published by Reed Books (Auckland) 1989. Copyright © John Cranna 1989. Reprinted with permission.

ALAN DUFF. Extract from *Once Were Warriors*. First published by Tandem Press Ltd 1990. Copyright © Alan Duff 1990. Reprinted with permission.

FIONA FARRELL. '*A Story about Skinny Louie*'. First published in the *New Zealand Listener*. Copyright © Fiona Farrell 1991. Reprinted with permission.

JANET FRAME. 'Insulation' from *You Are Now Entering the Human Heart*. Copyright Janet Frame 1983. Reprinted by permission of Curtis Brown Ltd.

MAURICE GEE. Extract from *Prowlers*. First published by Penguin Books (NZ) Ltd 1987. Copyright © Maurice Gee 1987. Reprinted with permission.

PATRICIA GRACE. Extract from *Potiki*. First published by Penguin Books (NZ) Ltd 1986. Copyright © Patricia Grace 1986. Reprinted with permission.

RUSSELL HALEY. 'Fog' from *Real Illusions*. First published by Victoria University Press 1983. Copyright © Russell Haley 1983. Reprinted with permission.

KERI HULME. 'Te Kaihau/The Windeater'. Published by Victoria University Press 1986. Copyright © Keri Hulme 1986. Reprinted with permission.

WITI IHIMAERA. Extract from *Bulibasha*. First published by Penguin Books (NZ) Ltd 1994. Copyright © Witi Ihimaera 1994. Reprinted with permission.

LLOYD JONES. 'Swimming to Australia' from *Swimming to Australia and Other Stories*, first published by Victoria University Press 1991. Copyright © Lloyd Jones 1991. Reprinted with permission.

ANNE KENNEDY. 'The Road to Damascus'. First published in *Islands Magazines* 1986. Copyright © Anne Kennedy 1986. Reprinted with permission of author.

FIONA KIDMAN. 'Hats' from *Unsuitable Friends*. First published by Random House (NZ) Ltd 1988. Copyright © Fiona Kidman 1988. Reprinted with permission.

ELIZABETH KNOX. Extract from *Pomare*, first published by Victoria University Press 1994. Copyright © Elizabeth Knox 1994. Reprinted with permission.

SHONAGH KOEA. 'Mrs Pratt Goes to China' from *The Woman Who Never*

Went Home and Other Stories, first published by Penguin Books (NZ) Ltd 1987. Copyright © Shonagh Koea 1987. Reprinted with permission.

SUE McCAULEY. Extract from *Other Halves*. First published by Hodder & Stoughton Ltd, Auckland, New Zealand. Copyright © Sue McCauley 1982. Reprinted with permission.

MARGARET MAHY. 'The Bridge-Builder' from *The Door in the Air and Other Stories*, published by The Orion Publishing Group Ltd 1988. Copyright © Margaret Mahy 1988. Reprinted with permission.

BILL MANHIRE. 'Ponies' first published in *The New Land: A Picture Book* 1990 and then in *South Pacific* by Carcanet 1994. Copyright © Bill Manhire 1990. Reprinted by permission.

OWEN MARSHALL. 'A Day with Yesterman' from *The Lynx Hunter and Other Stories*, first published by John McIndoe 1987. Copyright © Owen Marshall 1987. Reprinted with permission.

GREGORY O'BRIEN. Extract from *Diesel Mystic*, first published by Auckland University Press 1989. Copyright © Gregory O'Brien 1989. Reprinted with permission.

VINCENT O'SULLIVAN. 'The Last of Freddie' from *Palms and Minarets: Selected Stories*, first published by Victoria University Press 1992. Copyright © Vincent O'Sullivan 1992. Reprinted with permission.

EMILY PERKINS. 'Not Her Real Name', first published in *Sport 11*, 1993 then as part of collection *Not Her Real Name* by Picador 1996. Copyright © Emily Perkins 1993. Reprinted with permission.

MAURICE SHADBOLT. Extract from *The House of Strife*, published by Hodder & Stoughton in New Zealand and by Bloomsbury Publishing in the UK, 1993. Copyright © Maurice Shadbolt 1993. Reprinted with permission.

C.K. STEAD. 'The Dreamtime' from *All Visitors Ashore*, first published in 1984 by the Harvill Press in the UK and by William Collins Publishers in New Zealand. Copyright © C. K. Stead 1984. Reproduced by permission of The Harvill Press.

APIRANA TAYLOR. 'Te Tohunga Makutu' from *Ki Te Ao*, first published by Penguin Books (NZ) Ltd 1990. Copyright © Apirana Taylor 1990. Reprinted with permission.

NGAHUIA TE AWEKOTUKU. 'The Basketball Girls' from *Tahuri*, first published by the New Women's Press, New Zealand 1989. Copyright © Ngahuia Te Awekotuku 1989. Reprinted with permission.

IAN WEDDE. Extract from *Symmes Hole*. First published by Penguin, 1986. Copyright © Ian Wedde 1986. Reprinted with permission.

PETER WELLS. 'Outing' from *Dangerous Desires*. First published by Reed Books (Auckland) 1991, acknowledgement also to Michael Gifkins & Associates. Copyright © Peter Wells 1991. Reprinted with permission.

ALBERT WENDT. 'The Balloonfish and the Armadillo' from *The Birth and Death of the Miracle Man*. First published by Viking 1986. Copyright © Albert Wendt 1986. Reprinted here with permission from Curtis Brown Ltd.

DAMIEN WILKINS. 'Cable' from *The Miserables*. First published by Victoria University Press 1993 and by Faber & Faber 1995. Copyright © Damien Wilkins 1993. Reprinted with permission.

FORBES WILLIAMS. Extract from *Motel View*. First published by Victoria University Press 1992. Copyright © Forbes Williams 1992. Reprinted with permission.